KU-749-827

Spiritual Perspectives

Spiritual Perspectives

Maharaj Charan Singh
Answers Questions:
1960 – 1990

Volume I
Understanding the Basics

RADHA SOAMI SATSANG BEAS

Published by:
J. C. Sethi, Secretary
Radha Soami Satsang Beas
Dera Baba Jaimal Singh
Punjab 143 204, India

First edition 2010

17 16 15 14 13 12 11 10 8 7 6 5 4 3 2 1

ISBN 978-81-8256-931-7

Printed in India by: Thomson Press (India) Ltd.

Contents

Volume I
Understanding the Basics

Volume II
Walking the Path

Volume III
Living the Life

Preface

The master lives among us to raise our consciousness to his own level. Both by example and precept, the spiritual master teaches us to withdraw our attention from material concerns of body and mind and awaken to the truth, power and beauty of the divine.

In olden times, a master would have a small number of disciples and communicate with them through personal interaction. His disciples would mostly be from the area where he lived, and his influence would reach them as he would travel to see them or they would travel to be in his company at his spiritual centre.

Since the early part of the twentieth century, the masters at Beas have attracted a growing number of disciples living in countries outside India. After Hazur Maharaj Charan Singh assumed the responsibilities of mastership in 1951, more and more overseas disciples began to seek his spiritual guidance. As increasingly they visited him in India, an International Guest House was created at Beas, and in 1961 he took the first of many tours to foreign lands to meet his disciples and seekers. At all these meetings, question-and-answer sessions in English were held at which the master would patiently respond to his disciples' questions. Fortunately for us, heirs to his legacy, many of these meetings were tape-recorded.

This book contains a selection of those questions and answers drawn from almost thirty years of Hazur Maharaj Ji's mastership, recorded between 1960 and 1990. In reading these exchanges, which have been organized according to subject, it is evident that the master used these sessions to create a bond of friendship, love and trust with us. The answers reveal that Maharaj Ji never acted as if he felt superior to us; he acted rather as one of us. He understood our problems and wanted to help us. But above and beyond, he did not create dependency; he taught us to think for ourselves and stand on our own feet. He wanted us to grow in confidence and understanding, and he guided us to come to our own conclusions.

Spiritual Perspectives offers an important foundation for people just embarking on the spiritual path, and serves as a comprehensive and practical guide for all disciples attempting to live according to the principles taught by the master. It is our great pleasure to present this three-volume collection of Maharaj Ji's responses to our questions so that we may all benefit from his wisdom.

J. C. Sethi, Secretary
Radha Soami Satsang Beas

Introduction
Any questions, please?

All mystics and saints have the same message to give, the same spiritual truth to share with us, but everybody has a different approach, depending on the audience they want to reach. Some mystics have a very mild approach, and some mystics – unless they just shake you from the roots, you will not understand. But they all have the same message; there's no difference in their message, there's no difference in the spiritual experiences they want to share with us, or the spiritual path they want to show to us.

– MAHARAJ CHARAN SINGH

Understanding the intellectual approach of his overseas disciples, Hazur Maharaj Charan Singh began holding question-and-answer sessions from the early days of his mastership in the 1950s until the time of his passing in 1990. For those of us fortunate to meet with the master in these small, informal gatherings, or who have heard tape-recordings of them, these sessions were the highlight of our relationship with him. "Any questions, please?" "Any new questions?" Those familiar words evoke memories of uncharted evenings of self-revelation, as Hazur Maharaj Ji would take our minds beyond the boundaries of habitual thought and preconceived ideas, challenging us to live our lives with greater love and confidence, free of fear and self-imposed limitations.

Maharaj Ji used the evening meetings as a way of creating an intimate bond, a relationship of love and support, and a deep sense of friendship with his sangat from abroad. Everyone had the sense of being taken care of, on every level of their being. The words of the master became a cocoon of safety and a prism of beauty and light through which we could look at our lives, and our world, with fresh eyes. In his gentle, humble, yet regal manner, Hazur Maharaj Ji imbued every moment in his presence with a magnetic energy that immersed us in his love.

When people would step up to the microphone to ask a question, they would feel that they were the only ones in the room with the master; time would literally stand still as they interacted with him. Maharaj Ji would intently focus his attention on the questioner, and in his response he often touched on an unexpressed, perhaps unconscious aspect of the problem being presented. He once commented, "I'm trying to understand you, rather than the question."

Why do we ask questions? Hazur Maharaj Ji would often say:

> *We have so many books written in detail that if you read these books and try to digest what is written in them, I wonder if there will be any questions left at all. The books are beautifully written from the Western point of view, from an intellectual point of view, from a creative mind's point of view, and we can know the answers to most of the questions just by reading and studying them. In fact, we always know the answers, and only that answer appeals to us which we already know. Otherwise, the answer that we do not know will never appeal to us. I tell you, we always know the answer when we*

> *ask a question. It is in our subconscious. The answer is always there, but we only want a corroboration of that which we think is right, and we are happy when we find that it is right. That is all; otherwise all our books are full of answers.*

No problem, no person, was too unimportant for Maharaj Ji. In his unstated humility, he treated everyone with complete respect. He saw beauty in us all, as if we were uncut diamonds; and he shone his brilliant light into us, to polish us so that we might manifest some of that beauty. To adapt a metaphor he often used, he created the hunger in us for spirituality, he prepared the food and served it, and then he helped us to eat it by pulling us to him and keeping us in his radiant presence.

Maharaj Ji indulged us tremendously in those question-and-answer sessions. No doubt many of the questions were just excuses to stand before the master and have his attention, but he welcomed it. He showered his affection on us like a father playing with his infant child, lifting him overhead with pleasure and hugging him gently. He reached down to us on our level, and brought us up to his.

Those evening meetings sometimes felt like a wonderful game, a courtship between lover and beloved. We wanted to keep him there for as long as possible, and he wanted to be with us. As he once said:

> *I am quite conscious that many people don't have a question, even when they come to ask a question. And even if they do have questions, they are not interested in the answer, and they don't want any answer. And whatever answer I may give them makes no difference to them. They only want to talk; they only want to keep me here; they only want to hear me. I am quite conscious of it.*

When I find seekers, real seekers, I do give the answer, and with clarity. Sometimes I know their real purpose behind it, so I put it off, in one way or another.

So this game is going on. And I know every day it will be the same. It's not one session or two sessions, or one meeting or two meetings. For the past thirty-five years, this question-and-answer is going on. No dearth of books have been printed, no dearth of tapes recorded; same questions, same answers.... I don't know what is the reason, but it is going on. They want to be here and I want to be with them; they want to be with me, and we are here. You can explain it in any way.

Hazur Maharaj Ji nurtured our capacity to understand Sant Mat as a practical spiritual path to guide and govern our daily life and actions. He covered a comprehensive range of topics during those lively meetings, which brought breadth and depth of understanding to the questioner and everyone in the audience, no matter how narrow the particular question.

Although everyone knew that the ultimate answer to every question was "meditation," few could hold themselves back from taking the opportunity to engage him in dialogue.

Q: A lot of us, including myself, want to ask you specific questions, and generally we get a response to do our meditation and have faith. Should we try to avoid asking these questions? Should we just concentrate on our simran?

M: Well, brother, you can ask me any number of questions, but I am sorry to say, I have only one answer. You see, I don't mind attending to your questions, but my answer will be the same in a nutshell. Whether you take it in a simple word or whether you take it in a more complicated word, or whether I explain it to you intellectually or in a simple way, there is no difference. The answer will be the same.

In responding to questions, Maharaj Ji often illustrated his answers with examples from mundane topics, such as the weather, agriculture and domestic life. As his overseas audience in those days was largely Christian, he would also quote the familiar parables and sayings of Christ, as well as tales and poetry of the Indian and Persian mystics. In illustrating the relationship of the soul with the Lord, he would sometimes use examples from domestic life, particularly the idealized love of the wife for the husband in the traditional Indian family. Thus he was able to reach audiences with diverse religious and social backgrounds and also to convey the universal truths at the heart of all religions and spiritual teachings.

These three volumes represent Maharaj Ji's answers drawn from the entire period of his mastership: the hundreds of sessions he held at the International Guest House at Dera, his tours abroad, and the Delhi and Bombay sessions of the 1980s (when Punjab was closed to foreigners). Most of the questions and answers in the books *The Master Answers* and *Thus Saith the Master* appear here, interwoven with previously unpublished material.

Transcribed from original recordings, the questions and answers have been edited lightly to eliminate excessive repetition and correct the English syntax and usage. It was the master's wish that his rough spoken material, when presented in print, be edited into a smooth and readable text. Continuing guidance on the process of editing has been provided by Hazur's successor.

The editing of *Spiritual Perspectives* reflects contemporary English usage. Because these volumes are intended to nourish satsangis and seekers for many years to come, a lowercase approach has been taken – a radical departure from the older Sant Mat books, in which many terms were capitalized to indicate their spiritual sense. It was felt that this approach is no longer necessary, as the spiritual meaning is evident from the words themselves and the context in which they were spoken. Only terms designating the Lord himself and common epithets for God, the personalized supreme Father, have been capitalized.

In citing the teachings of Christ or the Indian saints, Maharaj Ji would sometimes quote the scriptures, but more often than not he would paraphrase the teachings of past saints and weave them into his responses. For the sake of simplicity, we have presented these references as paraphrases and have not enclosed them in quotation marks. The actual quotes appear as Endnotes at the back of each volume. They are arranged in the sequence as they appear in the Bible and are numbered accordingly. The superscript numbers in the text, therefore, follow the biblical sequence rather than the order in which they appear in the book.

The material presented in this three-volume collection has been organized into sixteen chapters, which mirror the spiritual journey of the disciple. Questions range from the practical issues of everyday life to cosmic principles such as karma and reincarnation, the role of the master, and the practice of meditation and its power to transform our lives. Accordingly, Volume I is titled "Understanding the Basics"; Volume II, which deals with meditation and the inner struggle, is called "Walking the Path." Volume III, "Living the Life," concerns the disciple's relationship with the master, the support to be gained from satsang and seva, and living a balanced life in the world. The final chapter, "The Real Miracle," presents responses that touch largely on the transformation that takes place in us as we follow the path to the best of our ability. The answers emphasize the positive attitude that will sustain us throughout our journey, and explore the spiritual qualities that rise to the surface naturally, like "cream on milk," as Maharaj Ji used to say. The chapter culminates with a restatement of the miracle of the master's grace that has brought us on the path.

While the book's wealth of spiritual guidance has been arranged in topics and, taken as a whole, is an overview of Sant Mat, its essence is the personal, individual exchange. Each question and answer reveals the dynamic connection between a living master and his disciples. The book therefore may be read either as a sequence of topics or in random fashion, by taking a question and its answer from any part of the book and pondering on it as though we, too, were sitting in the presence of the master, reflecting on how his words relate to our own life and spiritual journey. Most of the time Maharaj Ji's answers touched on several themes at once, inviting listeners to reflect on not only the particular subject under discussion, but other, related topics as well. So although the answers have been arranged in chapters according to their primary topic, a subject index has also been included to allow the reader to research a chosen theme throughout the entire collection.

The title *Spiritual Perspectives* aims to convey the sense that the master's answers, taken as a whole, provide many perspectives of a subject, on various levels, thus offering a richness and depth that reach far beyond our own finite understanding. But even as we read, we see that the master's words, whether spoken or written, only hint at the spiritual reality. The experience of spirituality is something entirely different, beyond human language. There has always been a tendency to confuse the words that the saints utter with their inner teaching, and compartmentalize and limit that deeper truth. We ossify the saints' teachings by taking their words literally and arresting them in scriptures and doctrines. But scriptures can only hint at the reality the saints experience and want to share with us. At best, human language is merely a pointer to the truth. Only when we have expanded ourselves to the infinite, as the master has done, can we really understand the deeper meaning of his words.

This collection of the words of Hazur Maharaj Charan Singh, drawn from more than thirty years of his selfless ministry, is a testament to the miracle of the living master. Ever ready to meet us at our level, encouraging us to ask questions, and then – with affection yet firmness – answering us in the simplest and most down-to-earth manner, the master is always present for his disciples. His unbounded kindness, love and patience inspire us to do what is important in life so that we might rise up to meet him within.

> *At that level of consciousness, what questions will you ask? You're not interested in the world; you're not interested in this creation at all. You're so much absorbed in your love and being with your beloved, what questions will you ask? You may have a list of a thousand questions in your hand, but you forget everything, and all your questions are dissolved. Love helps you to rise above all those questions. Definitely he answers all your questions, but you will hardly have any question to ask.*

Spiritual Perspectives

Volume I
Understanding the Basics

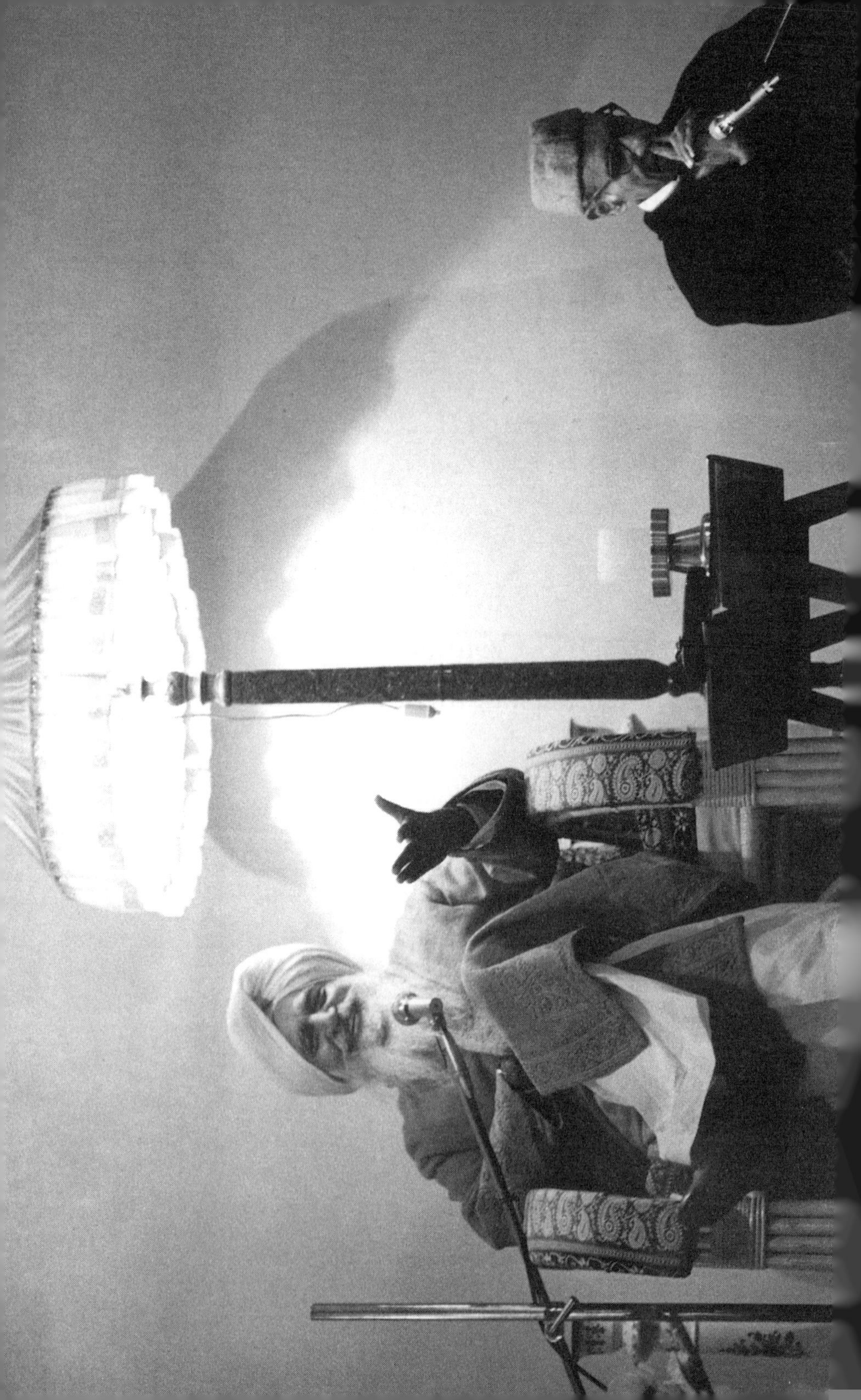

1

Mystery of Creation

Mystery of Creation

1 *Why did we ever have to come down here?*

We can ask the Lord who has sent us here when we go back to him. He knows best. We have to go to that level of consciousness where we can understand his purpose of creation. With this intellect, we can never understand. It has its limitations; it doesn't lead us too far. We cannot understand the purpose of his creation with this mind at all.

Actually, to the real questions, there are no answers at all. I don't think we ask questions because we need answers; we more or less ask questions to show off our own intellect, that this much we know. A child – when he starts learning, when he starts talking and admiring things – how many questions he goes on asking you. He never even waits for the answers. He doesn't want any answer at all. He wants only your patience and that you know that he has learned to ask these questions. He doesn't want your answer, and there is no answer anyway. If you try to answer the child, you will not be able to satisfy him, nor is he bothered about the answers.

The real questions are very difficult to answer, because there's no answer to them. Why God is there, why we are here, why he has made all the trees green – what answer will you give? Why vegetables have so many colours, why flowers give off fragrance – what answer will you give? There's no answer, and these are real questions.

All other questions, about which we have written so many books, are superfluous. There's no answer to a real question. These questions have to be dissolved, so we go to that level within ourselves. Then these questions don't bother us, they don't exist anymore. It's not that they are answered – they don't exist.

2 *Master, why was it that we came down from the Father?*

We will ask him when we go back to him. The fact is that we are separate from the Father, and why he has separated us we can only inquire when we go back to him. We have to spiritually grow to understand the purpose of this creation. In other words, why this creation at all? This mystery of creation can only be solved when we go back to the one who has created this whole mystery, not before. Now we try to grasp everything with our intellect, with our mind, and both have their limitations. We have to go beyond those limitations in order to know.

Hardly any mystic or saint has tried to describe the purpose of this creation. If a child asks the mother how he was born, the mother definitely knows the answer, but she would always like the child to grow to understand how children are born. Then the child never asks the mother at all. So we have to spiritually grow to understand the purpose of creation. We definitely realize that we are separated from the Father and there is a necessity to go back to him. When we are able to solve this mystery of going back to him, then we will also be able to solve the mystery of why we had to come here in the first instance.

3 *Isn't it a contradiction that we want to get out of this creation? Why was this creation made in the first place, and why were we given the senses which make us sensuous?*

You see, the senses have been given to us so that we remain part and parcel of the creation. And the creation is there because the Lord wants this creation to continue. It is his design. And we want to get out of this creation because he wants us to leave this creation and come to his own level.

Why does he want us to come back?

Let us go back and ask him. Let us go back and ask him why he is so anxious that we should come back to him. Brother, intellectually it is very difficult to understand all these answers, and it's very easy to ask these questions. You see, saints generally have not tried to explain the reason for this creation. There must be some reason. But they have definitely explained to us the necessity to leave the creation and go back to the Creator. You see, it's not that they don't know the purpose of this creation. But even if they tried to explain it to us, with our limited intellect we would never be able to understand. The intellect has its own limitation, and we have to understand everything with that intellect. But it cannot take us high enough to give us that understanding that can explain the purpose of creation.

If a child wants to know how he was born, he can never understand. Even if he asks the mother, the mother will put the child off with one excuse or another. But once the child grows up, he will never ask the mother, "How was I born?" He knows how he was born. So similarly, we have to reach or develop that level of spiritual consciousness within so that we can understand the purpose of creation. And then perhaps we won't have to ask anybody at all the purpose of creation. We will know it ourselves. There must be some purpose. It is very clear to us that we are miserable in this creation and we want to get out of it.

Great Master used to give us an example: Somebody has fallen in a well, and he's crying and telling people, "I am miserable, take me out of the well." Taking pity on that man, someone throws down a rope and tells him, "Take hold of the rope and I'll pull you out." But the man starts questioning him, "Let me know whether this rope is strong enough, how was this rope made, where did you get the jute, how much did it cost?" You see, he can ask all these questions when he comes out of the well. First he must realize that he's miserable in the well and that he wants to come out of it. Then he can ask all these questions. But if he starts with that inquiry and the questions, he will never come out of the well at all.

Our main purpose is to come out of this creation because we are absolutely miserable here. Some people are comfortably living in misery, some people are horribly living in misery, but everybody is miserable in this world. Nobody can say he's happy in this world. When we are able to come out of this misery, then we will know the purpose of this creation. We are too low to understand these things at this level.

4 Why was there ever creation, if God is perfect?

In order to know the purpose of creation, we have got to know the Father who has created us. Because even if we try to understand it at this level of intellect – why the Lord has created this creation – we will not be able to solve that problem at all.

The purpose of creation cannot be understood at the level of intellect. You have to rise above the level of intellect; only then will you be able to understand the purpose of creation. So saints generally do not try to explain the purpose of creation. But one fact is before us: This world was created, we are separated from the Father, and we are condemned to this separation. Unless we merge back into him, we cannot escape from birth and death.

We have to grow spiritually within ourselves to understand the purpose of creation. And then perhaps you won't even ask the Father why he has created you, because you will be one with the Father and will understand. In order to know the purpose of creation we must seek the Creator first and then ask him why. Guru Nanak was a great Indian mystic. He said that even if you spend a million lifetimes trying to solve this problem, you will not be able to solve it. Instead of wasting your time in this direction, try to find the Creator and your problem will automatically be solved.

5 *What causes the soul to descend from its original home?*

The Creator has created the creation. And the Creator knows best why he has done so. We can only understand this when we become part and parcel of the Creator. Even if we are told why he has created this creation, we will try to understand it with our intellect and the intellect has its own limitations. Still we will not be able to solve and understand that problem at all. In order to solve this problem, we have to go to the Creator. Then our soul will merge into and be the Creator. By then, perhaps we would not like to know why he created this creation.

The fact before us is that we are part and parcel of the creation. We are separated from the Creator, and unless we become one with the Creator, we suffer. We are suffering the pangs of separation. We are condemned. We are miserable in this world without the Creator. So the fact is before us that we must go back to the Creator. And when you go back to the Creator you can ask him all these questions.

6 *Would you explain to us what is meant by the creation of Adam and Eve in the Garden of Eden?*

What should I explain about Adam and Eve, sister? You see, they have tried to give an explanation of this creation. But I must say they are all myths. There was neither Adam nor Eve. It's all a myth to explain to us how the creation has come into existence. Forbidden fruit are the senses. The mind runs to the senses and collects karmas and becomes the slave of those karmas. So these are all myths to explain the purpose of creation, or how the creation has come into existence.

7 *The question I am going to ask is very difficult to ask and very difficult to answer by anyone, except perhaps by the master. This question has been asked many times before but without an adequate and authoritative answer. The question is: Why really did we leave our home in Sat Desh? Did our souls have some imperfection that made it necessary for the supreme Father to send us out to lower regions? Were we unconscious or conscious? And did we want to leave the Father's house?*

I think I have discussed this question many times in the meetings. You want to know why the Lord has created this universe? Why we are here? If we know why we are here, we will know the Lord. To know why he has created this world and why we are away from him, we have got to know him. And when we know him, perhaps we will not bother to ask him why he has created us. Now we can explain things only with the limited knowledge of the intellect, but that will also be through the mind. The mind can neither explain nor understand why this whole universe has been created. He knows best why he has created it, because in the beginning nothing existed besides him.

If anybody else had existed besides him, then the other being would have known why he created it. Only he is the beginning, and he is the end. He always was, is now and always will be. Everything that we see is his projection.

The question of imperfect souls there does not arise. Nobody is imperfect in the realms of the Lord. Everybody is perfect there, because he is the Lord himself. There, nothing exists besides the Lord, so the question of imperfect souls there, having been sent here, does not arise at all. In order to know why he has created the universe, we should make our way up to reach him. That is the only way to get the proper answer to our question. With our limited knowledge we may go on trying to analyze, but by mathematics or by scientific means we can never reach any decision at all. That is why we are working day and night in meditation – to know why he has created this universe. Even if the saints explained why he has created it, we would not understand it. We would have to take it on faith. We have nothing to put a test to, nothing which can be used for proof or comparison. So why just flirt with our mind and our own intellect, wondering why we are away from the Lord? We should take a practical view and try to make our way up to merge back into the Lord. Instead of trying to analyze why we are here, let us try to return to him. And then we will also know why he created us.

8 Is it true that every soul in existence will at some time get back to its Father's house?

Only the Father knows how long he wants the universe to go on. If he does not want it to go on, every soul will go back to him. If he wants the universe to continue, every soul cannot go back to him. When he wants the universe to be nonexistent, naturally the souls have no other place to go to but to merge back into him. But so long as he wants the universe to go on, all souls cannot go back to him. Some will have to be here.

9 *Does all humanity eventually arrive at the final goal, without any exception?*

When he wants to finish this play, ultimately everybody will go back and merge into him. We do not know how long he wants this play to go on. If he wants to finish it, and if he wants to save us, he can save us tomorrow. He will just finish what we see in this world. But as long as it is going on, we are a part of the agony and we are trying to escape it.

Will he eventually save us?

We cannot question him. It is entirely up to him. He knows his plans. He knows himself.

10 *Master, one time in the past, when creation was started, the Lord sent us souls down here for his purposes. Now, through the grace of the master, we're on the path of Sant Mat to go back home. But I'm wondering, or am somewhat afraid: Would the Lord decide to send us back down here again? Do we have to go through all this again?*

You see, if the master is pulling the soul back to the level of the Father, he is not doing that without the permission of the Father. He is doing as asked by the Father. Masters don't do anything of their own will at all. They have merged their will into the will of the Father. So they do what the Father wants them to do.

Why would the Father pull us to his own level if he has to send us back to this world again? Where's the necessity, and who's forcing him to pull us? He is the one who is pulling us to his own level. The very fact that he wants us to come to him naturally means that he will keep us with him. Why should he send us back at all? If that is what he wants, we are already here. Why should he pull us? Master is taking you to the Lord, and you think the Lord will send you back? They are not two entities at all.

But we were sent here once at the beginning.

Yes, but that is why he's pulling you. You won't be sent back at all. Don't bother about it. Our effort should be to go back to him and not to worry that he will push us out again.

11 *Master, is there anything gained by the soul coming down and viewing the play of life and then returning? Is there anything gained, or has there just been an interlude?*

These are all justifications, I would say. What do we gain by coming back from the Father? We hardly gain anything by separating from the Father. What does he gain when we are in this condition? We have lost what we had; we had everything when we were with the Father, and we lost what we had when we separated from him. We can justify our existence here in that we have gained so much experience by separating from the Father. But actually, what is this gain? There is no gain at all.

12 *I would like to know how you account for the increase in population in the world and where these souls come from and whether there is a fixed amount of souls in the world.*

Brother, it may look as if there is an increase in population, but if you take the entire universe as a whole, I do not think there is any increase in population at all. If there are more humans, there will be fewer insects, fewer animals and other species. Nature keeps its own level – sometimes there are more humans and sometimes there are more of other species, but in the entire universe, the number of souls remains the same.

And there is a fixed amount?

There is a fixed number of souls in the creation and they remain at the same number, unless they go back to the Father. Comparatively speaking, those who have gone back to the Father are very few, of course. So practically the balance remains the same – whether they are human or whether they belong to other species.

God as reality

13 *Maharaj Ji, could you give a concept of the Lord? It is such a wide one, you know, and difficult for all of us. Could you expound that in some way?*

You mean, concept from the point of view as to what he looks like?

Yes. He is omniscient and so on?

You see, he is a power. Give him any name. We cannot even say he is a power. We cannot say he is a person. It is difficult to describe him. I think it is for us to know him rather than to describe him. We all try to think with our own limited intellect what he would be like. What are we? Have we ever thought about ourselves? This body, of course, is comprised of the five elements, but there is something in the body which keeps it going, and that is the soul. The body is composed of earth, water, fire, air and ether. When the soul leaves the body, all these five elements decompose or merge back into their own origin. When the soul is in the body, we are alive, moving about, doing everything that you see. What is the concept of the soul? We have seen many people dying. Have we ever seen anything going out of a body at the time of death? We have no concept of the soul, and that means we have no concept of ourselves. Then how can we have a concept of the Lord?

The concept that we have of ourselves should be the same as our concept of the Lord. The Lord himself gives his devotion within us. He gives his own concept. He himself is within us. I do not think we can explain that with words, but intuitively we know it is the Lord. It cannot be explained logically that he is one. He exists. He is in every one of us and we are part and parcel of him. We have come from him and we are trying hard to go up and merge back into him. This is the natural inclination of our soul towards God. He has put that natural inclination within everyone. And that natural inclination is compelling us, working within us towards him. Without it we would never even think about the Lord. He himself implants in us his devotion or his yearning or his longing for himself. So it is very difficult to describe the real concept.

14 *You started off and now you have to evolve to a higher form of life. What is the basis on which you must start off with a liability and then prove yourself for the higher form?*

No possible logical explanation can prove the existence of the Lord. But he gives his own proof when he creates that loneliness within us, and we find that this feeling of loneliness doesn't leave us, no matter what we may achieve in this world. That is actually the inclination of the soul towards its own origin. It will not rest unless it goes back to its own source, its own origin. So the very soul in the body proves the existence of the Lord.

15 *You say that the mind is not mature enough at this level, and that the intellect is too limited to understand God. But then you also say that the intellect has to be satisfied in order to have faith and to practice. So how can the intellect be satisfied?*

You see, the Lord himself gives his conviction from within that he exists. Logically, you can never convince anybody that God exists. The Lord himself gives his conviction that he exists, he's the Creator, he's within every one of us, he's controlling us and we need him. He himself gives his own proof. It's not by reasoning that we know about the Lord. Reasoning will never be able to convince you. The soul is within the body and that is the essence of the Lord; potentially every soul is God. So he himself gives his own proof when the soul starts yearning towards the Father, because the inclination of the soul is always towards its own Father. It can never be happy without him. It's always yearning for him, for something unknown which we call God. So automatically you get proof of that.

Logically you can't convince your mind that God exists. The pity is that what we see, what exists, actually has no reality. What we don't see is the reality. What exists, what we see in this creation, has no reality. What we don't see in this creation, that is real. Logically you can't convince anybody about the Lord, even about the creation. But the Lord himself gives proof that he exists even to those who don't believe in him. But for that yearning nobody would search for him, nobody would ever think of going back to him.

It is not by reading books or attending meetings or discourses that we are being pulled towards the Father. He's the one who's pulling us from within. He worships himself through us. Then we get convinced about him. Nobody needs any proof at all of the existence of God. That conviction is already there within us. We try to set aside that conviction and tell ourselves that he doesn't exist, that there's no God. But you can't get rid of that conviction, no matter how logically you try to explain about his not existing. You'll never be at peace with yourself with that way of thinking. Something within you will always tell you that he exists.

16 *If God has projected himself in all the different forms here, then God is in everything, right?*

Yes, God is in everything. God itself is reality. Wherever God is, is a reality. But the house in which God lives is not real – that will perish. This body – you call it real, but it will become ash, flame, just merge into the dust; it will be no more. Where is the reality then? It is unreal. And God is not burned along in the fire. God is not buried along in the grave. God is real. Other things will perish, they will decay. God won't decay. So God is real, but other things are perishable.

The pity is that what we see, what we feel, what we touch is not real. What we don't see, that is real. What we don't touch, that is real. That is the pity of it. And we can love only what we see, what we feel, what we can touch, what we can hold. So we are in love with the creation. And we cannot love what we don't see, what we can't hold, what we can't feel, and yet we have to love the Lord and detach ourselves from this creation. That is the whole struggle.

That will be real – what you will see with your inner eyes. But that's not physical. These eyes can't see it. These hands can't touch it. That is real. What we see with these eyes and touch with these hands is not real.

17 *We are told that all things in our life are an illusion or a dream. Is that right?*

What it means is that what we see has no reality – reality in the sense that nothing will exist, nothing will remain, everything is perishable, it's not everlasting. Where is Christ now? Where is Nanak now? Where is Moses now? They were all reality when they were in the flesh, but where are they now? Flesh is no more, so flesh is not reality. That spirit in them was real, not the flesh that is made of five elements, that merges back into the five elements and then you cease to exist. Where are those old civilizations now? New civilizations are coming up; old ones are vanishing. What is real here? Everything is perishable, nothing is everlasting. In that sense, it is illusion.

Only he is real, whom we do not see, whom we do not know. What we see, what we are supposed to know, what we think we know has no reality at all.

18 Is this world really here or is it a dream world?

This world is perishable. You will not be able to stay with this world forever. This world is perishable.

Does it really exist?

It exists in a manner of speaking. When you are in a dream, everything looks real to you. When you wake up from a dream, then only you realize that there was actually no reality at all. It was just a dream. While being in this world, we think it is absolutely real. When we leave this world, then we know it was just a dream.

Are we in the world or aren't we?

At this time we are dreaming! When we wake up from this dream, then we will know that this world is perishable.

Well, if it is a dream, why is it so necessary to make such a great effort?

Because it's a dream that has no reality. You want to be one with the reality. We are miserable here, being separated from the Father. So we want to escape. If we had been happy here, we wouldn't have thought about the Father at all. We would not want to go to him if we were happy here. As Christ said, blessed are they that mourn, who feel the separation from the Beloved, who are missing their Beloved.[8*] They are the fortunate ones. Having come to this creation, they miss the Creator. They are the fortunate ones, the blessed ones. The teachings are meant only for the blessed ones, for the fortunate ones.

Those who are happy in this dream will remain part and parcel of this dream. And those who are the blessed ones will realize the travesty of this world and will want to go to their everlasting home, their permanent abode. They will feel his separation. They will miss him. They will try to get to him.

19 What about the people who deny the authority of God and even his existence?

If the Lord needed our democracy, he would not have got a single vote at all. He's there because he doesn't need our vote. He doesn't need our support. Whether we believe in him or whether we don't believe in him, he's very much there and we can't escape him. We can't run away from his authority. He doesn't need our recognition at all. So those who deny his existence, let them deny. The Lord has not given them the understanding to know that he exists. Those to whom he has given that understanding, they believe in his existence. It is not the people's fault. If he makes us blind, how can we have eyes to see his authority? If he gives us the understanding, then we will realize that he does

[*] References to Bible quotes are numbered according to their order in the Bible and appear in a separate index. The Ten Commandments appear in their entirety at the end of the index.

exist and then we will accept his authority. It is entirely in his hands how much he wants to reveal himself to anyone. Whether we accept it or not, that doesn't affect his authority at all.

Creation as a Projection of the Lord

20 *You said once that the Creator sent down the souls to have an experience of this empirical world, and now, when they are going back, they will forget all this experience. It will be as if they never had come down.*

We are here because the Lord wanted a creation. We had no option. He has projected himself and we are part of this creation now. What experience are we having here? We are not having any experience at all. We don't know what our past was, what our future is. Even if we are suffering now, we don't know what we are suffering for. We are absolutely blind. We are just suffering. We can't even learn from our past mistakes, and yet we are paying for our past mistakes. What type of experience is this? We have no option but to be part of the creation. So he has created us, and we are part of the creation. The real experience of bliss and happiness we will have only when we go back and merge into him again.

You see, you bring together all the flames of the candles. The fire is one, yet every candle has a different root. You become God – then you become the Creator instead of the creation. That is the real experience.

21 *Somebody has said that although it's one sea of love, each individual soul still maintains its individuality in a sense, and has its own particular shabd. Is it true?*

Who wouldn't like to become a Father, rather than a soul? Who wouldn't like to become a sea, rather than a drop? There is no question of any individuality at all. We all merge into one. You see, as Christ said in Saint John, before the creation nothing existed, only he.[72] Only the Lord existed before the creation and all we see is his own projection. Everything has come out of the Lord and the whole creation is nothing but his own projection. When the grand dissolution comes, everybody will merge back into the same source from where they have come. There will be only one. When there is one, there is no individuality. When he has projected himself in the form of a creation, then so many individualities come. Our whole endeavour is again to become one, to lose this individuality which we have got by becoming a part of the creation and to merge back into the Creator and become one with the Creator. That is the effort, and that is the purpose of meditation. If we will still preserve our individuality there, then what is the point of our meditation? We have so developed our ego in this world, our individuality, that we cannot intellectually conceive of the idea, "How can I lose my individuality?" Now we are limited, then we become unlimited. Then we become one.

22 *Maharaj Ji, you say that all this creation is done by God. Sometimes this thing bothers me that there is nothing to explain who created God.*

If we try to find out who created God, we will have to find out who created that which created God, and there will be no end to all that. There was and is nothing beyond God, and God created everything. That is what is written in all the books also. No one has yet been able to find something beyond God. He is his own Creator. He is everything.

23 What was in the beginning?

First, there was only the Lord, who is without beginning and without end. He has projected himself everywhere. There was nothing besides him. He was the only one. All that we see is just his own projection. Everything is projected from him. If we admit that there was something besides him, then the Lord is not one. He is the only one – he always was, is and will be. He is everywhere, and everything is his own projection.

24 Maharaj Ji, does all human life start in lower forms and evolve upwards? I mean, in animal forms, or even lower?

He created the whole thing. The creation did not develop slowly from one thing. He simply projected himself, through his word, the shabd, and the whole world and everything in it was created at once.

25 Then there is no life in a stone, and yet it is held together by spirit?

If we analyze it on a still larger scale, there is something in it to hold it together. There is something that holds the whole universe together. When the Lord withdraws that power from the universe, this whole universe will dissolve. Earth will dissolve in water; water will be evaporated by fire; air will consume the fire and merge back into ether; and ether will go back to God or the Lord, and there will be nothing but the Lord. So there is something to hold this whole universe together, to prevent dissolution, and you can give it any name. We call it shabd or nam. That is why I say that with the help of shabd or nam this whole world is moving. The Lord has created this universe with that word, as you have read in the Bible, in the first chapter of

John. It is through that word of the Lord that he brought this whole universe into existence.[72]

26 Was there a creator of the creation?

The Lord created this whole creation and shared the same life which he had with his creation. His creation is living because he has shared that life force with it. Nothing existed before the creation and nothing exists which he has not created. So he has created everything.

Does this not seem to contradict the evidence which has resulted from scientific research into the human mind?

It is the research of Christ; it is the experience, the spiritual experience of all mystics. Of course, we are human, and the research has been made at our level; but Christ says that having come to this level, we have access to the Father.[135] This is the spiritual experience that mystics try to share with us in their scriptures or books. Just as scientists or philosophers share their experience and experiments in their books, so similarly the saints or the mystics also have experienced certain things within themselves which they share with us in their scriptures.

It may be that they have seen something, but they show very little proof of it.

Well, you must test and prove it for yourself. You see, scientists tell you that a certain combination will give a certain result. You will say, "I have no proof of it." But you can have proof by doing it yourself – testing it for yourself. In the same way, you can also do research on the basis of the given formula. Then, only then, will you be convinced of the accuracy of the formula.

Similarly, the spiritual experiences which the saints share with us in books and scriptures can only convince us when we try to follow their teachings, live their teachings, and make our own research according to these teachings. Then we can say whether they are right or wrong. How can we tell, otherwise, unless we give them a fair trial?

I'm not convinced.

Because you have not made any research within yourself.

Maybe.

You see, in our very presence, scientists have gone to the moon, and we who have heard about it believe that they have gone to the moon. But if you had never heard about it, you might say, "I am not convinced that they have gone to the moon." Well, you may think whatever you like, but ...

No such experimental proof exists about the soul.

What is in the body now that gives it life? The body is the same after death, so what is missing that it cannot move around? I'll tell you what gives life to this flesh.

Maybe that's the creation of a new life, soul.

That is what I'm asking. What leaves the body and what comes into the body which gives it life?

There may be nothing.

If there is nothing, then how is it that today we are running about and tomorrow we are dead? What is in the body? After all, there must be something in the body which gives us life and something in the body without which the body becomes useless. What is that? I mean, as a scientist, you must have made such research. What is it? Give it any name. You can't just say coincidentally you are living and coincidentally you are dead.

There's something which is giving you life, something which, when taken out of the body, leaves the body useless.

After you are dead, the body is still made up of the same elements as when you were alive: earth, water, fire, air and ether. The elements remain the same. So what is there that is missing from the body when we are dead?

Maybe you are right.

27 How can we end our loneliness?

There is no permanent happiness to be found in this world. Some are comfortable in misery, others are uncomfortable in misery, but nobody can be happy in separation. That loneliness cannot leave you. It's the yearning of the soul to become one with the Father. You cannot overcome that loneliness.

Is the Lord lonely?

Well, maybe that's why he's calling us.

28 Is God lonely? If he created us and we're all him, then there is no one to keep him company.

You see, he has projected himself in this creation. He is everywhere. How can he be lonely when he is everywhere? He's within everyone; he's with everyone. He's everywhere in this creation. He has the best possible company because he is everywhere. He's everyone.

He enjoys his creation at every level. There is no difference between his enjoyment and bliss, peace and happiness wherever he may be, on whatever level he may be. We have to come to his level to share that bliss, peace and happiness.

Continuation of the creation

29 *Maharaj Ji, all the religions say, and all the saints say, that God is all powerful, that he is all knowing, and above all, that he is all love, that not a single leaf falls from a tree without his will. The Lord is the creator of this grand universe. He has created man with certain passions, with biological necessities, with biological urges, with instincts. He has created certain natural laws, which he knows man will break. And then he punishes man for breaking these laws over and over again until mankind is so deeply mortgaged into karmic debt that he can't see the light of his true home. The saints all say that when we get back to the Father, we will understand all this. But from my limited perspective, from my very nearsighted perspective and confused mind, I feel that I want to protest to the Lord about this situation. I want to complain about it. Even earthly manufacturers are responsible for their own product. Maybe God should have a product recall. I'm not trying to be funny. I wonder when God will end this charade, this amusement, and bring us back to his bosom.*

Well, brother, your protest is justified. Nobody can doubt it. Because if this creation is to continue, then those weaknesses have to be there. Otherwise nobody can remain attached to this imperfect creation. Everybody would go back to the Father. We are only here because we are imperfect. The moment we become perfect in this imperfect creation, we cannot stay here for a moment. We go back to the perfect being. And now it is entirely in his hands, who he wants to make perfect. He makes them perfect, pulls them to his own level, and saves them from birth and death. Our protest is not going to make any difference to him. But the main thing is that we are separated from the Father and we want to go back to the Father. He may be responsible for our misery, or we are responsible for our misery, or our weaknesses are responsible for our misery. These are all intellectual gymnastics. The main fact is that we are suffering in his separation and we want to put an end to this separation. With his grace, we want to go back to the Father. So we seek his forgiveness, we seek his grace, that he should give us admission into his court and save us from all this misery.

30 *Master, in the Bible, many people say that the end of the world is coming. Is that so? What happens to the ones who are waiting for initiation?*

I think that if the end of the world comes before their initiation, their object is achieved and they no longer need initiation. Where do we go when the end of the world comes? We go back to the Creator. There is no other place to go. Why should we be frightened of the end of the world?

The end of the world comes for us when we quit this body. What difference does it make to us whether the world lives or the world perishes, when we are no longer in the world? It hardly makes any difference. People are just scared and frightened about the end of the world. You see, we should only feel frightened if others will live and we will go. When the end of the world comes, everybody will go. At least you will be in the same place. Don't worry, in our lifetime this good opportunity won't come.

31 *Why does the Lord conceal himself?*

If he didn't conceal himself in this creation, nobody would stick to the creation; everybody would want to be the Creator. The creation is only going on because he has concealed himself in the creation; if he exposed himself in the creation, who would stay here? Everybody would run to him and become part of the Creator; then the creation would come to an end. If he wants this creation to go on, he has got to conceal himself. There's no other way.

32 *Will there ever be a time when souls advance enough to have a Golden Age? I have heard that when all souls are advanced there will be spiritual enlightenment on the earth.*

So long as this universe exists, whatever spiritual advancement there may be, it will only be to a certain extent. If there were to be total spiritual advancement, this world would cease to exist. We would all go back and merge into him. Nobody would be here. As long as the creation is to exist, some souls have to stay in it, so spiritual advancement in this world can only be comparative. In some ages more people are thinking about the Lord and fewer people are devoted to the world. In other ages more people are material-minded and fewer are devoted to the Lord. But the real Golden Age will only be when we all go back up and merge into him, and that will only be when he decides that there is no need for the existence of the whole universe.

33 *I read all about the several ages – the Golden Age and the Silver and Copper Age – when people lived for a million years and were promised a thousand elephants. I think the point is not made literally. Could you explain what that really means?*

Well, brother, we are only concerned with this age. We're not going to live a million years, and neither are we concerned with how long they used to live. The names of those ages are just a way of dividing the years – they're just comparative terms. They're all myths you see, a way of explaining certain things. We are more concerned with what we are going through now. Let scientists find out and prove how long a man used to live. What little experience we have in fifty or sixty years. People just pop off between fifty and ninety – that's all that we are concerned with.

You see, the mind is such; it either runs back or runs ahead and doesn't want to live with the present. We normally don't like to live with the present. Either we are thinking about the past or we are running ahead; we don't want to make the best use of the present.

34 If the world is becoming worse and worse, after it becomes so evil, will it destroy itself?

No, sister. The world was like this, is like this, and will remain like this. History does not encourage us to believe that there was ever peace in this world. Nations always have been fighting against each other. People always have been killing each other. Tribes always have been fighting one another for existence. The fate of the world will remain the same. There will never be peace in the world, there never was peace in the world. As long as the mind is there, human conflict will remain the same. The question is one of degree, sister. Sometimes there is a little more conflict, sometimes a little less. The purpose of the saints is to take us away. We are all prisoners here. The purpose of the saints is to unlock the prison house, to set us free. That is their mission, their purpose, and that is what their teachings tell us.

35 Will you please tell us what is meant by dissolution, and the grand or major dissolution?

I think that all this is mentioned in our books. By dissolution is meant the end of the physical universe. Grand dissolution is the absorption of everything, even beyond the astral plane, back into its origin. The final dissolution, when he is finished with this 'play', when and if the whole creation ceases, will be when everything is merged back into him, the source of everything. Saints have tried to explain this to us through the medium of language, but the intellect cannot comprehend all this, so we should not get confused. The saints do not want us to get entangled by thinking about these things. We should concern ourselves only about this physical universe and make use of the means which the Lord has provided for our escape from it and our ultimate return to him.

36 What does Dr Johnson mean in The Path of the Masters *by the grand dissolution of the soul?*

He doesn't say that souls will die. Dissolution means when the whole world comes to an end. Then all souls go to the third region. The grand dissolution is when all souls remain between the fourth and the fifth regions until the creation starts again. But the soul never dies.

37 What is the reason for not remembering what has happened?

If you remember what has brought you back into this world, you will not repeat those mistakes. And that means you will never come back to this earth again, but will go back to the Lord. In that case, eventually everyone would do so, and the creation would come to an end. If we all knew why we are here, which bad habits or which bad karmas have brought us here, we would stop doing those bad karmas. Kal has received certain boons, prerogatives, certain advantages. That is why this whole universe is going on. One of the boons granted to him was that all creatures would forget their past. Another was that wherever we take birth, we would like those surroundings. There are others about which you have read in *Spiritual Gems*. Those boons to Kal are essential for the continuance of this universe. Otherwise, nobody would commit sin, and nobody would do all these things again if they knew why they were being punished, why they are here. The universe would come to an end. Since the Lord wants this universe to go on, naturally we have to forget all that has happened in our previous lives, for which we are here now.

38 Why does this world exist in the first place? Is it that we must come here to learn these lessons? Why is there a world?

We are learning lessons if we remember what we have done before, so that we can avoid making the same mistakes. When we have forgotten what we have done in the past, what lesson can we be remembering? We are not learning any lessons. The world has to be like this, to a certain extent, as long as it is to exist. If we try to solve the problems of the world, we can never succeed. We can just rise above them.

Creation as the Lord's play

39 We are told that this whole business is a dream. Would you comment on that, what you mean by that?

Well, it is a dream in the sense that there's no reality in this body – and so the dream consists of 50, 60, 70, 80 years. Where are our forefathers, where are they now? Haven't they quit the stage? It was just like a dream; they came and went away. They don't exist anymore; they don't exist permanently. Anything which doesn't exist permanently is just like a dream. When we are in a dream we don't realize we are in a dream. We think everything is real in a dream. We weep, we cry, we are happy, we are miserable in dreams but we only realize that it was all a dream when we get up from sleep. So when you leave this stage, then you realize it was all a dream. Now we are a part of the dream, so we don't realize it is a dream. When we quit the stage, only then will we realize it was just a dream. Our past relationships, the role which we played in the last life as a husband, as a wife, as a child, as a friend, isn't that a dream to us? Where are they? We've forgotten everyone. It was just like a dream. So this will also become a dream after we leave this body. There's no reality. Saints say there's no reality to that which you are attaching so much importance. A real thing always exists – it doesn't perish, it is stable.

We're all in a dreamland. We have to be awakened from this dream and find the reality, and when you are with the reality then you will know that you have got to get up from this dream – not before that. Mystics want to explain to us not to give so much importance to all these things because they're not going to last. They're going to leave you.

40 What is meant by the word 'leela'?

You see, mystics have tried to explain with our Indian term that it is all a play, his play – *maya, leela*. You have seen a puppet show. A man comes. He brings everything, lays all the puppets on the table, and the puppets start dancing. Every puppet has a string behind it. The man is behind the screen, and all those strings are tied to his finger, and he just moves his finger and all the puppets start dancing. The realized puppet knows that there is a string behind her and that somebody else is pulling the string – she is just dancing to the tune of somebody else.

The unrealized puppet doesn't know that there is somebody at the back. She thinks she is dancing. Who can make her dance? She is dancing. Actually, the whole world is a play. When the puppeteer finishes the play he collects everything, puts it all in his bag and goes. There was no reality to the puppet show.

As long as the puppet show is going on, we think it is a reality. But when the puppeteer finishes it, puts the puppets in the bag, we see there was no reality. So unless we reach that stage when we are all put into the bag, we cannot know. Now we are just dancing like puppets. Our karmas, they are the strings – they are making us dance. And we think, who makes us dance? Ego is the attitude we have in life. We think we are doing it. We forget the string behind us, our karma, actions which we have done in the past causing the reactions now. That we have forgotten. So we have become egoistic.

Those who have realized the reality, they also dance like the others, but there is a difference. They have realized that whatever they have to do is according to their karmas. Somebody's making them dance, and they are waiting for the time when the puppet show is over and they can go back to him. But they are better off because they have realized the reality. So we have to realize the reality of the soul and try to go back to the Creator. And then we will also know the reason for this whole play, this whole creation.

Now we try to understand with our intellect why he has created it. But intellect has its own limitations. We may be able to solve nine, ten questions but those nine, ten questions may give rise to another twenty or thirty questions. So we'll always be a victim of this intellect in trying to solve the problem. Instead of thinking why he has created this universe, if we try to think about the Creator and go back to him, then we also will know why he has created the universe, and then perhaps we won't even care to know.

You see, a child asks a mother how he was born. She definitely knows the answer. But a child has not developed that intellect to understand. He has a limitation as a child. So she just puts him off with a smile. She wants him to grow to understand. When he grows and understands, he never asks his mother how he was born. Similarly, we have to spiritually grow and understand why he has created this universe. Now we know that we are part of this universe, part of this creation; we are not part of the Creator. So now we want to become part of the Creator, and that is why all this prayer and all this meditation.

41 *When the disciple is trying to produce love for the physical master, is that really in the disciple's power, to manifest that love, or is it up to the master to just give it?*

Yes. He puts the desire in us; he is the one who is pulling us; he is making us receptive. Actually, he is doing everything. We're all puppets, and our greatest realization is that we are puppets – that is the greatest realization we can have in this life. By meditation we learn that we are puppets, that we are helpless. The ego goes and we begin to learn that whatever is being done is being done by him.

Guru Nanak gives a very beautiful example. He says that the one who is making a puppet show, he has all the puppets in his bag, he takes his puppets from the bag and places them on the table and sits behind the screen. There is a string at the back of every puppet and he is holding that string in his hand, and he is sitting at the back, he is pulling from the back, and the puppets are dancing.

There are two types of puppets. One puppet knows that the string is behind me and he is the puller and I am dancing to his tune, and the other puppet thinks, "Who can make me dance? I am dancing – there's nobody at the back, I am dancing."

Gurmukhs realize by meditation that the Lord is the one who is making us dance in this world, that the string is entirely in his hands. So they dance according to his tune. The other people, they're tricked by the ego. They say, "Who can make us dance? I am doing it, I am dancing, I am behaving like this, it's a credit to me." That's the only difference. To the world, they're both alike.

42 *The other day you spoke about us being puppets. Does the puppeteer like to play with the puppets?*

Sister, the problem is the puppet doesn't realize that it is a puppet. The puppet doesn't realize that there is a string attached to him that is being pulled by somebody behind the curtain. He doesn't realize that at all. The puppet takes pride in its dancing. That is our condition. We are all puppets; we are dancing according to our karmas and we all feel, "Who can make me dance?" We think, I have done this and I have done that, and we are not at all conscious of what makes us do all that. It hurts our ego to realize that anybody can make us dance. We have built up our ego so much that we think that I am independently thinking like this and I have done that – that is ego. The gurmukh also is dancing, he's also part of the creation. All who take birth, all human creatures are dancing. But some are gurmukhs, some are manmukhs. Those who have consciousness and have realized about the string and the man behind the curtain, they're gurmukhs. Those who are not conscious about the string and the man behind the curtain, they're manmukhs. But to a spectator, they are all dancing.

43 *I have a question regarding discrimination. The whole creation – not this particular world, not just this earth –*

> *is his world, your world. I see the whole creation just as a creation of the Father. So, if you discriminate between the people on the outside, so to speak – those whom we see today – those in the other worlds, all of this being the creation of the lower chakras, then there is no good or bad karma. In other words, everything is his world, everything is perfect and at that point the intellect dies because we can't intellectually understand this whole thing. We have to spiritually grow in understanding through meditation. It requires years of beating our heads against the wall, so to speak. There is no intellectual answer to any of this, just love and devotion through your grace and the grace of the Father. Yet we feel so helpless and it seems so futile at times, and we babble, and we say things that we know will lead to nothing in terms of intellectual understanding. What can we do?*

Well, brother, the creation actually is not bad. Sometimes we are bad, sometimes we are good. It's our attitude, the way we look at the creation, that makes it bad and good. The creation itself is not bad. You see a play on the stage – the whole play is not bad at all. Some people play the part of the villain, some people play the part of the sick person, some people play the part of a very noble doctor. The whole play is all right, very beautiful, very good. By seeing a suffering man you cannot say the play is bad, by seeing a noble doctor you cannot say the play is good, because they have been given certain parts to play which they are playing on the stage. They have individual parts to play. On the whole, the play is all right. It is our attitude when we get ourselves attached to a particular character. We say he is a good man, and we think he is the reality, and we say the play is very good. We start hating the villain, who has been given that particular part to play – he can't help it. We start hating that person: "He is very bad; he acted like this; he behaved like this; he should not have done this." He can't help it. He has been given a part to play that way, but as an individual, he is all right – when he gets off the stage, he is all right.

So we should not get attached to people or obsessed with their miseries and start looking at the creation as if it is good or bad. The Creator has created it; he has given certain parts to certain characters to play in this creation. So it is our own attitude which makes the creation good or makes it bad. We start hating a person; we start loving a person; we start praising some; we start looking down upon some. It becomes bad for us or it becomes good for us. If we just see it as a creation of the Creator, as a whole, then nothing is good or bad here at all. We are only concerned with the Creator, who, as the director, has given people parts to play. So there is nothing wrong with the creation. But we have our own angle through which we see it.

KAL

44 If everything really is a part of God, and Kal is a part of God, how did he become such an evil enemy to man?

This is all God's creation. In order to run the universe, he needs all sorts of forces to keep people here. If Kal had not been here, we would all have gone back to the Lord again. This universe would not have existed. In order that the universe should go on, he wants such things, so that we get under their sway and forget the Lord; but still, he has also kept a way or path so that we can get release from this domain and go back to him. If he does not want this universe, it cannot exist even for a day. It is here because he wants it to be here, and whatever you see, all forces have come from him.

A limited example is a state: Everything comes from the head of the state. All the rewards and all the punishments come from him; the courts come from him; even the police come from him; the jails come from him – all departments are under him. If you do good deeds, you get meritorious awards. If you do bad deeds, the police treat you harshly, perhaps put you in prison, and you have to account for what you have done. But we cannot condemn the president or head of the state for all that. He is all good. He does not say anything to anybody about what we are doing here. We are getting merits, we are getting punishments, according to our actions; but he, the president, has to lay out all sorts of administration to run this, so he needs police as well as those who give rewards, and jailers and executioners, too. He needs all these officers in order to carry on. Similar is the case on a universal scale, as long as the Lord wants the universe to go on. But those people who are good citizens are not afraid of the jails and the police. Those people who commit crimes are always conscious of them and feel guilty and frightened of the police and the jails.

In the same way, if we remain good citizens of the Lord, if we are doing our duty in this world as well as our spiritual practice, then we are not frightened of, nor giving any thought to what Kal is and what mind is, or what any other forces are, because these are required for the people who are not rightly making use of their time, who are enjoying themselves through the senses and worldly pleasures and who have forgotten the Lord.

45 What is the force that seems to keep us from spirituality? What is the negative force?

The mind. The Lord has created this whole universe, and he has entrusted the working of this creation to Kal, or as Christ called it, Satan or the devil. The 'prince of this world' also refers to the same negative power. As long as we are under the prince of this world, we cannot go back to the Father. Unless we rise above the realm of the prince of this world, we always remain attached to this world. And the mind is the agent of the prince of this world. The mind has taken hold of the soul, and the mind is fond of sensual pleasures; so whatever actions the mind performs under the influence of the senses, the soul also has to come to the mind's level to reap the results of those karmas, those sins. Hence the mind is keeping us attached to this world, attached to this creation.

When the Father wants the soul to go back to him, he sends somebody from his level. And when he comes to our level, he is one with the Father and has no load of his own, no karmas of his own. He puts us back in touch with the spirit again, and then the soul will be able to go beyond the realm of the prince of this world and will be able to merge into the Father. So it is the prince of this world who is very anxious to keep the souls tied down to this world. That is his duty.

46 Does the prince of this world manifest in the human form the same as the Father manifests in his essence?

No, it's not like that. The prince of this world deceives us by so many tricks. He will send us to the wrong people, he will keep us involved in rituals and ceremonies. He will deceive us in so many ways that keep us tied to this world.

47 How much control of the mind does the prince of this world have over an initiate, and can he use this against another initiate?

The prince of this world – that is, Kal or Satan – becomes more active with the initiate than he is with the noninitiate. When he thinks the soul is escaping from his clutches, he becomes more active; so we should also become more cautious when we are initiated, because we have to escape from his clutches.

48 Does Kal recognize the mercy of the Lord?

You see, satsangis don't have to bother about Kal at all. They have to live with the teachings of their master. They're not to live with Kal at all. Kal plays tricks to pull you out and to deter you from the path. But if you live with your path and with your master, nobody can bother you. So we are in the realm of Kal, being here, but he is not controlling our destiny. Our destiny is in somebody else's hands, who stands as a ransom, though of course we have to pay for whatever we have sown. We have to go through our destiny. But somebody has taken responsibility for us, to clear us from all that destiny and take us back to the Father. So we are not worried about Kal or anybody else.

A good citizen doesn't bother about the police. A good citizen doesn't bother about jail and tortures in jail. It doesn't bother him, it doesn't affect him at all. He doesn't know whether they exist or not. Criminals are always scared of police and about the jails and the courts, because they know what they have to face. Good citizens never even bother to think about these things. So if we are a good satsangi, a devotee of the Father, why should we bother about Kal or anybody else? We will have to do our own duty and live in love and devotion and our meditation.

You see, even if a child commits a mistake, the mother or father never hands over the child to the police. The mother may spank the child, may discipline the child, may punish the child, but the mother would never hand over the child to the police or to the jailer. So we are not handed over to Kal for punishments and all that. But we have to be disciplined. We have to pay through our destiny, pay through our karmas and get rid of them and rise above them. So we're not worried much about Kal.

That is why Christ was assuring us at every step: I'm with you for a little while, and I'll be with you again. If I leave this body, you're not going to become an orphan. My guidance will still be with you, but I will be playing from a different level. I'll be within you, helping you and guiding you. After a little while, I'll again be with you, he said.[127] Master has placed himself in the disciple when he initiates him and he becomes responsible for taking the soul back to the Father. He has to account to Kal, whatever is due to Kal, and then take the soul out of that. That is why Christ said, I stand as a ransom, because Caesar must have what is due to Caesar.[66] When we are willing to pay to Caesar what is due to him, then why bother about it?

With meditation, our willpower becomes strong and we cheerfully go through our destiny. And then with his grace, there is so much remission also. But if we are always frightened about Kal we'll never be able to take a positive approach. We must have a positive approach. As I have said, we have to light our own candle and not worry about the darkness. Why curse the darkness? Light your own candle. We have to light our own candle within rather than be frightened of the darkness unnecessarily.

49 *Would it be correct to say that Kal is just a lower manifestation of the supreme Father?*

Nothing has come into being without the Father. Nothing existed before creation but the Father. What we see is the projection of that supreme Father, the supreme being. So Kal has also come from him, and he has an allotted task, which he is doing. Saints also have allotted tasks, which they are doing, and we all have allotted tasks, which we are doing. This has come from the supreme Father.

50 *Kal cannot do anything on his own? He has to obey orders from the supreme being?*

Whatever he is doing, he is doing by orders of the supreme being. If we admit that Kal does everything independently, it would mean that he is more powerful than the Lord. Everything is under the command of the Lord, the supreme Father. Nothing is beyond him. For example, you have a president, you have an inspector general of police, you have an inspector general of jails. They each have a duty to perform, but they derive their powers from the president. They are not independent of the president. Each one derives his powers from the same source. They have different duties to perform, and they are faithfully performing their duties. We cannot abuse them. Why should we worry about the police when we are good citizens? We cannot abuse the jailer either. He is to do his duty. So Kal does his own duty, and we are not concerned, not bothered about him in the least.

51 *We satsangis are very much acquainted with the ruler of this physical universe as Kal. Many of us are pondering over the question of whether he is a being with a soul or whether he is just universal mind, activated by a spiritual current from the supreme Father?*

You want to know what he looks like?

Well, we are trying to imagine a possible outline of his form, if we can. Of course, he does not mean much to a satsangi.

I think we had better not analyze what he looks like. We should not try to bother about it at all. It is a power. It is our mind. Universal mind is Kal. The Lord actually is shabd, and shabd emanates from the Lord. Similarly, the mind emanates from Kal, and the mind ultimately is Kal.

We should not try to formulate any opinion of what Kal looks like. Why you should even want to think about him, I do not understand. For instance, if we are good citizens, we never bother about the police; on the other hand, criminals are always frightened of the police, as to what they will do to them, how they will punish them. They are always worried and feel guilty because they know that they have done something for which they are bound to be punished. When we come on the path and are attending to our meditation, what fear can we have left about Kal? What is there to think about him? We are all good citizens, and we have a guide to lead us. Why should we even think about what he looks like?

52 Maharaj Ji, because Kal is just, he must be quite happy?

If the Father wants this creation to continue, this creation has to be imperfect. There must be some laws which govern this creation. And Kal is there to see that this creation is continued. But Kal is suffering in the sense that he can't go back to the Father as long as the creation exists. You see, Kal is not independent of the Father. Now, we have so many prisoners in a jail. The jail warden is also appointed by the president. He has been appointed to keep them in jail. He has been given a certain authority and power to keep them in jail and to punish them if they are not disciplined. But he derives his power from the president. And the judge who sends them to jail also derives power from the president. He derives the power to acquit them or to send them to jail. So everybody derives power from the president. They are all just doing their duty. We can't condemn Kal. It is our own actions which are keeping us tied down to this creation. We can't plead our own innocence and put all the blame on Kal. Kal is just. Whatever you sow, so shall you reap.[133] Don't sow, don't reap. But we cry at the time of reaping or harvesting, not at the time of sowing. Kal is just.

53 *When we become initiated and the master takes over our karmas from the Lord, who administers the karmas to us generally, how come we still get tempted by Kal? Why doesn't Kal leave us alone, since he doesn't administer our karmas anymore?*

That is his duty. A satsangi has to account for all his karmas before he can go back to the Father. Whatever karmas we have done already, we have to account for them. For that we have to meditate.

The master helps us. He gives us strength to go through those karmas or, with the help of meditation, helps us to rise above those karmas and go back to the Father. Kal will always be tempting every soul in this creation. And master is helping us through meditation to account for all our karmas and save us from the temptation of Kal.

Does Kal have the same power over initiates as non-initiates?

Even initiates. Everybody. That's his duty. He tempts everybody in this creation because he doesn't want a single soul to get out of his clutches. He doesn't loosen his grip after we are initiated. His grip is the same, but we are not caught by his grip, you see, because there's somebody else who is holding us now who will be able to pull us out of the creation. But he will only do it after having given all of what belongs to the negative power, to Kal, here. Not before that.

GOOD AND EVIL

54 Maharaj Ji, how did evil come into the world?

You see, minus goodness is evil. When there is light, there's no shade; and minus light, there is shade. It has to keep the balance equal. But for the evil, the creation cannot go on – this creation cannot exist at all. If today evil is taken away from this creation, everybody will merge back into the Creator. By 'evil' I mean the negative power, the Kal which is tempting us toward the worldly objects and worldly places, which is always trying to keep us away from our destination, keep us away from the Lord. That is evil. It has to be there if the creation is to go on, otherwise the creation will come to an end. If the Lord wants this play to go on, there must be something that attaches people to this world. Guru Nanak says: When the Lord created this universe, his creation, he put ego in it, and due to that ego this creation is going on. Call it evil, call it ego, call it negative power – they are all practically the same thing.

So due to that ego this creation is going on, and when the shabd saturates you, or you are attached to that shabd or nam, then this poison of ego is eliminated from you and then you go and merge back into the Creator.* So ego, or this negative power, or attachment to the world is keeping us tied down to this creation. The moment that is eliminated, we go back to the Creator. That is why Christ said that I have come not to create peace but I have come with a sword.[39] By sword he means that I have come to cut your attachments which are binding you to this world. You see, we are bound to this world due to these attachments with each other, and mystics or saints just come to cut those attachments, to detach us from one another. The

---

* *Haomai bikh paae jagat upaa-i-aa, sabad wasai bikh jaae.* Guru Nanak, Adi Granth, M1, p.1009.

moment we are detached from one another, we are attached to the Father, we go back to the Father. It is that ego or evil which is keeping us attached to this creation. If the Lord wants this play to go on, if the Lord wants the creation to go on, that has got to be there. The moment he takes evil out from the creation, everybody merges back into the Creator.

55 Maharaj Ji, since Kal is an authority created by the Lord himself, how can we attribute evil motives to him?

You see, it looks like evil to us, but perhaps it doesn't look like that to the Lord. It looks like evil to us because we have to suffer for it, being separated from him, being condemned to this creation. The sun is always there, but then shade is also there. It doesn't mean that where there is shade, the sun is not shining. The sun is always shining, but shade is there. So the Lord is all good, but then so-called shade is also there, so-called evil is also there. So I don't think we can analyze these questions or solve these problems of creation. I don't think we can question or even have any right to question. And even if we question, who hears us? It's only mental gymnastics. I don't think it will have any effect on Kal or on the Lord.

Ultimately we have to come out of this well. Maharaj Ji used to give a very beautiful example. Somebody falls in a well and somebody comes to pull him out and says, "I am throwing a rope into the well. You get hold of it and come out." The person in the well says, "No, no. First tell me where you bought this rope and how this rope was made and where you earned the money to buy it." He asks all sorts of questions. But let him come out first, and then he can ask questions. Let us get out of this misery, these temptations of Kal, and then definitely we will question the Lord about all this. There will be enough opportunity to question, but let us get out of it first. That is the main thing.

56 *I wonder if this world was not in the beginning a Garden of Eden and we people were just like children playing with our toys and having a happy time, until we got jealous of each other, wanting each other's toys, and so forth?*

Maybe, but whatever seed of jealousy came in us, it also has come from the Lord. Nothing has come from outside.

That is what seems so confusing, because it all seems so wrong.

We often feel that when God is all love, from where did evil come? That is what we mean. The sun is always in the sky and it is always shining; then from where does the darkness come? It is only when that side of the earth is facing the sun that there is sunshine; and even then, sometimes the clouds interfere, but we have daylight just the same. When there is negation of light, there is darkness, and the darkness is in proportion to the negation, the obstacle which prevents the light from shining through. Similarly, when we have no love for the Lord, when our face is turned away from him, there is evil.

57 *This may be a very silly question, but it has troubled many minds. In the lower animal kingdom, which does not have the power to discriminate between what is right and what is wrong, what power has placed in the lion or the tiger the instinct to kill other helpless animals in order to survive – and why is it so?*

Brother, this whole world is a field of killing and being killed. You cannot live in this world without killing something. There is a constant struggle for existence, and all creatures are always killing and being killed. That is why all the saints tell us that this world is not worth considering as our permanent residence at all, and we are simply passing through it in order to pay off our karmas, and at the same time trying not to make new ones so that we may not have to come back again. In this world one is either killing or being killed. So the saints say, "Leave this world and come back to the Lord with us." We cannot reform this world, and this world will never become a heaven, but will remain at daggers drawn and there always will be killing in this world. Saints do not come to reform this world. They just come to take us away from this world. We should not be concerned with this world. It will continue like this, for it is a place of imperfection and has to remain that way as long as it exists, as I have explained many times. But through the help of the saints, we have the opportunity to detach ourselves from it and go back into the lap of our Father, the original home of perfect bliss, never again to return to this field of struggle and killing.

58 Master, if we are lords of this creation, and the Lord resides in us, why does the Lord make us commit sin?

If the Lord is perfect, then why is the creation imperfect and why are we part of the creation? That is why we are imperfect – but for that, this creation could not exist at all. If this creation is to exist, it has to be imperfect. The moment anybody becomes perfect in this creation, he goes back to the perfect being. We're only here as long as we're imperfect. That is his divine law. He has created this creation; he has got to make some law to continue this creation. So he has made the law: Whatever you sow, so shall you reap.[133] Mind has been attached to the soul so that the mind may attract us to this creation in order for this creation to continue. That is also his divine law. Mind, or the negative power, doesn't derive power from somewhere else: That is also his divine creation. So as long as the mind is there, sin has to be there, imperfection has to be there.

When we become perfect we go back to the perfect being – the Father; then we don't stay in this imperfect creation. But we can only become perfect when the perfect being wants us to become perfect. Without his will, nobody can become perfect in this imperfect creation. Those whom he marks, only they will become perfect, not others. Others will remain part of this imperfect creation. It is in his hand to fill us with his love, with his devotion. We feel that we love him, that we are in love with the Father, full of his devotion. Actually, he's the one who is pulling us from within and creating his love and devotion within us. But for that pull, nobody would think about the Father at all. So he's the one who is pulling us, he's the one whom we are trying to worship and he's the one who is giving us the opportunity, facility and environment to worship him. He's the doer of all that. Without his grace, we can do nothing in this imperfect creation.

I often say that if there is very delicious food on the plate but we have no hunger, that food is of no use to us. And if we are hungry and there is no food on the plate, what will we eat? We will eat only if we have hunger and good food on the plate. He is the one who gives us hunger, who gives us food. You can take the credit that you are eating, but you start eating because he's the one who has given you the hunger and he's the one who has given you good food, and it's so delicious that you are automatically putting in an effort to eat. He's the doer of everything.

We are full of sins because he wants this creation to continue. Unless we collect sins in this creation, this creation could not continue at all. We collect so many karmas during one span of life that we have to come back again and again, in one species or another, to discharge or to account for those karmas. So this creation is continuing.

59 *Master, sometimes it seems cruel to me that I was separated from the ocean of God in the first place; and yet I am told that God is love and I should want to go back to the Father. I can't put these two things together, sir.*

You see, if this creation is to exist it has got to be imperfect. The moment anybody becomes perfect in this creation, that soul goes back to the perfect One. We can only exist here as long as we are imperfect. Imperfection keeps us tied down to this creation. The moment we are perfect we go back to the perfect being. What made God create this creation, I'm nobody to say. He knows best why he has created it. But the fact is, we have been created by him and we exist in separation from him. We are separate, and we cannot get peace and happiness unless we go back to him. Since our soul is a part of that divine ocean and it has taken the association of the mind, and mind is a slave of the senses, due to those karmas – whatever you sow, so shall you reap[133] – we are part of this creation.

God is all love. But due to the mind, we are in love with this creation now. God is not anything evil or bad. He is love, but this is our mind which makes us feel that God is not love – because our mind is so strong that it does such heinous actions for which we have to come back to this creation to pay or account for all those actions. Since we suffer due to all of those actions, we think, how can God be so cruel? God is not cruel. We have done these actions, and we are suffering for those actions. The president is all-forgiving, but criminals are sent to jail and it is the duty of the warden to keep them in jail. So criminals can't say that the president is so cruel for keeping them in jail. They forget what they have done to come to the jail. If they keep that in mind, then they won't accuse the president at all. They will accuse their own actions. So similarly, it is our actions which are responsible for the cruelty which we are facing every day, the misery which we are facing every day. But since we do not know what we have done in the past for which we are suffering, we blame the Father – look what he has done to us, that we have to suffer so much. Otherwise he is all love.

60 How must we accept the world conditions of today, the wars, the destruction, losses and suffering?

This world can never be perfect. If the world is to continue to exist, it can never become perfect. It has to remain imperfect. The moment one becomes perfect he goes back to the Father. So if the Lord wants the creation to go on, the suffering will be there – broken homes and tragedies will be there.

We come here into this world, in this body, due to a combination of good karmas and bad karmas. When we get the result of good karmas we are happy, and when paying the result of bad karmas we suffer. If we had only good karmas we would be in heaven and if we had only bad karmas we would be in hell. It is always a combination of good and bad karmas which brings us into a human body. So when it is a combination of good and bad, naturally one cannot always be happy in this world. He has to suffer also.

If the world is to go on, it has to be imperfect. If it has not become perfect yet, we should not hope that we are going to make this world a perfect one now. So many saints and sages have come in different countries and different times, yet the world is still imperfect. I don't think it will ever become perfect.

The purpose of saints is not to make this world perfect. They come to take us out of this world, back to the Father. They don't come to improve the lot of people here. They tell us that this suffering will go on in this world. If you want to escape this suffering, there is only one way and that is to go back to the Father. So their purpose is not to improve this world; their purpose is to take souls out of this world.

Christ said that he did not come to create peace in this world. He came with a sword.[39] His purpose of coming to this world was not to make it a paradise, but to cut his disciples' attachment to this world with the sword of truth. He did not come to create peace – that is not the purpose of mystics at all.

61 *Master, last night Professor read about how the world is an evil, sinful and disgusting place. It confuses me to hear that, because the Lord created this world. What's the best attitude for a satsangi to have towards the world? Even though we don't love the Creator yet, what should our attitude be towards this creation?*

You see, the world is imperfect and we, being part of this creation, are imperfect. So we are all miserable, unhappy; we cannot get peace and happiness in this creation. When we become perfect in this imperfect world, we do not stay in this imperfect world. We go back to the perfect being. And being with that Being, we will become happy, we'll get that eternal peace and bliss. Now, in order to put our mind to meditation, the imperfection of this world has to be explained so that your mind will not run to these things for pleasures – because ultimately it will rebound back. A child is always told, "Don't touch the hot iron plate. You will burn your finger." His mother doesn't want him to touch it and burn his finger and then realize the plate is hot. We are always told, "Don't touch the live electric wires," so that we don't have to give our life to learn the lesson.

We are always told, "Don't take poison." Our parents don't want us to taste poison to learn the lesson. So saints tell us, "Don't unnecessarily waste your time in these foolish pursuits. You will never get peace of mind or happiness in this creation. Turn your mind to the Father; only then will you get bliss and peace within." But if we don't believe in them, if we think that they are not correctly explaining this imperfection, then we will go into it and try it. You will come to know its reality. You will come back again. You will learn the lesson through your own experience. Actually, we all learn to some extent, if not to the full extent.

So parents have to give the right advice to the child. But still some children want to have their own experience before they can learn. Others take advantage and make use of the experience of the parents. So it's up to us whether we believe in our parents or not. Either we want to experience, to learn the lesson, or we can take advantage of the lessons of the mystics. So that is why sometimes they are very drastic in explaining things to us.

62 *Can't we make the world a better place?*

I think he has created this world as imperfect. You see, nothing existed before the creation. Only he existed. All that we see is nothing but his own projection. He has projected himself in an imperfect way, so to say, because otherwise this creation cannot continue at all. When anybody in this creation becomes perfect, he becomes a part of the perfect being, he does not remain with the imperfect at all. So if this creation is to continue, there's no other way but to keep it imperfect. Why has he created it? He knows best. But definitely this creation is imperfect. That is why there are so many wars and jealousies and so many miseries all around.

We cannot collect the thorns of the world, but we can definitely wear shoes so that the thorns of the world do not bother us at all. We cannot make others perfect in the creation at all, but we can become perfect ourselves. We have only to look to ourselves to become perfect, so that we may merge back into the perfect being. You see, the creation will remain like this – imperfect.

63 *Maharaj Ji, we often hear people talk of hells and heavens. Are these just metaphorical, or are they really in the domain of God?*

You see, there is heaven, there is hell, but the word 'heaven' is used very loosely. We also call our Father's residence heaven. Actually, heaven is something different than where the Father lives. If we do good deeds, we are sent to heaven to reap the result of our good karmas. That is only for a certain time. And when we finish the effects of the good karmas, we are sent back to this universe again. If we do bad deeds, wicked deeds, we are sent to hell. That is also just for a certain time. When we finish all the effects of our bad karmas, we come back to this world again.

But we have to rise above heaven and hell and to go back to the Father. We have to rise above this cause and effect, the karmas – good karmas and bad karmas. This heaven and hell have a connection with the mind, because mind does the good karmas and the bad karmas, so we remain within the realm of the mind. But a devotee has to rise above the mind. He wants the soul to be separated from the mind. He doesn't want to go to hell; he doesn't want to go to heaven. He wants to go to the Father.

Rabia Basri, a very famous Muslim mystic of Persia, writes in her beautiful books: If it is in my power, O God, I'll burn all these heavens you have made, and I will drown all these hells that you have made so that the people may not worship you out of the fear of hell or for wanting to go to heaven. They should worship you for yourself. It means we have to rise above this heaven and hell. We have to have the real love to go back to the

Father, not do good deeds with the motive of coming back to get their fruit, their result.

64 *Master, are heaven and hell situated on this side of the first stage, of earth?*

This whole world is a heaven and hell. You can make this world a heaven, you can make this world a hell. They exist within you. If you make yourself hell, you are in hell here. If you make yourself heaven, you are in heaven here. Why think about hell and heaven? Make this world a place of heaven. Have that peace within yourself and this whole world will be at peace with you. If we are able to build that heaven within ourselves, then the whole world becomes heaven here. And if we make ourselves miserable, the whole world is miserable to us.

2

Shaping Our Destiny

Shaping our destiny

65 *Would you quickly explain the three different types of karmas?*

Karmas are of three kinds. As you know, a farmer goes to a field to sow seed. He goes again to get the results, to reap the crop. Let us say he brings home and consumes half of it within a year, and the other half he puts in storage. Then again he takes from that store to sow the next crop. And again he brings in the crops. He cannot consume the whole, so whatever is not used he again sends to storage, from which he takes in the future.

Similarly, we have three types of karmas. Whatever actions we are doing here now we will have to come back to get the result thereof in the next life. But in one life we cannot reap the result of all the seeds which we have sown in that particular life. There is always something left which we cannot account for in one life. For example, if you kill a thousand chickens in one life, you cannot pay for all the thousand killings in the next life. You may be able to pay for a hundred or two hundred killings in the next life, and the rest of the account will be sent to your store of karmas. Unless all three types of karmas are cleared, you cannot escape from this world of Kal, the negative power.

Whatever we have sown in the past, we have come now to reap that portion allotted to this life. Whatever we cannot go through from what we have sown in the past is thrown into our reserve or store of karmas. So that portion allotted to this life has now become our fate karma. That is our destiny. We have to go through it. Whatever we are sowing now, whatever karmas we are performing now, that will become our destiny in the next birth. And whatever we cannot go through in that next birth will be added to our store of karmas.

Since all types of karma have to be cleared before you can escape from this realm of Kal, and destiny you cannot change, the saints advise that if you meditate and live according to the principles of the spiritual path, your willpower becomes very strong and you are not affected by those fate karmas. You will be able to go through all that cheerfully, without losing your balance. And, in the future, you won't sow any new seeds for which you may have to come back into this world again.

Whatever you have already collected as stored karmas, these are related to the mind only and can be cleared by meditation. So if you meditate, your mind becomes pure and the soul gets released from the mind; then the whole store of karma becomes ineffective and cannot pull you back to this world.

By meditation we go through the fate karmas without losing much balance. By meditation we become so strong as to not sow any new seed. By meditation we make our mind pure, the soul gets released from mind, and then all those stored karmas cannot pull us back to this world. So we have to clear all three types of karmas by meditation.

66 *I can understand how karma can account for the inner qualities and attributes of an individual, but not how it can account for outer circumstance. Please explain.*

I don't know what the questioner means by inner experience, outer circumstances.

> *What it means is that the person is born with certain qualities, and it is because of his karma. But outside circumstances – whether he is born in rich conditions or poor, is that his karma?*

All is karma. According to our karma we get our parentage, we get that atmosphere, environment, educational facilities, the citizenship of a particular country – it is all due to our karmas.

67 *Is it true that our life's destiny, the things that have and are to happen to us, had already been planned in advance? Is it the result of past karmas?*

First, I will take your first question. What is destiny? Destiny is something with which we are born and which we have to face during our life's span. We call it fate or pralabdh karma, another name for destiny. You know that we have three types of karma. Kriyaman karma is that which we do now, and for which we will have to pay in the future. That which we have done in a past life has become our destiny, our fate in this life. And then we have a store of karmas, which is called sinchit. That is the accumulated reserve, because in every life it is not possible to pay for all that has been done in the previous life, so we have also collected a huge debt of reserve or sinchit karmas, to which we have been adding in every life, for many ages. Supposing a man has killed a thousand chickens in one life. Naturally, in one more human form, he cannot pay for all these one thousand lives. So some of the account will still be left. In this way, in every birth, we have not been able to pay for what we have sown in the previous birth. Thus some huge stocks are left, which are known as stored or sinchit karmas.

Unless all types of karmas are cleared, our soul cannot merge back into the Lord. So we have to face this destiny as the will of the Lord. When you devote proper time to spiritual practice, you will become so strong that you can smilingly and calmly face your destiny. You will not feel much of the ups and downs of the world, and you will be able to account for everything quite gracefully. It is difficult to say whether you will be able to change your destiny through spiritual practice, but you will definitely be able to face it gracefully, without losing much of your balance.

As to the kriyaman karmas, every day when you are meditating, you remind yourself of your destination. You are trying to travel that path. You are trying firmly to remain on the principles while travelling on that path. Then, naturally, you will not be sowing any seed for the future, so you are making no new or kriyaman karmas.

The sinchit, store or residue of karmas can be burned only by meditation. When, with the help of shabd, our mind goes back to its own origin, at which time the soul gets released from the mind, at that stage all the karmas become ineffective, and in this way all of our karmas are cleared. Then only can the soul go back to the Lord.

So destiny is pralabdh karma, which we also call fate. We are reaping what we have sown, and we also have the option of sowing for the future, but we can never differentiate whether we are reaping the old crop or sowing a new seed. Therefore, with the best of intentions and to the best of our ability, we have to try to do only what is good. If then everything does not happen to our liking, we can presume that it is destiny. In the lower stages we can never know whether it is destiny or whether we have sown a new seed. After you cross the first stage, only then will you know what is your destiny and what you are sowing for the future. We are living in our destiny, which we created in the past, and we are creating our destiny for the next birth.

68 *Maharaj Ji, if a soul's life is very short in this birth, would it return again? Why is it that life was cut short? Their karmic debt must have been very light, but does that mean that they have been initiated already and will not return anymore, or will they have to come back in another life and pay off some more karmic debt, which they have not been able to pay off in this life?*

Our span of life depends upon our karma, and if one dies at birth or at a very young age, it is because that was the fate allotted to that particular life. That does not mean that after having this human form, that soul goes back to the Lord. Even though that soul has had no opportunity to make new karma in this life, there is still the sinchit or store or reserve load of karmas from which the fate of the next life is determined.

Our karma can take us down to a lower species and our karma can also bring us back to the human form. It depends upon our attachments, our desires and cravings which we have not been able to fulfil or sublimate during the life span, the seeds which we have sown and have to come back to reap the fruit thereof. All this determines where we have to go – it does not mean that if we die young, we must go back to the Lord. No, that is a wrong conception. It hardly makes any difference whether we die young or old. Our karma, our desires and our attachments determine where we have to go as well as the span of that life and whether to a lower species or whether to come back to the human form.

Without initiation, without spiritual practice, nobody can get release from birth and death. Whether we die young or whether we die old, we have to pave our way, we have to travel on that path, we have to reach a certain stage before we can get rid of this birth and death, and that we can do only by meditation. So it makes no difference whether we die young or old.

Sometimes in our life span we are reaping the fruit of what we have sown in the past, and sometimes we are sowing new seed, but we have to come back to reap again. Those who die young naturally get little chance to sow for the future; but all the same they may have reserve karmas, and they have to come back into this world in order to clear them.

69 The world is a place in which we learn. Do you think that is called karma?

What do we learn in this world? To feel unhappy? To be a part of this agony? What are we learning? What advantage are we taking now from our experiences in our previous births? Do we remember them? Are we not repeating the same mistakes which we repeated in our last birth? How much have we learned from those mistakes? Nothing. So how are we learning? We are just reaping the fruit of what we have sown. We do not even learn from our mistakes in this life, not to speak of our past lives. This world is a field of karmas. Whatever we have sown, we reap, and whatever we sow now, we reap here in the future. We have come here again and again to fulfil those desires, to reap the fruit of the seeds that we have sown in our previous births, and while reaping we also sow for the next birth, and the excess also increases our stored lot. That is karma.

70 I would like to know if it is correct to think that the karma of our health is, perhaps, the heaviest one?

Sister, every karma is heavy. The karma which binds us to this creation is heavy because the soul wants to go back to its Creator, it is yearning to become one with its Creator. Anything which keeps it tied down to this creation is a burden on the soul. And that load is naturally heavy, as long as the soul is separated from the Creator. Every karma is heavy. What difference does it make whether it is a small brick or a big boulder hovering over a needle, when the needle cannot go back to the magnet? The weight is there, whether it is light or heavy. As long as the weight is there, the needle cannot be attracted by the magnet.

Every little load on the soul is heavy. So some people feel that anything concerning health is heavy karma. Some people think anything which concerns the mind is heavy. Some people think, perhaps, that the poverty they have to face is a very heavy load. Some people are rejected in love, and they think this karma is very heavy. So it is an individual way of thinking. But from my point of view, every karma is heavy as long as it keeps the soul tied down to this creation – even to the last, last wrapping.

71 *If you bring somebody into this world and you are on the path, and you do not feed him according to the path, who suffers the karma, you or the child?*

If you do not put the children on a vegetarian diet, then it may be due to the karmas of both of you. The child and you yourself are both responsible for it. But it is his karma. If it is not in his karma, he will never eat meat, even from birth. If he is destined not to eat meat he will be born only in that family where no meat is served. For example, I have never tasted meat or eggs in my life, and my father never tasted meat or egg. Luckily we were born in that family. We could not have done anything about it if we were born in America. So the karma is there. That becomes destiny. That karma brings us automatically where we are to face that particular type of karma. When one's time comes, he will automatically shed all fears and will be on the path with a vegetarian diet.

72 *It is sinchit karmas then which prevent us from seeing the form of the master when we do meditation whilst doing dhyan?*

It is mainly the fate karmas. We have sown such seeds in past lives that we are reaping their fruit now, and we are so busy in reaping the fruit that we have no time to come to the eye centre – we have no environment or source of strength for meditation to lead us to that eye centre, where we can see the radiant form of the master. Because we have already sown such seeds in past lives, which have formed our fate karma in this life, they are a hindrance in our spiritual progress.

If a person takes birth in a satsangi family and happens to have good parents, good friends, a better environment, and he meets the master, keeps his company and is influenced by his company, then he naturally has an advantage over another person who is living far away and always is surrounded by evil influences and environment, and undesirable friends who are always pulling him towards the senses. There is hardly any opportunity for him to get any strength from anybody, and whomsoever he meets knows nothing about the Lord. So he can't have these advantages and he is here due to his fate karmas.

Both persons are satsangis. The one who is filled with love and devotion and is meditating is doing so due to his fate karmas; and the other is struggling under difficult circumstances, also due to his fate karmas. So fate karmas help us onward and also come in the way of our progress. Unless we clear all our karmas we can never go back to our Father. Christ said: Repent, for the kingdom of heaven is at hand.[3] You have to repent for whatever you have done in the past and in this life.

Through so many lives you have passed and so many seeds you have been sowing, and now you can't help cutting the crop and burning it. We have to repent for whatever we have done, and repentance is meditation. You have to bring that rusted knife near the sandstone, then only the rust can be removed. You may have collected a lot of rubbish, but if you have a match, you can burn it all. If you have no match and no fire, the rubbish will go on piling up. The master gives you the match and he tells you how to light it and he helps you to burn that rubbish. Without burning that rubbish, you can never go back to the Father.

73 *It is my understanding that when one dies and the soul goes to one of these regions, one spends perhaps about fifteen hundred years there before one comes back into a human body. What does one do during these fifteen hundred years?*

I cannot set the time limit as to how long you have to stay there, as that all depends on how much karma remains to be worked off. But having a master, we may not have to come back into the human body at all. We can always make our way up from there. We only come back into a human body if we have certain attachments left in this world. That alone brings us back to this world. Otherwise we do not have to come back.

74 *Am I correct or do I have a misconception in thinking that we have certain karmic positions that are relative, say, to the different reincarnations through which we travel, and that the teachings of Sant Mat affect that relationship of karma and reincarnation, in that some reincarnations can be avoided, say, because of following the teachings?*

Sister, with those people with whom we have a relationship in this world, we may not have a relationship in the future world or in future incarnations, so there is no question of reviving karmic relationships at all. We are husband, wife, child, brother, sister, and so on, according to our karma. When we have played our part, we have no relationship left with them; it is cut off completely, and it does not bother us.

75 *Maharaj Ji, what is the meaning of a newborn baby that comes into this world and dies immediately? Would you please explain?*

Sister, that is also due to a karmic relationship with the mother, with the father, with the doctor, with the world and with so many people. It was not in that baby's destiny to see life; yet he has had karmic relations with so many people in the world in the past, for which he has to come back into this world, but not to live here. This is all according to previous karmas. For example, when the mother has conceived, she has to go for help to so many people – the doctor, friends, relations, hospital, and so forth. That is all due to the karmic relationship of the child with those people, through the mother, through the father and through their friends, in addition to that relationship with the mother and father. That all has to be cleared; and yet the child is not destined to live, so it dies at or soon after birth.

76 *Will you please explain why certain people seem to be born with aversions to certain things? Like in my case, ever since I can remember, certain things bothered me very much until I was able to rise above them, almost without experiencing them, from the time I was very young.*

This is what is called karmic reactions, karmic connections, karmic relations. Sometimes we come across people and we just like them for no rhyme or reason. Sometimes we just cannot pull together, for no rhyme or reason. It is all due to karmic relations.

Sometimes we do things without any intention or motive, just under impulse, and when we try to reason it, we have no reason for it. Yet we do it. Certain things we explain by karmic connections or past connections of a past birth.

77 *If you have attachments to a certain country that you have never been in, with certain feelings that you do not understand, could you have been born in that country?*

Either you were born in that country or you may be thinking that to be born in that country may be your ideal. Some people are fond of worldly achievements and worldly riches and all that, and they are so envious and jealous of those people who have it that naturally those desires and cravings to have all those things may take them there. We take birth due to our karmas and due to desires, which we create every day and which we cannot fulfil in this life; so we have to be born again to fulfil those desires. We may have karmic relations of a past birth in a different country, or we may have unfulfilled desires to go there.

78 *How can we tell when something happens because of fate? People say "I am paying off karma" when it happens to be an event that they do not particularly like, or an event that is particularly unfortunate.*

Most of the things we say are just to justify our weaknesses, to justify our not having made any effort. That should not be the attitude at all.

79 *What are the karmic relations between identical twins?*

You see, their whole attitude towards life is different sometimes, and they have to pass through different types of lives. One may become a very noble person; the other may become a wicked person. I have seen twins, and they don't act the same way. Everyone has a different type of karma which they have to face in this life. Their destiny is not the same. Their destiny is only to take birth together because there must be some strong attachment, or some karmic relationship. But otherwise, they have their individual destiny – their destiny is not the same.

80 Is there any karma created when satsangis who are neighbours share rides and exchange driving their cars? Also to go out to dinner together and wonder who paid last, and so forth?

That is just like asking, when we breathe, do we add to our karmas? I do not think we should analyze these things to that extent. In love there is nothing of the sort. We should not analyze these petty things.

81 Maharaj Ji, if someone owes a bill and does not pay it, should you write it off or should you take legal steps to collect it? How would karma come into that?

We should not try to analyze these things in too much detail. We have to take a practical, objective view in life. If you think he owes, you can go to the law court. If it is in your karma to collect, you will get it; and if it is not in your karma to get it back, you will lose your case.

82 Master, when we are approached on the street by alcoholics or beggars, should we give them money?

If you know that your money is going to be misused, you should never give it. When you know that the beggar is going to drink, and misuse the money, I don't think it's wise to give him any. If you know that he's going to put it to good use, then of course there's no harm in helping him.

Could we take on someone else's karma that way?

Well, if you give the money knowing that you are encouraging him to do something which you don't want him to do, you are becoming a part of him to some extent.

83 *About injustices and merciless treatment, how can you tell whether what happened was an injustice or whether that person was not better off having been killed, or perhaps staying in the concentration camp was the means for him to come to the path? I do not think at our stage of development our vision is broad enough to tell us whether a thing is for our own benefit? It may seem to be for our benefit and it can be very detrimental to us?*

The thing is that we can only know whether justice has been done to us or injustice has been done to us if we know what we have done in the past. If we can know what we have sown and what we are reaping now, only then can we determine the difference.

84 *When you did something bad and you know you did something bad, you have a bad conscience and feel guilty. But what about when you do not feel any problem at all, and all of a sudden somebody cuts your head off?*

As you sow, so shall you reap.[133] That is what it proves.

The individual has no idea of what he did?

That is right. He does not know. We are meditating and trying to know what we have sown.

Is not the argument the same, like last week forty-four people got killed in an airplane and as long as we do not know them, as long as we were not attached ...?

That is right. Thousands of insects are getting killed under our feet every day. When we are breathing, God knows how many souls we are depriving of life. We feel affected only by our own friends and relatives, because we are attached to them. But everything belongs to the Lord, so if we analyze like that, we are led nowhere. Whatever we think, we do not know whether there is justice or injustice. To us, with our limited intellect, it looks like injustice because in our presence these poor souls never did anything wrong, for which they have been killed. But ours is a limited vision. We do not know what they have done in their past lives, whether an old debt has been paid or a new seed has been sown. Until we have reached that stage where we can know, the Father alone knows, as far as we are concerned.

So, actually there is no injustice, ever?

These are the fruits of karma. As we sow, so shall we reap.

And is it not that some people in groups, like in an airplane, all taking the same trip, their time calls for being beheaded or killed, and when it comes, they go in groups?

That is right. They have some associations from the past – that is the reason they all have to die together; or that some are killed and others survive. It is all karma.

85 Maharaj Ji, some Western teachings, philosophies or schools believe in group souls. In other words, souls also merge in one group?

There is nothing like group souls. Some souls have associations from the past that cause them to be born together, certain karmic associations; but you cannot call them group souls. They are individual souls and for a certain time they are together; but they may go different ways. They may not go together all through even just one physical life.

I guess there are some professors who teach that there are group souls, but I do not go along with it. They seem to think all of us are a particle of this, whether it is a human being or …?

No, no, that is not right.

All are individual souls?

This karmic association brought us all together for a period. We also have karmic associations with some other group, or some other associations to fulfil. So it is not true that we will always be led together everywhere. Each soul has its own karma to fulfil; but eventually, all those who are progressing on the path will merge back into the Father.

86 *Maharaj Ji, every morning when you open the newspaper and you find some mention of souls in trouble, would you call this national karma? Is there such a thing as national karma?*

You see, karmas of some people are combined together, you may give it any name. But actually, we are only concerned with individual karmas. The relationship of the soul with the Lord is an individual relationship, but when all those souls have karmic relationships among themselves, you can call it a national karma then, national calamity, national situation which they have to face. But actually, the relationship of the soul with the Lord is an individual relationship. It's not a national relationship with the Lord or a combined relationship with the Lord. But when such souls do come together, you can say they have to face the same type of karma, every one of them. So you can call it a national karma.

87 *Master, we think of karma always as an individual matter, but it seems there's group karma too. For example, the Jewish people, over hundreds of years, have suffered rejection, murder, and torture. Why does one particular group of people go through similar experience?*

Because people are interconnected with each other. Karmas are always individual, but since they're so interconnected with each other, karma can become collective. They're suffering collectively, because they're so interlinked with each other, but karmas are all individual. For example, if ten people conspire to kill someone, the karmas will be individual. All ten are responsible individually for that crime, but since they have done it together, they have been interconnected with each other in relation to that crime, so they may suffer collectively. They will be suffering individually, but may suffer at the same time, so it looks like they're suffering collectively. In war, you kill a thousand people with just one blow, one bomb. They have all died together. Karma is individual, but since they have died together, they're interconnected with each other. They may be together to reap the fruit of that karma. They may be together to take revenge on whoever killed them. So in that way we can look at karma as collective, but actually karmas are all individual.

88 *Maharaj Ji, we often read in the paper about tragedies caused by bursting of river banks and people dying in boat or train accidents in which so many people die in one tragedy. Can we reconcile that with their karmas, that all these people die at the same time?*

Yes, some sort of connection is there for them to die together. In war, many people die together. With one bomb, how many people can be killed? They die together. So some sort of karmic relationship is there, for them to quit this state of life together.

89 Is there such a thing as group karma?

No. There is no such thing as group karma, but definitely people's association with each other forms a type of a group. A thousand people are fighting together and trying to kill another thousand people in the army, so each side has made a group. They have a karmic relationship with each other, but everybody will have individual karma, and any individual can escape from that group. It's not that the whole group has to escape or be condemned. Any individual can escape from that group according to his own karma. So there is no group karma, but they have an association with that group, they are all interconnected in relation to that karma.

90 Something still bothers me mentally. I came originally from Europe. In Europe there were twenty million persons who had to give their lives, innocently – some very fast and some by slow torture – seemingly for no reason except because they were born in a different religion. I think you are familiar with that. They were herded into concentration camps, gassed and killed. How can I face my God and say, why did you do a thing like this? To us people down here, it looks like a terrific injustice to kill people just like cockroaches.

Who is killing? It is the people who are killing each other.

Because God has power over his children even when they say, "Why did you produce me?" I would say you are not being produced by me but by the Almighty, and because you behaved like that, when he hits you back, you feel it. Now stop hitting him, and there will be no such reaction. Now why did somebody not stop all this slaughter in Europe? All these wars?

This is where the karma theory comes in.

You see, I come from the middle of this, so it hurts me deeply.

I know. I know the effect on the human mind.

I was saved maybe by you, by some miracle.

It must have been the Lord. This is all due to our individual karmas. What we think of as injustice, what we see as injustice – God alone knows whether it is justice or injustice. Besides, is not that same injustice being done every day to millions and millions of cows and other animals that are being killed for the food of human beings?

Yes, in our small way, we are beginning to stop that.

In this world, there is nothing but misery. As long as the creation exists, these things are bound to remain. That is why the saints say: We come to take you away from this world.

91 *Is there any karma involved if a person resorts to surgical sterilization? Or to effect birth control?*

If it is in his karma to go through a surgical operation and not to have any children, he will have to do that. Nothing happens without karma. So that was his karma which led him to that.

92 *I meet a lot of people who, I think, are very spiritual. I feel very good around them, and they are not satsangis.*

Still, I feel that they are better satsangis than I am. Why are they not satsangis?

Every good person is not necessarily a satsangi. Some people were so nice and sincere in their last life and have been so good to people that they are getting the reward of their good karma.

But these people who are so good and so nice, they may be living out their good karma from their past life, but they are also sowing and seeding good karma for the next life, and I thought …?

That is right, so they will get its fruit again, but all the same, they will remain in the cycle.

If I am living out my bad karmas and I am being not as nice as they are, then will I have to come back?

Then you should try to be like them.

Well, I think they may be getting …?

They will definitely get the advantage. They may come on the path if they are very sincere in their desire to meet the Lord. When we have a strong desire to meet the Lord and we have real devotion, even if we do not know the path, even if we do not know how to meditate, how to pray for his grace, then the onus is on the Lord to put us on the path. Our duty is to have a genuine yearning to meet him. Then we automatically behave in such a way that we find ourselves on the path leading towards him. That is why it is mentioned in the discourse that you have just heard that only by the grace of the Lord can we meet the master, and only through the Lord's grace are we on the path. We, by ourselves, can never do anything; but if we are really sincere and honest in our search, then, if not now, sometime in the future it will be for the Lord's grace to put us on the path. As Christ said: Not I, but the Father in me doeth all things.[120]

Clearing karmas

93 *Master, I've read in one of the books the master saying that a satsangi can go through a lifetime's karma in a matter of days. Can you explain that, please?*

Provided you are full of love and devotion and you are not attached to anything else in the world. There is a stage which we achieve by meditation – it is a stage of mind, which we receive by meditation.

You see, this thing is worth understanding. How do we account for our karmas? All karmas have association with the mind, and the mind is slave of the senses, so, being slave of the senses, it collects dross. The soul has already taken the company of the mind. So all these karmas have become the master. The soul has become the slave, and the slave has no option but to dance to the tune of the master. Due to these karmas, which have become our master, the soul dances from one flesh to another, from one body to another. Unless the soul becomes master in the house, it cannot get free from the clutches of the mind and become one with the Father. Since the mind is fond of pleasure, unless the mind gets better pleasure than the sensual pleasures, the mind refuses to leave the sensual pleasures. And that better pleasure the Lord has kept within every one of us at the eye centre, which has been referred to by different mystics by different names, as you all know.

So unless we withdraw the mind to the eye centre and it comes in touch with that divine melody within and we taste that nectar, that better pleasure within, the mind refuses to leave the senses. With that better pleasure, with the taste of that nectar, slowly and slowly the mind starts leaving all the sensual pleasures and has its direction towards its own origin, that is, Trikuti. When the mind reaches Trikuti, the soul automatically gets release from the mind. The knot between soul and mind has been untied. Now the soul is whole; the soul is free; the soul shines. Now the soul is no longer under the sway of the mind. Now the soul is the master, and the mind has become the slave.

You can say you have burnt all the karmas, you have destroyed all the karmas, or you have risen above the karmas. You can use any phrase. It is immaterial. You have accounted for all the karmas, Caesar has been given his due.[66] But until the soul leaves the mind, our karmic account is not cleared at all. Only then does the soul shine and merge back into the Lord. So this process helps us to untie this knot of soul and mind.

A needle is always anxious to be attracted by the magnet. The magnet is always pulling the needle, but if there is a weight of an iron over the needle, the needle becomes helpless. Similarly, every soul is anxious to become one with the Father, to go back to the Father. Every soul is being attracted towards the Father. The inclination of every soul is towards its own origin, towards its own home, but it has become helpless due to the weight of the mind and that of sins and karmas. So we just have to remove that weight of the mind from the soul. It will automatically go back to the Father.

That is why everyone is searching for the Father in one way or another. Everybody needs the Lord, in one way or another, because the inclination of the soul is always towards its own origin. Under that pressure, we all run here and there in search of the Father.

94 Master, what is the connection between the grace of the master and the law of karma?

By the grace of the master, we know how to get rid of karmas and how to rise above them. We can know this only through the grace of the master. And that grace, as explained by Christ, is to hear the spirit within, to be given a new birth, to be baptized with the holy ghost, with the light.[5] When he puts us on the path, he lays certain teachings before us.

If we live in the teachings, if we follow the teachings, if we withdraw our soul current to the eye centre and hear the spirit within, that is the grace of the master. Without grace we can achieve nothing. The more effort we put in, the more grace we get; the more grace we get, the more effort we make. They go side by side. And his grace means that, by following his teachings, we can rise above this realm of mind and maya, with which our karmas are associated.

We have three types of karmas. First, there are the deeds which we have done in past births, for some of which we have come to face the consequences in this present body. Then, there are the things we are doing now, which may cause us to come back to face the consequences later. And, since in one birth we cannot pay off all that we have done in the past, whatever is left over is thrown into the storehouse of our karmas.

Now, unless all three types of karmas are cleared, the soul can never get released from the mind; the soul can never go back to the Father. So masters tell us that if we are in touch with the spirit within, we will get the strength and the willpower to face our destiny, to go through the effects of the seeds which we have sown in past lives. And since we are attached to the spirit within and are steadfast on the principles and teachings of Sant Mat, we are not sowing any new seeds.

Christ also tells us what sowing new seeds means. Since we are not sowing new seeds and whatever we have sown in the past we are going through now as part of our destiny, whatever is left as a store of karma only has association with the mind. When the mind is attached to the spirit, then it is able to detach itself from the sensual pleasures and is able to go back to its own source. Once the mind goes back to its own source, the soul gets released from the mind. And then all these karmas become ineffective; they cannot pull back the soul. At that stage the soul is the master and dominates the mind; and the mind has become the master of the senses. But before that, the senses are the master of the mind and the mind has become the master of the soul.

The whole process is to be reversed. With the help of the grace of the master, we have to withdraw our consciousness to the eye centre. When we are able to hold our attention here at the eye centre, the mind is freed from the sensual pleasures and becomes the master of the senses. Then they cannot pull back the mind because it has become attached to the spirit. When with the help of the spirit the mind goes back to its own source – the second stage, Trikuti – the soul gets released from the mind and then the mind can no longer pull the soul down. Then the soul can rise above all these types of karmas; only then the soul shines, becomes whole and clean; and then alone the soul can merge back into the Father.

95 How does meditation help us to burn karma?

Sister, as you all know, karmas are of three types, pralabdh karma, kriyaman karma and sinchit karma. Fate or pralabdh karma, whatever we have sown in the past, we are reaping the result now. Whatever we have done in the past, that has become our fate karma now, which we have to go through during this lifespan. The point is: Don't sow any new seed, so that you may not have to come back again. We do this meditation from two points of view: First, so that under the influence and intoxication of the mind we may not sow any bad seed that would cause us to come back into this world. And second, whatever we have collected in the past births, our sinchit karmas, our stored karmas, they also have to be burned. Because unless they are burned, we can never go back to the Father and we can never get rid of these karmas at all.

As you know, if in this one lifespan you kill a thousand chickens, in the next birth you cannot account for all that you have done in this one birth. You will be able to account for some, and the rest will become your store of karmas. So from every birth a small amount becomes a very big amount of stored karmas. We have to clear all three types of karmas. Saints advise us that as far as fate karma is concerned, if we keep our attention in meditation, we will get strength to face those fate karmas without losing our balance much. He also sometimes redeems us from the intensity of those karmas; he helps us. Master also helps us to go through those karmas cheerfully, at least without losing our balance. But those karmas we have got to go through.

Since our attention is entirely in meditation, we are not worried much about worldly objects and worldly faces. And we don't hanker after them. Our real attachment is to the shabd and nam, so naturally we will not be sowing any new seed. We will not be doing any new karma which can bring us back to this world. If you get detached from the world, you have no karmas at all. It is the attachment which creates karmas, always. If you are not attached to this world, you have no karmas at all for the future. And whatever our stored karmas are, those we can burn only by meditation. All these karmas are connected with the mind. When the mind is attached to the shabd and nam and goes back to its own source, Trikuti, and the soul gets released from the mind, all these karmas become ineffective because they only revolve around the mind. The soul can only get released from the mind when the mind goes back to its own source, Trikuti, the second stage. So that is why we are attaching our mind to the shabd and nam, because that shabd and nam is much sweeter than the sensual pleasures. It's much better than the sensual pleasures. And mind is fond of pleasure. So unless the mind gets better pleasures, it refuses to leave the worldly pleasures. By attaching it to that sound or holy ghost, we have to bring back our mind to its own source – we purify our mind. Only then can the soul get released from the mind and we can get rid of these karmas.

96 Maharaj Ji, does the master arrange the disciple's karmas that he has to go through in such a way that the disciple can also learn lessons from them as well as go through them?

Well, brother, the first thing is that we don't know for what we are being punished. And then, by the time we reach the age when it's time to learn the lesson, it's too late. We leave the body and go somewhere else. I don't think we learn any lesson from our karma at all. We don't learn any lessons at all, because we don't know for what we're being punished. If I know that I am being punished for this particular misdeed, then of course I will at least think I shouldn't have done that and I will not do it in future. But when I don't know for what I am being punished – the seed may have been sown long, long ago, and I don't know what crop I am collecting – then what lesson am I going to draw from it? So you see, we have to repent in general, not in particular.

As Christ said: Repent, the kingdom of God is at hand.[3] So that repentance is general, for all our karmas, our collected karmas, the load of our karmas, not for any particular karmas, because we don't know about any particular karmas at all. And that general repentance can only be done by meditation. Meditation is the real repentance. Repentance means not to commit the same mistake again, to refrain, and to be sorry for whatever we have done in the past. That is repentance. But we don't know what mistakes we committed in the past so that we can avoid them in the future. So real repentance can only be done by meditation, because the mind commits mistakes by being a slave of the senses. We have to withdraw the mind from the senses and attach it to the sound, that melody within.

When the mind is able to go back to its own destination, Trikuti, and the soul gets released from the mind, then we are able to repent for all the past karmas. That is real repentance; it means that those karmas cannot pull the mind back to the creation because the soul is no longer under the sway of the mind. All those karmas become ineffective. That is real repentance for the past, and that real repentance can only come by meditation. It is a general repentance, it is not a repentance for particular karmas. You can repent for what you have done in this life if it is weighing on your mind, if a sense of guilt is there – naturally you can repent for that. But we can't repent for what we have done in the past because we don't know what we have done. So only meditation helps us to get forgiveness from the Lord. Forgiveness, repentance, meditation – ultimately they're one and the same thing.

97 Is it at all likely that we could clear all our debts in one life?

Fate karma you have to go through, and sinchit karmas, if you meditate, can all be cleared in one life. If your load is not much and your meditation is all right, it can be cleared in one life. Fate karma you have to go through, you are going through, but the sinchit karmas, which are dragging you to this world, you can burn them like a heap of grass. Either you take a little portion of it and burn it or you burn the whole of it. It depends on you. By meditation, either you just take a little portion of it and burn it and the rest remains to be burned, or you burn all of it. So fate karmas and sinchit karmas can be cleared in one life, with the grace of the Lord. But it depends upon how much we have to burn, how much effort we make, and how much help we get from our environment to burn it. Many things are not in our hand, also.

98 *If a master diminishes or decreases the karmic load of a satsangi, does the master's body always suffer the consequences?*

You see, generally the karmas which saints help us to go through, help us to get rid of, or share on themselves are the sinchit karmas, the store of karmas which are pulling us back towards this creation again and again. We generally get help in relation to those karmas. The fate karma we have to go through. We get strength to live through these karmas without losing our balance much. But generally the real help we get is with sinchit karmas, our store of karmas. We are trying to burn them by meditation, but sometimes you can't. So there you get help to burn them by meditation.

99 *Will master see that the things that should be brought up to be worked off during a lifetime are brought up and things that shouldn't be will be left? In other words, is he always controlling what we do work off as far as sinchit karma or anything else?*

Actually, master takes control of all your sinchit karmas, and he knows how to account for all that. Caesar must have his due – whatever belongs to Caesar must go to Caesar.[66] What belongs to Kal, we must give to Kal, and all these karmas belong to Kal. We have to account for all those karmas, so master stands as a ransom – he helps us to clear all those karmas. How he helps us – that is his job.

So our duty is to put in our time with faith, with as sincere effort as possible, and leave the control of the situation to the master?

Our only endeavour should be to attend to the meditation and not worry how many karmas we have. That is for him to burn; that is for him to take care of. They may be gone through even in the dream stage, in meditation, even in the physical body. He has so many ways and means for the disciple to go through those karmas, and we should not try to analyze them. Even if we try, we can never understand them. The only thing that we can do is attend to our meditation and leave all that to him to take care of, because we have already made a mess of ourselves. In order to clear our karmas, we should try to not make more mess. Sometimes I really feel if only we were to understand that everything is destined, we'd feel happy. If it had been left to us, what a mess we would have made. Everything is destined, and we have just to go through our destiny.

Maharaj Ji, there are so many stories about how the master will interfere or will help and lessen the pralabdh karma.

I don't think we should give any ear to these stories at all. They are exaggerated, they are twisted, they are imagined sometimes. They may be right, they may be wrong, but why bother about them? What is the use of these stories? We don't understand them, we can't analyze them and we can't take any lesson from them. So let us only attend to meditation. That is the best story.

100 Maharaj Ji, do we do meditation for good karma as well as bad?

Yes, for both. You see, it's a comparative word, what is good karma and what is bad karma; karmas are karmas. Whatever ties us down to this creation is karma, whether good karma brings you or bad karma brings you. Whether you come here as a pauper, whether you come here as a ruler – it's immaterial as long as you are part of this creation, because then again you will collect more types of karma, so you will remain part of the creation. So we have to get rid of all types of karmas, good and bad. It is our way of looking at things. Actually, whatever keeps us away from the Father is a bad karma. From the worldly point of view it may be very good, but whatever pulls us towards the Father is a good karma – sometimes many things are blessings in disguise for us. So we have to get rid of all types of karmas, good or bad. Whether you sow chillies in a field or whether you plant mango trees, you have to go to that field to collect that fruit. So we don't want to sow anything. We want to uproot whatever has been sown, whether it's a chilli bush or an apple tree, whatever it may be.

101 Well, I was trying to ask you whether by living a balanced life with regard to the good as well as evil you might commit, do the good and evil balance themselves?

Well, brother, neither your evil deeds can help you to escape from this creation, nor will your good deeds ever help you to escape from this creation. You have to account for even your good deeds. Unless all type of karmas are washed, cleared or accounted for, the soul can never escape from this realm. That does not mean that if we always do good karmas we'll be able to escape from this creation. You won't. You may come as a ruler, as a king, as a rich man, as a noble man. But still those karmas will bring you back to this creation, howsoever good they may be. We have to account for all karmas, good and bad both, and 'good' and 'bad' are also comparative words. There's no definition of what is good and what is bad. Anything which leads us back to him is good; anything which keeps us away from him is bad. These are comparative words. We are to go beyond the realm of good and bad. Only then can we escape.

102 Can we cancel out our bad karmas with good karmas?

Meditation is required to burn all karmas. 'Good' and 'bad' are comparative words. What you may call good, it may be bad. What you may call bad, it may turn out to be good. These are comparative words. But karmas are karmas. You see, when we are in a better situation, a healthy situation, we think that is the result of good karmas. When we are right in the middle of a miserable situation, we think it is a result of bad karmas. But that is our classification. Karmas are karmas.

103 If we die and at the end of this life we have no strong attachments, could there be strong attachments from previous lives that could pull us back, or do we need to be concerned only with this life?

Our past store of karmas also pulls us back. Those attachments also pull us back to this creation. Actually, all this meditation – 99.9 percent of it – is meant for the store of karmas, our sinchit karmas. Because with a strong willpower you can go through your destiny without losing your balance, and you can also discipline yourself not to sow any new seed in this world, but you can't control what you have done in past lives. You have no control over those actions. All those collected karmas are to your credit, and they pull you back to this creation, every time. So you have to burn all those. And meditation is actually meant to burn all those karmas. Meditation is nothing but repentance. Attachments also pull us back, definitely, to this creation. These attachments are new seeds. We can get rid of them by strong willpower also. But what about the seeds which we have already sown, over which we have no control now? We can't uproot them now. Time has past. We have to collect that crop of whatever we have sown, and we can only burn that crop by meditation. So meditation actually is meant for sinchit karmas.

104 *Maharaj Ji, there was a debate in our meeting one day about animals, and whether they are creating karma or simply paying off karma.*

Everybody is creating karma or paying off karma. But since discrimination is not there in animals, they are not much responsible for all that.

They are mostly paying karma?

They are creating also, but they are not held responsible so much because the sense of discrimination is not there. Christ says it very beautifully: Now you have no cloak and cannot claim you didn't know what you were doing.[125] The Lord has given you discretion with which to judge good and bad, and you cannot escape from the situation saying "I never knew." But animals can escape the consequences of their actions because they have no sense of discrimination. And you humans, being the top of creation, have no cloak now. You will have to pay for what you do.

When a human dies, you have often said that we go into the astral existence. Does this apply to animals also?

They don't go there at all. How can they go there? Human birth is the last rung of the ladder. From the lower rung you can't jump up to the highest – you have to climb rung by rung, step by step. Only from the last step of the ladder can you go to those regions.

They just go to another species immediately?

From being an animal you can't go back to the astral regions and then to heaven. You can't. You have to come back as a human, and from here you can go anywhere. This is the last step of the ladder. Either you slip down or you go up. From in-between, or from a lower step you can't climb to the roof at all.

105 *Maharaj Ji, our storehouse of past karmas, our sinchit karmas, are they made up only from past human lives?*

As humans, you see, we are punished for these karmas, because we are conscious of what we are doing. In those animal species we are not conscious of what we are doing, but we are still collecting karmas.

106 *Then God himself does not forgive us, if for every action that we do he gives us a karma?*

No, sister, the Lord is all love, he is all grace. We do not know, nor can we comprehend what that grace and love is. But if we are not good children, we have to pay for that. For example, if a child does not obey his mother, or tries to hurt somebody, if she cannot correct him by reasoning with him, she disciplines him. Not because she does not love him, but because she wants to set him right, to make him a good boy. Similarly, the Lord is just love, but we have to be receptive, we have to obey the laws of nature, we have to live as good citizens in this world. If we are naughty and we are not rightly behaving, he will punish us. That does not mean that he has started hating us. We have to be set right, and he has set up certain agencies which take care of all these things. But he is all love.

107 *Maharaj Ji, yesterday you explained the point that through meditation we clear our sinchit karmas, and what I was wondering is, say in this lifetime I cheat a man out of a million dollars and then it goes to my sinchit karmas and eventually I have to pay that back, and it goes to his sinchit karmas and eventually he has to collect it. Now say in the next lifetime that man is initiated and he is a good disciple and all his sinchit karmas are cleared. Well, then automatically a big portion of my karmas are cleared too, right? Who do I pay back?*

You see, it is not one individual karma which shapes our future. It is the combination of karmas which shapes our future. Not that you necessarily will have to pay that much money to the same person. But in some other way you will have to pay for all that. He's forgiven, he has escaped from the load of karma, but you have not. So you have to pay all that – that is the load for you.

Sometimes we want to do something, we have a desire to do something which we know to be selfish, but instead of restraining ourselves from doing that action, we tell ourselves that it's our karma to do it – that we have to learn something from doing it, whether it be the fulfilment of some ambition, some sense experience that we feel we have to learn about – and so we go ahead and do it and rationalize it. How can we avoid that?

Since you don't know, you're trying to justify your actions, saying that it must be in my fate. It is more or less a justification for doing things. If you can be sure that it is your karma, that is different. But you can never be sure. So we should take every action as a new seed. To begin with, our thinking should be that whatever we are going to do, we are going to sow a new seed. But still, if in spite of our efforts it does happen, you can presume to some extent that it must be in my fate. Still, it may be a new seed because your presumption is also conditioned by justification. So we can never know that. So from that point of view we should think that every karma is a new seed that we are going to do. That attitude should be there, at least. But we always try to justify our actions, more or less.

Maharaj Ji, would it be correct to assume that if you do an old deed, a karma, with relish that you are continuing that karma into a new seed and a further play of that same karma? You see, if you do it with keenness then you are prolonging or projecting that karma again, aren't you?

You are sowing seed after seed. You have sown one seed in the field; then tomorrow again you sow another same seed in the field. Again you sow another seed in the field. How many crops will come from it? Not only the one seed will sprout – every seed will sprout. So in the same way, every karma will be a new karma. It may be a continuation of that one seed or may be independent of that, but the seeds are all karma.

108 When an individual is initiated, does it take him a certain amount of time to burn his rubbish?

It depends upon how much effort he is putting in, how much the grace of the Lord is there, and the type of environment he has been brought up in and is living in. There are so many factors in burning that load of karma. Suppose he has just a small load but doesn't attend to his meditation at all; then how would he burn it? If he is trying to attend to meditation but his environment is such that his mind is not there in meditation, or if he has such worldly activities that he can hardly snatch any time for meditation or he's hardly in a mood to meditate, or if he is a victim of certain weaknesses which he can't get rid of, then how can he burn that karma? So many factors are involved in burning that load. That is why Christ said: The first may be the last and the last may be the first on the path to reach back to the Father.[62]

It doesn't mean that if we are initiated today, we will all go back to the Lord by seniority of initiation. There's no seniority in Sant Mat because everybody has an individual load of karmas. You can't say that there's any seniority on the path – that I was initiated forty years ago so I have first right to go and the other man was initiated only ten years ago so how can he bypass me. It's nothing like that.

The first may be the last and the last may be the first to reach there because everybody has an individual load of karma. This load is not what we have collected here; this load is the sinchit karmas, the store of our karmas. Everybody has to burn that – as Christ said: Repent, the kingdom of God is within you.[3] So we have to repent for all we have done in our past lives. And what is repentance? Not to repeat those mistakes again; whatever you have done, you are sorry for it. That is repentance.

The mind has done all those mistakes, and the mind has to repent. But the mind will repent or leave the sensual pleasures only when it gets a better pleasure than the sensual pleasures. Otherwise the mind refuses to repent, refuses even to realize our mistakes, our weaknesses. The mind is fond of sensual pleasures; the mind is running to sensual pleasures every day. So it has to be attached to something better, and that is the holy ghost, or spirit or that holy light which is within every one of us. When the mind is attached to that, then you can say that you have started repenting for what you have done in the past, what you have sown in the past; then you have started burning the rubbish, or trying to dry the rubbish so that it can be burned. So the real repentance is meditation.

You can't fix a time limit on meditation because you don't know how much you have to burn and how much effort you are putting toward the work and how much the Lord's grace is there with you, in what atmosphere you have taken birth, in what environment you are living. All these factors go a long way before we can repent or before we can attend to the meditation. Ultimately meditation will burn that load of karma, but there is no time limit at all.

109 What does it mean karmically when a child dies?

The very fact, sister, proves the karma theory. That very factor proves that the child has done something in the past for which he has to pay in this world and could not see the light and has to leave the body at once. You have read in the Bible about somebody asking Christ when a blind child was born: Whose sin is this, that of the child or of the parent? Christ said: None, as far as this world is concerned, as far as this birth is concerned.[101] Because at birth, the child had not done anything at all to be blind. And neither did the parents make him blind. Something which he has done in the past for which the parents and the child are now suffering caused him to be blind. So, you see, if a child is born and leaves the world at once, it is due to his past karmas. That is why we cannot explain why children are born mentally disabled or blind or have to suffer. They are so innocent; they have not done anything in this world at all. We collect sin when we come back into the flesh when we are conscious of what we are doing. But a newborn child is hardly even conscious of his own existence. What sin could he commit by coming into this world? That proves the karma theory – that he is paying now for something he has done in the past.

110 *Master, can we also assume that when we are initiated, we are now twice as responsible, that we have more responsibility after initiation to stay on the path?*

You see, after initiation we have two responsibilities. Not to commit more sins – "sin no more" – that is one responsibility, and to repent for whatever we have done in the past – that is the second responsibility. Sin no more, and attend to your meditation and clear all the sinchit karmas or store of karmas. Don't add more to your load and burn whatever you have already collected by meditation; those are the two responsibilities of the disciple.

111 *There is a type of karma which the perfect master cancels and pardons. And yet there is another type of karma which cannot be paid off until the body has gone through their results.*

You see, it's very clear; some karmas are part of our destiny and we have to go through them. Sometimes there is very little karma left before the soul has to leave the body. If it is in the interest of that disciple, if master thinks that for just a small amount of karma the disciple should not take another birth, master makes him go through those karmas in so many other ways, while being in the body. Some karmas you have to go through in the body – you have no other option, it is destiny. For example, you have to be born to a certain mother, a certain father. This karma can't be pardoned because it is interconnected with so many people. Some karmas may be just individual – that karma may be pardoned. But where you are connected in a chain with other people, those karmas you have to go through. So you can't draw a line, that this karma you have to go through, this karma will be pardoned. Only the master knows that which is in our best interest.

112 *Master, in regard to karma, must it be paid the same way that it happened?*

You see, it is not like that. It is the accumulation of karmas which determines our future. Individual karmas do not determine our future. It is the accumulated effect of those karmas that we have to go through. Not in the same way and not in the same kind. For example, if you have killed a thousand chickens in one life, you do not have to come back a thousand times to be killed by them. In one life, you can have a thousand pricks, painful pricks. And that will account for the killing of those chickens. So it can be cleared in many ways. The Lord knows best how that karma can be paid.

113 *Master, I have read in the literature where souls who are initiated are marked before their birth. Why is it that some of us reach the age of forty or fifty or sixty years, living lives contrary to Sant Mat, eating meat, and so forth? Why is so much of our life spent in a manner contrary to the teachings of Sant Mat?*

There are many barriers in our way. Unless we clear them, we cannot come on the path. There are so many karmic barriers which have to be cleared before we can come back on the path. And some people take a few years to clear them; some people take more years to clear them. Some just get a little time in Sant Mat, and some are initiated even two days before their death. This just depends on the individual. It does not mean that right from birth everybody can be put on the path, or everybody starts meditation. Whenever an individual's karmas bring around the proper time, he comes on the path.

Duty and karma

114 *In the case of people or children who are born with handicaps, cerebral palsy or mental retardation – if we try to talk to them or to educate them, are we interfering with their karma? Is it right for us to try to aid them, or should we not interfere?*

Sister, the question of interfering with karma does not arise at all. It is the mother's duty to set a child right, to explain to him the right way to live in this world. One is actually failing in one's duty by not trying to teach that child what is wrong and what is right. When the mother does her duty to the best of her ability and then she leaves everything to the karmas, they will take care of themselves automatically. But we should not think that we are interfering with their karmas if we are trying to explain to them their disability, or the right way of life, and are trying to help them in every way. We have to do our best to make them good and disciplined children, good citizens, to face life, and then leave it to the Lord. What comes out of them should be left to their karmas, after we have done our best to help them.

But we cannot justify our indifference under the garb of karmas. That attitude should not be there. In fact, we would be interfering with their karmas if we did not try to teach them and help them. We have learned by experience, by age and maturity, and it is our duty to impart the benefit of these experiences to them, even though we may sometimes have to be quite stern in disciplining them.

115 *If the purpose of life is God-realization, why do we have to have worldly duties? And does man have to have worldly duties? What are his duties towards his family, his society and his work?*

All these are karmic relationships. We have done certain karmas for which we have to come back to this world. Whatever we have sown in the past, we are reaping some of the results now. So we have certain karmic relationships with our mother, father, wife, daughter, son, friends, associates, country and the like. Those karmas have resulted in our birth in this particular body and at this particular time. We have to fulfil all the karmas, the destiny allotted to this life. You cannot escape from your karmas. So to discharge those karmas you perform your worldly duties.

But in discharging your karmas, you have a purpose in view; that is to go back to the Father. Otherwise, if you discharge your duties and at the same time continue sowing new seeds for the next life, you will again come back to this world. This you cannot escape, because the seeds you have already sown in the past, the results you must reap now. You are not supposed to sow any more seeds that would entail your coming back to this world again to reap the results. So, in order to avoid sowing new seeds, we have to travel the spiritual path leading back to the Father.

Whatever you have already sown, you cannot escape from that now. You have to get its result. So to go through that destiny is our karmic duty, which means our worldly responsibilities, our duties towards our parents, society, associates and so forth.

116 *Someone wishes to ask a question that his son has just asked him today at noon. The son is now going into the military service, because in Switzerland we have an obligatory military service. Every citizen must go through this. And now if he is going to the war and he has to kill somebody, he would like to know, if he kills somebody, would he not put on his shoulder all the karma of the people he is killing? And so suffer from it? And if he lets himself be killed, what will become of him?*

You see, one gets whatever one is destined to get. Everything is written in one's destiny, which he has to go through in that life. If he is not to be killed in war, he will never be killed in war. If he is to be killed in war, nobody can save him from the war. But since he is joining the army, naturally he is supposed to do his duty.

117 *Maharaj Ji, how can a person be in the army and still be a satsangi?*

You see, he has to do his duty. He is not wilfully trying to kill unnecessarily. And if he doesn't want to kill, the master will protect him, save him, and he will never get the opportunity to kill at all. We have so many people in the army – Baba Ji [Baba Jaimal Singh] himself was in the army. Huzur Maharaj Ji [Maharaj Sawan Singh] used to tell us that when there was a conflict with the Pathans on the Afghanistan side of the border, during the fighting Baba Ji would just sit off to the side in bhajan. The enemy would come and they would say he must be some mystic, some fakir; they wouldn't even touch his gun and they would pass him. The power is always at our back to save us. So, Maharaj Ji himself was in the military, and so was Baba Ji.

118 *If the soul wants to go back to the Father, should children and husband be considered an attachment?*

Well, sister, if you have some karmic adjustment with your children, with your father, with your husband, you can't escape it. You have to give and take in this world because you have certain karmic debts to pay and karmic debts to collect. Unless they are all cleared, the soul will not be able to leave. Caesar must get what is due to Caesar.[66] You have a certain amount of karma which has brought you here, which is your destiny. Now, you have to face that destiny. You can't escape from that destiny.

Saints say: Face that destiny, and then also try to find your way out of this world. You can't run away from your husband or from your responsibility to a child. You have got to face them.

TRANSCENDING KARMA

119 *If it is true that the saying "As you sow, so you reap" means that one has to be reborn to reap the fruits of not only his bad actions but also his good actions, doesn't that have a hampering influence on the deeds of mankind?*

No. In a sense, we are trying to get out of this creation. We are not trying to improve the working of this creation. We are not trying to improve the living conditions of humanity. That is not the main purpose of the saints, or a devotee of the Lord. His main purpose is to get out of this creation. For worldly people, naturally, good karmas benefit you. Whatever you sow in a field, you have to go to that field to get that fruit. You can't say that I will go to collect chillies only, and I won't go to collect mangoes. You have to go to the field whether you sow chillies or whether you sow mangoes.

So these words 'good' and 'bad' are very comparative. We cannot draw a definite line as to what is good and what is bad. All karmas pull us back to this level of creation. We have to come back to pay for all karmas, whether they are good or bad. Even the result of good karma may bring suffering in the end. Due to your good karmas, you may become a king, a leader, or an officer at the top of a certain firm. But then there's a different type of suffering there, too – you're not happy there either. This world is nothing but suffering, whether you come here to reap the result of good karmas or whether you come here to reap the result of bad karmas. The purpose of the mystic is to take us out of this realm of Kal. Unless all types of karmas are cleared, the soul can never escape from the realm of Kal.

Maharaj Ji, my question is this: If I am anxious to advance in my spiritual career, then do I have to avoid doing not only bad deeds but also good deeds?

No, you don't have to avoid doing good deeds. You just don't want the result of the good deeds.

How to achieve that?

You see, you don't want any result. For example, you give something in charity. You don't want to come back to collect that charity. We give things in charity to people and we expect that in the next birth we'll get repaid tenfold. We always have some desire to do good works. I am going to help my friend, and in my time of need he's going to help me. So I have sown a seed. I have created a karmic connection with him. But if I have done a good deed for my friend and I forget about it, then I have not sown any seed at all. If you have given a thing in charity and you forget about it – you don't want its result – you are not sowing a seed to come back.

May I take it then that if I wish to do some good turn to friends or relations or even to the general public, if I do so without any desire or intention ...

That's right. Then it is all right. You have to be good and loving and kind and compassionate and helpful to people but without desiring any reward. If we want a reward, then we have to come back. But as long as we are in the flesh, we can't help doing karmas; we can't exist without doing karmas. Either we have to go through them or we are creating new ones. There's no other way to remain in the flesh. So we don't want any results even of our good karmas. We need to have a loving nature. We have to not be attached to anyone, we have to have a general loving nature. We are not kind to people so that they will be kind to us, but we need to have a general habit of being kind to others. That type of attitude should be there.

120 Master, is it true that when the soul transcends the second stage, Trikuti, the law of karma no longer applies?

I'll tell you. Association of the karma is with the mind. When the mind comes back to its own place and the soul gets release from the mind, then those karmas can't pull the soul back because karma is associated only with the mind, not with the soul. So when the mind is attached to the shabd and comes back to its own source, there the soul gets release from the mind. When the soul is separated from the mind, those karmas become ineffective; they cannot pull the soul back because the soul is no longer associated with the mind.

Yes, but in dissolution and grand dissolution up to the regions and including Brahmand, the soul can be brought back?

There are certain deep karmic impressions, which still are impressed upon the soul after Trikuti. But generally those impressions on the soul don't attract it back to the world. All the deep impressions of those karmas are washed in that pool of nectar in the third stage. But in the grand dissolution, then everything is dissolved. In the grand dissolution everything is finished and goes back to the Father. But in dissolution also, souls remain in the fourth stage; they don't come back to the world. They are immune from birth and death.

121 Does the higher mind have the seeds of karma in it?

Mind is all karma, nothing else. Mind is all wrapped by karmas. Whatever karmas we have committed in the past we are reaping now; they are all wrapped around the mind. Even higher mind has karma. Karmas follow us even right till Trikuti. Even after the soul has escaped the mind, has gone beyond the realm of mind and maya, still we have fate karma which we have to go through during the span of life. But then you have control over the karmas. Karmas are still there; without karma nobody can remain here for one minute. When the soul gets release from the mind, it shines, it becomes whole, but that doesn't mean that all karmas are finished while your destiny is still there to go through. Without karma we can't exist even for a second, but then you're master of the karma, you're not a slave of those karmas. As Christ said: I can leave this body when I want to; I can take this body when I want to.[108]

122 Master, if a person were to become desireless and without attachment, does it mean that he is karmaless?

No. You see, karmaless is something very different. The moment we become karmaless the soul goes back to the Father – you can't exist in this creation. The very fact that we are in the body means that we have some karmas which are attaching us to this body. If we had no karma we would not be here at all. It is karma, fate karmas, which are keeping us bound to this flesh, this body. The moment we become karmaless we go back to the Father. If you can become desireless, you can become detached from the world. But you can't become karmaless by being in the flesh. Whatever you do in this world is karma. You drink, you eat, you walk, you talk, they're all karmas. They're all actions. So you can't become karmaless. You can have desireless actions – you're helping somebody, you have given something in charity, you are not desiring a reward. You can say that you have a desireless karma. But you can't become karmaless. It's impossible as long as you are in the flesh.

123 I know master is always with us, but driving on the highway one wonders: Does sudden death ever happen to a satsangi?

It depends upon the individual karma. It doesn't mean that a satsangi can't meet with an accident, a satsangi can't meet with an air crash. It depends upon the individual karmas. Whatever seeds we have sown, we definitely have to reap. But we will get the strength and willpower to face those karmas smilingly and cheerfully. We won't lose our balance on such occasions. The grace is always there, and the help is always there. Still we have to go through such karmas if we are destined to do so.

124 The lost sheep cannot help going astray. But what about the shepherds?

Nobody can exist in this creation without karmas. He has to select a father, a mother, a brother, a relative, and there is so much give and take in this creation. Nobody can live karmaless in this creation at all, whether he's a god or not. The moment you come to this creation, you have karmas. The only difference is that the saints are not slaves of the karmas; *we* are slaves of the karmas. With us, sins are our master and we are the slave. With them, they are the master and the karmas are the slave. Ultimately, that is the purpose of meditation.

So, actually, nobody can help anything in this world. It is all in his hand, by his grace that we can rise above the realm of karma. Nobody can help anything.

125 *Is karma itself an illusion, devised by Kal to delude our mind, our higher mind?*

That's right. You see, karmas are accumulations of the mind. They can only be gone through here. They are not something which stays. They come; they go. You collect karmas; you get rid of those karmas. So it's not something stationary.

Are they only real as long as we believe in the karmas?

My definition of real is that it never changes. That which is true, only that is real. All else is illusion. Only the Lord is real. The soul is real. All other things change.

126 *When we are a satsangi, aren't we always under the protection of the master?*

You feel the protection of the master in many ways. It doesn't always mean saving you from an accident. Protection is something very different. If it is in our karma to meet with a certain accident, which involves so many other people's karmas also, then how can we escape? We are only a part of a long chain. The grace of the master is there in many other ways – you may not feel the full effect of that accident, you may get immediate help and medical aid or you may be healed quickly. But you can't say that you will escape from that accident in any way. You have to go through that because it also involves so many other people.

127 *I'd like to know if our life span is shortened when we become satsangis?*

No, sister, our life span is not shortened at all after we become satsangis. Whatever fate we have brought with us, we have to go through. We have to give to Caesar what is due to Caesar.[66] We have to account for whatever we have collected in the past. So our life cannot be shortened. You read in the Bible where Christ prays to the Father to make his disciples one with himself.[129] He is leaving the world, but they are still in the world. So he is asking the Father to look after them. He means everyone has to go through his destiny, his karma. Our life is not shortened, but we get the strength and willpower to face the ups and downs of our life cheerfully and without losing our balance.

128 Is it possible for someone to change his karmas?

We cannot change the pralabdh karmas, which is our fate or our destiny. But by spiritual practice we can develop to such an extent that we are not much affected by those fate karmas. We go through them, but our will becomes so strong that we are able to rise above them to the extent that we can go through them gracefully, without upsetting our balance too much. They do not bother us. But we have to face all that. And naturally, when we are meditating, when we are in love with the Lord and his devotion is within us, we do not sow any new seed for which we have to come back to reap its fruit. And the sinchit, which is all the stored karma, is burned or washed away only by meditation.

129 When we seem to be drawn into helping people, how can we tell if we are paying off past karmas or building new karma?

That question was also brought up before. It is very difficult to know whether we are reaping what we have sown or whether we are sowing. By meditation, we develop ourselves to that extent that after a certain stage we know that this is due to our past or this is a new seed we are sowing. So what we can do is to always try to do good to the best of our ability; but if it happens the other way, we can take it that this is due to our past karmas. This is just a crude way of discriminating.

SANSKARAS

130 *Maharaj Ji, just before death, why does one person simply feel he is in a state of sleep while another person sees beautiful things? This can also happen to one who has died and has been brought back to life.*

Everybody has individual karmas; and some people are spiritually advanced. So they will have different experiences after death, or at the time of death, or even in an unconscious state. Other people will have different experiences according to their own spiritual, emotional, or worldly background.

Everybody has different experiences in the state of unconsciousness. For example, when we sleep, we each have a different type of dream. Everybody doesn't have the same dream. According to their own background, their personal life, or their suppressed thoughts, everybody has a different type of dream; but everybody sleeps. Similarly, in unconscious states, everybody has a different type of experience. Our experiences can't be the same, because our backgrounds are different and we have gone through different types of karma during our life span.

131 *A friend of mine has a little grandchild of three and that grandchild has never been told that they are vegetarian, but he will not eat meat and he tells his grandmother it is not right to eat meat. Is that a memory?*

This is due to associations with a past life. We call them 'sanskaras', impressions of a past life. Sometimes they come along with us into this world and we automatically have such an abhorrence for these things that we cannot do it in spite of our best efforts.

132 *Some people can concentrate better than others on studies or on other worldly problems. Do such people have any advantage over those who cannot, in regard to spiritual achievement?*

Spiritual concentration is different from worldly concentration. Some people are intellectual, born intellectuals, according to their karmas. Some people are spiritually inclined, and they do not care much for worldly things. They are only happy to be one with the Lord. They always try to follow the path. So it depends upon the individual karmas.

133 *Is there a difference between karmas and sanskaras?*

To some extent. Sanskaras are deep impressions on the mind; karmas are actual actions that we have done. The desires we create in our mind – our wishes – they create deep impressions on our mind, and then actually they become karma for the next birth.

134 *Is a sanskara a groove made upon the mind? I have read in the teachings that when we come to this birth we have to go through a remedial hell – we come to those grooves on the mind and have to live through it. But I was wondering if those sanskaras could also be caused from, let us say, a desire from a past lifetime?*

Same thing, there is no difference between them. Sanskara means impressions of your last life on your mind. Whether you call it desires of the last life, those desires are being fulfilled now – our very existence proves our past desires. The very existence of this creation proves our past desires, past karmas.

135 Do we ever commit karma by waiting and not doing anything in a situation that's very difficult for us?

Your mind is involved in karma. First the thought comes, then the action comes. All these desires are nothing but strong thoughts. These strong desires – even if no action follows – they are all grooves on our mind. And those grooves pull us back.

First comes a strong desire. If you are obsessed with that, that obsession will bring you back. You have sown a seed to come back, to fulfil that desire. It is the karmas that will bring us back, but it is also the strong desires that will bring us back. That is why Christ said in the Sermon on the Mount that if you look at a woman with lustful eyes you have committed adultery.[17] No action was there. He says you have already committed adultery, which means that desire can become very strong in you; you may be obsessed with that desire and that very desire will pull you back into this creation. That is what he means to say, when he says that you've already committed adultery.

By meditation all these desires just disappear, they just evaporate. They become meaningless for us.

136 If our thoughts are not loving, does that create karma? Do our thoughts have to be spoken in order to create karma?

Sister, if you have malice in your heart against somebody, even if you don't express it, slowly and slowly it will go on creating a groove on your mind. It will lie dormant in your subconscious mind. It will rise to the surface sometime or it may make such a strong desire that the desire may pull you back. A thought comes and goes. If thoughts just fade out, they're all right. Sometimes some thoughts remain so dominating in our mind, we can't get rid of them. They become our obsessions, howsoever we may try not to express them. But they dominate us always. And they take root as strong desires, and then we may have to come back to fulfil those desires.

Sowing seeds of karma

137 Master, can you give us some light on original sin?

Actually, it is very difficult to say what our original sin was. Because when the Lord created this creation we had no sin at all. Only he existed before the creation, and he has created everything. Nothing existed, and nothing exists in the world which has not been created by the Father. So, since we came from the Father, we have been separated by his will. We had no sin. It's not that we sinned there and that is why we have been sent to the creation. After having come to the creation, our soul became attached to the mind; and since the mind runs after the senses, we started collecting stains on our soul.

It is very difficult to say what the first step was that the soul took after taking on the association of the mind. But before the creation, we had no sin at all. This world is a divine play, so to say, that he has created.

We had no free will at all to be separated from the Father. But he has created us and, after having come to the creation, we have been tempted by the senses. And once we yielded to temptation, then, of course, whatever we sowed we had to reap. That was the start of action and reaction, and now we have become helpless and have become part and parcel of the creation. But I don't think we had any original sin.

138 What determines our karma?

Whatever you sow, so shall you reap.[133]

In the beginning, when we were brought here?

When we were created, we had no karmas at all. If you play a game of chess, the first move is up to you and all the other moves will be conditioned by that first move. Then you have no choice at all. So in the beginning, when we were created, we didn't have any karma when we came to this world. The Lord wanted us in the creation. But having come to the creation, naturally we cannot remain without creating karma. We perform good karmas and bad karmas, because a mind has been given to us and that is always running after the senses. So we are always forced to create some sort of karma.

139 Maharaj Ji, doesn't sin imply a choice? And, at the beginning, when the souls came down, there really was no choice for those souls.

No choice, brother, absolutely no choice.

So, can it be considered a sin then?

Well, you have to give it some name. Even good deeds are sins. You can call them good deeds, but even to account for all those good deeds you have to come here to this creation. So Indian mystics have found the word 'karma', which covers good deeds and bad deeds. You see, we have no free will to start with. The Lord has projected himself in this creation, and we are part of this creation. We were never consulted. We never wanted to come. Because who would not like to be with him, rather than go through the agony of separation? Why we are here has to be explained in some way, so the saints have explained it this way.

140 *From what you have said, Master, there is still one big question unanswered – the question of the creation. You said that we will find the answer once we go back to our Lord, but I would like you to tell me if birth is the consequence of original sin.*

You see, original sin only came after the creation, not before the creation. There was no sin, even according to the Bible. At the time of creation, there was no sin in Adam and Eve. After that, original sin came. So before that, they had no sin at all.

Saint John said: Before the creation, nothing existed. Everything was with the Lord. In his creative power, he's created all that we see, and all that has been created has been created by him.[72] And before the creation, nothing existed at all; only he existed. So he has projected himself into this creation, and all that we see is nothing but his own projection.

Once we have been created, then naturally, since mind is there, our soul has taken the association of the mind, collecting sins, and that is why those sins started becoming our master and we became the slave of those sins. According to those sins, we have to shift from place to place, from body to body, from house to house. So that is how the creation came into existence.

But before the creation, there was no sin at all, because we were with the Father, and nothing existed besides the Father. There can be no sin with the Father. But after having been created, then naturally we came to this realm of maya and mind, and mind is fond of pleasures. That is how the Lord has created this creation. But for that weakness within us, there would be no creation at all; nobody would be part of the creation at all. He has made us imperfect. And the more we remain in this creation, the more imperfect we become, the more sins we collect, and the more we remain attached to this creation, and so this creation continues.

The moment he wants anybody to become perfect, he pulls that soul and it escapes from this creation. Without him, nobody can escape from the creation. And if everybody becomes perfect, this creation could not continue at all. This creation would cease to exist. The moment we become perfect, we merge back into the perfect being. This creation can only continue if it remains imperfect.

141 *Is it our attitude towards our actions that creates good or bad karma? If something devastating happens, for example, do we have a little bit of free will in how we regard that?*

Sister, motive goes a long way. Our intentions, our motives go a long way. For example, you want to do a good deed. You want to help somebody with your best intentions. But it turns out the other way. Instead of helping him, we may injure him. You have made him more unhappy, more miserable. But your intention was all right, your intention was good. Even in the law, nobody is punished without motive. You have to prove the motive of a person before any punishment can be given, even in the physical world. So motive is very essential, with what motive you were doing the actions.

142 *If we do something for someone and it turns out badly, and we find out that we were wrong and are truly sorry, does that rectify anything?*

That is what I tried to explain to you just now. We should honestly, with the best of intentions, try always to do good. Then if it turns out differently, we should not worry. We should take it as our pralabdh karma, fate or destiny. There is nothing to rectify. The thing that had to happen has happened. Our conscience is clear. We have not done it knowingly. But we should not try to justify weaknesses. When we are honest in our efforts to do good, then it is up to the Lord to take care of it. We cannot help it if it takes another shape.

143 *It is written in the books that it is impossible for us to understand karma entirely until we reach the first region.*

Yes, it is not possible for you to know from what karma you got this and from what karma you got that. You cannot discriminate whether it is a new seed or whether you are reaping the fruit of an old seed. At this stage it is not possible for us to differentiate, so we should take an objective view, a practical view. We should try to do good and then leave the results to the Lord.

144 *Does a particular soul have any free will in the karma it commits? Now, for instance, some of them do good karmas, some of them do bad karmas. Why should one soul do bad karmas and another do good karmas?*

It depends upon where you have been sent. In the beginning, the Lord gave us good or bad karmas and we had no choice where we were being sent. Some souls may have been sent to a better atmosphere; they are conditioned from that point of view. Other souls may have been sent to a comparatively bad atmosphere, so they were conditioned accordingly. So they initiated karmas according to the atmosphere to which they were sent. So their karmas differ from each other. For example, say a dacoit adopts a child and brings him up. That child will pick up the same behaviour from his father, from the atmosphere in which he has been brought up. At the same time, a noble person goes to an orphanage and adopts another child. The father is so religious, so noble, so kind, so good: The child is brought up in that atmosphere. Now both children have come from the same orphanage, but their way of thinking is different. You can understand yourself what difference there will be in their upbringing, in their way of thinking, in their deeds, in their behaviour. Neither child had an option to select where he would go when he was adopted. So this is a very crude example. In the same way, wherever souls have been sent, they are brought up in that atmosphere, start behaving the same way, and their minds become conditioned accordingly.

145 *All those years of committing karmas – I don't see the point in it. We're not even aware of them. We learn nothing from them. So why bother?*

No, we don't learn anything at all. If we learned any lesson from our past mistakes, we wouldn't commit them. We're absolutely ignorant of what we have done in the past, so how can we learn anything here? We don't learn anything at all. We only suffer for what we have done. And that too is through no fault of ours. We have been thrown into this creation, and the creation is such that you can't help doing actions. And then you become a victim of those actions.

146 *Is it possible to know what desire has brought us back to this particular life?*

It's not one particular desire that brings us back to this world. It is the accumulation of so many desires, so many suppressed wishes or desires, and so many karmas which we have committed. It is because of the accumulated effect of all these that we got this human body. So it's not one particular desire that pulls us back to this world.

147 When we drive a car and we pay full attention, but we happen to kill someone, what is our karmic debt?

Well, brother, in this world you can't escape from killing. When you walk you kill so many insects. When you breathe you kill many germs and when you drink you also kill many bacteria. All this is done unconsciously, without any intention to kill. Still, it is a load of karma. Even if it is a small or insignificant load, still killing does involve karma.

You had no intention to kill and you have tried to avoid it. On the one hand it may be due to your past karma that he had to be killed by you, or maybe a new seed has been sown by you unintentionally. When there is no intention to kill, the penalty is not so great; but still it is a karma.

Even in our laws in this world there are degrees of punishment according to the crime. If you kill a person knowingly, or you kill him by negligence, or you kill him by accident, there is a punishment in every case, but there is a different degree of punishment in each case. So there are three types of punishment, depending on whether the act is done by negligence, whether it is intentional or whether it is just by coincidence. There is a different degree of punishment in each case.

148 What about killing insects in the garden?

You can't remain in this world without killing. When we walk, we kill so many insects under our feet. When we breathe, we kill so many germs. When we drink water, we drink so many germs along with it. You cannot live in this world without killing. Saints tell us that while we have to remain in this world, we should try to collect the least amount of karmas. As you all know, all living creatures can be divided according to the five elements: earth, water, fire, air and ether. Plants have only one active element – water. So if you eat vegetables you are collecting the least amount of karma. No doubt we are collecting karma when we are killing insects under our feet, when we are eating vegetables, when we are tending our garden. No doubt we kill all those insects. But we are collecting a very small amount of karma. If you are running and have only a shirt on your body, you will hardly feel any weight at all but if you have 100 pounds to carry, you are just crushed under the weight.

We cannot remain in the world without collecting karmas. So saints advise us to collect only the least amount possible of karma.

When you are meditating, this small amount of karma is automatically taken care of. So you should not worry if you are eating vegetables, or if you are doing hoeing and weeding in the garden, or plucking flowers. You shouldn't unnecessarily analyze these things to this extent.

149 I don't understand when you said everything is destiny. Couldn't being evil be our destiny also?

If you have sown evil seeds, you must come to this world to get the results of those evil seeds. If you have sown good seeds, you will come to this world to get the result of those good seeds. Christ says: A corrupt tree gives you corrupt fruit. A good tree gives you good fruit.[31] So you must know, when you are sowing a seed, whether you are sowing a good seed or whether you are sowing a bad seed. When the fruit comes, you cannot say, "I do not want the bad fruit; I only want good fruit."

Be careful when you sow a seed. Whatever you have sown in the past, you are here to reap the result of both the good and the bad seeds. Therefore don't sow any bad seed now. And that you can avoid only when you are attached to the spirit of God within yourself. So sometimes we have to reap a harvest from the evil seeds. We have to go through these karmas, because they have already been sown in the past. You can't escape them.

150 *Master, the most helpful thing I have received from your lips is when you said that you get only what you deserve.*

What I mean by "we get only what we deserve" is that whatever we have done in the past, we have sown certain seeds to deserve what we are getting now. We reap what we have sown in the past, and now we deserve it. Therefore, we should always do those actions of which we want to reap the desired results.

151 *Maharaj Ji, there seems to be a fine line between desires for worldly accomplishments and destiny. Can you explain or give a suggestion about how we can more easily determine what our destiny is as opposed to adding to our worldly desires?*

Well, brother, at this level of consciousness we can never know what is in store for us, or what we desire. We can never know at this level of consciousness. We can only know when we have gone beyond the realm of mind and maya. When the soul becomes whole, leaves the association of the mind and all its coverings are removed from the soul, then the soul knows whether the karma I'm going through is according to my past seeds that I have sown or whether I'm creating new karma. You know only at that stage, not before. But some instinct does come in us that allows us to start discriminating that this is not right, I should not do it, I may have to suffer for it. We have a higher level of consciousness so to say, but still we can be deceived. It may be due to our destiny or we may be creating a new karma. It's very difficult to say. So any karma we commit we should always think that I'm going to commit a new karma, I'm sowing a new seed. We should approach every action from that angle. But still, if in spite of all our best efforts a particular thing happens, you can console yourself by saying that it is due to my past destiny. But still we may be wrong. At least we can't object, because we've done our very best. But still the mind can be so powerful as to deceive us and tempt us to do it. So any action we do, we should always think that we are going to sow a new seed. That approach should be there.

152 *Master, does this include interpreting the meaning of events? Often there's a lot of discussion and theorizing about the meaning of particular events karmically or within the context of Maharaj Ji's will.*

Actually, there's no necessity at all. We should do our best honestly, sincerely, to do what we think is right. Then we should leave it to the Lord, whether it was destiny or whether we have sown a new seed. It may be a new seed, but that may be your destiny also. We can't differentiate at this stage at all. So there's no need for analyzing whether it was my destiny or whether I've sown a new seed. You see, we should try to forget about it. We should just be honest and sincere in our actions. Then if we succumb to weakness we should forget about it rather than carry the guilt on our mind. We should attend to meditation rather than try to justify to the mind that it was my destiny, or carry guilt in our mind that I have sown a new seed now.

Meditation will take care of it – what you feel about it is immaterial. Meditation itself will take care of everything. At this stage we can never know what is destiny and what is a future seed. So we should approach every event and every step of life as if we are taking a new step, sowing a new seed. But still, if in spite of our best effort something happens, then you can say it is your destiny – but still we may be wrong. So it's better to forget about it and attend to meditation.

153 Maharaj Ji, if we sow new seeds in this life, will meditation also clean that up – if we attend to our meditation regularly?

Definitely, whatever we do even in this life, meditation takes care of it. Even our seeds which we are sowing now, they also can be destroyed by meditation, even now. Christ said in the Bible: Go and make up with your adversary, lest it may be too late for you.[16] He means that when your adversary leaves the body, or you leave the body, the karmic relationship between you will continue. But now, when you are both in the body, you can make up for whatever you have done to him. Otherwise meditation will help you to do it. Meditation always helps.

154 Will we ever be aware when we're creating new karma in this life?

You should always assume that every action you are going to do is a new seed. That is the maximum you can do. You can never know whether it is your destiny or whether you are sowing a new seed. It is impossible to know at this level of consciousness. So always try to think that whatever you are going to do, you're sowing a new seed. This can be the maximum safety factor.

155 Is it not possible that a newly sown seed can change the destiny?

You see, whatever new seeds we are sowing, that is for the next birth, not this one. Destiny is what we are going through now. New seeds are always for the future, can become our destiny for the future. But even if we have sown new seeds, we can destroy them by meditation while being in the flesh now.

We should think that anything unpleasant I do, I am going to sow a new seed. That should be our concept. If in spite of that it happens, you can say that it was your destiny, but still you can be wrong, still it may be a justification. So everything we do, which we think is not right for us to do, we should take those actions as new seeds. That concept helps us.

156 Maharaj Ji, do we have any choice in choosing our marriage partner, or is the choice predestined?

It could be destiny or we could be sowing a new seed. This is true of every action in this life, not only of marriage. Many things we have to go through are due to our destiny; many things we do are new seeds we are sowing in this life. Marriage could fall into either category.

157 Will meditation help my destiny?

Naturally, you are the maker of your destiny. As stated in the Bible, if the tree is good, it will give good fruit. Otherwise, it is hewn down and cast into the fire.[4] So if by getting this human birth you are sowing good seed, you will get good results. You are making your destiny. If you are meditating, you are creating your destiny to go back to the Father. And if you are doing evil deeds, you are creating your destiny to come back to this world. So you make your own destiny. Meditation will take you back to the Father. And if you are against the holy ghost, as Christ says, it means you will have to come back again to this world.

158 Are we responsible for evil actions?

We are responsible in the sense that we have to pay for them. God does not make us do them. It is our mind that makes us do all that. In the Bible it is also stated that whatever you sow, so shall you reap.[133] A farmer plants seeds in a field, and he reaps the fruit thereof when the crop matures. If he sowed chillies, he is bound to reap chillies; if he plants a mango tree, he is bound to get mango fruit. So this whole world is a karmic field, and whatever actions we do, whatever seeds we are sowing, we have to come back to reap the fruit thereof.

Destiny and free will

159 Would you talk about free will?

I think all the books are full of this subject about free will. You must have read them. If anything is not clear to you, ask me and I will explain it.

First, we never had free will when we became a part of this creation, because nothing existed before the creation but the Creator. All that we see is nothing but his own projection, and since he has created this creation and he has projected himself in this creation, by his will we have become part of this creation and we are not part of the Creator anymore. And after having come here, now the soul has taken the association of the mind and the mind is dominating the soul, and the mind, being fond of sensual pleasures, is a slave of the senses. Whatever karmas the mind is doing, the soul has to pay for those karmas. We are all slaves of this creation.

If you take it from a higher point of view, I don't think we have any free will at all. You are born in a certain family, with a certain background, certain environment; you are brought up in that atmosphere, and your whole way of thinking, way of action, is according to your environment, according to your heritage, according to your relations, your friendships in the beginning and in childhood. All those things go a long way to shape your future actions, to shape your decisions. So whatever decisions you take, in any situation, it is according to your heritage and environment and atmosphere in which you have been brought up. So you can't say that you have taken the decision by free will. But if you eliminate all that, then you can say that you have free will.

So we have nothing but conditioned free will, limited free will, because you can't select your country, you can't select your parents, you can't select your school, you can't select your friends, you can't select the atmosphere in which you have been brought up. Whatever you are doing now, whatever you are thinking now, is according to all that background. You can't eliminate that background at all. Your mind has been so conditioned right from birth to now, that you can't help thinking in that way. So that is why we say we have absolutely no free will at all; but if you eliminate all that, then of course you have free will. When you start playing chess, the first move is in your hand, but all the other moves are conditioned by the first move. You have done certain karmas in the past life – good karmas and bad karmas. Now you have no free will but must reap the results of those karmas.

You have free will before you sow any seed in a field. Once you have sown the seed, you have no free will to get a different crop from that field now. The same seed is going to sprout and you have got to taste the same fruit. At the time of tasting the fruit, you can't say that you don't want this fruit. You have to eat that fruit. At the time of sowing you had a choice of what type of plant you wanted to plant there, or seed you wanted to grow there. So seeds are already sown in the past lives. Three-fourths of what we go through in this life is nothing but our pralabdh karmas, seeds which we have already sown. One-fourth, practically speaking, are new seeds we are going to sow, and they are conditioned by our parentage, our environment, our education, our associations. Our new seeds which we are sowing today are influenced by all that. So in the long run you can't say that you have any free will at all. If you sow chillies you have got to gather chillies – you can't say, "I want a sweet apple."

So where is the free will? It is at the time of sowing chillies, but that time has gone out of your hand. Now you can't undo whatever you have sown in the past. There's nothing you can do. That is why Christ said in the Bible: Repent, the kingdom of God is within you.[3] Whatever you have already sown in past lives, whatever you have collected in past births, repent for that. The Lord is nowhere outside, the Lord is within you, but what you have done is between you and the Father. Unless you are able to eliminate what you have sown in the past life, you can't see the Father. Repenting means not repeating the same mistakes again, being sorry for whatever you have done.

But how can we be sorry when we don't know what we have done in the past? If we know what we have done in the past, we can, with strong willpower, not repeat those mistakes. But you don't know what you have done in the past, and that is why we meditate. Meditation makes us repent for mistakes done in past lives. The purpose of meditation is to repent for the past mistakes, which are absolutely out of our hand now. Saints give us a certain pattern of life which we have to follow and tell us not to sow new seeds for the future. If you lead this type of life, you will be saving yourself from sowing new seeds. For those seeds you have already sown, there is only one remedy – meditation – to burn those seeds, to escape from the fruit of those seeds which you have sown. So, when sowing new seeds, you can say that you have free will, but seeds which you have already sown in the past lives – you don't have free will, and you are going to taste the fruit of those seeds. Meditation helps us to clear the past, and it gives us strength not to sow any new seeds at all.

We have free will only when the soul is released from the mind. As long as the mind is dominating us, forcing us towards the senses, we can't say we have free will. What do we mean by 'we'? 'We' or 'I' doesn't mean the body. It means the soul. Soul has no free will now, because it is dominated by the mind, and the mind has no free will because it's dominated by the senses. The senses are controlling the mind, and the mind is controlling the soul. So how can we say the soul is free to do whatever it wants to do? The soul is not free now. The soul can become free when it controls the mind and the mind controls the senses. When we reach that stage, we go beyond the realm of mind and maya. Then your soul gets release from the mind, and all coverings are removed from the soul and you will have free will.

Only when 'you' is your self, your soul, not aligned with mind, not aligned with senses, can you do what you want to do. It's a pure soul, a shining soul. Then you are living in the will of the Father. Now we all live in the will of the mind. So from that point of view, as long as mind is dominating us, we don't have any free will at all, because mind is influenced by our heritage, education, friendships, associations, and the atmosphere in which we have been brought up. Mind is always influenced by that, and we act accordingly. So when mind is dominating us, how can we say we have any free will? It's very hard for any modern generation to digest this fact that we have no free will because we do so much to inflate our ego, and then we find that we are absolute puppets. It's very difficult to believe, but actually we are.

160 How much free will do we have?

We have no free will as far as our destiny is concerned. Whatever seeds you have sown in the past have become your destiny now. You have to reap the harvest of the seeds which you have sown. But as to the seeds you are to sow now, you have limited free will to sow these seeds. Whether to sow or not, you have that choice.

So what is destiny? Destiny is something with which you are born and which you have to face during the span of your life. That is destiny. We have no option here. That is why Christ says you can't even add a hair to your body.[38] He indicates that you can't add anything to your destiny. But if we are attending to our meditation, if we are attached to the spirit within, we definitely get strength to face that destiny cheerfully, without losing our balance. And sometimes, by his grace, remission is also there. But we have to face our destiny, and in that we have no free will at all.

However, when we are attending to that spirit within, that word within, we become so strong-minded that we do not sow any new seeds which can bring us back to this world. So there you have some choice, whether to sow that seed or not. But since you cannot know whether what you are doing is a part of your destiny or what you are doing is sowing a new seed, you can only do your best. You can think like this: "I am going to sow a new seed and I should not sow this seed." Then, whatever happens, you can say it was your destiny. That can be a justification – it may also be wrong, and may be the weakness of the mind. But that is all we can do.

Actually, we can only refrain from sowing new bad seeds when we are attached to the light within, when we are attached to the spirit within. When we live in the light, then we do not sow evil seeds. As long as we live in the darkness, we sow bad seeds.

161 Since we can do nothing unless God wills it, why are we subjected to the law of karma?

In the beginning, no doubt, we had no will of our own because we were not consulted when the Lord brought forth this creation. Our will was not there at all. He wanted to create, and we are part of the creation. But then he gave us the mind, which is fond of the senses. So whatever karma the mind creates, the soul also has to go through.

Practically speaking, we have no free will now at all. But we have a limited free will. Whatever we have sown in the past, we are reaping the harvest now. Whatever we are sowing now, that will be our future in the next birth. So whatever we are sowing now, for that we have some free will. But whatever we have sown in the past, in the reaping of that we have no free will at all; we have to face the results of those karmas.

We can only act freely when we actually are free. Now we are not free. Mind is dominating us, and mind is the slave of the senses. So we are all helpless before the senses, before the mind. Whatever we do, we are not doing with our free will at all. Whatever we may think, the mind is always forcing us to do all these things. So we are not free at all.

In order to become free from that karma, the soul must take leave of the mind. Then whatever you do, you do with free will. Now we are sowing seeds for the future, and whatever we have sown in the past, we have to go through that destiny now. We are helpless, as far as our destiny is concerned. But we have a limited free will. We can avoid sowing seeds now. However, it is very difficult at this stage to know if we are sowing a new seed. So that is why we say we have conditioned free will, we have limited free will. We cannot say we have absolute free will. Because whatever we do, it depends upon the environment in which we have been brought up, upon our heritage, our parentage, our education, and so forth.

So many things influence us to commit certain types of karma. And under the influence of those things, we now do these things. We think we are free. Actually, we are not free at all, because our mind is conditioned by all these associations. That is why Christ said in the Bible: Even the hairs on the body are numbered.[38] It is not free will that determines that we should have five hairs less or more. Even they are numbered. Every little thing, every detail is destined. That is why we are all puppets in the hands of destiny. But we are the makers of our own destiny, because we have committed these acts; we have committed these karmas in the past for which we are reaping the results now.

When you play chess, it is only the first move which is in your own hands. All other moves are conditioned by the first move which you have made. Similarly, in the beginning we had the free will to do anything. But now we are all victims of the karmas that we have done.

That is why saints advise us to rise above these karmas. And we can only rise above these karmas when we are attached to that holy spirit within. With the help of that spirit, that word, that nam, our mind becomes purer. Then we do not sow any seed in this world. And we get the strength to face whatever we have sown in the past. Our willpower becomes strong enough to face these karmas without losing our balance.

162 Maharaj Ji, we do what we have to do, so why are we responsible?

Because what we have to do, what we do, that is also our own doing. We are responsible for it. Nobody writes your destiny. You are the maker of your own destiny. Whatever karmas you have committed in the past, you are collecting that very crop now, you're harvesting that very crop now. But who sowed it? Whatever you sow, so shall you reap.[133] Who sowed? You have sown it. So you are responsible. So you suffer. Nobody has written your destiny. Nobody has carved your destiny. You have shaped your own destiny. Soul was absolutely shining and pure when it was with the Father. I often give an example: When you play chess, the first move is in your hand. All other moves are conditioned by the first move. Your circumstances force you to move in that direction. You become helpless. But who made the first move? One wins, the other loses; both had the option to make the first move. So we are responsible – we have to suffer and we have to pay for it.

163 *Why were we given free will in the beginning, since God knew that it would be suppressed in this plane of weaknesses, desires, suffering, and so forth?*

Actually, we had no free will at all even in the beginning. If there had been free will, nobody would have wanted to be separated from the Father. Nobody likes being a part of this creation and suffering in this world. Everybody would like to be a part of the Creator and be happy and have that bliss and joy. But we had no free will. That is why we are all part of this creation.

164 *If evil is predestined, and if it's the will of the Lord that man commit evil, why is man punished for this?*

I don't say your evil is destined, but the result or effect of the evil is destined. You have sown certain evil seeds. Now you must come to have that corrupt fruit, that evil fruit. You must come to taste the bitter fruit that you have sown. If you have sown bitter seeds, you must taste bitter fruit. If you have sown good seeds, you must come to taste good fruit. We must face our destiny.

I have done evil deeds, Master. Why was I chosen for this path?

Well, sister, ask the One who has selected you for the path. The Lord has chosen you and the Lord may have pulled you from within. So you ask him about your being on the path. Why ask me?

165 *I see that when a child is born he is perfectly pure. So it's environment, and the physical conditions that make a man spiritually ignorant; the older he becomes, he loses all his spiritual power.*

The child is pure when he is born [as far as having committed any sins in this life is concerned], but he is born with a certain destiny. He is not absolutely pure when he comes into this world. He has a load of karmas which he is carrying from past births. And he has come with all those sins, with all those karmas. He will be given an environment according to those karmas. He will get his parentage, education, and friends. He acts in his life according to those things.

166 *Should a human being leave everything to his destiny and not work? For example, if somebody is destined to be a doctor or an engineer, or it is written in his destiny that he is going to commit a murder, and if he thinks that he is going to do so, if it is written in his destiny, can he become a doctor even if he did not work for it?*

When it is in his destiny to become a doctor, he will automatically work to be a doctor; otherwise, he will never become a doctor. We have to do, with our limited intelligence, what we think will be the best; but only that will happen which has to happen. We cannot think why should we do anything if it is already written in our destiny and we will get it automatically anyway. If a thing is in your destiny, then your way of thinking will be to develop it. We always have to do our best under all circumstances, and then naturally only that will happen as he wants it to happen. But we cannot excuse ourselves by taking shelter or not doing anything and letting the Lord do whatever he wants to do, because that is just another trick of the mind.

For in order to be able to act according to the will of the Lord, we have to be receptive, we have to submit ourselves to the Lord. And that we cannot do until we have controlled our mind and made it our own – we cannot submit anything that does not belong to us. As long as the ego is there, the I-ness is there, we have to observe, we have to work; but only that will happen which he wants to happen.

We are all just like puppets who are dancing, and the strings are being pulled by him according to our karmas. The realized souls and the unrealized souls are all dancing in the same way. The only difference is that the realized souls know that he is pulling the strings and the unrealized souls think that they are dancing by their own effort. So we have to act in this world with detachment from our role in life, knowing that he is pulling the strings and whatever is to happen will happen, but all the same doing our best under all circumstances. Thus we make ourselves receptive and become good puppets in his hands.

167 Master, what percent do we have free will in this life and what percent are our lives predestined by our past karmas?

Well, brother, we all know how much free will we have. We know that we should avoid certain bad things. Have we any control of our mind to avoid them? We at once become tempted by them; we do those same things. We repent: Why have I done it? But again we do the same things. We have no free will even in our thoughts, even in our actions here in this world. We don't want to hurt anybody; we don't want to say anything bad to anybody; we all logically know the right thing. Yet how much do we do everyday? We have no free will even in our thoughts, even in our actions here. So, on a grand scale, what free will can we have? To begin with, we never had any free will to part from the Father and to become part and parcel of this creation. We had no free will at all.

I often give an example: When you play chess, the first move is in your hand, but after the first move every move is conditioned by the first move. You have no choice. So similarly, after having come to this creation, we have started action and reaction. We have no free will at all. We can't select our parents. We can't select our heritage. We can't select the environment in which we have been brought up, the atmosphere in which we shape our thinking. We have no control over these things, and all our decisions, all our thinking is conditioned by the environment in which we are brought up, conditioned by our parentage. You are born in Russia – your way of thinking is very different. The same soul is born in America – its way of thinking, its attitude on life is very different. But the soul has no choice to be born in Russia or in America. After that, you see, due to its environment it starts thinking in a certain way. If you eliminate all that, then you can say you have free will. But if you include all that, then we have no free will.

We are puppets. In our life we see that we are all slaves of the senses. We have no free will. The mind runs to them like a wild animal and has no control over them. We know they are bad. We want to avoid them. We know they are weaknesses, but we have no control over them. Being here in the body we have no free will. So, right from the beginning, if we consider our way of thinking and parentage and heritage and all that, then we have no free will at all. But if you eliminate all that, you can say that you have conditioned free will, you have limited free will.

168 *Master, would you please explain regarding choice? How we are to know when we are making this choice or when there is a karmic result? When we make a choice, is it karma to do something we cannot help?*

We cannot think from this point of view, that we should make a choice according to our karmic background. We cannot know what is our karma or what is in store for us. With our best efforts, honestly and sincerely, we should try to do our best and leave the results to the Lord. If it does not happen according to our best intentions and efforts, we should take it that this must be the will of the Lord. We should feel happy in that. We should never try to justify our choice by saying it is in my karma to do this. It is difficult for us to know what is the right choice, according to our karmic background. Karma will take care of our choice automatically. We need not try to analyze what is our karma or what is not our karma, for that will take care of itself.

169 Even in our daily life we all face problems. If it is not the work that we want it to be, should we try and force the issue or just sort of go along with it and take it as it is? Things will come?

We should do our best and leave the results in the hands of the Lord. We should not feel dejected if we cannot achieve that for which we have worked. It simply was not destined for us. In that case our destiny was only to work and not to get its fruit. Other people do not work, and yet they get the fruit. That is their destiny. It is all individual karma.

170 Maharaj Ji, I know that there is no accidental death but would you comment on that, such as when an airplane goes down and all the people are killed?

Brother, everything is destined. We will live only as long as the span of life which our destiny holds for us. After that we have to leave this body, whether we leave it in a natural death, as it is called, or an accidental death, if you want to call it that, or in a hospital or in any other way. We cannot live longer than what is destined for us.

171 *If children are born with a special knowledge – they know more than the average child – and they grow up to be physicists or let us say great men, has it anything to do with their previous lives? What made them superior to the average person?*

What we are and what we are going to be naturally has something to do with our past life. That is what is known as destiny or fate. We bring it with us into this world. Destiny or fate is something with which we are born, which we are going to face in this life span. Naturally, it has an association with our past life.

In other words, it is true that there is something in his capacity from before that makes him superior, from a previous life?

Yes, that is right.

172 *Master, sometimes you speak of the will of God, and in many countries they speak of the will of Allah. If a drunken driver comes around a corner and kills an innocent child of three or four, or a bomb goes off in Ireland or the Middle East or anywhere and kills and maims innocent women and children – is this the will of God?*

It's very difficult to define the will of God. These are our own karmas which we face, our own sins which we have committed in the past, and we are facing their effect now. If we take them as the will of God, we go through them without losing much balance. However, it's not what God wills; it is what we have sown. The will of God is: Whatever you sow, so shall you reap.[133]

You have to go through your destiny, which you already shaped in previous births. According to his will the whole creation is going on, and we have to face our own karmas here because our karmas have become our master. Actually, we have done those karmas. It's not that God has written what we should face. We are the maker of our own destiny.

I'll give you an example. A case goes to a judge. He takes the evidence of the complainant and accordingly he sentences the accused or acquits him. Now, the judge has not used only his discretion – he's bound by the file of evidence before him. The whole record of the accused is before the court. Accordingly, the judge sentences the person. He acquits him or he sentences him, but you can't say that the judge has punished him. The criminal's own sins are punishing him. There's only one word the judge writes, but there is a big file, a big record of that criminal behind it, which forces the judge to sentence the accused accordingly. Similarly, our record – whatever we have done in our past lives – is before the Lord. And accordingly, we are facing our destiny. You can call it the will of God, but he has not indiscriminately written that you face this, you face this or that. He has written it according to our past records. So we have to go through our destiny. We have no option – there is no sense in accusing the Lord.

173 By saying that you have no free will, blaming the way you were brought up and so on – is it not possible to use this as an excuse for doing anything we want?

When we don't want to do anything, we always say, "It is my destiny, I had no choice," which is just an excuse, I would say. We have to do our best, and then if in spite of our best effort things don't happen to our liking, we can say it was destiny. We have to put in effort. How do you know it is not in your destiny to put in effort, rather than just getting something by the way? It may be in our destiny to put in effort. For another person, it may be in his destiny just to inherit. For me, it may be in my destiny to work hard to get that.

So we don't know our destiny; we have to put in effort. We are not to use this way of thinking just to justify our weakness, our laziness. We have to do our best. When in spite of all that something doesn't happen to our liking, then we can say that I was not destined to have it.

174 Maharaj Ji, do we also have some free will?

We have the power of discrimination, not free will. If we had free will, we would not be here. It was his free will to create this universe. So we are here not by our free will but by his free will. Now, what we think is our free will is ego. We have forgotten the will of the Creator. We think we exist; this I-ness and we-ness which has come in us is ego, and this is the veil between us and him.

So when we eliminate this I-ness, ego or attachment to this world, then again we will have no free will. Then we merge back into him and merge into his will; we lose ourselves.

Mentally we're not prepared to think that we have no free will at all. We have developed this instinct of possession so much that intellectually it is very difficult for us to grasp that we have no free will at all. And that is why we are not willing to lose our idea and concept of free will – because we are so attached to it. Actually, we have no free will at all, from the higher source. But from a limited source, we do have a limited free will.

As long as we are blind, we think we have free will. But when we realize how the whole is being governed, then we realize we're puppets; we have no free will at all. This realization – that all that is happening is his creation, that he is the one who is making this whole universe or this play go on – this realization is our escape from this world. That is eliminating the ego. This ego is making us always think that we are doing it. And who can make us do this? It is my free will to sit on this sofa or that sofa. But I forget: How can I sit on this sofa or that sofa unless I enter the guest house? And was it up to me to enter the guest house? There are so many circumstances leading me to this particular place where I have to exert my so-called free will to sit on this seat or that seat. And even after my coming here, if the seat is already occupied, then I have to sit somewhere else. Even here, I have no free will. You see, all this free will that we have is conditioned, limited.

175 If we sow a new seed, is that also in our destiny?

A new seed can't be a part of destiny. Circumstances may force you to create new destiny for yourself; you will be forced to sow a new seed under those circumstances. But still, it's a new seed. Destiny is something with which we are born, which we have to go through during this span of life. A new seed is something which we are creating for the next life. But destiny plays a great part in our sowing a new seed also. A person, according to his destiny, may be born in a thief's house – his whole environment encourages him just to steal, commit theft. That may be his destiny. But still, his upbringing is such that he may even be sowing a new seed for the future in that atmosphere. So to some extent, destiny is responsible for our attitude, for our sowing new seeds. It may be due to our past life, our destiny, that we are brought up in very immoral, bad company. Our attitude, the development of our mind causes us to start leading that type of life. Some of the acts we commit may be new seeds. So it affects us, but destiny by itself doesn't cause us to sow new seeds.

176 *Is destiny a series of specific events or is it just the fulfilment by any means possible of our karmas?*

What is destiny? Destiny is something with which you are born and are going to face during this span of your life. Destiny is not coincidence at all. When we say it was destined it doesn't mean it is a coincidence. Destined means it was to happen. You have no option – that is destiny. In coincidence you have an option – something may or may not happen. In destiny it must happen. So destiny is something with which you are born and which you are going to face during this span of life.

177 *If we are so helpless, will the Lord take care of us?*

You see, we are very fortunate that the Lord has kept the reins in his own hand and that he chalks out a certain destiny for us to follow. If we had been given free will, I don't know what mess we would have made. It's lucky that all decisions already have been made and that we are just puppets dancing to the Lord's tune. It's very lucky. Even when we are confronted with a little decision, we can't make it. And if we had to make a decision at every step in our life, I don't know what mess we would make. So it's better that the Lord is doing everything and we just remain a puppet.

No more mess then?

It's less mess. Actually, there is no mess. It is only our way of thinking that has made a mess. If we leave that way of thinking, then there is no mess at all. Our way of thinking has made quite a mess.

178 *Good afternoon, Master. I would like to ask a question more concerned with karma, or the way I see karma. If*

you meet up with a person or maybe get into a situation where you feel that this just brings a lot of unhappiness, you could walk away from it, but you feel involved. If this continues for a very long time, and you feel that maybe it would be better for you to walk away from this – even if that would be very difficult – would this be avoiding karma? Should we stay and live through this, or is it okay to just walk away?

Brother, we can never walk away from our destiny. We can never walk away from our karma. Everybody has a bond with a certain destiny which he has to go through. Whether he likes it or not, he has to go through it. It is not our choice to accept it or reject it. We are a slave of our destiny, whether we accept it cheerfully or otherwise. We have to go through our destiny.

179 Is the amount of love we experience for the master something that's bounded by destiny, or is that totally a matter of grace?

Destiny itself is a grace. If he has planted in our destiny the seed of love, by his grace it becomes a part of destiny.

180 Master, if everything in our life is predestined, then is the amount of meditation we do predestined? Or can the master alter our destiny by giving us more opportunity to meditate?

To some extent our amount of meditation, our tendency towards meditation, is destined.

You get a certain atmosphere or certain shocks from the world that break your attachments to them; you don't want them. So that is also part of the destiny which moulds you towards meditation. Otherwise such events would have been different. We would have never thought about the master, or even about the Father. All these things go a long way towards our meditation. So the time we give to meditation depends a lot on destiny. We get a certain beautiful atmosphere, environment around us, a satsang atmosphere around us so that automatically we feel like meditating; those surroundings and atmosphere are part of our destiny. All these are prompting us towards meditation, so we should try to make use of that.

181 Is the time of our death already set?

Yes, it is definitely set. You cannot increase even a breath. You cannot change even the place where you have to die. It's all set. If all little detailed things are set for us in this world, if we have no free will, death cannot be in our hand, cannot be our choice. Even that is destined.

182 Master, I have a question concerning free will and destiny. There's a prayer – I think it's by Saint Francis – called the serenity prayer, and it says, "God grant me the serenity to accept the things I cannot change, the courage to change the things I can, and the wisdom to know the difference." My question is: How does one develop the wisdom to know exactly what we can or cannot change in our lives?

You see, our destiny is interconnected. It is not independent of the events of life. One has to take a birth. One has to have a father, a mother. One may have sisters, friends, doctor, nurses – when you have to become sick and to be admitted to the hospital – medicines, chemists, your admirers buying flowers, sending you cards of sympathy.

These are all destiny in which they have to play their own part. If one event is withdrawn from your destiny, what about that chain? It will break. What will the doctor do? What will the nurse do? What will the hospital do? What will the chemist do? What will that flower shop do?

Our destiny is interconnected, but its effect can be minimized. If one has to break one's legs, he may not feel the pain at all. But you cannot avoid breaking your leg if it is in your destiny. We can't change the events of our life. We can adjust to those events of life so they don't affect us.

183 *A lot of times we think, or I say I think that I'm owed something, that I worked hard for something and I should get it. But when I look back at my life, if I had gotten what I wanted, I don't know that I would be here today. What can I or anybody in that situation do to better accept things you get that you don't want or situations that don't go your way?*

Brother, we always pray for those things which are not in our destiny. What is in our destiny will automatically come to us. But we are more anxious to get what the Lord has not written in our destiny. Then we feel frustrated. Why not leave everything to him? Let him give whatever he thinks best, and we should just go through it.

184 *Master, are there ever situations where we can change the course of our destiny?*

You see, this whole life is nothing but destiny. We are all born with a destiny and we have to go through that destiny during this span of life. What do you mean by changing the course of destiny? You can't change the course of destiny. You may not be affected by the events of destiny, you may be able to rise above the events of destiny, but you can't change destiny at all. You have to go through it. With the help of meditation, you are not affected by the events of destiny. You don't lose your balance. You face it smilingly. There may be some remission, as far as its effect is concerned, but you can't change the course of events.

You see, in destiny there's not much interference. If you have to bump your head, you will have to bump your head. But you may not be affected; you may not feel the pain when bumping your head. But you can't change the course of events. There may be a little remission here and there, but normally, you don't change the events of destiny because our course of karma is not independent, it's connected with so many people. If one has to have an accident, it's not just an accident. Now the car is involved, the passengers are involved, the hospital is involved, the doctor is involved, the nurses are involved, relations are involved. The person who's sending flowers is involved. So many people are involved with that person's destiny. So if his course of action is changed, what about the destiny of the other people? That will also have to be changed.

So saints never interfere with the destiny of anybody at all. But it's possible that there may be an accident and you just laugh over it and not feel affected by that accident at all. You may take it very easy and may not feel any pain about it and take it very lightly. But you can't say that accident should have been avoided because I've been meditating. Our load of karma is not independent, it's always interconnected with other people. There's a long chain, so all that can't be changed. The mystics never interfere with the destiny of any person.

185 *At a certain level of consciousness, can you exercise some control on your destiny? If you know what your destiny is going to be, can you change it?*

No, you can't change it, but you can face it very boldly and smilingly. You won't be affected by that destiny. Your attitude towards that event changes. You see, it depends upon the attitude. You take two people. Both have lost their dear ones. One is weeping and crying and even wants to commit suicide. He can't stand the separation. The other man just accepts that as the Lord's will and smiles over it and starts doing his work. The same event has happened to both of them, but they each have a different attitude. Our attitude towards that destiny which we are going through is absolutely changed by meditation. Not that you are able to change the destiny, but you are able to face it with a smile. Without losing your balance you can accept it as the will of the Father. And by his grace there may be some remission sometimes. But you can't make it a principle that you will definitely get remission by meditating. He may give you some remission, but you have to go through your destiny smilingly in any case.

186 Master, is it possible to short-circuit or stop your destiny?

No, sister, you can't make any short cut, but sometimes, in our interest, when master takes command of us, he changes the course of our destiny. For example, you may have to go through a certain amount of karma in two births, but he thinks that you are quite prepared to bear all that heavy load in one birth, and he thinks that his guiding hand is there to help you, and you are quite strong enough to face even two birth's karma in one birth. He may help you in many ways. Some karma may be burned – some by meditation – and some he may make you go through in this very life with little suffering and may not bring you back at all into this world. So he may change your course of destiny in your interest, not from any other point of view at all. Or he might think you are too weak or too feeble, and he may even give you another birth to clear all these things. He may think that if too much load is put on you, you may even leave meditation, go away from the path. So the master may prolong your journey and may give you another birth to face all that. In that way he can change the course of our destiny, but destiny we have to go through.

187 Maharaj Ji, to what degree should we follow astrology?

Well, brother, it is a science. To what extent it is correct depends upon the interpretation of the person who is doing it. If we all know and realize that everything is destined, nothing can be changed. Then why run after astrology to know what is going to happen? We are curious to know what comes next, what I am going to face. But can you change it? You can't change it. Everything is destined. You have to go through it. The first fundamental principle of astrology is that your destiny is destined, and astrologers try to tell you what you are going to face. They presume that your life is destined, and they try to read your destiny. But if it is not going to change, then where is the necessity to know beforehand? We'll face what comes. Why create worry unnecessarily about those events, whether they are going to happen or not? We'll face the situation when it comes.

So why run after astrologers? We do it just to satisfy our curiosity about what is in store for us next. But that may or may not be right – nobody can correctly say, 100 percent. So it is always better to leave it to the Father and face our destiny smilingly. Whatever comes, we'll face it. Why worry about astrology? There is nothing wrong with it. It's a science. Some people have the knowledge to interpret, to some extent. It's all right if they are interested in it.

188 *Astrologers claim that when one is born in a certain month of the year, one is given a certain type of life and guaranteed a certain way of living. Is it true or not?*

If you know what is going to happen to you, what difference will it make? Nothing can be changed. We will have to face what is in our destiny. So why add to our agony by knowing beforehand what we are going to face? If one is told that he is going to have an accident two years before it is to happen, he lives in anxiety and agony for two years; whereas if he did not know in advance, it may have bothered him for perhaps only two or three hours. What is the use of it all? Even if we know beforehand, that does not help us in any way. Astrology is a definite science, but very few have mastered it, so mostly their predictions are not correct. But one should not dabble in these things. Whatever has to come will come, so why bother about it?

189 *I have found a very good remedy in a particular case of aggressiveness. I try to find out the month and day of that person's birth and then see, more or less, what his traits are. Sometimes you will see that they are completely antagonistic to the particular sign that you were born under. And this will help you to understand the person, when you know his traits.*

But, sister, you will only know by that horoscope the trend of that man towards you, which you already know by personal experience.

Yes, but doesn't it also help?

The question of knowing does not arise when we have to improve ourselves. In every situation, whatever the other person's view may be, we must improve ourselves. That is all. It should not affect us even if the other person slanders or otherwise abuses us.

But I think if you know what sign he is under …?

I think the other person makes you know him much better than whatever you can try to know by these methods. When you meet a person, you know where you stand as far as he is concerned, as far as his likings for you are concerned. Sometimes these scientific or mathematical calculations may deceive us or may be wrong, but the human touch does not deceive us at all. We know where we stand.

190 *Maharaj Ji, you've told us that once we're initiated, and once we are able to go within, we will understand all of the past karma that is creating our present life circumstance. There are many metaphysical sciences and teachings today that can help us at least partially penetrate that barrier, help us understand maybe the details of the karma of our present life. It often seems that some of that understanding can be a tremendous benefit to people in a counselling situation, in understanding the whys and wherefores of their present karmic situation. It seems to give them a great deal of relief to know that these particular situations have been perpetuated by karmic grooves that have been created in the past.*

But how to know why we are going through this destiny, what we have done in the past to face these situations, these events of life? Science can never lead you to that point. There is a school of thought in India where they tell you about your past lives, about your date of birth, about your father, mother, and what you're going through in this life – bare facts, bare events of life, not the details. Why you have to go through that event they don't tell you. That only proves one thing, that what you're going to go through is already destined. And if it is destined, then what is the necessity to know? If we can't change the course of the events of life, then what is the necessity to know the events of life? Anyway, we're helpless, we have to go through them. Why know them? Why know the trouble beforehand? After all, one's whole destiny is not very pleasant.

You see, this inquisitive mind only helps people to exploit us. Because we have an inquisitive mind, we want to know our future. This helps people to exploit us, nothing else.

REINCARNATION

191 I have a question about karma, reincarnation and transmigration of the soul.

As far as transmigration is concerned, I have just discussed that passage in the Bible where Christ says that your sins have become your master and you have become the slave of your sins.[99] A slave or servant has to go where the master commands. He cannot stay in one house. It means that when our karmas have become our master and we have become the victim of those karmas, then we cannot stay in one body forever – we shift from house to house, from body to body. Our karmas force us to do this. Not only in the Bible, but in other holy scriptures as well, we find: As you sow, so shall you reap.[133] So in order to reap the fruit of those karmas, we have to shift from body to body, in the species in which we can best fulfil that karma. And that is transmigration of the soul.

192 *If one fails to reach God-realization in this life, will he have another chance?*

The Lord does not find excuses to send us back again and again. He gives us quite a fair chance to make progress on the path. In fact, it is our attachments that are pulling us down every time. Generally, if we are not much attached to the world, even though we may not make much headway towards home, we are given another chance to loosen those attachments. But we have to do that by means of spiritual practice while we are in the human form. However, if we have not found a living master and refuse to travel that path, refuse to think about the Lord, have absolutely no devotion for him, have no desire whatsoever to go home, we will not continue to get a human body; we have to go down into a lower species. We then get that form in which we can satisfy all the unfulfilled desires and cravings that come in our mind every day.

It is our karmas and desires coupled together that bring us every time into birth and death. Whatever seeds we sow, we have to come back to reap. Whatever we desire and crave and do not get or sublimate while in this world, we have to take birth to satisfy those unfulfilled desires and cravings. So unless we clear our karmas, unless we clear ourselves from all these desires and cravings, we cannot escape from birth and death. We do get a chance. The Lord is merciful. He always helps us and gives us chance after chance to make the best use of our life. But if we refuse to make use of that chance, naturally we have to go down into the lower species.

193 *Does memory go with the soul after passing on? After we move on to the next plane, does memory go with it?*

You forget the past when you take birth in another life. All the things which you committed in the past birth, you completely forget. And I tell you, it is fortunate that we forget our past. It is not possible to know now even of our last life, what we did then. And if we were to remember what a mess we made in our previous lives, it would frighten us and put us to shame.

194 *When we reincarnate, is it just because of the bad karmas, or is it both good and bad karmas?*

Both good and bad karmas; both pull us back to this world. Our good deeds and evil deeds both pull us back to the world.

Do we only come back as a human being?

No. You may go anywhere, according to your load of karmas. For example, let's say you give something in charity and in your mind you are thinking: I gave that man a hundred rupees; the Lord should give me ten times this amount. Now, you have done a good deed, sown good karma. You have been concerned for someone else. But you have sown a seed to come back to this world again, to get the reward you desire. You want ten times more than you have given. So even your good karma brings you back to this world. You have to rise above all karmas.

You can't tell whether you'll come back as a human being. Is that what you are saying?

It depends upon our karmas. Wherever we can fulfil those suppressed or unfulfilled desires, wherever we can best reap the fruit of our actions, that is where we are sent.

There are human beings who could come back in an animal life?

We can come back in an animal form. There are certain desires which can only be satisfied in those species. So we have to come back in those species.

Does the animal reincarnate the same?

They also get the chance to come up, slowly.

195 *Maharaj Ji, does every human being go through the 8,400,000 species before it attains the human form?*

It is not essential that you must go through the whole cycle. When you get this opportunity, if you don't make use of it, then you can scale down. Not that you must come through the cycle of 84 again. No. Wherever your karmas will pull you, wherever you can fulfil those karmas, you will go to that level. After that, you will get to come up again.

That means you could get another human form again, after ...?

That's right. You see, the Lord doesn't find excuses to push us down. We are given every reasonable opportunity to improve. But if we refuse to, then nobody can keep us from going back into the creation.

196 *I am thinking in particular of reincarnation. How can one satisfy oneself about this, intellectually, without first going back and meeting or seeing our former life? How can we justify reincarnation intellectually?*

When we find so many ups and downs in this world, when we find so many disparities, the rich and the poor, so many diseases, so many born blind, crippled, mentally disabled, we definitely start thinking: "Why is everybody not equal in this world, why does everybody have a different destiny and different fate?" We ponder and wonder, and then we think about the past. We can find no other explanation but reincarnation, karma. They must have done something in their past life for which they are in that condition now. Otherwise, how could the Lord be so unjust to them and good to others? Whatever they have sown, they are reaping now.

What is destiny or fate? It is something with which we are born, something that we have to face during our life's span. That is the 'original sin' with which we are born, the reactions of past deeds that we have to fulfil in this life. If we accept the theory of original sin, destiny or fate, we have to accept the karma theory also, and we will accept reincarnation too. There is no other explanation.

But one cannot accept it intellectually. There is no proof?

You see, all these things you are only trying to understand intellectually. I have just said that to know the teachings of the saints we have to experience them. We try to think with the intellect. We have to satisfy the intellect with the intellect. I said that the intellect is a great barrier in our way. We have to pierce through it with the intellect. So these are the logical explanations of our intellect about reincarnation.

197 *A scientific or technological problem can be solved so that we can actually see the result. But the theory of karma is so abstract. It is hard to believe.*

If you don't believe in the theory of karma, how can you accept the fact that one person can be born blind, another mentally disabled, another in a very good family? How can you account for this discrimination in their births?

What I mean is, we cannot just base our ideas on some faith or something we don't know.

If we don't know something, we should try to know it.

198 *This evolution, we are told, comes up from the grain of sand, plant life, animal life and the human – are we to understand that every material thing in this universe will finally have to get back to God?*

Only the souls.

Is there not a soul in a grain of sand?

No. For example, there is no soul in this water, no soul in this stone, no soul in the air, no soul in the fire; yet all of these things are made up of one of the five elements. The whole creation is made of five elements. Yet, if you take those elements individually, they have no souls. Plants have souls, insects have souls, birds have souls, the animals have souls, and of course human beings have souls. They can make their way up to the Lord, after having attained the human form; but not this metal, for it has no soul.

Have these other creatures the same soul as human beings have?

Oh yes, the soul is the same. That same soul can be in human form or in any other living form.

199 *Master, do you believe in retrogression, degeneration of a soul into an animal?*

Yes, why not? Our own karma also decides that. According to the karma theory, man can merge back into his source, the Lord from whom he originally came, and he can also go back into a lower species, such as an animal or even below that, to which he may have descended in a previous life and came up to the status of a human being again.

The Lord does not find excuses to send us back. He gives us opportunity after opportunity to improve, to go ahead. But if we refuse to make use of this opportunity, we can go back. Our attachments, our unfulfilled desires, our karmas can pull us down. We do not like to think so, but that is a fact.

Master, in other words, if a man acts like a beast he may have to come back as a beast?

He may have been a beast in his last life and is still carrying all those instincts in him. Or he may come back again as a beast. Why not?

200 How can one believe in the Bible and also believe in the transmigration of the soul?

If you believe in Christ and read the Bible thoroughly, you'll be convinced about the transmigration of the soul. If you prefer another mystic, read his works, and you'll find the same thing.

Is it not an imaginary law, imagined by the mystics?

No, it's not an imaginary law.

201 In regard to the Resurrection, are we supposed to take that literally or …

The soul is always immortal. The soul never dies. It is only the body that dies. The Resurrection, according to my understanding, is for that particular soul, at the time of death. You see, we are judged by our fruits. Whatever we have done during the span of our life, according to these deeds we'll be judged at the time of our death and that is the resurrection for that particular soul.

If the deeds are good, if the soul has been in touch with the spirit within, then with the help of that spirit, it will be raised by the mystic and will go back to the Father. If the deeds are corrupt, if the deeds are bad, if we have spent our life in sensual pleasures, remaining a slave of the mind, living in sin, then according to those deeds we will be condemned, we will have to come back to this world.

Whatever is to be decided will be decided immediately, at the time of death. We don't have to go anywhere for that decision, which is the Lord's judgment. Judgment is immediate, at the absolute moment of our death. It is decided at once whether the soul is going upward or the soul is coming downward. That is the resurrection for the soul.

202 *Is it ever necessary for a satsangi – that is, one who has been initiated by a true master – to reincarnate into an animal form?*

Even if his karma was bad, he will not be sent lower than the human birth. It is not necessary for that soul to come back into the animal form. We do not come down. We go up. Such a person may get another human form, and in that form he will have to go through all those bad karmas, but he will not go down into a lower species.

203 *If people do wrong, do they not come back as animals?*

Not initiates. Of course, otherwise, one has to come back according to his karma, into whatever species our karma designates. But you had asked whether it was necessary for a satsangi. It is not necessary. He can improve right from there.

204 *With this population explosion, as well as the explosion of other births and so on, there will be a need to have a very large number of souls, to give them life. Will there be new ones coming back here from the Lord, or will those souls be taking birth again?*

Brother, no new souls are coming at all, and you can never count the limit of souls in this creation. This whole room is full of souls. Even bacteria, every living thing has a soul, and the whole atmosphere is filled with souls, even what you can only see with a microscope that is not visible to the naked eye. As for the whole population, we see humans in only a limited way, but the overall population of souls remains the same.

Sometimes there may be more birds; sometimes more humans; sometimes more insects. But overall, generally the number of souls remains the same in this creation, except for those who go back to the Father. No new souls are coming every time. The souls which have come right from the time of creation, only they stay here; they are here in one form or another, except those who have gone back to the Father.

205 Master, if the master is gracious enough to allow you to leave this particular plane at your death, and he grants you another three lives before you go forward, what is the timing? Could these lives be hundreds of years? And, what opportunities do you get for advancement in the new places you go to, when you don't come back here? Do you meet a spiritual guide, or your master?

You see, it depends upon the karmas of the individuals. Some people immediately take birth in this world – I'm talking only about satsangis. Some people take birth immediately to fulfil their karmic accounts, and then they come in better facilities, better opportunities, better environments to make better progress in meditation. And some people may not take birth at all. They may be kept inside in those regions, and from there they make their spiritual progress back to the Father. But whatever decision is taken, the decision is taken at once, at the time of your death. It's not that souls are put into some cold storage, and slowly and slowly a decision is made about them. The decision is made at once, according to your karmas, according to your past spiritual progress.

206 *There has been some question about how long it takes the soul to leave the body when a person dies.*

It takes no time at the time of death. What do we mean by leaving the body?

Being taken out of the body.

It depends upon from where the soul starts to leave. If it has already reached here [the eye centre], it takes no time to leave the body at all. And it can only leave when the soul comes here. Without reaching here, the soul can never leave the body at all. It may take more time for the soul to come to this place – that's different. But when it leaves the body, it leaves in a second. At the time of death, it takes no time for the soul to leave the body.

Is that for nonsatsangis, too?

For everybody.

It is believed, Maharaj Ji, in the West, that a person who dies must not be cremated or buried for two or three days because the soul is still in the body. I think that is the reason why this question has been asked.

I think this belief has been created in the minds of the people from many other points of view, because their relations and friends are scattered and they need two, three days before they can gather and put the body to rest. That belief has been created in them that the soul is still hovering in the body, so there should be no hurry in cremating it, so that other relations and concerned people may come and collect there.

Otherwise, once the soul leaves the body there's no question of keeping the body. That is just made of five elements, you see; there's nothing there, it has no life at all. You can keep it forever, or you can cremate it in the next second – it makes no difference. The soul never hovers in the body, and even if it is hovering over the body, it can't come into the body. Whether you bury the body or cremate the body, the soul can't enter the body at all after death. Once it leaves the body it may become a ghost, a spirit. It may take another birth or go to higher regions, but it will never in any way be able to come back into the body. So it's immaterial how long you keep the body before cremating or burying it.

207 *We are told in the teachings that the human infant, before birth, suffers in utero and thinks of the Lord and sees light and so forth. At what stage would the soul in that infant become conscious?*

You see, before birth, when the child is inside, he's conscious of that light, he's conscious of that sound. The moment he takes birth, he forgets everything. That is why, generally, a small little babe will always go on gazing at the light. I don't know about your country, but in our country there's still a custom that when any child is born, people create noise outside. They beat a drum or any utensils or anything, just to make the baby familiar with that sound, and they always put a candle in his room, never keep him in darkness, just to make him familiar with that light. Now people don't know the background of all that, but that was actually the meaning behind it, to get the child used to seeing that light and hearing the sound, so he would be made familiar with these things, before slowly and slowly he forgets everything.

208 *If we do our meditation, even if we haven't seen the light or heard the sound, will we have to come back?*

If a satsangi is faithful to his initiation and faithful to his meditation, then nobody can pull him down. Even if he does not have much concentration, has not made much progress within, nothing will pull him down if he is honest about himself. If he is honest in meditation, honest in following the teachings, honest in his way of life, nothing can pull him back.

209 *Can you please tell me if it is possible to remember something from your previous life?*

You can always recollect what has happened in your previous life, provided you go within yourself to a certain stage. Sometimes you do get reflections, visions of your past life, but they may be right or may not be right. You can only know about your past birth when you have crossed the first stage inside and made your mind pure. But then you won't even worry about your past birth. You always try to look ahead. There is so much to look forward to that you hardly have even a thought for looking back, because it's not pleasant to know from where we have come. It is pleasant to know where we have to go. But we can definitely know about our past births.

210 *Master, sometimes do certain members of families keep coming back in the same family circle due to attachment?*

Sister, naturally, because they're so attached to each other in one way or another, they come into the same surroundings, same atmosphere. But they can leave also. Some people in the family are hardly attached to anybody. They're different than all the others, they cannot stand even their own family. So it differs, but normally, naturally, yes.

211 *We are told we will have a minimum of four human births after initiation. Is that right?*

A maximum of four births is for those who are attached to this world and who want to come back, who are not trying to follow the right path, who are not trying to make any spiritual progress inside, not trying to attach themselves to the shabd and nam and still trying to revive their worldly attachments. They may have to come back to fulfil those attachments. But one who has detached himself from the world and has attached himself to the higher self inside, he will not come back to this world at all.

212 *Master, when a satsangi dies, and if that soul has to return to this world for a rebirth, will that soul be born into a satsangi family?*

You see, once we are on the path, we never go outside of the path. We always continue to go ahead. If we don't have much spiritual progress to our credit now, and certain desires or karmas pull us back to this creation again, we will definitely be born in a better environment, better situation, from the point of view of meditation and making further progress. We'll definitely be on the path again. Whether the family is satsangi or not, it's immaterial. The main thing is that we will get an opportunity to attend to our meditation, we'll be in a position to attend to our meditation, and the Lord will pull us from wherever we may be. It's not essential to be born in a satsangi family. Some other families are so good, so noble, that you may get the chance to attend to your meditation even in those circumstances, those environments.

213 *Master, speaking about desires, I and many other satsangis have noticed that every time we want something,*

we get it, so we have to be very careful what we wish for. The other day I heard that it is not the master that fulfils those desires but our mind.

You see, all desires are fulfilled, but they may not be fulfilled in this life. You may have to take another life to fulfil those desires. He is a good giver. Whatever you want from him, whatever you ask him for, he will give you. He will never be tired of giving to you, but you have to come back again and again and again and again to get all that you want. So don't think that all that you are desiring you will get in this life. You may have to take another life to get all that.

Desires will be fulfilled because desires are pulling us back to this creation. Desires make a strong groove on our mind, and then we have to come back to this creation. They will be fulfilled, if not today, then tomorrow, next birth. So we should not desire anything and accept what comes. The mind creates the desire, and we are praying to the Lord to fulfil those desires. We are not trying to explain to the mind to live in the will of the Father. We are trying to explain to the Father to live in the will of the mind. We are devotees of the mind. But we want to become devotees of the Father. So we should try to live in the will of the Father rather than the will of the mind.

So we should not create any desires, you see, or try to fulfil those desires. We should not even think about those desires. Because then there is no limit to these desires. Hardly you fulfil one and the mind creates still more. You hardly tackle them and there are thousands more before you. Mind is never tired of these desires. So we should try to train the mind to live in the will of the Father rather than to create desires, and training of the mind can only come by meditation.

214 If at some time in our lives we have a very great desire which is not fulfilled, and then we grow away from that desire, are we still bound by that desire?

You see, either that desire will be satisfied or the desire will be driven out of you before you die. The master, in one way or another, will satisfy that desire during your lifetime. Or by meditation he will drive out the desire, before you leave your flesh, so that you may not have to come back to this world again. But we have to get rid of these desires before we can go back to the Father.

215 What does the saying mean: Neither a borrower nor a lender be?

Sister, we should never knock at the door of the court as either a debtor or a creditor. You should be neither a debtor nor a creditor. If you owe a debt to somebody, you will have to come back to this creation again to pay the debt, and if you are a creditor and you want the debt back from the other person, you'll have to come back to this creation to collect the debt.

So whether you are a debtor or a creditor, you will have to come back to this creation, whether to pay or to take. So you should be neither a borrower nor a lender. If some people owe you, you should forget about them, not have the desire to take it back from them. If you knock at the door of the court, whether you go as a creditor or a debtor, you will have to go there again, because you want justice.

216 Do satsangis have to come back, after being initiated?

If it is in the soul's interest to come back to this creation, it will be brought to this creation. If it is not in the interest of the soul, it will not be brought to this creation at all. Sometimes it is in the interest of the soul not to come to this creation, where it will get so entangled and attached, so from that point of view, master may not send the soul down. He may make the soul a little more worthy inside, in certain mansions within, and then bring it back to the creation and then take the soul back to the Father. It depends entirely upon the individual. There are no hard and fast rules about it. The responsibility is entirely his to make the soul whole, make it shine, make it clean and take it back to the Father. How he does it, that is his job.

217 Maharaj Ji, I have heard it said that when a person gets initiated, his load of karmas is light enough so that there is a possibility that he may not have to come back here again.

Well, it depends upon the individual soul. The endeavour of every soul is to make best use of this life span and to reach back to its destination. But there may be so big a load of previous karmas, so many human failings, so much attachment, that the soul may have to come back. But it will pick up from the same thread and make further progress. It won't scale back. It will go forward.

218 Master, if we do not see the inner master in this lifetime, does that mean we have to come back again?

Sister, it is only our attachments which pull us back to the level of the creation. If we are not attached to anything in this creation, nothing can pull us back. If, on the other hand, no matter how much spiritual development we may have within, how much we may have achieved within, we have some strong attachment in this creation, it will pull us back – even in spite of our spiritual development – to account for that attachment. So the main thing is the attachments. If we are not attached to anything in this creation and we have no spiritual progress within to our credit, nothing can bring us back. We will find our place in those mansions from where we can make spiritual progress within.

I have read, Master, that it's even more difficult to make spiritual progress from those regions.

That is right. It is. It is easier to do it here than there. It is quicker here than there. The progress is very slow there.

Only attachment will pull us back to this creation, nothing else. But unless we are attached to the divine melody within, it is impossible to detach ourselves from this creation, from objects of the creation, faces of this creation. Only that attachment can create detachment within us. Ultimately, meditation helps us to be attached and remain attached to that divine melody within. Then these worldly attachments automatically will fade out. They won't exist anymore. Sometimes we have many attachments of which we are not even aware. They remain in the subconscious mind. At the last stage, at the time of death, they all appear before us as on a movie screen, and no matter what you may think, you cannot get rid of those faces which come before you. They remind you of your past and all of your attachment to them. They remain dormant within you, in your subconscious mind. Only meditation helps us to rise above all that.

219 Maharaj Ji, it is said that it takes four lives for a satsangi to reach Sach Khand. Can a satsangi reincarnate in another life to another species?

Well, unless the karmas are very, very heavy, generally not. Satsangis generally are never allowed to scale down from this human birth. They are always improving. Once the seed [of nam] is there, it's always coming up and up and up. It's never destroyed. So since it has to grow, the question of going down doesn't arise. We have to grow and grow and grow to become one with the Lord.

220 During our many rebirths, are we sometimes reborn on other planets, or are we always bound to this planet?

Generally we are bound here. We can go anywhere, but generally we are bound to the same planet because our attachments are here. Our attachments from generation to generation, from house to house, from time to time, are on this planet. So we come back to this planet, in those very same surroundings, to those same attachments. But there's no bar – we can be sent anywhere. For the Lord, the whole creation is the same, is one. But generally our attachments pull us back to this level of creation, and our attachments are all here. So automatically we come here.

221 Will there be a time when this will all be over?

When you leave this creation, your dream is over. That is why the saints say that the creation is not real, because we don't stay permanently in one form here. So many times there has been a dissolution or evolution or whatever name you give it. That is why nothing is real. Everything is subject to decay. Everything is impermanent, not everlasting. So it is unreal. Soul is immortal. Soul neither dies, nor can it be killed. It just changes shape – from one flesh to another flesh, from one body to another body, from one form to another form. So soul is immortal.

3

What Are We?

Relationship of the soul to God

222 *What is the final goal? Is it where God and I are one? What does this mean, exactly? Is there a sense of individuality?*

You see, the idea is: I and God are one, I and my Father are one.[111] The soul is the essence of the Lord. It has come from the Lord and it will merge back into the Lord, and it will become one again. A drop in the ocean becomes the ocean, but when the drop leaves the ocean by evaporation, it becomes a cloud; by rain it comes to the ground, merges into the ground, and it becomes dirt. It doesn't realize that it was a pure drop of the ocean. It thinks of itself as just dirt, but with the heat, with the sun, it again evaporates and leaves the dirt. Then it realizes that I am something different than this dirt. Unnecessarily taking the association of the dirt, I had lost my identity, my individuality. So then it thinks about its own origin. It finds that it's, you see, clouds in the sky. It goes back and merges into the clouds, and perhaps goes back into the river again.

That's exactly the condition of our soul. It is the essence of that universe, of that Lord – the supreme Father. We are a slave of the mind here, and according to our karmas we are just a part of this agony, but when – with the help of meditation – we unknot the knot of the soul and the mind, the soul again goes back and merges into the same supreme Father. Then we can say, "I and the Father are one." As long I am different from the Father, and I am a slave of this cage, I cannot say, "I and the Father are one." Actually we are one because we were one, and we can become one again, and we have a link to be one.

As I have just explained to you, a drop when it's mixed with the ground can say, "I and the sea are one," but actually it will become one when it goes back and merges into the sea from where it has come. Similarly, what Christ meant by "I and the Father are one" is that I have come from him and I have gone back to him again. I have realized him. And so all of us and the Father are one. There was nothing besides the Father when he created the universe. Everything was one, and now what we find is his projection, and when he withdraws everything into himself again, it again becomes one.

So, ultimately there is no difference between the soul and God?

Ultimately there will be no difference, but there's a great difference between a drop and an ocean. But when the drop merges into the ocean, then of course there's absolutely no difference.

223 *In the Old Testament we read that God on the first day created the light. On the third or the fourth day – I can't remember exactly – he created the sun. That light that he created was the logos, the shabd.*

Our soul is that divine spark of that creator, that divine light which is giving us life. The moment that is withdrawn, we cease to exist. This body is made of five elements and that soul is holding the five elements and has given life to the five elements. The moment that soul is withdrawn from the body, the five elements are there but we cease to exist, we perish. So that soul gives us life, and that soul is the drop of the divine ocean.

So potentially everyone is God; potentially every drop is a sea, but it has to grow to become the sea. A soul has to spiritually develop and grow to become God, to become part and parcel of the Creator. Somebody called Christ God, and he said: Why call me God? You are all Gods,[112] because potentially every soul is God. It has the capability to become God.

224 Maharaj Ji, one time I heard that Guru Nanak said that earth has to return to earth, water to water, fire to fire, and so forth. I never heard any explanation of how this takes place.

It's very clear, brother. When the body is cremated, where does it go? When it decomposes, where does it go? We no longer exist then; where does it go? Then it returns to its own origins. Earth goes to the earth; water goes to the water; air goes to the air; fire goes to the fire. Then we're just not there anymore. It is only the soul, that ray of shabd that is holding these five elements together. The moment it leaves the body, the body becomes useless and it decomposes. Then it just goes back to its own origins.

225 Why do we want to go back and merge into him?

It is very clear that unless we merge back into him, we will never get release from this worldly bondage. Nobody is truly happy in this world. With all the achievements to our credit, we are not happy. There is something in us which is always disturbing us, something within us which always makes us feel that we are lonely in this world. We feel that we are missing something, and that which makes us feel that we are missing something is nothing but a natural inclination of the soul towards its Lord.

Unless it merges back into him, we can never stop that feeling of missing something.

A drop, by merging into an ocean, becomes an ocean. So we are a drop of that ocean. Unless we merge back into the ocean, we can never escape from birth and death. We can never escape from this world. This world is filled with misery, agony, howsoever much a paradise we try to make it. I do not think we have become mentally happier than before. Despite so many worldly achievements to our credit, I do not think we have made this world a paradise. We are more unhappy than before, I would say – more unhappy than those whom we call the uncivilized people. They had much better and sounder sleep than we do. They had much better health than we possess today. They had a much longer life span than we have today, and they were a much happier lot than we are today. So I do not think we have improved this world in any way, from the happiness point of view. Every day we are becoming more and more unhappy. The more we run out to achieve happiness, the more frustrated and unhappy we are becoming. So I think our pursuit is in the wrong direction. If we just pursue that happiness within ourselves, we can become happy. And unless we find that happiness within ourselves, life is not worth living. The true and lasting happiness we can find only when the soul merges back into the Lord, merges back into that ocean. Just to find that happiness, we want to go back and merge into him.

Some saints explain the relationship of the soul with the Lord as that of the son with the father. In the relationship, the son is absolutely carefree. The Lord is also referred to in the Bible as the one God and Father of all. Some saints have explained this relationship of the Lord with the soul as that of a wife and a husband. The wife is happy only when she is in the company of her husband, when she is with her husband. Whatever you may give her, even all the comforts of the world, if she is separated from her husband, she can never be happy. So some saints explain the relationship of the soul with the Lord as that of a wife and a husband. Many saints have explained this very relationship as that of a son and a mother. For example, Ramakrishna and Vedantic saints say the relationship of the Lord with the soul is that of a mother to a son, for when a son submits himself to his mother, he is carefree, he is happy, he has a sense of security. He does not bother about anything in the world.

Unless the soul merges back into the Lord, we can never have that sense of security or of happiness; we can never get release from birth and death. And as long as we are separated from him, we are in this world, we are very unhappy and miserable. Our lot is despicable. That is why we search for him. That is why he is our objective; he is our destination. And this human form, as you have just heard, is bestowed upon us, is given to us for that very purpose. That is the only duty of the human form because only in the human body can we travel on that path to reach our destination, to achieve our goal. In other forms we can never do that. That is why the human form is known as the top of the creation, the temple of the living God.

We have got to find that living God within the body, as this is his temple. We have to make a search within this temple. He has made this temple himself, he resides in it himself, and we have to search for the Lord within this temple. We can be happy only when the purpose of our coming into this body has been achieved. And the purpose of our coming into this body can be achieved only when we invert our attention within this body and try to search for him there. Unless we meet him, we can never be happy and we can never be saved from birth and death.

It is difficult to know why he created this world, but it is very clear to us that we are separated from him and we have got to make our way up in order to reach him. Then, when we reach him, we will know the reason for this creation too. It can be explained, but you would understand it only with the intellect, which cannot comprehend it, and so would lead you nowhere. We have to go beyond the mind and intellect, reach the state of direct perception by the soul, and then experience will explain everything.

226 Is the whole physical world his manifestation?

Somebody asked Christ: What are your commandments? He said, remember two commandments. The first commandment is to love thy Lord, thy Father, with all thy heart, with all thy mind, with all thy soul. This means to try to realize the Lord within yourself in this body. And once you are able to achieve or follow this commandment, then, he says, love thy neighbour as thyself. For when you are in love with the Father within, you will be in love with him outside also and you will see him everywhere in the world: The whole world will become your neighbour. Christ says the teachings of all the prophets and saints hang on these two commandments.[67]

We have to search for him within, because unless we search for him within, we cannot find him outside, yet he is everywhere. He is not confined to our body; he is found in every part of his creation. But we can see him in the creation only when we are able to realize him within. First, this body must become the temple of the living God. Then, once we are able to achieve this, the whole creation becomes the temple of the living God. That is why Christ said, I live in the Father and the Father lives in me.[132] The Father is always living in the disciple, everywhere he goes. But we cannot realize this until we are at one with the Father inside.

227 If God is a spirit and there are many spirits, are there many gods?

There is only one God, sir. There are no gods at all. All spirits and all souls are drops of the same ocean, but there is only one ocean. God is one and all souls are rays of that same sun.

There is no difference between God and the spirit?

There is no difference between the rays and the sun. The rays come from the sun and merge back into the sun. So the soul comes from God and merges back into the same God. Potentially, every soul is God, because its origin is the Creator. Ultimately, every initiated soul will merge back into the Creator and become one with him. But there is only one God. He is everywhere, yet he is separate from everyone and everything.

But is there a difference between the spirit and God?

The spirit is within every one of us. We have to become one with that spirit. Call it the spirit, call it the voice of God, or nam. It is God. In Saint John, Christ says there is no difference between the word and God.[72] They are one and the same thing, just as there is no difference between the rays of the sun and the sun.

Then in what way is the soul separate from God?

The ray has its root in the sun. It comes from the sun and merges back into the sun. It is the sun. Potentially, every soul is God, but we have to realize that potentiality and become God, to be one with the Father.

228 Is it spirit in everything that holds it in shape and that goes back to God? How does one differentiate between soul and spirit?

These are only different terminologies. Some people use them very loosely. Some people mean different things by these words.

Some philosophers never differentiated between the mind and the soul. They just took it to be one. But now, some modern philosophers have differentiated between mind and soul. Indians always have done so. Consequently, sometimes these terminologies are used vaguely. In the Bible the 'holy spirit' or 'holy ghost' is used to denote the shabd or nam, and the word or logos means the same thing, as is also the sound current or the audible life stream. So, the word 'spirit' can mean the shabd and it can also mean the soul. Some people may refer to it as mind, but mind is not soul; it is something entirely different, as previously explained.

I tell you, actually, that wave of the audible life stream or word or logos or whatever you want to call it – that is soul, and it is that which keeps us together. Without that, neither the body nor the mind can function, for it is the very life of the mind and the body. This body is made up of the five elements – earth, water, fire, air, and ether. All these five elements are inimical to each other. The earth dissolves in water, water is evaporated by fire, and so on. Yet with the aid of the soul, the ray of the Lord – or you may call it spirit – all these elements are collected together to make the human body and we are functioning in this world. The day that the Lord withdraws that spirit or soul from our body, all these five elements will again separate and merge back into their own individual origins. The earth merges back into earth, water into water, and so on. It is the spirit, nam, shabd, soul or whatever you may call it that keeps us alive. That is what enables us to function. So we are concerned with that thing, whether you call it soul or spirit. It is the soul that is the life and activates the body and the mind. The moment the Lord withdraws the soul from the body, it becomes useless and decomposes. The words 'soul' and 'spirit' are simply different terminologies to express the same thing.

229 *Maharaj Ji, are there two instincts of the sound current, one in a living being and one in the …? In other words, the sound current holds the universe together, but it leaves a living being when he dies. Then this human being is here and the sound current has left the human being for …?*

That shabd has created this whole universe and it is sustaining this whole universe. The whole universe is existing on the strength of that power, and the Lord has kept that power within every one of us also. The privilege of getting in touch with that power is given to human beings only, and that has to be contacted within under the guidance of a living master in order to get deliverance from birth and death and eventually become one with the Father. Otherwise, that power is everywhere, but it is of no use to us unless we can contact it within.

The moment the Lord withdraws that power from this universe there is dissolution. Everything comes to an end. The earth is dissolved in water, water is dried by fire, fire is taken away by air, the air disappears in the ether, and everything comes to an end.

Then that's the way with the body?

Just as the shabd is sustaining the whole world, so also it is sustaining the body. After death all the elements of the body will merge into their own origin: earth to earth, water to water, fire to fire, air to air. Only the mind and soul have left the body, but the elements of the body are still in this world.

230 *Master, I would be very happy to hear you talk to us a bit about shabd, but more in experiential terms. And also I would like to hear you talk about you being the embodiment of shabd yourself, if that's …*

As I often say, all the mystics, no matter when they have come and from where they have come, have the same spiritual truths to share with us, to teach us. And that creative power is known by so many names. Unless we attach ourselves to that creative power, which Christ called the word, the holy ghost, the spirit, the name, we cannot get rid of this human birth, this flesh. That is the only thing which can relieve us from the bondage of karmas and can take us beyond the realm of mind and maya. And that shabd is within everyone, irrespective of caste or creed. Whomsoever the Lord has created, that shabd is within every one of us. And masters also project themselves in the radiant form within their disciples, project themselves from that shabd. The Lord also is nothing but shabd. Christ said, the word is God.[72] That shabd itself is God. The same shabd is in humans, same shabd is in the master, and same shabd is the Lord.

Shabd automatically will make you believe its reality within. It will not leave you with any doubt at all. It becomes so absorbing and pulling that you have no other choice but to believe in it. You don't have to find any sign to test it.

231 *Master, I would like to hear in your own words: How did the soul first descend into matter?*

You see, naturally, it is the Lord himself who has projected himself like this in the universe. Naturally, drops have no intention to leave the sea unless, with the heat, the water evaporates from there. Drops have no intention to leave the sea at all. Souls have no intention to leave the Father. It is the Father who has projected himself in this creation. So originally soul has no karmas at all. It is absolutely pure. Souls shine because they are with the Father. Otherwise, if they had any karmas, they would not be with the Father. No soul can stay with the Father if it has even the slightest impression of any karma. Only a pure soul can be with the Father and can be the Father. So naturally, souls have no karmas of their own at the time of creation. It is the Lord who has pushed the souls to this level of the creation. And they have been made to take the association of the mind. And the creation is such that mind has been filled with weaknesses for the senses. So the ball starts rolling. It is all his design for the creation.

232 *When the drop merges into the ocean, then we leave our personality?*

Sister, who would like to be a drop, remain a drop, and not become an ocean? Who would like to be a part and not become whole? These questions are bothering us as long as we are victims of this flesh – we don't want to lose our individuality. This is another form of ego. We think we are something higher, we don't want to lose what we have, and this is actually an obstacle in our way to the Father. This very concept, this very thinking, is an obstacle in our way to the Father. So ultimately we have to become a drop and merge into the ocean and become the ocean; we have to become him. So this body we will leave; this flesh we will leave; this individuality we will leave. This feeling of individuality is there only as long as we are under the sway of the mind. There's no mind there. You go beyond the mind, far higher, and yet to some extent you're separate. You bring two candles – their flames – together, the flames merge with each other; you cannot distinguish which is which. The fire becomes one, and yet the two flames came from different candles. So ultimately all souls merge back into the Father. The Father is just a higher soul.

Everyone is the Lord. As long as we're in flesh, we're prisoner of the flesh. When we get release from this flesh and know our reality, the soul shines and becomes pure, we become the

Father, we become the Lord. Potentially everyone is the Lord. So we have to merge back into that ocean. Nobody would like to retain individuality there.

233 *Master, carrying the same thought forward, when we do merge with the supreme Father, do we merge to a state where we lose our consciousness, as in the overall consciousness, or do we maintain individuality?*

Who would not like to merge back into him? Who would like to retain his individual consciousness while being in the presence of the Lord? These questions come only when one is under the sway of the mind. Due to our ego, we think we are greater. Why should we merge into anything else? But when we reach that stage, there is no ego; there is only merging. You get peace in losing yourself, losing your identity, in becoming part of the other, in becoming part of God. No drop would like to remain away from the ocean; yet a drop is something different from the ocean. We merge into him; still we are separate from him. But nobody likes to retain his individuality at that stage. Even in our human love we always like to do what pleases the other person. We take ourselves out of our 'self'. We feel that we are the other person. We feel that it is not our self moving about, it is the other person. When this happens in the physical human love, what of the love where there is no mind and we are just attracted to him, we merge back into him, we just forget our self – there is no 'self' left there. Who would not like that stage?

234 *After merging back into the Lord, does man maintain a separate consciousness?*

In merging, it is still separate. Being in it, you are separate from it. But you are not conscious of your consciousness. There, you just merge yourself. Even in worldly love, when you are with your beloved, you forget yourself completely and want to please only the beloved. You are so absorbed in the beloved that you do not even think about where you are or what you are, even in these physical or worldly emotions. The spiritual is much more fascinating, absorbing; it is much more sublime, nobler. The bliss of merging into the supreme being cannot be expressed in mortal language. There is no thought of individuality, consciousness, or anything else. It is all love, all bliss, for in merging we become the supreme being, and he is all, he is everything.

Then there is just one consciousness?

The Lord is one. When we merge back into him, we become the Lord. We become a part of him. A drop has its own identity when it is in the mud. When it leaves the ground by means of evaporation, it still has its own identity, separate from the ground and separate from the cloud. But when it merges back into the cloud, it becomes the cloud. That minute part of the cloud becomes the cloud by merging into it. When we love the Lord, we do not like to remain away from the Beloved. We lose our identity by merging back into that, and yet we remain separate from that. For instance, if you merge the flame of a lighted candle into the flame of a fire, can you differentiate whether it is the flame of the fire or the flame of the candle? When you take the candle away from the fire, you have an independent, individual flame. But when you take it back into the fire, it merges into the fire and is no longer the light of a mere candle. Similarly, the soul merges into the Lord.

235 Master, you said that God is love, power, and wisdom. Is one of his characteristics also that he separates and merges back into himself continuously?

Love means to merge into another being, to become another being; to lose your own identity and to become another identity. God is love because we lose our own identity, our own individuality, and merge back into the Father and become the Father. He has separated us from him because he has created us, and with that feeling of love, we can merge back into him again.

But will he separate us again?

The saints say he won't. That is our only hope. Don't worry about another separation.

236 Master, are all souls the same – the souls of people?

Sister, all souls are immortal; all souls are a drop of the same divine ocean, but some have merged into the dirt; some have fallen onto stones, where they still shine; some drops have fallen into the leaves. They look just like pearls from above. But all drops are the same. Some fall into the dirt and become part and parcel of the dirt, but when they evaporate, there's no difference in that water. Similarly, there is no difference between souls at all. Each is a drop of that divine ocean – it is only the mind which makes it dirty. So more or less, we are all dirty; some souls are more and some are a little less. Otherwise we wouldn't be part of this creation. But once we leave the mind and go beyond the realm of even the impression of our karmas, then we are all alike, and there is no difference.

237 What kind of form can an individual soul have beyond form?

The Lord has no form. The soul has no form. We are so used to the idea of forms because of the fact that everything here is made up of elements, physical elements. But the physical elements do not go beyond form.

Why do you call it individual then? In what way is the soul different from the Lord?

I'll tell you. As long as the soul is with the mind it is separated from infinity. When you withdraw it from the body and bring it to the eye centre, it is still attached to the mind. It has not yet merged into the infinite and still retains its identity. Even when it leaves the mind, the impressions of karmas are still over the soul, and they keep that soul away from the infinite.

Between the mind and Sach Khand?

Between the mind and Sach Khand there are still the impressions of those karmas which, of course, cannot pull the soul back to this creation; but those impressions are still with the soul. That is why, at the time of initiation, it is explained that there is a darkness we have to pierce before we can reach Sat Lok, Sach Khand. Unless the soul becomes so pure that it is able to go through that darkness, it will not be able to merge back into the infinite. It is only in the company of the shabd form of the master that the soul is able to go through that darkness of Maha Sunn, as we call it, and merge into the infinite.

Then how does the soul know without seeing at that time?

It is a realization. There is no question of seeing, touching or feeling. The mystics call it direct perception. The soul gets that inner perception. It is a realization. It is very difficult to explain these things intellectually. I am just trying to tell you why, after all the coverings are removed, the soul still doesn't go straightaway and merge back into the Lord. After all, when the soul reaches the third stage it has no coverings. Why is it then separate from the Lord? Because it still has to pierce through that Maha Sunn, the intense darkness, but it cannot go with its own light. That is why, when the mystics explain the teachings, they always say that without his grace the soul can never go back to the Father.

When crossing that blackness, is the soul accompanied by the master?

Always.

Then how does the master appear there?

You must have read in the books that the soul has its own light, but still it is not sufficient to enable it to cross that veil of darkness. Then the master's light, which is much brighter and is sufficient to pierce that darkness, has to envelop the soul, so to say, and merge back into the infinite light. This is just a way of explaining things which really have to be experienced, to be realized.

238 After the third or fourth life does every soul return to God? Is there such a thing as a lost soul? That is, if a soul does not find a master in his fourth life, is he lost?

Every soul does not go back to the Lord after the third or fourth form. That is absolutely wrong. Only those souls which are destined to go back to the Lord, which are the souls marked by the Lord, will go back to the Lord. And whenever they will go back to the Lord, they will go back through his sons, through the masters who initiate them, who put them on the spiritual path. With his grace, with his help, when they spiritually advance, when they clear off their karmas, when they drive out their desires, when they root out their attachments, then only do those souls, with the help of their masters, go back to the Lord.

From the time of initiation, this may be accomplished within one birth, within two births, within three births; but at the most it will take four births. It depends upon the individual, as to how much he has to clear, how much he is required to develop himself spiritually.

But those people who do not follow the path, those people who have no desire to go back to the Lord, those people who do not drive out the desires and attachments of the world from themselves – the question of their going back to the Lord does not arise at all, whether they come into this world a hundred times or two hundred times. They will always be a part of this huge chain. They will come and go. It is only when we have a desire to go back to him that we think about him or can go back to him.

239 Is there such a thing as a lost soul?

I think we are all lost souls. By lost souls, I mean the souls who have forgotten the Lord. From what I understand, probably the lost soul means that soul which has forgotten its origin. We have just given ourselves to the world, have forgotten our real home, have forgotten our own real Father. We are all lost souls and we are all struggling souls. But we should not remain lost. We should try to find out the purpose of the soul being in this human form, for only then can we get rid of this condition, this sad state of affairs.

240 Can a soul ever destroy itself, and can the master save it after ...?

The soul never dies. The body in which the soul resides, that body changes from one form to another form, but the soul never dies. The soul is eternal.

241 *Master, the whole universe is contained within our own bodies. Is that correct? So, within each body, there is a complete universe, a complete everything?*

This is a different meaning actually. I often have explained that all that we see is nothing but the Lord's own projection. Everything has come out of God. The whole creation has come out of the Creator. And now the Creator is within us. So the whole creation is within us. The whole creation is in the Creator and the Creator is within us. So, when we realize the Creator, we realize the whole creation within us. So everything is within us.

Do you follow my point? You see, actually there is no question of within or without. Because we are searching within, we say it is within us. But if you do a post mortem examination on anybody, you won't find any creation, any God – nothing – but concentration within makes us have that realization of the Lord. And because we started from within, we say the Lord is within. This whole creation has come out of the Creator, and the Creator is within us. So the whole creation is within us because the creation has no other source to come from. All that we see is nothing but his own projection. Since he himself is within us, his projection, the whole projection is within us.

242 *Maharaj Ji, when does a soul enter a body – directly after birth, or before?*

When the life enters the child, it is the same thing. Some call it life, we call it soul. Without the specific order from the Lord or intention of the Lord, no soul will go into any body at all. Every soul that comes is marked for a particular relationship which brings it here. Actually the soul comes at the time of conception. It comes, but is inactive, and it becomes active after the third month.

243 *Are there any words or teachings in Sant Mat that relate particularly to women?*

Well, sister, Sant Mat does not discriminate at all between a woman and a man. Sant Mat is concerned with the soul and not with the body, and soul has no sex at all. But when the soul comes into the body of a woman, you can call it a woman. And when it comes into the body of a man, you can call it a man. But it is the soul, and not the body, that has to go back to the Father. So there is no question of any difference between the teachings for a woman or teachings for a man. The teachings are the same for everyone.

244 *Will you tell us the definition Sant Mat has for us about soul mates? Whether it is in marriage or without marriage, and how we will recognize it?*

As I have mentioned in some other places, many times I have received letters, especially from American satsangis, indicating that there is a certain idea among some people that we have some kind of soul mate, and unless we meet that soul mate somewhere inside or outside, we cannot merge back into the Lord. That is a wrong notion, for every soul has its own individual relation with the Lord. There is no such thing as a soul mate. That idea is simply a justification for certain weaknesses. Absolutely, we have no soul mate. We are working our way back to the Lord independently. We have karmic relationships with people that come and go, but that does not mean that if we do not have any karmic relationship with a particular person, we will not go back to the Lord. Every soul is independent.

The human form

245 *You said, and it comes up in a letter also where you give the impression that it's relatively easier to be born again in the human form than Maharaj Soami Ji says in* Sar Bachan, *where he says it's very difficult to get the human form again. In fact, you certainly will not get it again unless you are devoted to him.*

I didn't say anything is easier. I said the Lord doesn't find excuses to send us back into the creation. Our attachments pull us back. We are given an opportunity to improve if we want to improve. But that doesn't mean that if we won't make use of that opportunity, we will definitely get a human birth. We may have to go down a step. I just said the Lord doesn't find excuses to send us down.

But once we go down, once we slip down, then it's difficult to get a human birth again. But when we have got it and we are sincere, are trying to make best use of this human birth, naturally we'll get a human birth in our next life. But if we slip down, then it may be difficult to come to the top again. But once we are at the top, though we don't go up to the Father, and we are very sincere, we are trying to do our best, trying to lead a good life, then definitely the Lord won't find an excuse to send us down just because we have not met him. He will give us an opportunity again – that's what I mean.

Good karmas are enough to entitle you to get this human form. A good heart, pure heart, forgiving heart, always trying to help others, good deeds, that's what I said. The Lord doesn't find excuses to push you down. He's more generous to give you another opportunity. What Soami Ji said also may have been in response to a particular suggestion. Sometimes you like to frighten satsangis when they are not trying to make best use of the opportunity – you will not get this opportunity again if you won't make use of it. That doesn't mean that they are not going to get it. Saying that is a way of putting in their minds, reminding them that they should make best use of this opportunity of a human birth.

246 *Maharaj Ji, in this morning's discourse it was mentioned that some people waste the human body, a very precious thing. Now, would it be considered to be wasted by a person who has lived a good life according to his own spiritual views, as opposed to someone who has not done so – would that person automatically have to go back on the wheel of eighty-four [8,400,000 species], or could he possibly return in the human body to go on spiritually?*

Yes, he can. By waste we mean not attending to our meditation, not making use of this human form to realize the Lord. If our direction of travel is not towards him, but is reversed towards the senses, we are wasting our human form. But if we are not a slave of the senses, and yet we are not doing anything to realize the Lord, we are doing good things, we are trying to be helpful to people, we are doing everything that we can for the masses, then we are building good karmas which will take us back into the human form again. We are given chance after chance to make the best use of this human form, but unless we make use of the human form in the right sense, we can never get out of the cycle of transmigration.

247 *I believe the discourse said that we are fortunate to be in this human form because this is the jumping-off place – from here we can go up or we can fall back down – but that once we lose it, we might have difficulty in getting back to it. Perhaps this is clearer to some people than it*

is to me, but I do not understand: If there is a reincarnation, would this reincarnation perhaps be in some other form because of the karma that was accrued in this life?

If we do not make the best use of this human form, we can be sent back into a lower species. It is our attachments, our unfulfilled low desires, longings, cravings and our karmas coupled together which take us back to the lower species. We are sent back into those forms or to those places where we can satisfy those unfulfilled cravings and desires, and can give an account for our karmas, for what we are doing now. We have got to make our way up; otherwise we can be sent down. The Lord does not find excuses to send us down. He gives us a fair chance to make the best use of this human form. If we are really sincere and we do not want to come back, he does not send us back. We will get opportunity after opportunity to improve ourselves, to make the best use of this human form. But unless we make our way up, we cannot escape from births and deaths. We can be sent back. That is why we have got to make the best use of this form at this time.

After a fruit drops from a tree, it is very difficult, if not impossible, to put it back on the branch again. Similarly, if we lose this opportunity now, we may find it very difficult to get such an opportunity again. We should try to make the best use of this opportunity which he has given us. You have several references in the Bible to the effect that we have to face our destiny in this world. That destiny is something which we bring with us into this world and which we have to face during this lifetime. It is the same as fate, or what we call pralabdh karma.

248 *Master, yesterday the professor was speaking about this life and that you can't have a human life another time if you don't take this opportunity. There are sometimes some propositions, some ideas in Sant Mat that are very,*

very deep. Very deep. And sometimes it angers me a little bit because these ideas are too deep for me, too deep in the consequences.

You see, the Lord doesn't find excuses to throw us down. We are given sufficient opportunity to make use of this human opportunity. But if we refuse to behave like humans, if we have made up our mind and are determined to behave like animals, then where is the justification to get the human form? We have to go down. We have to satisfy our desires in those bodies, in that flesh; so we scale down. But the Father doesn't just find an excuse to throw us down. We are given sufficient opportunity to improve ourselves, but we can go down also.

Those animals also have a soul. They also live and breathe like us, eat like us. But since we think we are the top of the creation – and we are the top of the creation because we can reach to the very top after this opportunity – we refuse to accept the possibility that even we can go down. But we have to go down if we don't behave and make use of this opportunity. That is why Christ said, I can work in the day. When the night falls, nobody can work.[102] This is a day. Human birth, the human opportunity, is a day. After death we can't work; we can't find the way leading back to the Father. We can always find our path, our way, during the daytime, but not in the darkness, not at night.

249 *A few nights ago you made the comment that our meditation will make us more human, more normal, and I was wondering if you could explain that. Do you mean more human in the higher sense or in the ordinary sense?*

What is ordinary? They say God has made us in his own image. Do we reflect God? Being in this body, do we reflect God? Or do we reflect the devil? When we attend to meditation, we become more human. Then we reflect God. Now we don't reflect God. We reflect the animal in us, animal instincts in us. So we're not humans. We're only carrying the body of the human. But when we meditate, we become real humans. Then the purpose of getting this human birth is achieved.

Guru Nanak says: Your body becomes that of gold. He means it becomes pure. Christ says: As long as your mind is slave of the senses, you are a leper, you are crippled and you don't know how to walk straight. And I've come to help those lepers. I have come to help those people who are walking crooked. I want them to walk straight in life.[43] Humans have to walk straight in life. So when we're not straight, we're not humans. Some other instinct is working in us. When we meditate, that makes us really human. The purpose of getting this human birth is achieved; then we become normal. Now we are all abnormal. We want to cut each other's throats. We are always blackmailing each other. We are always backbiting each other. We try to deceive each other, cheat each other; we let each other down, hurt each other. We are fond of sucking each other's blood. You read the papers, you hear the radio. Is this the work of humans? People behave worse than animals. Even animals know better how to live together in one room, but put two, three people in one room and see what is the result.

Where is that human feeling in us? If we become real humans, there won't be any war, there won't be any jealousies, there won't be any letting each other down. We'll be really helpful to one another, loving to one another. We'll see the Lord reflected in everybody.

Is that ever possible?

It happens. Yes.

250 Great Master said: Man's the strangest of all strange things. Would you comment on that?

Aren't we strange? For what purpose has the Lord sent us here and given us this opportunity to be in human flesh? Yet we have absolutely forgotten our goal, our path, and have given ourselves to sensual pleasures and worldly pursuits and enjoyments. Aren't we strange creatures? Man can be God, man can be a villain. We have the potential to become God. Potentially everyone is God. And yet we can be worse than animals, worse than beasts. We read history and we see every day to what degradation man can go and to what heights he can fly. Isn't man a strange creature? When he's generous, he's just generous, and if he becomes a miser, or stingy, he can't give even a pin to anybody.

We have a strange combination in us. We can give our lives for certain causes, but for another cause we may not give even a pin to anybody. Isn't it a strange combination in a human form? We can be so low and we can be so high. In another species, if they are low, they are low; if they are high, they are high. We have God in us, we have beast in us. We are so sympathetic that we give our life to somebody. We are so cruel as to kill thousands with a bomb. Don't we have strange characteristics in us? We can't bear to see a child crying, and yet we don't mind killing thousands. We will give *lakhs* [hundreds of thousands] in donations, and yet we don't hesitate to adulterate the most essential things in life and kill people. I don't think there is a stranger creature than a human. I don't know in what reference Great Master has written, but I think whatever he said is right.

251 What is the purpose of life?

The main purpose of life is to realize God. This privilege the Lord has bestowed only on human beings. The human body is the top rung of the ladder of creation. From here we can either drop down to lower species or we can go back to the Father and escape from the cycle of birth and death. Everything else we have been getting every time we have come into this world, in any form, in any species.

But the privilege of going back to the Father can be achieved only in the human life. So we should always be mindful of our destination and try to follow the spiritual path which leads us back to him. While working out our destiny, our karmic accounts or adjustments – our other duties, responsibilities – we should not forget the end and purpose for which we have come into this world.

252 Must the body change for spiritual growth?

This body has been given to us for meditation, for going back to the Father – then the purpose of getting this human body has been accomplished. That's all. The body remains the same to look at; there is no change in the body. The attitude of the mind changes and, due to the happiness of the mind, it reflects through the body. The same body reflects misery on our face sometimes and sometimes happiness. The body is the same, but there is something in the body that reflects either happiness or misery, and that is the attitude of the mind. The body remains the same.

253 It is said that we were created in the image of God. Does that mean that our imperfect human form is a copy of a perfect form and this exists in the universe somewhere between Sach Khand and Trikuti?

You see, the idea behind this is that we are the image of God or we are the top of the creation. The idea is that whatever the quality of God is, so is the quality of our soul in this body – we can become God. This privilege has been given to the human form, this is the last step of the ladder – we can go back and merge into him. Whatever he is, so are we. Christ said, I and the Father are one.[111] That means the soul and the Lord are one.

Whatever his image is, so our image is – image of the soul, image of the Lord. That does not mean this Lord also looks like a human body. That is about the soul. The soul and the Lord are one. You see, sun and the ray, drop and the ocean – their image is the same, their qualities are the same.

So this is the top of the creation. From here only can we go back and merge into him. From no other form can we go back to him. So this is known as the last rung of the ladder. This is known as the top of the creation. He has created us in his own image – we can become his image from this step. He's pure, the universal supreme Father. From here we also can make our way up and become the universal Father, become his image, become him, merge back into him. That is why he said that we are his image.

254 What does 'top of creation' mean?

The opportunity to go back to the Father is given only to humans. This human form is known as the top of the creation. Unless we are in this human flesh, we cannot make progress to go back to the Father at all. We have to come as a human before we can become one with God. From here, we can reach to the top.

We are made of five elements, which means we have a sense of discrimination. This whole creation can be divided into five elements: earth, water, air, fire and ether. Plants have only the water element. Insects have fire and air. Birds have three elements: water, fire, and air. Animals have four elements. They don't have ether, the sense of discrimination. Humans have all five of the elements. Since we have five elements, we are the top of the creation. The Lord has given us a sense of discrimination, which is denied to other species. This is why the human body is known as the top of the creation. From here we can rise above or we can scale down.

255 *When they speak of one initiation, I was wondering if there are not more than one initiation and if some of these initiations cannot take place on this earth but have to take place in the spiritual world? If you initiate someone, does he have the same status as you after having undergone hundreds and hundreds of initiations in previous lives?*

Brother, the seed has to be sown while one is in the human form, and once this seed is sown, then that initiation, that help, can also take place inside us, on the internal stages. But first the seed has to be sown while in this physical form. Unless that seed is sown in the physical form, we do not get internal initiation at all. That is why this body is known as the top of the creation. Only by being in this body can we be shown the light, the wisdom, the path.

Whether we have made much spiritual progress or not while being in the body does not make any difference. If the seed has been sown while being in the body, we can make spiritual progress inside. But it must start while being in the physical body.

256 *Could you explain to us why we should want to return to the source?*

Brother, it is very clear that since our separation from our source, we have not been happy in this world. Even in the human form, which is known to be the top of the creation, if you analyze, you will not find anybody happy in this world. Some are suffering from diseases, some due to lack of children, some due to too many children, still others due to lack of security in life; some are frustrated in their love affairs and some in their domestic life. If you go to the prisons, you will find that they are filled with prisoners. Go to the courts and hear the details of the victims, the criminals. If you look around in the whole world, you will not find any peace anywhere. When, in this human form, which is known to be the top of creation, we cannot find peace, then what is the use of this form? We will find peace only when the soul merges back into the Lord. That is why we all seek him. Without meeting him, without merging back into him, we will never find eternal peace. We cannot be saved from the cycle of birth and death, from the wheel of *chaurasi* [8,400,000 species] unless we merge back into him. That is why we want to return to our source, who is the Lord himself.

If we could be truly happy in this world nobody would ever even think about the Lord. You know the Lord may give us anything in this world. Go to the richest people in the world, go to the healthiest man in the world, go to these politicians who command [they say] the whole world – are they happy? Perhaps they are more miserable than we are. We often sleep six or seven hours or more at night, but they have to depend upon pills, tranquilizers. No one can ever be really happy without meeting the Lord, without merging back into him. Unless our soul goes back, merges back into the Lord, we will never get that peace of mind, that happiness, nor can we be carefree or save ourselves from the cycle of birth and death. But for that, nobody would search for him; and that is why we seek him, our source.

257 *The lower animals seem to be living a happier life and seem nearer to God's life than human beings are.*

As a human, you may think that they're living a happier life. But how can you say the lower animals are living a happier life? You see their conditions. They are tortured; they are killed for our palate. Every day thousands and thousands of animals are being killed, just for our food. Is that living a happy life? They are being shot, hunted, caged, and tortured. They are used for our own selfish ends, for their skins, for our shoes; how can you say that lower animals live a happy life?

I didn't say a happy life, I just meant whether they were living God's word more than us.

They cannot be in touch with God's word at all. That opportunity is only given to a human form.

258 *Master, I have often read in Sant Mat literature that it is said that angels yearn for a human body because it is only in the human form that we can realize God. Yet religious Christians regard angels as being spiritual entities, with no coarser admixture of materiality. Can you explain this?*

You see, actually this word 'angel' is from *devi* or *devata*.

Yes?

These entities may be higher than humans, but from their level they cannot go back to the Father. Only from this human species can one go back to the Father. That form is only a reward for good works, good deeds, good karmas they have done in this world. It is just a reward for a certain time. After that, they again come back in the human form, and then they may make progress and go back to the Father. And this privilege, mystics say, is given only to human beings. So even these entities are yearning for this. They may be better off than humans in some ways, but they can't go from there back to the Lord.

So 'angel' actually is a wrong translation of *devi* or *devata*. It is actually very difficult to translate the words 'gods' and 'goddesses' and all that.

> *Yes, it sometimes says gods and goddesses – and sometimes angels.*

These deities are known as gods and goddesses. Those terms have been translated as 'angels'. The human form is better than they are because from those species or forms they cannot go back to the Father.

SELF-REALIZATION AND GOD-REALIZATION

259 *Radha Soami. Often we talk about self-realization and God-realization, and my question is regarding self-realization. I'm wondering if part of that is trying to face your faults, face the things that are wrong with you, and correct them and try to rise above them. And what beyond that is self-realization? How do we really attain self-realization before God-realization?*

Sister, that's what we talk of every day. Self-realization is essential before God-realization. What is self-realization? Going beyond the realm of mind and maya; trying to bring the mind to the eye centre and to its own destination, so the soul can get release from the clutches of the mind. Separating the soul from the mind – that is self-realization, that is knowing ourselves. That is the whole purpose of meditation.

Our mind is fond of worldly pleasures, worldly pursuits, sensual pleasures. Unless the mind gets some better pleasure than the worldly pleasures, it refuses to leave the worldly pleasures. So we withdraw our consciousness to the eye centre and get in touch with the shabd within. When we taste that nectar within – Christ called it the living water which will give you everlasting life[82] – when we taste that nectar within with the help of that shabd and nam, we come back to Trikuti, the second stage. When the mind comes to its own source, the soul automatically gets release from the clutches of the mind. And the soul and mind are separated. That is self-realization. That is knowing ourselves.

260 *Master, in the morning satsang we heard you say a phrase in English: "Self-realization before God-realization." Would you share some thoughts on that with us?*

Well, we have discussed it so many times. Books have even been written about it – *Die to Live,* for example. You see, when the soul gets released from the clutches of the mind, it is self-realization. When it goes back to its origin, the Father, it's God-realization. So unless there is self-realization, how can there be God-realization? Soul has forgotten its home, soul has forgotten its identity, after taking the association of the mind. Mind, too, doesn't know itself. It has become a slave of the senses. So we have to withdraw our mind from the senses by attaching it to the shabd and nam within. And then with the help of shabd and nam, mind becomes pure and comes back to its own source. Then soul automatically gets release from the clutches of the mind. That is self-realization.

You see, there is water in the clouds in the sky, but when it rains the water comes onto the ground. It merges into the dirt. It stagnates; it gives off a foul smell. It has forgotten its identity. It is thinking itself part and parcel of this dirt. But when a hot wind touches that water, it evaporates. Then it realizes: The dirt is something different from me; unnecessarily I was thinking of myself as part and parcel of the dirt. It realizes its own origin – it is a cloud in the sky. It goes back and merges into the sky, the clouds. That is the condition of everybody's soul. Our soul becomes whole when it goes beyond the realm of mind and maya. We are not complete; we are not whole as long as the soul is within the realm of mind and maya. Because mind dominates it, and the senses dominate the mind, we are not whole. We become whole only when we go beyond the realm of mind and maya.

That is why Christ, when he was initiating someone, advised him to abstain from all sins. He said: Ye have become whole, sin no more lest a worse thing can come unto thee.[85] Since I've put you on the path, you are in the process of becoming whole now. If you continue on the path, you become whole, provided you don't add more to your karmas, more to your sins. If you do, a worst thing can come unto thee. You can again be condemned to this creation. So unless we become whole, we cannot merge back into the whole. Unless we become pure, we cannot go back to the purest One. That is why Christ said: If you love your parents more than me, then you are not worthy of me[42] – that is, worthy to become me, worthy to become part and parcel of me. Because Christ is pure, Christ is whole; to become worthy of Christ is to become as pure as the Christ himself, to become him. And unless we become him, we cannot become the Father. To become him is self-realization. To become the Father is God-realization. That is the nutshell of self-realization.

261 Is it only in meditation that we become aware of our soul's progress?

Not only in meditation, but when we reach a certain stage where we are able to remove the veil of mind from our way, when we are able to unknot the knot of soul and mind knotted together. I'll give you a little example. The water in a cloud is very pure, but once it becomes rain, it mixes with the dirt of the ground and it becomes very dirty, it stagnates. It forgets its origin. It forgets that it was pure, very pure. It just starts thinking that it is a part and parcel of this dirt and loses its identity even. But when with the heat of the sun it evaporates, leaves that dirt, it realizes: I am something different and this dirt is something different. Unnecessarily, having been in the company of the dirt, I was thinking myself dirt, a part of it. So the moment it leaves the dirt it realizes that it is something different and the dirt is something different. Then it thinks about its own origin, which is the cloud in the sky. It goes back, merges back into the cloud.

The same is true of our soul. It is a part of that ocean divine. Having been in the company of the mind – and the mind is already a slave of the senses – we have lost and forgotten our identity. We have to reverse the process. In other words, our mind is to control the senses and the soul is to control the mind. When we withdraw our mind from the senses, we take our mind back to its original home, Trikuti, the second spiritual stage. Then the soul gets release from the mind. There we know who we are and we think about our origin. Then the soul, freed from the mind and senses, goes up and merges back into its own origin.

Socrates said: Know thyself. Self-realization is essential before God-realization. Unless we know who we are, how can we know who God is? How can we conceive of him? We have got to control our mind, subdue it, before our soul can realize its own self or we can get rid of the intellectual barrier and merge back into the Lord. All these barriers and obstacles are instincts of the mind, and when the soul is rid of those coverings, it is pure; it is free to merge back into its source.

262 *Master, in trying to come back to the fact that we don't exist, many times I've thought of a large pomegranate. It sounds awfully silly, but I can think of God as a large*

pomegranate, and each one of us is one of those seeds. We don't really exist, but the total exists, which is God. Would that be a good example?

You see, take any seed: The reality is in that seed though we don't see it, but ultimately it comes out. The seed of a banyan tree is so small, but ultimately it becomes a banyan tree; the whole banyan tree was in that seed, it hasn't come from anywhere outside. Potentially the seed contains the whole banyan tree, but then it has to grow to become the banyan tree. So potentially every soul is God, but we have to become God. We have to grow spiritually to come to that level. Potentially every soul is God, every drop is an ocean, but it has to evaporate to become a cloud and then to become rain and to merge into the sea.

263 *Master when we have self-realization, does that mean that we will know everything that is buried in our sub-conscious mind?*

Yes, sister, then you can know everything about yourself, about your whole past, about others – but you are not interested in anybody. Neither are you interested in your past. When we become old and good, we never think about our evil days or bad times which we have passed through. We never think about that. We are so happy in that happy moment, we never think about the misery of that time. When you are happy, you don't think about miserable days. So when you realize yourself, when you go beyond that realm and know yourself, you are not interested in knowing what you have gone through, from where you have come, and what mess we have been making. You are not interested because you are so happy in that bliss and that peace. You can know, no doubt – you don't forget that memory. But you are not interested in that at all.

So Master, in the subconscious mind, we have the memory of all our previous lives? What is the subconscious mind?

No, the subconscious mind consists of whatever memory we have in this life – all our impressions that we have collected in this span of life. That is the subconscious mind, psychologists say. It is not about past lives. But the mind is carrying all the past karmas, all the sinchit karmas. We can know about those karmas only by meditation, but then we are not interested at the stage when we can know.

264 *Maharaj Ji, in the process of going back, the memory that is recorded on the soul, is that all recalled when we see the radiant form of the master? Does one then get the realization of who one was from the beginning of the creation? In other words, the reason for the various karmic debts and so on …*

Your past has absolutely no value at all. Only your future is of value. When you are in the presence of the lover, the beloved, you are not interested in the past at all; you are only interested in the master. You ask the moth, when she goes to the light, what her past is, who her parents are, who her brother and sister are – she has no time to think about it, she is in love with the light. She is one with the light, she is not one with those people at all, she is not one with the past at all. The past doesn't bother her at all, neither is she interested in the past. It is only our curiosity that makes us want to know what our past was and what we have come through. But when you get to that stage, you are not interested because you are so much absorbed by your love and devotion in that being – you never think about the past. If you are still thinking about the past, it means you are still not there, you are somewhere in the past.

I think that the nature of the divine design is such that we don't know our past; otherwise it would be horrible to live with the present. It would be just horrible to live with the present if we knew what we did in the past and from where we have come. Everyone would be a mental case. The best part of this design is that we just forget what we have done in the past. Even if we remember our heinous deeds in this very life, what we have done, if we always remember them, we can never live with ourselves at all. We are so ashamed and we feel so small and we are so sorry and we always feel tortured and burdened; thank God that we forget all that. So imagine all that we have come through, imagine if we had to carry the memory of all that, what would be our fate? Another good thing the Lord has done is that he has kept everything in his own hands; otherwise we would have made a mess of ourselves if he had given us any free will at all to do anything here.

265 Loving can be a gift, but it also comes from meditation?

You see, I have discussed many times, the inclination of the soul is always towards its own origin. The needle is always attracted by the magnet. The needle is always in love with the magnet. But if you put weight on the needle, the magnet cannot attract it. It cannot go back to the magnet. That doesn't mean that if the weight is there, the love has become less. Love is always there. The inclination of the soul is always towards its own origin. That is love. But if we have a weight on the soul – the weight of the mind, of karma, of our sins, of our actions – the more we remove that weight from the soul, the more that love for our origin shines.

When the Lord marks a particular soul to become whole or to become part of him, the weight starts being removed from that soul. That love starts shining. Then we become whole and then we merge into the whole one. So love is always there. Potentially every soul is God. But we have to become God; we have to go to that level of consciousness. Potentially every drop is the ocean, but it has to evaporate and become the cloud and the rain before it can be one with the ocean.

So love is always there in every soul. But for that love, nobody would worship the Father. You find all religious places full of devotees. All the holy places are full of devotees because the pull is there from within to the Lord. And that is love. Whether rightly guided or wrongly guided, that is a different thing. But the inclination of the soul is always towards its own origin. When he marks it, then the weight starts being removed from the soul. The coverings start being removed from the soul, so it starts shining.

That is why I say that meditation not only creates love, it strengthens love. It helps you to grow and grow to become one with the Father. That is the love which helps us to become one with the Father; which helps us to lose our own identity, our own individuality; which helps us to become another being. That is love. And that is why we say that love is God and God is love, because love has the characteristic of becoming another being. To lose your own identity, lose your own individuality, that is the characteristic of love. Love never wants that the other one becomes like you. Love makes us want to become like another one. In love there is submission, there is merging. So that is why they say that love is God and God is love.

266 If we are the temple of the spirit, we are also one with that light that has never had a beginning and never will have an end?

That is right.

Why do we need the advice and counsel of a human if we are one with that light?

Because now we are not one with it. We need the counsel because we again want to be one with that light.

We never cease to be and we never will cease to exist. There is no beginning and no end?

That is right. Actually, do you see that light? Do you know that you are part of it now?

If we are the temple of the spirit, we are automatically one with that light.

That is what we think intellectually but, practically, we want to be one with it.

But we are one with it? We are one with it and we do not know?

I and the Father are one.[111] I can say I am God. But I am a prisoner here, and I will be God only when I get released from all these prisons and go back and merge into him. That is God-realization.

I do not feel that I am a prisoner. I feel that I am a part of that light, serving his purpose.

We are all part of that light.

If it takes one hundred incarnations, I am serving the purpose of that light, so why worry when it ends?

Oh, no. We are all serving the purpose of this creation. Without serving the purpose, the creation cannot exist.

I realize that, but if we are automatically the temple of the spirit, we are automatically that light, and there should be no contemplation of when we leave, as we are here to serve that light?

We are part of that light. We are part of that Lord and that power, that Lord God, whatever you may call it. But now we are separated from him, or caged in this body. We can say theoretically we are God, but there is a difference now, as long as we are a prisoner here. When we develop our consciousness to that stage that we again see that light and merge into that light, then we can say we actually are that light, that we are God.

> *But I do not feel that I am a prisoner. I feel that I am serving that light with every breath that I take.*

How do you know that you are serving that light? You see, we are under the sway of the mind and the senses.

> *I am that light that existed millions of years ago and will never end?*

It will not end. From this body you will go to another body, and then to another and so on.

> *We are all one with that light?*

The whole creation is one with the Lord.

> *And we mix it up with our physical mind and wonder what to do, but we do not have to do anything if we know ourselves?*

No, no. The same light is in animals, the same light is in insects, but we would not like to be that.

> *But each person is his own interpreter of that light. He does not have to seek outside counsel, as the light tells him what to do?*

But the pity is, it does not tell us what to do.

> *It does tell us?*

We have that light within us, but unless we see that light within, unless we merge into that light – as Christ said, if thine eye be single, thy whole body shall be full of light[23] – we are not aware of it.

But nobody can tell another person?

You have to open that single eye in order to see that light. The light, of course, is there, and it does not come from anywhere outside; but we have to develop that consciousness to open that eye which sees that light. Without the actual experience, this is just a way of explaining that I and the Father are one. Naturally we are one, but unless we remove all these stumbling blocks, all these walls from our way, we cannot become one with him. Intellectually it is all right to say we are one. We can all think like that, but practically, it makes all the difference between us and the Lord. We are all rays from the same light and we have come from that light and we have got to go back to merge into that same light. That is what we are all striving for.

Master, if we were able to use that light, as we should, the whole time, every moment, we would not need to be here, would we?

No. We would be in that light.

We could not be in this world then, could we?

We would merge back into him. Who would like to remain away from him? A drop of water would not like to remain merged in the dust and dirt, nor does it enjoy the separation from the cloud or the ocean from which it came.

We are, then, masters of our life and death.

Yes, and that is the purpose of meditation. Now the mind is controlling us. We are striving to control the senses and the mind, for only then can we become a conscious part of that light.

RELATIONSHIP OF THE SOUL TO THE MIND AND SENSES

267 *We speak of mind a great deal. Can you tell us exactly what mind is and its relationship to the soul, and why it causes us so much trouble?*

Soul is the essence of the Lord. Mind also is not a small thing. Its source is in Trikuti, the second spiritual stage. The soul, having separated from the Lord, has taken the company of the mind. Mind itself is not independent, for it has become the slave of the senses. The senses always keep the mind under their sway. Being controlled by the senses, the mind does so many karmas – good and bad actions. The result is that the soul also has to reap the fruit of what the mind does, as long as it has the association of the mind.

Mind is the agent of Kal, the negative power, and Kal does not want any soul to get out of his reach. So with one trick or another, the mind always likes to keep us in the cycle of birth and death. The mind is a very obedient servant of its master. In its present state it is such a slave of the senses that it does not want us to go back, merge back into the Lord. Sometimes, as a friend, it tries to deceive us. Sometimes, as an enemy, it tries to threaten us. The purpose of the mind is to keep us astray, not to let us go back to our own original home. So we have to release our soul from the clutches of the mind.

Yesterday I tried to explain that in our body the seat of the soul and mind, knotted together, is in the centre just behind our eyes. From here our mind is being pulled down to the senses. Mind is fond of pleasures, and unless we give our mind a better and superior pleasure than that of the senses, it will not detach itself from the senses. And that superior pleasure is the word, the holy ghost, the shabd or nam, which is within every one of us, right behind the eyes. When, with the help of simran and with the help of contemplating on the form of the master, we try to withdraw and hold our consciousness at the eye centre, only then can we be in touch with that sound, with that shabd, with that nam. That attachment automatically detaches us from the senses. For example, a river is flowing. If you put a dam in that river, how long will you be able to hold the water? Perhaps a week, perhaps a month, and when there is too much water, the water will break through the dam. The water will rush out over the banks. But if you put a dam there and you also direct the channel of the river into another direction, then the dam is permanent and the river starts flowing into another direction.

So we cannot place our mind in a vacuum. We cannot control it by austerities. We cannot control it just by analyzing it or merely by suppression. By just withdrawing ourselves from situations, we cannot control it. We can only get temporary relief in that way. Just as you take a criminal and hand him over to the police, as long as he is in a police lock-up you are safe from his vicious doings. But as soon as he is released, he does the same thing, if not worse. If, instead of handing him over to the police, you try to correct him to be a good man and explain to him, he is reformed, and you are safe permanently from his vicious doings. Similarly, we are not to suppress our mind in an attempt to detach it from the senses. Unless we attach it to something better than the senses, the mind will never be detached from the worldly pleasures. We may try to control it by running away to the forests, by reading holy books, by giving alms, by going into seclusion or by rushing about, by escaping from situations, but in this way we get only temporary relief from it, and the moment it gets an opportunity, it reacts and rebounds and again makes us dance to its tune.

We can only control our mind when we attach it to that word, that shabd, that nam. Attachment to that automatically detaches us permanently from the world. Then the mind goes back to its own origin, and the soul gets release from the mind. It is only then that the real love and devotion of the soul takes it back to the Lord. Socrates said: Know thyself. It is only after the soul is released from the mind that it really knows itself. Only then do we realize who we are. Only when we know ourselves are we capable of knowing the Lord. Till then, we do not know our self, much less the Lord. We are just under the sway of the mind.

Now the mind is our guide, our guru. Wherever it wants to go, we run after it. We are just following the dictates of the mind. Even our devotion to that Lord is also under the sway of the mind now. But when we know our real self, it will be pure devotion, pure love, pure faith of the soul in the Lord. That alone can take it back to the Lord.

268 What is it that directs the mind in that direction?

You mean, what is it which pulls the mind from the senses and takes it towards its home? First, we have to understand why our mind runs to the senses. The reason is, it is fond of pleasures. Unless we give our mind better pleasures and better enjoyments than the sense pleasures, it will never leave the senses. The real enjoyment which can make us forget the sensual pleasures is that word or logos, or audible life stream, which is in every one of us. When we concentrate our mind at the eye centre and attach it to that, that attachment automatically detaches us from the senses. That is what pulls the mind away from the senses and will take it back to its own origin.

Unless the mind is attached, it can never be detached. I will give you an example: If a beggar is asking for a penny and he gets the penny, if you try to snatch the penny from him, he is prepared to fight and die for it. If you give him a dollar or a pound, he will just drop the penny. That is the nature of the mind. Unless it gets something better than the sensual pleasures, it will never leave the senses. We try to detach it by austerities, by secluding ourselves, by running to forests, by analyzing ourselves. We think we have conquered the mind. Actually, we have just got temporary relief from the mind, and that is the great deception, for the moment the mind gets a chance, it makes us dance on the hot coals. If we run to the forest for three or four years, we think we have conquered the mind. When we come back to the world, we face the same faces again, and our condition becomes even more abnormal than what it used to be. Suppression does not help. The more we suppress the mind, the more it is aroused when it reacts. If we direct it into a different channel and attach it to something different, then it automatically detaches itself.

For example, if you say to a girl that as you want to marry her to some person, she should forget her mother, her father, her sister, she may try hard, but she cannot succeed. However, when she falls in love with somebody, she forgets everybody else. That one attachment detaches her from all the other faces. She used to think that probably she could never live without her parents and it would be impossible to forget them, but this one attachment makes her forget everything else. This is the nature of the mind. Unless we attach it to something better than the worldly pleasures, it will never get detached from them.

269 How can we tell the difference between love that comes from the soul and love that comes from the mind in regard to spirituality?

Well, first, the mind will feel love. Actually, it is that love of the mind which is the love and devotion you feel for the Lord in the beginning. It comes in the mind and ultimately, when the soul leaves the mind, then it is the real love of soul for the Lord. So when you are able to withdraw your consciousness to the eye centre and be in touch with the spirit, then your mind will be filled with love and devotion for the Father. And that love and devotion for the Father, in the mind, helps the soul to get released from the mind, and that will be the real love and the real devotion of the soul. Real love and devotion of the soul means that the soul is able to merge back into the Creator.

The characteristic of love is to lose one's own identity and to become one with the being that is loved. So the soul merges into the Father, becomes one with the Father. That is the real love of the soul. But it has to start with the mind.

270 *Is spiritual love different from emotional love, and if it is, does it grow out of emotional love or can it come from just an intellectual understanding and a devotion to the master?*

Sister, you want to differentiate between emotional love and spiritual love?

Are they the same thing, or are they different?

To begin with, they are same. You see, devotion must come with the mind, and the mind is becoming spiritual, so to say. But you have real spiritual love only when the soul gets released from the mind. When the soul becomes whole, when it becomes pure, then you realize yourself, then you get that spiritual love. But that spiritual love is also mixed with emotional love. You see, unless there is love and devotion in the mind, the soul will never be able to go back to the Father. The mind is an enemy as long as it pulls you downward towards the senses. But the mind is your best friend when it is at the eye centre and is in touch with the shabd and is being pulled towards the second stage, Trikuti. Without winning the friendship of the mind, the soul can never go back to the Father. So when the mind is attached to the shabd, you can call it emotional love, devotional love. But in that, love of the soul also comes in. That is also spiritual love. But pure spiritual love will only be when there's no mind at all, beyond Trikuti.

271 *Is it just the mind that thinks sometimes that it doesn't have love, but actually there's always love between the disciple and the master?*

First, love has to start with the mind. The soul is always in love with the Father. There is no question that the soul loves the Father. It is always anxious to go back to the Father. Instinctively, it is always yearning to become one with the Father. It is only the weight of the mind that makes the soul helpless. So to think that we are trying to create love in the soul is a misnomer because it's always full of love for the Father. We are trying to create love in the mind so that the soul gets release from the mind. And then automatically the soul will go back to the Father.

272 *Master, I'm trying to understand something a little further. You said to me the other night that everything's based on the pull of the master in meditation.*

The pull of the Father.

When we aren't able to meditate as much as we'd like to, or we don't feel the pull as strongly as we'd like to, is it our karmas that are blocking it, or is the Lord withholding that grace until certain karmas are over?

Well, brother, we cannot analyze these things at all. If you start analyzing that today I'm not feeling the pull – karma has come in my way so I won't sit in meditation – you will never sit in meditation. We have no business analyzing these things at all. If his grace were not there, there would not have been any marking at all. It is his grace that he has marked us, his grace that has brought us on the path, so now we have to do our job, do our duty. We cannot analyze these things, thinking that I have to wait for my pull today to sit in meditation.

I'm not trying to get out of meditation, but the feeling of the pull – is it always the same, no matter how heavy the karma? Is the pull always there and always the same?

You see, the pull is not always the same. Sometimes it is less, sometimes more, but we have to train our mind to sit in meditation every day, irrespective of whether the pull is there or not. Sometimes willingly, sometimes unwillingly, we have to sit in meditation. The soldier has to go out on parade every morning. Sometimes he is very happy to do it, and sometimes he doesn't want to do it, but he has to. That's part of the discipline he has to go through. So we don't have to do everything happily. Sometimes we have to do our meditation even by force – we have to force our mind to sit, we have to fight with our mind.

I'm aware of the fight at this level, but I'm really scared when I look at where I am today and how long it's taken me to get even here in fifteen or sixteen years. I don't have a chance, by the time I die, to go to the eye centre. You said the other day that if our mind was always pointed in one direction, that even after we die, where else would it go?

Naturally. Meditation means that we are training our mind to go inward and upward. We are creating a tendency in the mind to go inward and upward, withdrawing it from outside and bringing it back to the eye centre. To create that tendency in the mind is the purpose of meditation.

I know you say we shouldn't expect results, but what part do results play?

Results come and go. Often you may not even see anything within, but you feel so happy, so contented, so at peace within yourself. You feel the effect of meditation within yourself – you feel detached from everything.

And that is enough at the time of death to take us up?

That is more than enough. Because your tendency is not towards the creation now.

I have another question, from a slightly different angle. You said that the mind is a separate entity and that the soul does not want anything to do with this creation, that it doesn't remember anything of its past.

No, the soul remembers all of the past. It remembers each and every one of its past experiences. The mind doesn't remember any of its past experiences.

So at this stage, it's all mind?

Actually, the soul's tendency is towards the Father, not towards the creation. The soul is not interested in anything in the creation. It is always yearning to go back to the Father.

So the mind has its own power that's actually drawing the soul down?

Yes. The mind is pulling the soul down to the creation.

So as I walk through this world and live from day to day, that's mind?

That is mind – 100 percent mind.

So I have absolutely no awareness of who I am.

The soul is part of the mind because the soul has taken the association of the mind. It's not that the soul is somewhere else – the soul can't escape from the clutches of the mind, the soul is being dominated by the mind, the soul is helpless before the mind. It's not that the soul is interested in this creation – it's that she has no option but to take the part of the mind.

> *Is it mind or soul that gives us the will to sit or the will to do anything?*

Mind.

> *So there is actually no action in this world from the soul?*

No. No.

> *So from that point of view, there's no reality of ourselves here, there's no experience of ourselves here.*

All this experience is through the mind. Without the mind, nobody can exist in this creation.

> *Is there a part or a feeling, be it love or devotion or willpower …*

Everything's in the mind.

> *Everything?*

Everything's in the mind, because the soul is only yearning to go back to its own destination.

> *So even love is the mind?*

Mind takes all the powers from the soul, all the devotion from the soul and then pulls the soul downward. Mind takes its power from the soul.

So if I say, "I want to meditate," or "I want to go home" – it's not me, it's just the mind saying that?

It's the mind. Because the soul is part of the mind, you can also say that part of the soul is saying that. When the soul is separated from the mind, then when you say "I," that means the soul. Now when you say "I," it is 99 percent mind.

And yet when you say the soul is only yearning to go home, it's absolutely helpless in this …

Absolutely helpless.

So the mind actually is stronger than the soul.

At this stage it is, until Trikuti. Once you go beyond the realm of mind and maya, then the soul dominates the mind – then the soul is stronger than the mind. Then mind becomes the slave and soul becomes the master. Now mind is the master and soul is the slave.

So the mind, which sometimes hates to sit in meditation, is forcing itself to sit in meditation?

That's mind.

And it's the mind that feels the yearning or the love …

That is also mind.

Even emotions are the mind?

Everything comes through the mind. The mind also is not happy in this creation. The mind also gets frustrated with these sensual pleasures, becomes miserable after some time in the sensual pleasures. It also wants more peace, more happiness. And the mind also gets peace when it goes back to its own source.

The yearning to go home – that's coming from the Lord?

Yes. This is all for the mind. The satsangs, the meetings, the books, the discussions – they're all for the mind.

So when you talk about limited free will, if it's all the mind, then there really isn't any free will.

I say the soul and mind are knotted together. When we talk about the mind, the soul is there with the mind. But the mind is dominating the soul. The soul is helpless.

When you say the mind is dominating the soul, does that have anything to do with the weight of the karmas on it?

Naturally. Mind means a combination of karmas. When the karmas have been cleared, the mind becomes pure. A noble mind, higher mind, friendly mind means that karmas have been cleared. Otherwise, all karmic effects are there on the mind.

And this meditation that we're asked to do, although our action itself isn't really clearing our karma, by performing it, does our karma get erased?

What do you mean by erasing karma?

Well, you talked about the karmas covering the mind like the weight of a stone on a needle …

That's right.

So in one lifetime, we can't possibly clear all those accounts …

No.

But there must be something that's actually erasing the karmas.

No, no, no. You can't clear them in one lifetime. Nobody says you can clear them in one lifetime. Soami Ji says that will happen in no more than four lives. Every soul which has come on the path ultimately has to go back to the Father, he says, but the soul will come back to this human body a maximum of four times.

But even in those four lifetimes, is there an erasing of karma? I mean, if we've been here for millions of lives, it would be quite impossible to clear it even in four lives.

He knows best how to clear it.

So that's being erased either by the Lord or …

It's all grace. Guru Nanak said that if you look to our karmas, there is no end to them. If you go on scratching the earth in order to reach water, even in a million years you can't reach it. And that is just the position of our karmas. All that we need is grace, the Lord's forgiveness.

We may not be able to clear all the karmas in one life, but you said that if we're starting to turn inward and upward, then that's where we would go at death. So I wouldn't have to come back?

Karmas won't bring you back.

But the meditation may not erase all the karmas.

That's right. It is our attachment to the creation which brings us back. You see, even if you have no progress within, but you are not attached to anything in this creation, nobody can bring you back here. If, on the other hand, you have a certain amount of progress to your credit within, but you are attached to something in this creation, you may have to come back to clear that attachment.

As Christ said: If you love your father and mother more than me, you are not worthy of me.[42] 'Worthy of me' means you are not worthy to become part of me. And unless you become part of me, you cannot become part of the Father. If you are not attached to me, you cannot be attached to the Father. If you're attached to your relations more than to me, you cannot become me and you cannot become God.

So our best action in this life would be to do everything we can to become attached to the master.

You can't do that mathematically, by calculating or thinking. You have to take a positive step to attend to your meditation, and that automatically detaches you from everything.

Automatically?

Automatically. When you are attached to something, you are automatically detached from other things. If you want to detach from each and every friend of yours, each and every relation of yours, you can never succeed. But if you fall in love with some girl, you will forget everybody. That is the nature of the human mind. So attachment can create detachment in us. Detachment doesn't create any attachment in anybody.

That is the difference between Sant Mat and philosophies whose followers try to run away from the world – they leave their wife, their children, their business, their house, and run away to the jungle to avoid facing them. They build up a lot of suppression. And sometimes they become even more hopeless than normal human beings. Sant Mat is very different. Attach to nam and automatically you'll get detached.

But you have to get to the eye centre before you can attach to nam.

Yes. All that we're doing every day in meditation is attaching to nam. We are trying to create a tendency in the mind to come upwards toward nam.

But you may still not be actually attached to it if you're still struggling just to reach the eye centre.

There are certain phases one has to go through – you can't start running the day after you are born.

273 Is the body in the mind, or is the mind in the body?

The mind is in the body.

When you meditate, you see things as forms and objects not only in the outside world but also in the body, and therefore the question: Is the spirit in the body, or is the body in the spirit?

Your mind and, as a result, your soul currents also are spread into the whole body. You have to withdraw the mind up to the eye centre and then you are out of the body. Now your consciousness is spread not only in the whole body but through the nine apertures of the body into the whole world. Your mind is not only within you, your mind is also in the whole world.

274 You mention that the mind and soul are different and inimical?

I discussed this in the evening meeting yesterday, that the mind is our enemy as long as it is pulling us down, pulling our soul down. Soul and mind are knotted together, and in the body their seat is behind the eyes, what you call the third eye or the single eye. From here we are being pulled by the senses – the trend of the mind is towards the senses. Mind has become the slave of the senses, and the soul, having taken the association of the mind, has become the slave of the mind. So the soul has also become the slave of the senses. As long as the mind is the slave of the senses, it is our greatest enemy. When we are able, by meditation, to withdraw the mind from the senses and attach it to nam or shabd or the audible life stream inside, the mind starts taking the soul along with it back to Trikuti, the origin or home of the mind, and in doing so, it becomes our best friend. Once the mind has reached its home, it stays there and the soul is free to go up and merge back into the Lord. The mind and the senses are the dross, the filth and the coverings of the soul, and when it is released from these coverings, it is its own pure self and merges back into the Lord.

275 Do you approve of ascetic practices as a means of purifying the body and soul? And if you do, what kind of practice do you recommend?

Brother, when we withdraw from the body, the body is automatically purified. It becomes sublime. There is nothing wrong with the body, it is when the mind runs to the senses that we say that the body is bad. When we withdraw the mind to the eye centre, the same body becomes pure. So we have first to make this body pure. Then we have to make our mind pure by attaching it to the shabd or nam inside. When it returns to its destination, its source, the mind becomes pure.

In our body, the seat of the soul and mind knotted together is in the centre behind the eyes. From here our mind is being pulled down by the senses. As long as the mind is a slave of the senses, you can say that the body is impure. When you withdraw your mind from the senses and take it back up to the eye centre, you can say that the body has become pure; but still your mind is not pure because it can be drawn back to the senses again. However, when you attach your mind to that shabd or nam, that attachment detaches you permanently from the world, and your mind starts going back to its own destination or home. Then the mind becomes pure.

As long as your mind is being drawn downward, towards the senses, it is your enemy. When the mind starts withdrawing from the senses and goes back to its original home, which is Trikuti, the second stage on the spiritual journey, then the mind becomes your friend. So we have to convert this enmity to friendship, and when the mind goes back to its own source, to its own destination, then only the soul gets released from the mind. At this stage the soul also becomes pure, as all the coverings and influences of the mind are removed. And when there is no particle left on it and it becomes absolutely pure, it shines in its own pristine glory and automatically merges back into the Lord again. So it is by meditation, the spiritual practice, that we make our body pure, we make our mind pure and we make our soul pure.

276 How can a seeker control his lust?

In the body, the seat of the soul and the mind knotted together is at the eye centre. From here our mind is pulled down to the senses. Unless we are able to withdraw the mind from the senses, unless we try to hold the mind here at the eye centre, unless we try to attach the mind to the spirit within, give it a taste of that nectar within, it refuses to leave the sensual pleasures. We cannot control lust by fighting with the mind, by disciplining it, by running away to the forests, or by performing austerities. But if we are able to withdraw the mind to the eye centre and give the mind a taste of something better, a taste of that spirit, that nectar within, it will automatically discard worldly pleasures. That is the only way to take the mind away from lust permanently. There is no other way.

277 Can soul and mind ever overcome Kal?

Yes. In the body, the seat of the soul and mind knotted together is just between and behind the eyes. From here our mind is being pulled down by the senses. So, our mind has become the slave of the senses, and the soul has become a slave of the mind, for through the mind it also is being drawn to the senses. Now we are to reverse the process. When mind wants to go to the senses, it will go there, but if it refuses to be attracted to them, it will leave the senses. When the mind leaves the senses, it becomes our friend. Why do we want to withdraw our mind from the senses? Because the soul is under the control of the mind. When, with the help of shabd, our mind comes back to its own home, the soul gets released from the mind, and the process is thus reversed. Then the soul is controlling the mind, and the mind is controlling the senses.

It is with the help of simran and dhyan that we have to withdraw the mind from the senses, and by attaching our mind to the shabd, we have to withdraw the soul from the mind. As long as the mind is running towards the senses, you cannot have a worse enemy. When the mind withdraws from the senses and is attached to the shabd, we cannot have a better friend. Unless the mind goes back to its origin, the soul can never get released from the mind. We have only to convert this enmity to friendship, by the grace of the Lord, by means of meditation, as imparted to us through his saints.

278 How can soul be aware of itself without mind?

It can be. The soul has the power of direct perception and the mind is supposed to be only its instrument for functioning in this world; but the instrument has taken the upper hand and has itself become the slave of its own instrument, the senses. So that is why I say, unless the mind merges back with the universal mind and the soul gets released from the mind, the soul will never know its reality. But at this stage, as long as the soul is a prisoner of the mind, it is only with the help of the mind that the soul can go back to its origin. Mind is our greatest enemy as long as it is the slave of the senses, for it is constantly being pulled down from the eye centre to the senses with one excuse or another. Its tendency is always towards the senses, and it is always trying to find justifications for this, not realizing that it is a slave of the senses and our worst enemy.

When, through meditation or concentration, the attention collects at the eye centre, and with the help of nam or shabd it returns to its own original home, there can be no better friend than the mind. When it is on its way back to its own home, it becomes our friend because only when the mind is on its way home can the soul also be on its way along with the mind. They are knotted together until the mind reaches its own home, and it is only then that the soul is released and is free to go on up to its source. We have to convert this energy into the channel leading upward instead of downward. Mind is a very powerful friend when it has devotion for the Lord. The master gives us the key, puts us in touch with the sound, and with the help of that we have to convert this enmity into friendship. Then the soul automatically goes along with the mind to the mind's origin, leaves the mind at its own source, and continues onward to its true home. Therefore, ultimately we have to leave the mind – drop it. Only then can we go back and merge into the Lord.

279 *Maharaj Ji, what about the force sometimes exerted by the universal mind – for instance, when the power of love is greater than the love of power? Are the supreme Creator and the universal mind the same, or are they two different things?*

You can say mind, pure mind, and still purer or refined mind. After all, mind is mind. We can say soul or God. Soul and God are the same, ultimately. Mind and universal mind are the same thing. The individual mind comes from the universal mind and merges back into the universal mind. You can call it essence of the mind; ultimately it comes to the same thing.

280 *Maharaj Ji, I have a question about the mind. Mind is said to be the agent of Kal and, as such, it has to carry out the orders of Kal so as to prevent the soul from following its true path of going inward and upward. So far so good for the mind, but if on the other hand the mind listens to the advice of the soul and does not perform its duty of preventing the soul from going upwards, then so far as it does that, isn't it guilty of dereliction of duty to its master, Kal?*

Mind listens to the senses. Senses are always attracting the mind because mind is fond of pleasure and tries to seek those pleasures in the senses. So it is always a slave of the senses and the soul is absolutely helpless. It just is a way of explaining – the soul is trying to explain to the mind. The soul is always yearning towards its own origin and the tendency of the mind is always downward and outward. The tendency of the soul is always upward and inward. But shabd is such that it pulls the mind upward. There is no question of the mind not doing its duty to its own master because that is the divine design. Mind is also not very happy in the senses. Mind is also frustrated – that is why there are so many suicides, so much frustration and misery, because we become frustrated by always being slaves of the senses, frustrated because of something we can't achieve or something we have done. We want to get rid of them – the mind is not very happy in these things. Yet mind is also seeking pleasure. And when it gets into the taste of a better pleasure, automatically its tendency becomes upward, inward. And that is the divine design by which the soul goes back to the Father.

Then the mind gets peace. Even the mind doesn't want to live in misery; the mind also wants peace. When we are happy, it is our mind which is happy. When we are miserable, it is our mind which is miserable. The mind is seeking happiness. That is a characteristic of the mind – to seek happiness. The moment it finds a channel for happiness, it diverts to that side. In seeking happiness, it has become a slave of the senses. But when it becomes frustrated by the senses and it finds another channel through which it can seek some internal happiness, naturally its tendency becomes inward.

It is not a question of discussion, it is a way of explaining, you see. The tendency of the soul, inclination of the soul, is always towards its own origin; only it is helpless under the weight of the mind. There is no question of discussing anything with the mind.

In seeking happiness, the mind is persuaded by happiness. That is why the tendency of the mind becomes upward, inward. It wants happiness. It wants peace. It wants bliss. It is very, very miserable, being a slave of the senses. That is why there are so many suicides and mental cases and all that, you see – that is all the mind. Everybody is living miserably here in this creation; some may be living comfortably in misery, but everybody is miserable.

281 *I have read that the soul, when it came into the creation, is sort of sleeping, is not conscious, and it took on the mind and ego and other coverings. Does the soul actually suffer in this creation?*

The soul suffers along with the mind – the soul doesn't suffer without the mind. When the soul has no association with the mind, the soul doesn't suffer at all. But then it takes the association of the mind, and of course it is suffering.

You see, the soul has an inclination towards its own origin. It's always yearning to go back to the Father. So that suffering of separation is always there. But it forgets the Father because it has taken the association of the mind, and the mind has become a slave of the senses. The soul starts suffering, being a slave of the senses. Even when it starts going back to its own source, the suffering of separation is always there.

The mind is also suffering. Being a slave of the senses, the mind also suffers. Because the mind runs to the senses to get pleasures and happiness, and it rebounds back because it doesn't get happiness there at all, it becomes miserable. It runs to the senses to find happiness and peace, but it becomes more miserable by being a slave of the senses. So the mind is suffering also. And since the soul and the mind are in the body, the body is also suffering. As long as the mind is there, as mind and soul are in the body, the body is also suffering. When the soul and the mind leave the body, then there's no suffering in the body. When the soul leaves the mind, then there's no suffering of the mind. When the soul merges back into the Father, then there's no suffering for the soul. The body is at peace then, the mind is at peace and the soul is at peace. Until everything merges into its own origin, it's always suffering.

This body is made of five elements. Unless the five elements [that together constitute the body] merge into the five elements [that constitute the creation], the elements suffer. Because the soul and mind are keeping these five elements separate, suffering is there. They also want to merge back into their own source; then they will get peace. So as long as the soul and mind are in the body, this body is suffering. When the soul and mind leave the body, these five elements merge back into the five elements – then there's no suffering of the body. When the mind merges into its source, in Brahm, then there's no suffering of the mind. When the soul merges into its own Creator, then there's no suffering of the soul.

282 *I want to ask about suffering and pain and what their relationship is with the individual consciousness and with the universal consciousness.*

You see, when flesh and soul and mind don't synchronize with each other, then one of them suffers. If all three go together, they synchronize with each other. But when they go in different directions, then someone has to suffer. The soul suffers when the flesh becomes victim of the senses, sensual pleasures. The soul's tendency is toward a different side. Now the tendency of the mind through the flesh is on a different side. So the soul suffers, whether we are conscious of it or not. And when the mind doesn't synchronize with the body, the mind suffers mental illness, mental worries and problems. Unless all the three merge into their own origin, none of them can escape from suffering. The soul is suffering because it is separated from its origin, the Lord. The mind suffers because it is separated from the second stage, Trikuti, universal mind, and has become a slave of the senses. The body suffers because its five elements are separate from earth, water, air, fire and ether. When we die, what happens? All five elements merge into the five elements. The suffering of the body finishes. And when the mind merges into the universal mind, suffering of the mind finishes. When the soul merges back into the divine melody within – the Lord – the suffering of the soul finishes. As long as they are separated from their origins, they must suffer. There is no other escape for all three of them. In one way or another they suffer. It is a question of more or less.

283 *Master, I want to thank you for all the help I felt, and it is really devastating what our mind and the imagination can do sometimes in looking for happiness. I hope I'll remember this for the rest of my life.*

Brother, all these worldly pleasures, worldly happinesses, are short-lived. They are just temporary. They are not permanent at all. The real permanent bliss and happiness is when the soul merges back to its own source. Everything finds peace when it merges back into its own source. When the mind goes back to its own source, the mind becomes peaceful. When these five elements of which bodies consist merge back into the five elements [of the creation], the body is at peace. Now we sometimes have cancer, sometimes this problem, this pain and this misery, but once all the elements merge back into the original elements, all the pain vanishes. When the mind merges into its own source, all mental problems finish. When the soul merges into its own source, it is the most blissful and best happiness one can get. All others are short-lived temporary things – they don't give you any mental peace or happiness.

284 *Why would the soul want to come back here from the superior planes, knowing how much suffering and misery is here? Why would the soul want to come down again as an individual? Why would the soul want to come back at all?*

Even now, we do not want to go. We see suffering all around us. If anyone tells you to prepare yourself, you are going to die, are you prepared to die at once? We say, "No, we have so many things to do yet." Even now we are not prepared to leave, in spite of all the suffering in this world. We may think we are prepared to die but realize that we are not when faced with the situation. The Great Master used to relate to us a very humorous story: There was an old lady whose daughter was very ill, and she was praying to the Lord, "O Lord! Please take away my life. I cannot bear to see the suffering of this poor girl. Let her live. I want to die in her place." Just then a black buffalo came and took some food from a small black utensil which was in the courtyard. As the buffalo put its mouth in the utensil to get the food, its horns got stuck in the utensil and when it raised its head, just then the old lady looked out and all she could see was something black running towards her. So when that buffalo, running about in fright with the bucket covering its eyes, approached that old mother, she thought that the angel of death had come, and at once she said, "My daughter is in that room."

We may say that we are ready, but when the situation arises, then we know where we stand. Knowing that we are weeping and suffering, knowing that we must have done something in our past birth that we are so miserable and unhappy, still we are not doing anything to get rid of this condition. We are doing the same things again and again. We are not taking lessons from what deeds we have done in the past birth, for which we are suffering now. We are victims of the senses, just the same as we used to be. We are still doing the same things every day in our human life. How can we go back home? We will have to come back here. We are not taking any lessons at all from the past. Nobody does. When the situation arises, we do the same thing, and we are again sorry. We repent for what we have done, but when again the situation arises, we do the same thing, and we are again sorry. If this is so in this life, what about our past life? We have forgotten the reason why we are unhappy, and so we are doing perhaps the same thing, sowing the same seed every day in our life.

285 What is emotion?

It is an instinct of the mind.

So the label 'emotion' is a part of the mind?

Yes.

According to psychology and other teachings, this is not usually so.

That is unfortunate. I do not know about the old psychologists, the old philosophers; but now, especially in the East, philosophers think that the soul is an entity different from the mind. First, they always thought that soul and mind were one. They never differentiated the soul from the mind. But now, as a result of their research, they have begun to think that soul is something different from mind. Generally, they are mixed up, as in Freud and others, when they say that there is no soul and that mind is the soul, that the terms 'mind' and 'soul' mean the same thing. Actually, that is wrong. Eastern philosophers have always differentiated the soul from the mind. As Socrates said, "Know thyself." What is that self that we have to know? That is the soul, which is our real self. This concept is very, very old with the East. It was also so with the West, and with the Greek philosophers, but it has been absolutely forgotten.

We can only know our self when we get released from the mind. For example, you see the ocean. Some of the water evaporates, becomes a cloud, and goes up; it becomes rain and comes down again. It merges into the ground, becomes mud and dirt. At that stage the water absolutely forgets its real intrinsic value, its pure qualities, and thinks itself nothing but the dirt. But again, with the heat of the sun it evaporates and leaves the dirt. Then it begins to realize: That dirt is something else and I am something else. Unfortunately, having taken company of the dirt, I lost my identity. I thought I was part of this dirt. When it leaves the dirt, only then does it realize that its real self is something different from the dirt. Similarly, it is when the soul gets released from the mind that it really begins to know itself. Then it realizes where its origin is, which is that supreme Father, that cloud. Then it evaporates, leaves the dirt behind and merges back into the cloud.

Our soul is the essence of the Lord. It has taken the company of the mind, and the mind is a slave of the senses. Whatever we do through the senses, the soul has to take part in that because it is under the sway of the mind. So we have just to reverse the process by bringing our mind under the control of the soul and bringing the senses under the control of the mind. The centre between the eyes is the seat of our soul and mind knotted together in the body. From here, our mind is being pulled down. If you forget anything, automatically you will touch your forehead to remember what you have forgotten. We all know that this place, between the eyes, has something to do with our thinking; so we have to hold the attention of the mind here and not let it come down to the senses. But we cannot keep our mind blank here, we must have something to hold the mind. And that something must be superior to the pleasures of the senses because our mind is fond of pleasure. That superior thing is that word or logos, that shabd, that light, which is here between the eyes. Therefore, we have to withdraw the mind up to this place, to be in touch with that light, that word. The pleasure of that word or light is so great that the attention automatically stops going down to the senses.

286 *Master, we speak about love in the heart. How did this relationship between heart and love ever arise?*

The Lord has given every part of the body a certain function. Seeing is done with the eyes, smelling with the nose, eating with the mouth, and the feeling of emotion in the heart. So, love is felt through the heart. These are physical functions of the body.

On that question, I sense more feeling in the solar plexus or in my throat than in my heart. Perhaps I do not know where my heart is?

Sister, they are all combined. When the heart feels, the throat is choked, tears come in the eyes, and the face is flushed. So you cannot confine love just to the heart. Rather, you feel this sensation in the whole body – from the feet to the head – physically. You may feel it here in the throat, in the eyes or in the head – in fact in your whole being. That is different, but it arises from the heart. Of course the spiritual heart centre is the eye centre, and what we experience spiritually is felt with even greater intensity from there upward.

287 *Speaking of souls, is there any essential difference in the souls of, say, a person who is very bad and one who is very good? Is that not just the action of their mind, and there would not be any difference in the souls as such?*

Brother, a diamond is a diamond. If you throw it in the mud, it will be encrusted with mud, but the moment it is washed, it is again as brilliant as before. The soul is a diamond. Every soul is the essence of the Lord. It is pure in itself, but having taken the company of the mind, and the mind having become victim of the senses, it has covered itself with evil, darkness and filth. So when it leaves the mind, every soul is the same. There is no difference in their purity. Some souls fall into very dirty mud;

some fall on a little cleaner ground; some have only little specks and stains stuck to them; and some are completely wrapped in filth, so more drastic measures have to be taken to cleanse them. But a diamond is a diamond.

288 *Everything except the form that is God, is actually unreal, because only that which is eternal is real – is that right?*

That is right. How can we say anything is real when it is not permanent – here today and gone tomorrow?

> *And everything that we see out here is like a sunbeam, and it looks out, and that is the way we become mesmerized in this world? And only by looking back through the sunbeam can you see reality? Is that true?*

That is right. All that we see with the physical eyes is made up of one or more of the five elements, namely, earth, water, fire, air and ether. And all these five elements are inimical to each other. But with the help of, or due to that ray of shabd, the soul, which is also a ray of the supreme Father, all of the five elements are contained and active in a human body, each one manifesting them according to his own karmas – in that proportion. But all the five elements are active, to a greater or lesser degree, in every human body. We are moving about, but the day that the Lord takes the soul away from the body, all these five elements begin to decompose. The earth goes back to the earth, the water goes back to the water – each element merges back into its own origin. So it is a salvation for the physical body when these five elements merge back into their own origin. That is the physical death. And salvation from birth and death is attained when the soul reaches Trikuti, Brahm, and the mind merges back into the universal mind. Salvation for a soul is when it merges back into the supreme Father, its own origin.

For the purpose of functioning in this world, the soul has taken the association of the mind and senses; but, unfortunately the soul has not remained in control of the mind and senses. Mind is fond of pleasures, and so it has become a slave of the senses, dragging the soul down along with it to the extent that now the soul has become a slave of the senses also, through the agency of the mind. As a result, the mind as well as the soul has forgotten its origin and purpose.

We get a body according to our actions and reactions, whether it is in the human form or anywhere else. But we can find the path out of this mess, or out of this jail, only in the human form, and this grace is bestowed upon us by him [the Lord], just for this very purpose. So while being in this body, we should always keep our destination in view and try to tread on that path which leads to our destination. We should never forget it. We should perform our worldly duties and other responsibilities which we have to discharge while being in this world, according to our karma, so to say. But we should always keep our destination in view and try to tread on that path which leads to our home. The path leading to our destination should always be our main road. We should not deviate to the left or the right, but keep our goal always in mind while travelling straight on that path.

289 *When the senses enjoy something in spite of the mind, do we say that it is contradictory?*

No. The senses never enjoy anything without the mind. It is the mind that enjoys through the senses, for the senses in themselves are nothing. Unless the attention of the mind is there in the senses, there is no sensation whatsoever.

Can the senses not enjoy it?

No, no. It is the mind that enjoys it. Say your daughter or your son is in your lap. He has a body, you have a body, but your feeling is pure. It is not the bodies, but it is the mind in each body which is a slave of the senses. Unless the mind works, the body does not work. So it is the mind that has to be controlled.

Christ said: If thine eye be single, thy whole body shall be full of light.[23] Where is that single eye which we have to open to see that light? Everything is within the body, and that 'eye' is just between these two eyes. You may call it a single eye, or third eye, or give it any name; but it has nothing to do with the physical eyes. It is at this eye centre that we have to concentrate; it is this door which we have to open. There is no other door outside at which we have to knock and open in order to be in the church. This, right from this centre upward – the whole forehead – is the real church. And the single eye is the door of that church, which we have to open. Unless we open this door, we will not see the light, we will not find our path, we will not know our path, and we cannot seek the Lord.

When the door of a house is closed, you always knock at it from the outside, and it is always opened from the inside before you can get in. Similarly, the Lord is inside, and we are outside. We have to knock at this door, and when we knock at it by concentrating at this point, the door is opened and we get into the house of the Lord. Christ also referred to the human body as the temple of the living God.[132] He also said: The kingdom of heaven is within you.[3] We have to make a research in the laboratory of our own body by concentrating our attention at this point – knocking at that door, in other words – in order to travel on that path, in order to seek him, in order to find him.

290 Do the senses always misguide, or can the senses be of help?

As long as the mind is a slave of the senses, we are away from the destination. Our destination is upward. The trend of the senses is downward. Anything which keeps us away from the Lord, naturally, is misguiding us. A lover never appreciates anything that keeps the beloved away. We make karma under the sway of the mind and senses, and our karma keeps us away from our Lord, the beloved.

291 *Nature – the natural feelings that we feel – are probably the mind?*

I don't know what you mean by nature. It is the characteristic of the mind to run to the senses. That is the characteristic of the mind, and then it becomes a slave of the senses and then it starts justifying that it's right: "I can't help it. Nature has made people so beautiful and I must have it. It is meant for this purpose." Then mind starts justifying all these things, you see. And the same mind starts hating those things later on. If they are beautiful, they should always remain beautiful. Why do they become ugly then, later on? They should always remain beautiful. The mind thinks: That woman is very beautiful; I must marry her. And he marries her. The same mind starts hating her and runs to the divorce court. Where has that beauty gone now? Where has the love for that beauty gone? It is the same mind, same nature. First you justify this way, then you start justifying in the other way. Our whole struggle is with the mind.

292 *Master, last night Professor said that the mind is a slave to the senses, and if your soul is aware that you're doing something wrong, and your mind is agreeing with you that you're doing something wrong, and so your soul and your mind are both in agreement that this is not the right thing*

to do, but yet your senses are pulling you and you're going along with it, it's like you have no choice in the matter. Is that fulfilling your destiny? Is that paying off karma?

Sister, the soul has no voice. The mind is dominating, and the mind is a slave of the senses. The soul has no voice; it is helpless under the weight of the mind. All karmas are connected with the mind, not with the soul. The soul's inclination is always towards its own origin. The moment you lift the weight of karmas from the soul, it runs back to its source. So karmas, all karmas, are associated with the mind. And since souls have taken association with the mind, the soul is suffering.

It's not the soul, it's the higher mind. You see, the higher mind is what we call conscience. My conscience is pricking me for what I have done. It's your higher mind which is pricking you, your better mind, noble mind. Mind projects in many forms, many ways. Lower mind is running toward the senses and higher mind feels it. But it's the same mind. They're not two minds.

293 *Is it not the Lord's grace that what we experienced in a previous life, as sanskaras, as leftover experiences, may help prevent us from committing certain actions? We get a feeling in our next life: "Don't do that." Is that the Lord's grace?*

Yes, you see, conscience is there. It pricks us, it tells us, it warns us. But conscience is also part of the mind. Conscience is also conditioned, developed. Under certain circumstances, the atmosphere in which we are brought up, conscience is created, conscience develops. But then, mind is also so helpless before the senses. The mind projects itself before us in so many ways. The mind is the one who warns us "it's not right," and the mind also is the one who takes us to the senses. It projects itself in so many forms. It is the mind which is a slave of the senses, and it is also the mind which gives us wisdom, intellect and conscience. It projects in so many ways.

294 *Sir, you know how belligerent we Americans can be sometimes. In fact, we even have in our Constitution that we like to own guns. Is it improper for a satsangi to ever defend himself with a weapon, or to engage in such hobbies as target shooting?*

You can do whatever you like, but don't develop the habit of killing people. You see, the mind always likes to go further and further. There's a story – I don't know whether I remember the whole of it or not – in an old text, one of the Vedas. A passerby was travelling in the forest and he left his bow and arrow at a rishi's hut. He said, "I don't need it, I never hunt, it is of no use to me. I am going further, and when I come back, I'll collect it. I'll just leave it there and I'll pick it up when I come back. There should be no problem for you – I'll just keep it outside your hut." So he left it there.

Every day the rishi, when leaving and coming to his hut, noticed that arrow and bow. He said to himself, "What is the harm in just trying to learn how it works?" So one day he started trying it, just aimlessly shooting without any target, without any victim. And he said, "I'm not going to kill anybody, I am just trying to see how it works." So he started that. Then he said, "What is the harm even of killing? I won't eat the meat at all." And after a month or so, he found himself hunting animals. And then, ultimately, it ended with his eating the animals. The man came back – he was probably the rishi's guru in disguise. He said, "You are following all my instructions?" Naturally the rishi kept his eyes down – he couldn't say anything. The man said, "I told you to abstain from meat and shooting, and I hope you have not been indulging in that." The rishi fell at the man's feet and said, "I'm sorry, I became a victim of this mind, and it slowly and slowly started justifying everything, and now I'm absolutely a slave of it." I don't mean to say that you will become like that, but this is what can happen.

295 Why do we commit actions that we know are harmful?

Naturally first we see things, then a sense of possession comes in. We want to possess them, and then we do actions to possess them or to dispossess them. Unless the thought arises, actions will not arise. First the thought will come, then the action will come, and then we will be a victim of the action and reaction. Sometimes you are able to drive out those thoughts. But sometimes they become so impulsive, so strong that you become helpless and you try to put them into action. And then you become a victim of the reaction. The question of why doesn't arise at all. There is a difference between thought and action. Unless we think, we will not act. That is the mind. The mind creates a thought. Then we try to go through that thought to our senses, and that becomes an action. And once we have gone to the senses, once we have passed that thought through the senses, then we have to come back to bear its effect. That was the cause and this is the reaction. So then we are involved in the karma theory.

296 Master, mind and soul – how do they come together when we are born in this world? Does the mind come from the previous life together with the soul?

It is the same mind, same soul, because the karmas the soul is carrying are the effect of the mind. The burden of all the karma is on the mind, and the soul is under the sway of the mind. Same mind, same soul. They are just knotted together. We have to reverse the whole process by meditation. Now the mind controls the soul and the senses control the mind, so we are in this flesh, a prisoner of this flesh, of this house. By meditation we have to reverse the whole process. That soul should control the mind and mind should control the senses. The moment the soul controls the mind, the soul goes beyond the realm of mind. Then it cannot be arrested in any flesh because karmas only pull us to the flesh, pull us to some body. When the soul is beyond the realm of karma, who can pull the soul back?

297 Is it the design of the creation that human beings forget the purpose of having a human body?

You see, it is the mind which makes us forget the purpose for which this human body has been given to us. Mind is an agent of Kal. Kal doesn't want any soul to escape from the clutches of his realm. Mind is attached to every soul, and mind himself has become a slave of the senses. Being attached to the senses, you always forget the purpose of human life. That is the divine design, so to say. Otherwise, if you are not attached to this creation, nobody would be here, nobody would stay here. There's no other way that the mind could keep you attached to this creation if this creation is to continue. Those who, with the Lord's grace, get detached and go beyond the realm of mind and maya – they escape.

THE MIND

298 How can we determine the difference between promptings from our mind and the real promptings from you?

What you mean to say is whether it is the master inside who wants us to do things or whether it is our own mind. It is always the mind which has cravings and desires. We have to lean on the master within to get rid of those cravings and desires. All lower tendencies are always of the mind. Even the devotion, the emotions we feel for the Lord, are also of the mind. The origin of the mind is Brahm, in Trikuti, the second stage. In our body, the eye centre is the seat of the mind and soul knotted together. From here the mind is pulled down by the senses; and the soul, being knotted with the mind, is pulled down along with it and has become a slave of the senses. This is the condition of the soul as long as it is knotted with the mind. So we have to reverse the process in order to go back to the Lord. Our soul has to control the mind, and mind has to control the senses. Only then is the mind free to go back to its origin and the soul is released to go up to its original home, beyond the home of the mind.

Whatever desires and cravings come within us, actually, are the play of the mind. But there are some good desires also. The mind also desires good things – good deeds to do in this world. Whether good or bad, all desires pertaining to this world bring us back into this world. Our karmas, whether good or bad, bring us back here. When we do so many things in charity, help people socially, economically and in some other ways, with the expectation of reward, we are building good karmas; but we will have to come back to this world to reap the fruit of those good deeds. Good actions and bad actions both bring us back into this world. That is how we got this human form. If we had only good karmas, good actions to our credit, we would now be in heaven. If we had only bad karmas or actions to account for, we would now be in hell. But if we have good and bad combined, we get a human form. That is why you find so many ups and downs in this world. Some people have more good karmas and less bad karmas, so they are more happy and less unhappy, more rich and less poor. Others have more bad karmas than good karmas, so they have more unhappy days and fewer happy days in this world. It is the combination of good and bad karmas together which helps us in getting this human form.

So while being in this human form, we have to rise above these good and bad karmas; and we can rise above them only by devotion to the Lord, by attaching the mind to the sound or audible life stream. The mind is flitting, wavering, always running after worldly objects because it is fond of pleasures. That is why it is a slave of the senses. Unless we give the mind something better than sensual pleasures, it will not leave those sensual pleasures because detachment never creates attachment in us.

It is only the attachment to the sound that creates detachment within us. That sound, that audible life stream, is here at the eye centre, and when we withdraw our attention up to this place with the help of concentration and contemplation on the form of the master, we are able to hold our thoughts there. We attach our mind and soul knotted together to that shabd or word, that sound or logos. Its attachment automatically detaches us from the senses and pulls us up. That detaches us from all these desires and cravings. As long as the tendency of the mind is downward, these desires and cravings are always there. But when its tendency becomes upward, it automatically leaves these desires and cravings.

299 How can we determine if an impulse is coming from within or from the mind?

Sister, practically speaking, you cannot know. By meditation we have to develop to such an extent that we will know whether it is good or bad. Practically, sometimes, we do not know whether what we are doing is good or bad. We may think we are doing good, but actually we may be doing bad, harming ourselves.

So it is difficult to discriminate between what is good and what is bad. We can safely say that anything which is leading us to the Lord is good, and anything that keeps us away from him is bad. That is the only way we can determine whether this is right or that is wrong.

300 *Master, we were talking a while back about the difference between conversations with the higher mind and the sort of conversations we have when we think we are talking to the master inside ourselves. Is there a difference?*

You see, the mind can project in many forms. The mind can project or be at a thousand places at a time. Mostly we talk with our mind. And since we are talking about the master or the path, we are talking to a higher mind or a better mind.

So the only time we will be talking to the master is when we see him inside in his radiant form?

You will talk to the master only when he is there. How can you talk to him when he is not there?

But I thought the master could view every thought, that he knows every thought.

Of course, even when you are not talking, he knows your thoughts – that's different. As far as talking is concerned, we can only talk with someone when he is before us.

So we're never talking to the master when we're having conversations inside of our mind? It's just talking to the mind, not talking to the master?

Now we are all talking *about* God, but we are not talking *to* God. We're all talking about God-realization, his love, his devotion, but we're not talking to God. We are talking about him, his love and devotion. So even if you talk to your own mind about the master, it is definitely to your advantage, filling you with love and devotion for the master. You are so much in love with him that you just talk to him. Whether he is there or not is immaterial to you. But still it is the higher mind, better mind.

When we pray to the Lord, we don't see the Lord anywhere. We think he is there and that he is hearing us, so we pray to him. We presume that he is there, but we will only know that when he is really before us and we see him, and then perhaps we won't even pray. So there's no harm in talking to the master within, no harm in praying to the Father, but you can't say that you are talking to him unless you see him personally.

301 Is it possible to give and receive instructions on the astral plane, like when we are sleeping?

When you are sleeping, you are not on the astral plane. You are just at the throat centre. But we can sometimes get instructions in sleep. We think it is sleep, but actually it may not be sleep.

302 Maharaj Ji, oftentimes questions are answered inside during satsang. Are these questions which are answered inside always answered by the master or are they sometimes answered by our own mind?

Sometimes we are deceived. So we should never give any attention to any answer that we get within unless we are sure that the answer is coming from our master. Unless you see the master, unless you make yourself sure about the master, you should not put any reliance on any answer you may get inside. Sometimes the mind deceives us and starts answering our questions.

In the beginning your mind will tell you the right answer to the right situation. But having won your confidence, the same mind starts deceiving you and leads you astray. So it's always better not to listen to anything within yourself at all; not to give any importance to any answer until you become sure of the master – the method for which the disciple is always told at the time of initiation.

303 *Master, when we're having difficulty with the mind, when we're having a very bad struggle and we're trying to say the words, is it all right to stop and talk to the mind and tell it that it's not happy here, so why doesn't it go to its home in Trikuti?*

Talk to your mind in any way that it will understand, in whatever way it is receptive to you. The best way the mind can be receptive to your explanations is to attach it to the spirit within. Then it becomes receptive to whatever you want to say to it. The mind is fond of pleasures, and that is why it runs to the senses. Unless it gets a better pleasure than sensual pleasures, the mind refuses to leave the sensual pleasures. And you will only be able to give it better pleasures when you withdraw it to the eye centre and attach it to the holy spirit within. When it is absorbed in that light, then of course the mind will not run to the senses. Then it will hear you. Then it will be receptive to whatever you want to say to it. Not otherwise.

304 *The hardest task facing new seekers is that the mind can't be held so steadfast.*

It's not a question of new seekers. Even with initiates, the mind is not so easily subdued. The real struggle starts with the mind when you are on the path. As a seeker, you don't realize the extent of the struggle with the mind. When you become a disciple, an initiate, then you'll understand how real the struggle is.

Then the mind realizes that you are going to escape from it, so it becomes more active than before. We are all struggling souls on the same path. We shouldn't simply throw up our hands – we should try to do our best to control the mind.

305 *Maharaj Ji, in our literature we read very often that where mind and matter are active, there can be no peace. Would it be possible for you to tell us what are the contributing factors to this situation?*

This whole world, all these material things, are matter. And as long as mind is after this matter to achieve happiness, it can never find peace.

Then it is mind's ambition to enjoy this matter?

Our mind tries to find happiness in these outside material things, in this matter composed of five elements – earth, water, fire, air and ether. That can never be achieved because it cannot be satisfied with whatever it gets in this world. It shifts from place to place, from person to person, from thing to thing. It is always shifting, for nothing here is able to hold our mind permanently. When it is attached to shabd, only then does it detach itself from matter. That detachment in itself gives peace to the mind. One who does not desire anything is the happiest. Rather, he would explain that he does not need anything. But one who desires and is always hankering after things is even more frustrated when the desires are achieved. Matter does not give the mind happiness at all. Only the shabd gives lasting happiness. The spiritual path gives happiness to the mind and the soul. Matter is just another lure for the senses.

306 *Maharaj Ji, would you say that this disease of ego may be at least greatly attributable to the fact that we have*

become in the habit of identifying ourselves with the mind – a feeling that we are mind and not soul – and to the extent that we realize that mind is our instrument and we are soul, to that extent it consists in freeing us?

That is right. That is realization. Now we hardly differentiate between the mind and the soul, so we think that whatever our mind wants, our soul probably wants it. But then a time comes when we feel the soul never wanted it. It was something else that was wanting it. Otherwise, what the soul wants, it wants that always and it never wavers. The soul never feels frustrated with what it wants; but the mind does sometimes feel frustrated with what it wants. The soul is happy when it gets what it wants. It is always happy there and it never likes to change. The mind always wants change and it always shifts from one thing to another.

307 When we go inside and meet the master, even then the negative power will put many obstacles in our way. Even if we have the master, will we be overcome by these negative forces and ruin everything which we have gained?

The mind is the same, whether the tendency of the mind is downward or upward. The mind is not our enemy; it is our best friend. It is an enemy as long as it pulls us toward the senses. When it comes back to the eye centre and is attached to the spirit within, and starts enjoying the bliss of shabd and nam within, and takes us back to our own destination, then it becomes our best friend. Without the help of the mind, the soul would never be able to go back to the Father at all.

All your emotion, your devotion, your love to begin with are nothing but the outcome of mind. Mind is creating that love and devotion in you, and soul is taking advantage of it. So we have to win the friendship of the mind. From enmity, we have to get friendship. There is nothing wrong with the mind; its tendency is downward only because it's fond of pleasures. So we have to give our mind a better pleasure than sensual pleasure. And we have to create an upward tendency of the mind. When the tendency of the mind is upward, when it is full with devotion and love for the Father, then it is our best friend because the soul will become active only when it gets released from the mind. Till then, it is guided by the mind.

308 Master, a few days ago, you said that when love is directed downwards, it's passion. When it's directed upwards, it's emotion. Even a good speaker can create a mild emotion. My question is, can emotion be of value, is it to be trusted and of what value is emotion in Sant Mat?

Well, brother, there is only one word in English for love. Sometimes it becomes passion, sometimes it becomes devotion, so we try to differentiate. When the tendency is downward, then of course it's passion. When the tendency is upward, then of course it's devotion – call it emotion.

Love begins with the mind. The soul is already in love with the Father. We don't have to create any love in the soul for the Father – it is already there. It is yearning to become one with the Father. It is only helpless due to the mind because the tendency of the mind is outward and downward, to the senses. The soul is just helpless. We are not creating love in the soul; the soul is already full of love and devotion for the Father.

So first we have to create this devotion – or you can call it emotion – in the mind. That is just trying to lift the weight from the soul, and then the soul automatically goes back to the Father.

You see, my concept of emotion is not the downward tendency of the mind but the upward tendency of the mind.

The attitude of the mind is towards its own origin, towards the Father. That is my concept of emotion and devotion.

309 *Master, I wanted to ask a question about negative emotions, particularly the emotions of jealousy, envy, and anger or resentment. When the emotion is so strong it overpowers you, and when you struggle and you finally subdue the emotion, it seems to come out in other ways. It seems to always find a way out, like through thoughts. And the thoughts go into creating fantasies – using those same emotions, having to do with those same people – fantasies about abandonment, or betrayal, or persecution.*

Sister, the emotion is the same. When its tendency is downward, it becomes passion. When upward, it becomes devotion. So we should try to make its tendency upward. Our emotion should be for the Father and for his beloved sons. That emotion should lead us above the eye centre. If its tendency is downward, then naturally it becomes passion. Then jealousy, rivalry, and everything else will come along with it.

310 *You have mentioned the mind several times, but what can the mind do unless you have the emotional maturity to train the mind to do one thing or another? Are the emotions closer to us than our mind is?*

What is the mind and what is emotion, in your view?

The emotions are those actions which we perform in spite of the mind?

No, in spite of the soul. Emotions are nothing but the expressions of the mind. All these instincts are nothing but the expressions of the mind. The intellect is with the mind. The emotions are with the mind. The soul is just being dominated by the mind. We do not know what soul is, in fact, because we are so much a slave of the mind. We begin to think probably that our mind is the soul. Actually, the soul is something far superior to the mind.

What do you do then if you have a contradiction between your mind and your actions through your emotions?

That is a contradiction between your higher mind and your lower mind. What we call conscience is itself an attribute of the mind.

311 Master, will you speak of the different kinds of love there are and try to explain the confusion one feels about passion?

Brother, lust is something different from love. The quality of love is to lose one's own identity and merge into another being, to become the other being – that is love. When the soul merges into the Father and becomes the Father – that is the true love. That is why it is said that God is love, because only through love can the soul merge back into the Father. Now we have individuality and that is why we are separated from the Father. So to lose this individuality and to become another being, to merge back into the Father, that is real love.

Even in worldly love, we have so much love for the other being that we lose our identity and become the other being. We always do that which pleases the other person and never do anything which displeases him. So the higher love is to lose your own identity, merge back into the Father and become the Father. Otherwise, what is generally called love is nothing but lust.

312 Why is anger the most destructive perversion?

Sister, all perversions are destructive. We hold on to them dearly. They are all the instincts of the mind. When the mind becomes pure, all these perversions automatically leave us.

313 Temptations are tests, aren't they?

We test ourselves, actually. The mind is putting in an effort to become perfect, and the mind is the one who tells you, "You are the most imperfect one." These tests are from our own mind. On the one hand it is trying to become pure. On the other hand, it is reminding us every day, "You are the most impure one." In that way you can say that the Lord is testing us. But if he were really to test us, we would never be worthy.

314 Master, will you please tell us what happens when a person dreams?

Dreams mostly are projections of our own mind. Whatever our daily associations with the world are, they come in one form or another in a dream. But sometimes we have a very meaningful dream. For example, something which is going to happen with you, you witness all that in a dream, and that something happens with you after some time. We have no explanation why, as that cannot be an association of our mind because that thing has not happened and is yet to happen; so these are meaningful dreams. But dreams are, after all, dreams, and it is not in our power to get them. So we should try to work for reality rather than depend upon dreams. Good dreams are good dreams, that is all; but there is no reality in them.

315 Would you explain to us what spiritual dreams are?

That is what I tried to explain. Sometimes we have good dreams about things that have not happened so far, and later these very things happen to us. These are, we can say, pure dreams or elevated dreams. If we have love for God, and we attend to our meditation at the time of going to sleep in addition to our regular time, then generally we get very good dreams, like flying over the hills and trying to reach a certain destination. These dreams have associations with the soul. The soul tries to get release from the body and tries to fly back to its origin, and because we have so much karmic load that we cannot do that while in the conscious state, the soul gets a little release in the unconscious state of sleep. As a result we have dreams of flying. We cannot, however, depend upon these dreams in any way.

Supposing you have a dream that you have met a friend tonight, a friend whom you have not seen for ten years, and you even dream under what circumstances you meet him. You are simply surprised because you have not thought about him. Then suddenly you find the next day all that happening – you are going to that particular place and experiencing all those circumstances and you meet him. Naturally, psychologists cannot give any satisfactory explanation as to why such dreams occur.

> *Do you mean to say that these spiritual dreams have some connection with intuition? Meaning something you think about – it is not a dream but it is something that you think about – will happen, and it happens?*

After all, everybody does not have that intuition. It must be due to some purification of the soul that a thing that is going to happen, you feel that it is going to happen, or you know that it is going to happen. To some extent that comes as a development of your mind, development of your soul. You call it intuition. It happens sometimes, definitely.

316 Maharaj Ji, are fine works of art or music, which stir the heart and move us inside, reflections of higher spiritual regions, and if they are, does the soul create them?

Well, it is not the reflection of higher spiritual regions, but it definitely is the reflection of the higher mind, of a better mind. But still that is not the reflection of higher regions, but of a better mind.

317 What is imagination, and what place does it have in Sant Mat?

I don't know what the questioner means. Imagination is imagination. Sant Mat is Sant Mat. You can't imagine Sant Mat, you have to experience Sant Mat. Imagination can be wrong, but experience can't be wrong. So you have to experience the Sant Mat teachings. You cannot imagine the teachings of Sant Mat. The two have no relationship at all.

318 What is willpower?

The purer the mind becomes, the more it is attached to the shabd and nam. The purer it becomes, the more strength and power it gets. The more it is detached from the spirit, the more it is under the control of the senses, the weaker the willpower. As I often explain, in the body the seat of the soul and the mind is here at the eye centre. The more downward the mind's tendency, the less willpower we have. The more upward its tendency, the stronger is our willpower. So it is the spirit that actually gives you strength and willpower.

319 I would like to touch on another subject which I do not think anybody has questioned you about here. For six years I have studied psychology. I became one of the finest hypnotists in the business, if you want to call it that. And Brother Replogle told me that the master will not allow me to use this type of psychic therapy. Will you please elaborate on that?

This hypnotism, as you call it, is trying to dominate somebody's willpower, controlling somebody's mind with your superior mind, and to make him do what you want him to do. That is all. It is never good for the man who practices it and never good for the man on whom it is practiced. And this is far removed from spirituality. I do not think satsangis should ever dabble in these things at all. It is extremely detrimental to our spiritual practice as well as to the one who is hypnotized.

What about self-hypnosis, in which a second party is not involved? You put yourself in a state of suspended animation and you probe your own subconscious and you can reach a level where you can see your last incarnation. If you go back further you can see your previous incarnations. Now, in this state, are you going up to beyond Trikuti, or is this all residing in the subconscious?

No, no, absolutely not. You cannot be beyond the first stage at all in those circumstances.

Where is the knowledge that they are receiving? Is it false knowledge that the mind is feeding out?

All the knowledge is coming from the mind. It is control of the mind to some extent, a sharpening of the mind, nothing else.

Well, is there any value in practicing self-hypnosis to control the mind? One apparently can receive a high degree of control of the mind through self-hypnosis. Would there be any value in pursuing that as a steppingstone to …?

No. I do not think so. That would be a block in your way towards spiritual progress.

Because, for example, a person who has highly developed himself in this can sit still and immediately, with just his thought, stop all sounds. He cannot hear a thing from the outside. He can stop all body movement. If that could be achieved with the mind through self-hypnosis, could he not reach the eye centre quicker that way?

No. It is a block. It is a definite block in spiritual progress.

Why is it a definite block?

Because you would not go ahead at all. You would be lost, lost, just in that. At the most, you would see yourself. You would think that you are the master of yourself, you are God, and you would be just lost in that state and would not make any further progress at all.

So one should leave self-hypnosis alone then?

I do not think we should allow ourselves to be hypnotized, nor should we try to dabble in these things. Absolutely not. Those who do generally meet with a terrible fate. If we analyze what has happened to those who dabbled in hypnotism or spiritualism, we find that their end is tragic. It is difficult to describe what they have to face at the end of life, or even much earlier.

Master, would this also pertain to telepathy between two persons?

Telepathy is something natural. Sometimes you feel you are going to meet a friend, and suddenly you meet him at a corner. Something told you within that you were going to meet him or see him. It comes, but that is something different. This intuition, after all, is also of the mind. Call it intuition or give it any other name.

320 Is it possible that good can come from certain types of spiritualism? Can there be two spirits …?

In spiritualism you never contact any soul. All that you contact is your own mind. It becomes your medium and tells you all that. Initiates should not dabble in spiritualism at all. It is absolutely no good. The fate or end of the spiritualist is terrible.

321 What happens to the mind when we die?

Mind does not leave us, brother. The mind has piled up so many karmas, and according to our karmas, we are again given birth. The same mind and soul come back into another body. Another cage is ready for the mind and the soul, knotted together; another prison is ready for the unliberated soul and mind. You leave one body; another body is ready for you. Here your relatives are weeping because you have left them. In another place in this world, your new relatives are all joyful and happy and dancing because you have come. That is the only difference. Nothing else happens. We leave one house, we cut off our relationship with them and we get another set of relatives. We forget the previous ones and we are in love with the new ones. That is all. That is what the mind does to us.

322 Does the mind have no virtue at all? Are all our intellectual pursuits worthless?

No, I will tell you. The intellect is a faculty of the mind, but we have to use it in the right direction. I told you that as long as the tendency of the mind is downward, it is our enemy. When its tendency becomes upward, it is our friend. So we are not to use this intellect to destroy the creation of the Lord, or to hate each other, or to destroy each other, or to become the prisoner or the victim of the senses. We are not to use the intellect for that purpose. We have to use the intellect in the right perspective – to seek the Lord, for which this intellect has been given to us. To love the Lord, to love his creation, that is the purpose of the intellect. Intellect is a friend when it leads us back to the Lord, and it is an enemy when it keeps us away from him.

Yesterday I gave an example of the difference between an intellectual and a simple man. I said both of them want to go from Washington to New York. The simple man just asks anybody standing on the roadside for directions to go to New York. As soon as he is told, without making further inquiries, he just starts driving. If anybody else meets him on the way and says, "You are wrong. The road leading to New York is to the right," he just takes that turn. Somebody else comes along and leads him in still another direction, and he just takes that turn. He is so simple that he follows whatever anybody tells him to follow. But the intellectual does not follow, does not pay attention to the first man, whatever he may say. He wants another ten corroborations. Then he will see a map, a guide, to determine whether the nine or ten men have told him the right way leading to New York. Once he is convinced, he drives a little and then he sees a milestone. He is convinced intellectually that this road leads to New York. He has not seen New York yet, but then he does not bother. Once he is convinced, he just drives on. His intellect does not lead him to New York; his driving leads him to New York. But the intellect becomes a help, once it is satisfied.

Intellect in itself is a great barrier in our way. We have to pierce the barrier of intellect with our intellect. That is why all this investigation, all this research. We should never just close our eyes and jump into anything. We must jump with eyes wide open as to what we are going to do. Even if we spend our whole life in trying to understand what we have to follow, I say the time is not lost, it is gained. In so doing, we are just boring down deep for our foundation. We are building on solid rock, and the deeper the foundation, the stronger will be the building. So even if our whole life is spent in trying to understand the right path, we should not feel worried. We should give full time to investigation. We should never jump with eyes closed, never make our decision with emotion or to please our friends, or whatsoever comes our way we at once jump to follow it, for then we are deceived, then we are deluded, then we are unhappy. We must satisfy our intellect to the best of our ability. Whatever the Lord has given us, we must make full use of our intellect, but once we are convinced that this is the right path for us, this is the right guide for us, then we are not to worry with our intellect but should set it aside. What we need then is practice, faith and devotion. That alone will lead us back to him, and not the intellect. So intellect is a friend only if we know how to use it.

323 Master, Sant Mat is very straightforward and scientific. Why is it, then, that the mind entertains so many doubts?

It's very simple. The mind never takes simple things as they are. The mind believes in complicating things and then trying to solve those problems. If you can't solve them, you feel frustrated, and if you solve them, you feel happy. Otherwise, our whole life is so simple. We have complicated so much in this world. What do we need? How many clothes do you need? How much do you eat in a day? In how many places do you need to stay? We have complicated these three necessities of life so much. If we can complicate such simple things to the extent that we have to fight and kill each other just to satisfy these three needs, what to say of Sant Mat, how much we have complicated it. This is the intellect. This is the mind. The mind never accepts a simple thing in a simple way. After all, for what are nations fighting, people fighting? What do they need in life? Living is so simple. Christ has said that the Lord looks after even the insects and the stones.[25] Just to pass a life of a few years, what we don't do! We are sitting on a volcano every day. We are fond of complicating things.

324 How does one know when one is beyond the intellect? Can one be tricked in that also?

We will go beyond the intellect only when we are able to subdue our mind. The intellect is a faculty of the mind. So we have got to control our mind, remove the veil of mind from our way, for then only we go beyond the intellect and know ourselves, as Socrates pointed out when he said: Know thyself.

325 We have a desire for knowledge. Where does that come from?

I don't know what your concept of knowledge is. Real knowledge is only to know the Creator. Real knowledge is to know his creation, know the law which governs the creation and know the law through which we can go back to the Creator.

326 Are wisdom and love divine attributes? Are these not pure, and are they not complementary to one another?

I don't know what your concept of wisdom is. If by wisdom we mean to use our intellect to be one with the Father, then yes. If by wisdom you mean modern civilization, scientific inventions, then it may be contradictory to that love for the Father.

When we are filled with love and devotion for the Father, we get the real wisdom within us. When the mind is in pursuit of the Father, then we get the real intellect, real intelligence, real wisdom. When the mind is running to the senses and is taking us away from the Father, inventing things that destroy his creation, then from the Father's point of view, we are not men of wisdom. This is destroying his creation, not loving his creation. So we have our own concept of wisdom, but what is the right wisdom? Those who have invented bombs, fighters, tanks and guns also call themselves men of wisdom. So much destruction is going on, and they get Nobel prizes and awards. But from his point of view, they're not men of wisdom. A simple person who sees the Lord in everyone, in every part of the creation, he's a man of wisdom. However literate or illiterate he may be, however ignorant from the worldly point of view, he may have the real wisdom.

327 Can the intellect, properly used, feed the fires of love?

Well, sister, satisfaction of the intellect gives you faith. And faith creates that fire of love, and practice strengthens that fire of love. With practice it grows. The intellect doesn't give you the fire of love. To begin with it helps you to follow a path. It creates faith in you. Satisfaction of the intellect creates faith in you. There's no harm in being intellectual because then you can never be deceived. You are building on a rock and you cannot be shaken. A simple person can be easily led astray. He's so simple that he follows everything and everybody, and he doesn't know what is right and wrong. He may be the first to start, but may not have a deep foundation within himself. But once the intellectual person has satisfied his intellect that this is the path for him, nobody can shake him. He is building on a rock.

Real intellect is when the intellectual person uses his intellect in the right way. The people who have made atom bombs, fighters, tanks and guns are also intellectuals, but they're using their intellects to destroy each other, to kill each other. You call them intellectuals? If your intellect leads you towards the Father, to find the Lord, and you see the Father in everybody, you are helpful to society, to humanity, you sacrifice for their sakes, you have become very loving and kind – that is real intellect. It is the same intellect, but it is a question of how you use it.

328 On the subject of Socrates, what does the saying, which has come down to us and attributed to him, mean: He was wise because he knew nothing?

I think the wisest person is he who realizes that he knows nothing. Christ himself said: O Father, you have hid these things from the prudent and from the wise, and you have revealed them to the babes.[44] You see, this ego, this intellect, makes us think we know everything. When we eliminate that ego, we realize we know nothing.

The Lord has given us intellect in order for us to know him, to realize him, to find him. That is why this sense of discretion has been given to us. This discretion is not in animals. The greatness of man is that he has a sense of discretion. And if he doesn't use it in the right way, I think he knows nothing.

It is absolutely useless to have all the knowledge of the world if we do not know the Creator, who is within every part of his creation. When we know the Creator, then we realize that we know absolutely nothing. It is the Creator who knows everything. That's what Socrates was trying to say.

If you're full of ego or intellect, this will keep you from the real wisdom, from the spiritual experience and spiritual truth which the Lord has put within every one of us. He was probably trying to convey: I have realized the fact that I am nothing; in that is my greatness, because I see the Creator within myself, I see the purpose of his creation. I see the Creator everywhere in this world. I can do that only when I have been able to eliminate my ego and my intellect. That is the real knowledge, real wisdom. It isn't worldly wisdom.

Ego

329 Could you explain humility to us? I don't think that we Westerners understand humility.

Well, brother, we can only get humility when we are able to eliminate the ego. Ego comes out of the mind, so unless the soul leaves the mind, we can never realize the real humility at all. When we are able to eliminate the ego, then we are filled with humility because there is always humility in the soul, but there is none in the mind. Mind always wants to assert itself. It does not want to submit to anybody at all.

When we are able to purify our mind, and the soul gets released from the mind, only then can we realize or taste true humility. And humility has the characteristic of love because by it one merges back into the Father – one merges back into the other being. You want to lose your own individuality and become the other being. So unless we are filled with humility, we cannot merge back into the Father at all.

As long as the mind is in control, it always wants to be the master. Mind does not want to be the slave – it does not want to surrender to anyone. The mind always feels: I am better than everybody in the world; I am superior to everybody. So unless the mind becomes pure, unless we are able to eliminate the ego, we cannot be filled with humility.

330 I have often wondered about the meaning of "the meek shall inherit the earth."[1]

That means that meekness and humility are essential qualities for going back to the Lord. Meekness truly means elimination of our ego, of our self-importance. This ego holds us down and does not let us merge into the Lord. When humility comes in its place, we merge into the Lord and inherit the kingdom of heaven.

This ego is mostly the result of our attachment to things and objects of this world. Christ said that it is more likely for a camel to pass through the eye of a needle than for a rich man to enter the kingdom of heaven.[61] By 'a rich man' he did not mean a man of wealth, but one who is attached to the riches [things and objects] of this world. It means that those who are attached to worldly possessions and relationships cannot enter the kingdom of heaven. It is, in fact, these attachments that keep us away from the Lord and bring us back into this world again and again. In translations and interpretations by different men in authority, much of the true teaching is always lost.

331 Master, why is it that primitive people seem to be able to accept their destiny?

Because through so-called civilization, people have been able to develop their ego, so they don't believe in destiny. They have built up their ego so much that they think that nobody can make them do anything at all – it is through our effort that we have achieved everything, and with our effort we will be able to achieve everything. They have built up that much ego. The other people perhaps didn't get the chance to build up that ego so much.

We have become quite self-centred in modern civilization, and when we become self-centred, we become more egoistic. We don't feel the need for anybody at all. Then the habit of submission, resignation, is not there. We become very egoistic by becoming self-centred. Society, with its modern, scientific achievements to its credit, is becoming more and more self-centred every day. So we find it very difficult to come together, to understand each other. We are very good friends on the telephone, but if we are put together for ten minutes, we'll start quarrelling. We find it very hard to adjust to each other. That is why we have so many broken homes, broken families – parents, children, sister, brother – because everybody is becoming self-centred, they think they don't need anybody at all. That spirit of obedience and respect for elders and love for the younger people is going. So we are building ego through this so-called civilization. I may be wrong, but that is my analysis.

So we're digging our own graves? Is that what ego does?

Ego is a block between us and God. It is a definite block and a very solid block. Without elimination of ego, the question of meeting the Lord doesn't arise at all, because God is love. Love means submission. Love means losing your own identity. Love means becoming another being. Love means that the other one exists – you don't exist at all. Ego is just the reverse: Only you exist, and nobody else exists at all. They're poles apart. In ego you want other people to love you; in love you want to love another person. You want to submit to another person. You want to eliminate your individuality in another being. In ego you want other people to respect you, to love you, to praise you. The ego makes you think you're much higher than everybody. In love there's always submission.

332 Master, yesterday in the satsang, it was said that anger, lust and greed all come from ego. Would you comment on that?

The five perversions are all expressions of ego. Lust generally goes with anger. You can't say that you have no anger if you are a victim of lust. They generally go together, and all these five perversions are combined together in ego. We are attached to them. Through them we are attached to the creation, and that is ego.

333 Actually, it is the mind and not the soul that does not want to give up its identity?

That is right. Mind is the stumbling block. This ego does not like to lose its identity. We always want to observe that I am so-and-so, I am so-and-so, and it is the I-ness that we do not want to lose. We perhaps think that we have developed it in this modern world and that it is something quite unique; but the fact remains that the ego is a great stumbling block in our way. This is what we have to lose.

334 When we speak of 'I' this, 'I' that, is this particular personality speaking, is this a true 'I' speaking or is this a false 'I'?

Brother, it is mind that is speaking. All that we say is mine is 'I', is of the mind. Our soul is dominated by the mind. Mind has ego, and that ego brings the I-ness in us. But when the soul will have the upper hand over the mind, then everything will be thine. You see, absence of ego is all yours, meaning the Lord's; with ego, it is all mine.

Carry this a little further. Now, if we say I read a certain book, for instance, or I say I am going to do this, I am going to do that or I am going to get initiation, or I think this and so on; what is this? This has to be the soul making that decision, does it not? Mind would not want us to do that, would it?

Do not confuse language with I-ness. This is our way of speaking: "I am going to do ..." It is a mode of expression. But the I-ness, the instinct of possession, the ego, that is something different.

I see. In other words, then, whenever we use this personal pronoun, it does not mean that it is the ego or the false 'I' speaking?

No. When I say, "I am going today," it does not mean the ego is speaking. It is just an expression. After all, this body has to be referred to as something. But I-ness is something different. That is the instinct of possession: mine – "this is mine," "this is my son," "this is my wife," "this is my country," "this is my wealth." When the instinct of possession overpowers you, that is I-ness.

335 How is it that we can erase this veil of ego since, especially in this Western civilization, the 'I' seems to be the dominant pronoun? Can we erase it by praying with a 'we', with the thought of being united with others within?

Brother, first, I assure you that ego is not more in you or in the West than it is in Indians. You have the instinct of possession because you have possessions. We have the instinct of possession because we are trying to get them. We do not have them. But as far as the ego is concerned, it is the same here, it is the same there. There is absolutely no difference. Some people have possessions and some people are dying to get them; but practically, the ego is the same. It is the attitude of the mind. The ego is the instinct of the mind, so we have to conquer our mind. We have to subdue our mind before we can drive the ego from us. As I have said so many times, the mind is fond of pleasures. Unless we give our mind better pleasures than the pleasures of the senses, the mind never leaves the desire and craving for possessions in this world. Therefore, saints always advise us to withdraw our mind by simran, by dhyan, back to the eye centre and to attach it to that sound, to see that light. When we are attached to that, we are automatically detached from the senses, the desires and cravings for possessions.

The Lord has provided the means of attachment within us. When we attach ourselves to that, we automatically detach ourselves from the worldly things and worldly objects and faces. The ego will naturally, automatically, go out of us. Then we are not attached to this world. Then we are attached to that love, to that nam, to that shabd. Devotion to the Lord comes in. When devotion to the Lord comes in, that devotion, that faith, that love of the Lord drives everything else out of us. So we have just to develop that devotion, develop that love of the Lord within us. When that love is there, the question of ego does not arise. After all, mind is the same, whether you pull it down or whether you take it up. When the mind is up, it cannot be pulled down.

Then the way of diminishing the dominance of the ego, aside from that in ordinary life, is to think in universal terms?

The only process of driving out ego from within us is to attach ourselves to that sound, attach ourselves to that light. Unless we are attached to that shabd or nam, we can never detach ourselves from this world, from nation, friends, relatives, possessions, gold, dollars. Only attachment can create detachment. When the mind is attached to something better than the senses, then we do not have ego in us. Ego is in us only as long as the love of the Lord is not in us. When the love of the Lord takes its place, there is no place left for ego.

336 *I am a little bit confused. Do I understand that you speak of God as a separate entity, not dwelling within us, or someone that we pray to on the outside? My thought has always been that God lives within us?*

God is within everything in this universe. He is within us. Yet, though within us, he is still away from us. So we have to remove that barrier of away-ness from us. He is within us. When we realize him within ourselves, we will find the Lord everywhere. But unless we find him within, we will never find him without. God is not to be found outside. He is within us, but we do not see him within ourselves. We have got to remove this veil of ignorance which is between our soul and the Lord. The soul is within the body; the Lord is within the body. Yet the soul does not see the Lord. We have a veil or a barrier of mind between the soul and the Lord. We have to remove this ego, this mind, which is the obstacle in the way. Then only can the soul see the Lord within, and when we see the Lord within ourselves, wherever we look, we will see nothing but the Lord. That is what I was trying to explain by saying that the nearer we are to the Lord, the nearer we are to each other. The more we are away from the Lord, the more we find ourselves away from each other. We cannot come together on any political or economic or social platform. At least history does not encourage us. Only on a spiritual platform can we all come together. We are together. We are one. We can still become one. So when we realize him within, wherever we look we will find nothing but the Lord.

337 Individualism is central to the Western philosophical framework. In your view, what is the right use of individualism?

This – our so-called individuality – is keeping us away from the Father. This individuality is nothing but our ego. As long as the ego is there, the soul is separated from its source. When we are able to eliminate that ego, we eliminate our individuality, we merge into the supreme being. From there, we came at the time of creation. It's very difficult for an intellectual man to lose his individuality, because he has done so much towards maintaining it. But actually this very individuality – or in other words ego – stands in our way to our destination. With the help of that spirit or holy word within we have to eliminate that ego.

And ego is the offspring of the mind. So, unless our mind is pure, unless we are able to subdue the mind, the soul can never get release from the mind. And unless the soul leaves the mind, it can never merge back into its own source. So we have to lose our individuality.

Even in the world, when you love somebody, you always want to become the other being. You don't wish the other person to live according to your will – you always like to live in his will. You always like to do what pleases him. You never try to do what displeases him. You want to lose your individuality. You want to become another being. And you become another being. Love makes you do that. Similarly, by love and devotion for the Father, we lose our individuality, and we become the supreme being. We become the Father. So unless we lose our individuality, unless we lose our ego, we will not be able to achieve our destination. We will not be able to go back to the Father.

ATTACHMENT AND DESIRES

338 It has been said that detachment can come only through attachment. My question is: Should desires of the physical world be satisfied or fulfilled to get to the state of detachment?

No. By fulfilling your worldly desires, you will not be able to get detached from the world. The more fuel you put on the fire, the more it blazes. The more you desire these worldly things, the more hungry and thirsty you become for them. By trying to satisfy these worldly desires, you will never be able to detach yourself.

Unless you are attached to something better, it will be impossible to detach yourself from the world because the mind is fond of pleasure. Unless it gets something more pleasurable, it will remain attached to worldly pleasures. It always wants more and more, more and more variety. But when you are able to attach yourself to the spirit and get the pleasure of the nectar within yourself, you will find that pleasure so fulfilling and satisfying that you will automatically become detached from the senses; and that attachment will be able to detach you from the world. Not otherwise.

339 Is it even possible to fulfil our desires here?

Desires can never be fulfilled. If you go on putting wood in the fire, the fire will always go on burning. If you stop feeding it with fuel, naturally there won't be any fire.

You try to fulfil one or two desires, and the mind creates another twenty. We make a list of twenty, and the mind creates another thirty.

Desires can never be fulfilled. The mind has to rise above these desires and learn to live in the will of the Father. Whatever he gives, we should accept with gratitude. He knows best what to give us. We must have faith in him. Whatever he gives, that is for our advantage, and we should accept it. We shouldn't desire anything at all.

340 Maharaj Ji, could you please explain about desires and duty? I tend to get the two slightly confused – not just my desires, but my wife's desires and my friends' desires. For example, if you need a car for your occupation, do you get a Volkswagen, a Buick or a Mercedes-Benz? Where to draw the line between desire and duty?

You want to know the difference between necessity and desire? Well, you have to make up your own mind whether you can afford a Volkswagen or a Buick or a Lincoln. You have to make up your own mind, even whether you can do without all of them. It depends upon you. If you are becoming so obsessed to possess one, and it is bothering you, so have it. If you can afford it, buy one. If you can get rid of your desire and you can't afford the car, get rid of the desire. It depends on so many circumstances, whether we have to fulfil that desire or not. Many desires we have to fight – we don't want to fulfil them. Our mind is always pulling us to these desires, and we have to pull our mind out of them. But certain desires can be fulfilled if we have the economic means to satisfy them. It depends upon one's circumstances. If you have a desire to possess a Lincoln but you have no money in the bank, you shouldn't commit a robbery to buy one. One has to look at one's economic circumstances. Otherwise, you have to withdraw your mind from such desires.

341 Master, if before death a disciple had reached a stage where he has no strong attachments to this world, or feels that he has no strong attachments to this world, and yet has not been able to still his wandering mind, would that disciple have to be given another birth?

It is our attachments that pull us back to the world. As Christ said: If you build your treasure in the world, you come back to the world. If you build your treasure in heaven, you go back to heaven, because where your treasure is, there your heart will be.[22] So our attachments always pull us back to this world. Even if we have not made spiritual progress of any significance at all within ourselves, but we are not attached to this world, nothing can pull us back to this world. But you will not be able to detach yourself from this creation unless you are attached to something better. And that is the sound within, that light within, that holy ghost within. That melody automatically will detach you from this creation and from the senses.

The mind is a slave of the senses and this mind is fond of pleasures. That is why it runs towards the senses. So unless the mind gets something better than the sensual pleasures, it refuses to leave them. That something better is the holy ghost or the spirit within every one of us. When we are able to withdraw our consciousness to the eye centre and are able to hold our consciousness there, then we can be in touch with that spirit and that light. Attachment to that automatically will detach us from this world, from this creation. Then nothing will be able to pull us back to this world. So even if we have not been able to travel on this spiritual path and reach our destination in this lifetime, if we are not attached to anything in this world, then nothing will pull us back. According to our spiritual progress, we will find our place in the inner regions. And from there, slowly and slowly, we will make progress and go back to the Father.

In Saint John, Christ says: I will come and receive you. As there are many mansions in my Lord's house, I will prepare a place for you there.[116] This means, according to his inner progress, the disciple finds a place in those regions. He will escape from birth and death. He will escape from this creation. But he will still have to find a place in those regions before he can merge back into the Father. And from there he will make progress and slowly go back to the Father.

If you are not able to find your destination in this very lifetime, if you are not able to realize the Lord in this very lifetime, you can escape, even then, from birth and death. But you will have to remain in those inner regions in order to make spiritual progress upward. Only then will you become one with the Creator.

342 Should the satsangi who has not made much or any progress internally, at the moment of death, hold a small wish to return to earth in a satsangi family just to start on the path earlier in the next life, since I understand progress after death is more difficult in the beautiful regions above the eye centre?

It is not one particular little wish that can pull us back to this world again. Our desires build up slowly, and then they become so strong, and we become so attached to these desires, that they may be able to pull us back to this world. But when we are attached to the shabd and nam within, then slowly, slowly all these desires are washed out or they are fulfilled in one way or another. Or we become desireless by the time of our death. If we are attached to the world, whether we have made any spiritual progress or not, or even if we have made some spiritual progress but if we have very strong desires, strong attachments to this world, then we may very likely be pulled back to the level of those desires, those attachments.

Actually, it is attachment which brings us back; it pulls us back to this world. But we can only detach ourselves from these attachments or from these desires when we are able to attach ourselves to that holy spirit within ourselves. Without the help of that holy spirit, that shabd, that nam, it's very difficult for us to detach ourselves from this world or from these worldly desires.

343 What would constitute final liberation? Is it final liberation once you get there, or is final liberation the elimination of all desires on a lower plane?

Final liberation is explained generally from two points of view. One is, as far as birth and death are concerned, that we get liberated from that even if sometimes we cross only the first stage. This is so, providing that we have a competent master to save us from birth and death, if we are thoroughly attached to the shabd or nam, and we have no attachments left for anything in this world and have been able to clear all those attachments. We may not have made much progress inside yet, as far as the spiritual path is concerned, but as far as physical bondage is concerned, we will be saved from birth and death; however, we have yet a long distance to cover to go back to the Lord, to go back and merge into him. So we can only call it final liberation when the soul merges back into the Lord. But as far as final physical liberation is concerned, that you can achieve even if you have not progressed much inside, as that only depends on how much detachment from this world you have achieved. If you have cleared your attachments and you do not have very strong desires to bring you back into this world, you are saved as far as this physical bondage is concerned. But unless the soul merges back into the Lord, it can still drop back again.

So final liberation can only be when the soul merges back into the Lord; but from birth and death we do sometimes escape, even if we cross only the first stage, or even if we have not crossed the first stage but we have a perfect master and we do not have very strong desires or very strong attachments with the world. For example, if you are attached to a bulldozer, naturally you will be drawn wherever the bulldozer goes. So if we have attachments in the world, they will pull us back. If we are attached to the shabd or the master, our attachment to him automatically takes us back to our own home. But we may still have a lot of karmas to clear and a long journey to travel, and sometimes we do it after death, providing that we have been put on the path during our lifetime and have no desires that will bring us back into this world.

344 How can we know what our attachments are?

At the last moment they come to the surface. Many attachments just fade out – they don't possess you at all, you are not obsessed by them at all. But many attachments linger on, even in the subconscious mind, and you feel you are being possessed by them. You can't get rid of them – they have made such a strong groove on your mind. Those attachments definitely will pull you back. Many attachments are just on the surface – they come and go. But some make very deep grooves on the mind, and if you are not able to rise above them, they may pull you back. Meditation definitely helps us to rise above them. They become meaningless to us. Those very faces or things we thought we could not live without, we don't want to see them, we are not even attached to them.

345 *Are we usually conscious of our strongest attachments or sometimes are they so subtle that even if we're as honest as possible within ourselves, we still don't really know how attached we are inside?*

You see, there are many types of attachments. Some attachments fade out after some time and they don't leave any mark on our mind at all. And there are certain attachments which go with you right to the end of your life. You can't get rid of them, and even if you try to forget, they remain in your subconscious mind and spring up whenever they get the opportunity.

Can you give an example?

Suppose a person is very conscious of becoming rich, but he's been able to intellectually convince himself that he doesn't need much money. But to become rich remains in his subconscious mind, and he can't get rid of the idea though he has intellectually convinced himself that he doesn't need so much money. But that impression remains on his mind, and it may rise again at the time of his death, which can pull him back to the riches of the world. This is a crude example, but certainly in this way some sorts of attachments remain in your subconscious, which you sometimes can't get rid of. These desires are attachments. You want to fulfil a certain desire, but you can't, and slowly and slowly that desire is making a groove in your mind and can pull you back to its own level.

So is it a good idea, then, to try to go with your desires – if you want something, to let yourself have it?

No. It doesn't mean that by fulfilling a desire you have not created a karma. It doesn't mean that if you desire something and you do it, you'll be able to get rid of that desire. You have still sown a seed, and you may have to come back to reap its fruit.

Which is worse?

Both are worse. They are equally bad. If there is only a desire and you have not stooped to its level to fulfil it, there is a possibility that you can get rid of that desire by meditation and it will fade out. But if you've already sown a seed, then it is not in your hand not to reap its result. There are many desires sometimes that we feel are very strong in us, but at some point they may just become meaningless to us. At that time, they are very strong, but after a few months they become absolutely meaningless. So it is always a safer policy to refrain from giving in to these desires.

So you're saying that it's never good to use the excuse, "Well, I should fulfil this desire."

That is correct. It's wrong.

346 Is there such a thing as negative attachment to people whom one dislikes intensely? Will that bring us back to that situation again?

Do you mean hatred?

A negative attachment. We talk about attachment to things we love, but is there such a thing as negative attachment?

Hatred is another form of love. When we hate anybody, we are actually in love with him; otherwise, we would never hate him. How could others affect us if we were not concerned about them, if we did not bother about them, if we never thought about them? When you hate a person, you are always thinking about that person. You cannot drive that man out of your mind, you hate him so much. You are not analyzing yourself, for actually you are in love with him. You have not been able to make him according to your wishes, so you hate him; but all the time you are in love with him or you would not even be thinking about him. We have to drive that feeling out of us. We are just to forget all about it. Then the question of hatred does not arise in us. By hating anybody, we are attaching ourselves to him.

347 *To get to the point, these desires, according to your discourse, are tied in with our intellect and our senses. I read in some philosophies that we must eliminate all desires if we are going to reach this point. Yet it seems like we must retain a desire for this, which would seem to be a conflict?*

You mean the desire to meet the Lord? When the devotion or the real longing and desire to merge back into the Lord will come in you, all other desires will be automatically driven out of you. You have to create that desire, just to merge back into him; that desire should always be there. We have to channel our consciousness into that direction.

Then one ends up with a desire?

Yes, the longing, the love, the strong desire to return to him. For the lovers of the Lord, their only religion is love. They do not bind themselves to any particular religion. They believe only in the religion of love, which comes only from within and not from without. So it is immaterial to them whether you go to a church or to a temple or to a mosque. Their only concern is the real longing and love and devotion for the Lord. That comes by spiritual practice. That is what they want and that is what is required of us. That is the only thing which will lead us back to him, and that longing, that love, that desire we should always entertain.

348 Should one desire to be a master?

You get many things even when you don't desire them. I'm only doing that duty allotted to me by my predecessor. If it were in my hands, I would not stay, even for one second, on this stage.

4

The Soul Has No Religion

Give him any name

349 What is the name of the supreme being?

Give him any name. Call him God if you like. After all, the Lord who is remembered by so many names really has no name. He is also called the nameless one, and his abode is also known as the nameless region.

The relationship of mother and child is that of love, and the mother expresses her love by using different names. But it is the love and not the names which form the link between the mother and the child. All these words are just expressions of the mother's love. She may call him by any name or by a hundred names. The link is love; it's the common blood they share.

Similarly, you may call the Lord by any name. We have so many countries, and every country has so many languages. In one language alone we remember him by different names. Every name is good. Out of love and devotion you may call him by any name. It is the love and devotion that count, not the name. You can give him any name, it makes no difference.

350 Master, you always talk of the Father, and Christ also spoke of the Father. Who is the Father? Is he a person? Is he an entity or is he a power? I thought a power must be owned by a person or by an entity. I don't understand it.

Well, sister, how to name him who has no name at all? You call him Father, because the relationship of the soul and the Father is that of love and the relationship of Father and son is that of love. So Christ called him Father. Because the relationship of the soul and the creative power is that of love, he is known as Father. Some people call him mother; some people call him husband. But one who is known by so many names, a thousand names, has no name at all. He is a creative power, he is an entity. After all, he has to be explained with some word. But his power can't be limited at all.

Can he be seen inside?

You have to experience him. He is a being. When you cannot see yourself, how can you see the Creator? Seeing is what you see with these outside eyes. Hearing is what you can hear with your outside ears. Neither can he be seen with the outside eyes, nor can he be described with this tongue, nor can he be heard with outside ears. That is why Christ said, having eyes you see not, having ears you hear not.[69] And yet we are supposed to see him; we are supposed to hear him. There is another faculty which sees him, which hears him. We can't call it even a faculty. But these things have to be described, have to be explained. When we cannot explain the faculties of the soul, how can we explain the faculties of the Lord, the Creator? But he has to be referred to somehow. Sometimes people call him God or Allah. After all, these are the names we have given out of our love. Our relationship with him is that of love. Some people call him love. Even love cannot be described by words. It has to be experienced.

Christ said, God is love[136] – the word is God.[72] That word cannot be described because it is God, and God cannot be described. So this word also cannot be described. If God cannot be described, how can the word be described, when it is God? So we have to experience it. Many mystics say, if you ask a dumb person about the taste of honey, what can he say? So we are dumb – our language is a very poor expression for what he is. And yet there is no other media by which mystics can explain him to us. So Christ called him Father. As we love our father and a father protects his children, so God protects us. Sons look to the father for all types of protection, all types of help. So we look to him – whatever he may be – for all types of protection, all types of help. So we call him Father. Many mystics call him husband. Christ called him the bride. Some people call him bridegroom. These are just different ways of talking about the creative power which cannot be expressed in words at all.

351 Master, what strength is attached to the words Radha Soami?

It is just a name like any other name. You call the Lord 'God', 'Father' or 'Radha Soami' – there's no difference at all. Radha means the soul, Soami means the Lord – Lord of the soul. Or Radha means the surat, Soami means the shabd – surat shabd yoga. It's same thing, it's just a name for the Father. You see, the Father, who has been given so many thousands of names out of love and devotion by his devotees, actually has no name at all. A mother calls her child by so many names – the relationship of the mother with the child is not that of words but that of love, that of affection. These words only express her love for the child. So similarly the Father has no name at all – he is nameless. But devotees have given so many names to the Father out of their love and devotion for him. So these are just a means to that end. And in the same way, the words Radha Soami have no special significance at all. As you have given so many other names to the Father, so this is also one of the names of the Father.

The soul has no religion

352 *Did our forefathers and ancestors also have religions, and to find God they would have gone on changing their religions?*

I don't know, sister. That's why I asked you what your concept of religion is. If by religion you mean you follow the rituals and ceremonies of that social, political religion, then of course that is something different. If by religion you mean a way to find that path inside, within your body, which is leading back to the Father, then you don't need to change any religion at all. There's only one religion in this world: the religion of love – love of the soul for its own origin, for its own father. To follow that path which can lead us back to the Father – that is our religion.

When you arrest that path into organizations and that path is forgotten and not tread by anyone, then we have so many divisions. Then we are worried about changing religions; but it is immaterial then what religion we follow. Saints neither create any religion nor do they condemn any religion. They only point us to that path which leads back to the Father – you can give any name to that religion. They're not very anxious to give it a name. But followers do give some names to that organization, ultimately, when it grows.

We all know that the Lord is one, that the Lord is within every one of us, that the path leading back to the Lord is also within every one of us, and that we have to seek that path within us in order to find our destination. That is our religion. You can follow that path as a Zoroastrian, a Christian, a Muslim, or a Sikh – it's immaterial. If you're just sitting in your meditation in your skirt, in a sari, in a suit or in any other clothes, it's immaterial.

These religions have become just like clothing. They don't change your essential human values. They do not improve you, nor do they deprive you of anything. Our real religion is within us; it is to follow that path which ultimately takes us back to the Father; and that religion is that of sound and light, which you'll find is given by all mystics of the world if you go deep into their teachings. It is immaterial whether you follow that path by becoming a Christian or a Hindu or a Sikh. Whether you're attending to your meditation in a sari or a skirt, it doesn't make any difference at all. You have to become unconscious of what you are wearing; you have to become unconscious of all the religions in order to follow that path because your path, your meditation, is your main religion.

But we give more importance to these rituals, ceremonies, dogmas, parentage and environments with which we have been brought up because our mind has been conditioned by these things, and it becomes very difficult for us to jump out of these dogmas and rituals. Our religion is devotion to the Father – give any name to that devotion. But our mind becomes so conditioned by the religion in which we have been brought up that unless the same path is shown to us from the point of view of that religion, we refuse to follow it. Christians, if you show them the same path from the Bible, they'll follow it at once; if you show Sikhs the same path from the Granth, they'll follow it at once. The path is the same, but our approaches have become different.

353 Maharaj Ji, could you explain the difference between metaphysics, the universal God, and Sant Mat?

The God of Sant Mat is the same universal God. Sant Mat is the Hindi term for 'the teachings of the saints'. It is no particular religion; it is simply that path which leads us back to the Lord.

The essence of every religion is absolutely the same. We have different rituals and different ceremonies, of course. These are always introduced by the priestly classes after the departure of the founder, because after a certain period, the people forget the real teachings of the saints and lose the essence. All that they pay attention to is just rituals and ceremonies and dogmas. However, that is not actually the teachings of the saints. The teachings of the saints are meant simply to lead us back to the Lord. Every saint tries to tell us that there is one God – there cannot be two – that he has created the whole universe, and that God is within every one of us. The human form is given to us just for the purpose of realizing the Lord within our own body. And we have to search for the Lord within us, because this body also is referred to by various saints as the temple of the living God.

If the Lord resides within us, naturally the path leading to the Lord must be within us. If anything is lost in our house, we must search in the house to find it. If we start searching outside instead of inside, we cannot be successful in our search. If the Lord is within us, the path leading to the Lord must also be within us. We therefore have to search for that path within ourselves. And unless we tread on that path, unless we make a research on that path, naturally we cannot be led to the Lord, our true source or home. It is clearly stated in the Bible that Christ also referred to this body as the temple of the living God.[132] He also taught us to search within. He said: Knock and it shall be opened unto you.[29] We have to knock at the door of our house, our body, the door being the eye centre and the knocking at the door being our meditation, as instructed by the master at the time of initiation. When our attention is fully concentrated at the door, it is opened for us and we travel on the path by means of sound and light, through many mansions in our Father's house, and ultimately we merge into the one God.

354 *Maharaj Ji, on the first three days of Punjabi satsang, I kept hearing a few sentences a few times in English,*

and whenever I hear that, it makes me feel that there's something special I need to hear. So I'd like you, if you would, to speak briefly about the two sentences that I kept hearing. The first one was: "Though I have eyes I see not, and though I have ears, I hear not." And the other one was: "Blessed are those who mourn, for they will be comforted."

Well, brother, as is my habit, perhaps due to being a lawyer in my past, whatever I say I like to corroborate by giving so many quotations from different saints. First, having eyes you see not, having ears ye hear not;[69] this is to explain that divine melody and divine light within. Every mystic, every saint has tried to explain to us that this sound, this light cannot be seen with these eyes, cannot be heard with these ears, and that it cannot be written by these hands. They are different eyes with which we see that light, they are different ears with which we hear that shabd, hear that melody within. So I give quotations from Christ to confirm what I say. And I also give so many quotations from many other mystics and saints.

I also quote Christ as saying that the relationship of the soul and the Father is that of love.[137] This relationship is not based on any religion, any caste, any creed – it's just based on love and devotion. Every soul has the inclination towards the Father, is a drop of that divine ocean, is in love with that divine ocean. Unless it merges back into that Father, it will never get peace. And those who are yearning to go back to the Father, those who are full with love and devotion for the Father, only they are the blessed ones who will get peace ultimately, when they will go back into the lap of the Father. Without that love and devotion within us, no matter whether we are Hindu, Muslim, Christian or Sikh, nobody's entitled to go back to the Father.

Nobody is going to bother there whether you were a Christian, a Sikh, a Hindu, or a Muslim, nobody will ask you these questions. There what is judged is our love, the intensity of our love, our desire to go back to the Father, how strong our inclination is to go back to the Father, how much we have been able to withdraw from the senses, withdraw from the riches of the world, withdraw from this creation, and how anxious we are to go back to the Father. Those things will be weighed there. Our baptism will not be seen there; our religion will not be considered there; what type of dress we used to wear; from which country we have come; what colour we carried with us; what honourable degrees we had all through our life – nobody is going to bother about these things. All that counts is that love and devotion for the Father.

In that capacity I do refer to Christ. He said: God is love. Similarly, I quote him saying: Blessed are those that mourn, for they shall get comfort.[8] Every mystic has said this, every saint has said the same things again and again. Guru Nanak said: Only that wife can please her husband who has two qualities in her. First, she has great love for her husband. Second, she doesn't do anything to offend her husband. She talks the language of her husband, she always does that which pleases the husband, she never does anything which displeases the husband. Similarly, only that soul can please the Father who is full of love and devotion for the Father and who doesn't offend the Father with any excuse, always talks the language of the Father, and never acts in a way which can offend or hurt the Father, and so never hurts even his creation, lest he may be offended by our actions. The soul always does those actions which please the Father. Only that soul which is adorned with these two qualities is entitled to go back to the Father.

I quote so many mystics, just to elaborate that particular point, because in this modern time we lay so much emphasis on our religion. Whether you are Hindu or a Sikh or a Muslim or a Christian, people think that if I become a member of only this particular religion, only then can I be saved. So they are more worried about the conversion list rather than being filled with any devotion and love for the Father. But these things won't count there in his court. All that counts there is love and devotion for the Father. All these religions are concerned only with our body. Our religion, caste and colour will either be burnt along with the body, or they will just merge into the dirt. Nobody is going to bother about these things.

The soul has no religion. The soul has no colour, no creed. It is a drop of that divine ocean. We have to let it grow in love and love and love and love so that it will become one with the Father. The Lord has created humans. We have divided ourselves into so many religions, so many castes, so many creeds; and religion has become the base of so many countries, so much strife, so many wars, and we have become bloodthirsty, cutting each others' throats. Religion is the cause of all that. How can these religions take us back to the Father? The real thing which religions should fill us with they've absolutely forgotten. We have closed our God into brick and mortar, and every weekend we open the locks. We collect there. We talk about things for half an hour, collect money and come back home, satisfied that we have done our job as a member of that religion. These things are not going to count. We don't have to search for him in bricks and the mortar and water and jungles. He's right within us. We have to search for him within, nowhere outside at all. The Lord has given us a complete temple in which to search for him. That is generally the subject matter in which these references come.

355 Can people find spirituality through religion in these times?

For the lovers of the Lord, their only religion is love. They do not bind themselves to any particular religion. They believe only in the religion of love, which comes only from within and not from without. So it is immaterial to them whether you go to a church or to a temple or to a mosque. Their only concern is the real longing and love and devotion of the Lord. That comes by spiritual practice. That is what they want and that is what is required of us. That is the only thing which will lead us back to him, and that longing, that love, that desire we should always entertain.

It is not by becoming a Christian, or that from a Christian you become a Sikh or a Muslim. This conversion, this change of religion does not entitle us to go back to the Lord. The love, the longing, the desire to merge back into him, our spiritual practice, that alone entitles us to merge back into him, regardless of one's religious denomination. Saints give absolutely no importance as to what religion you belong to. They do not believe in conversion. Religions, as they exist today, are not practical religions from a purely spiritual point of view, as the essence has been lost, the truth has been lost. These religions are concerned mainly with increasing the number of converts from a commercial point of view. But the saints are concerned only with the human values of love and devotion for the Lord. The saints are open to everybody, always. No saint comes into the world to create a new religion or to tell you about a new practice or method for reaching the Lord. There are no short cuts here. It is the same path which was, is and will remain. Those who want to go back to him have to follow the same path. It is as old as the human race, and is only for those who long for him, desire to go back to him, want to seek him within. It is not for those who want to seek him outside.

356 Master, is there an incompatibility between one's own religious beliefs, like being Jewish, and becoming a satsangi?

Well, brother, I don't know. If by religious beliefs, you mean you really know the religion, then there is no difference at all if you become a satsangi. If by religion you mean organized religion, the bundle of rituals and ceremonies or misguided beliefs in which you have been brought up, then there may be a difference. But there also may be a difference between Christianity and the teachings of Christ. You will not move away from the teachings of Christ if you become a satsangi. But you may move away from Christianity if you become a satsangi.

There may be a difference between his teachings and the shape which has been given to his teachings today. So by becoming a satsangi, I don't think we have to leave our beliefs. But we do have to understand those beliefs in depth. We know the real beliefs which we have to follow, which we have to practice. I think if you follow the path you become a better Jew, you become a better Christian, you become a better Sikh; because every mystic has come to share the same spiritual truth with us. And the teaching of every mystic is the same.

If you try to find the path within yourself, then it is the same path which every seeker has to follow. If you try to find the Lord outside, then naturally you will just have an illusion of a path according to your own mental concept. You won't get anywhere at all. It won't take you to your source. If you try to follow the path within, then I don't think you'll deviate from your religious belief at all. But if you have been trying to search for the Lord outside first, and now, after becoming a satsangi, you are trying to find him within, then naturally you have to discard your old beliefs.

No mystic has ever told us to find the Lord anywhere outside. If the Lord is the same, and he has created everyone alike, and he is within every one of us, and we have to seek him within ourselves, then naturally the path leading to him cannot be two. It has got to be one. For those who search for him within, there is only one path. They may call themselves Christians or Jews, but as long as they are following that path within themselves, they are going to the same destination. There is no difference between them.

357 Are we all the same?

Yes, on the spiritual level there is no difference at all. People are always trying to get together on some social, political or economic platform, but they can never get together that way. However, if they would try to come together on a spiritual platform, then there would be no difference between them, because that platform is the same for everybody. Every soul has a yearning to go back to the Creator, and if people realize this fact and come on to a spiritual platform, then there would be no difference between anyone. But since that is not the will of the divine Father, they will never meet together as one.

Even on a religious platform they will never be able to come together as one, but they can come closer to each other. They can only become one on a spiritual platform and not on a religious platform, because organized religion has distorted the teachings of the mystics and saints and has exploited their teachings and given them different names, which we call Christianity, Hinduism, Buddhism, Islam, and so forth.

Christ never came to lay the foundation of Christianity. Buddha never came to lay the foundation of Buddhism. Neither did Nanak come to lay the foundation of any religion. They just came to share their spiritual truths with us. Their main purpose was to fill us with love and devotion for the Father and take us back to him. They didn't come to found religions. But after their death, people forgot their real teachings and established religions and started fighting and quarrelling with one another. So how can we come together on the basis of any religion? But if we try to grasp the real teachings of those mystics, we can all come together on one platform. However, since not everybody is destined to be filled with his love and devotion, everyone will not be able to be on the same level.

358 Would you be kind enough to explain the difference between the modern Buddhist religion and Sant Mat?

Sant Mat, brother, is no religion at all. It is the teachings of the saints, and by 'saints' is not meant a particular saint but all saints of the world. As I often say, the teachings of all the saints are the same. All the religions that we see have different types of rituals and ceremonies, but the essence of spirituality at the base of every religion is absolutely the same – it is not different. Saints are only concerned with the essence, the spirituality of the teachings. They are not concerned with the rituals and ceremonies.

Rituals and ceremonies generally come after the saints leave, when the organizations come and society takes over, when the priestly class and the professions come in. Then it becomes ritual and ceremony just to hold the masses, to hold the public. But the saints never bind us to any ritual and ceremony. They are concerned only with the real teachings of spirituality. Sant Mat literally means the teachings of the saints, not of any one particular saint. But whosoever has risen to that status, that height, his teachings are bound to be the same. They cannot be different, because if the Lord is one and resides within every one of us, we must search for him within the body. We cannot find him outside the body, and naturally the path leading to the Lord cannot be different. It must be the same. We human beings are all made alike, and if we have to search within, it is impossible and illogical to think that, physically alike as we all are, there is one way inside for Christians and another for Hindus and Sikhs. The path is one, though rituals or ceremonies may differ.

Buddha must have taught the same things which the other saints have taught us for attaining God-realization, but with the passage of time, the real teachings were lost. Only organizations and groups and so many other things are left, and they then make their own interpretations of the teachings of Buddha, and for that matter, of all other saints. That interpretation may be very different and far from the real teachings of Buddha or, as I find, of Christ or of Guru Nanak or of any other saint. The real teachings are something very different from what is being told through the organizations and churches and temples.

If, with an unbiased mind, we try to make some research and go deep to the foundation of different religions, we will find the same teachings in all of them. There can be absolutely no difference. Buddha believed in light and so did Christ. I often go to Buddhist temples and find their rituals to be absolutely the same as that in the churches or in the Hindu temples, or other temples. They have an everlasting light as they call it, a vigil light or candle. They always keep it lit – they do not let it go out – and that is a symbol to explain to us that light, that inner flame, inside here. [Maharaj Ji pointed to his forehead.] They also produce the sound of the conch while others use a bell, the sound of which is the same as that produced in the churches. The same light is produced in the churches and the same sound is produced in Sikh, Hindu and Jewish temples.

These rituals are the same, and they denote the same teachings of the saints, but we have forgotten those teachings and have become slaves of these rituals. The symbolic meaning we do not understand. So Buddhism as it is now may have a different thing to tell us, may be very different from the teachings of Sant Mat. But the real teachings of Buddha cannot be different from those of Sant Mat or of Christ. The real teachings of Christ are exactly the same as the teachings of Sant Mat. But as the teachings of Buddha or Christ are given to us today, we may find vastly different interpretations because the real teachings have been lost and forgotten. Only symbols, rituals, dogmas and priests are left with us – meaningless relics, debris of ages.

The difficult problem with the Bible is that Christ himself never wrote it; otherwise we might have had a true interpretation of his teachings. It was most probably written by followers of the apostles and that too not at the same time when he was delivering his lectures – probably long after he had left, and some of the apostles, besides, were not so fortunate as to have come in personal contact with Christ. Through his disciples they got his teachings, which you find in the Bible, but these teachings are not complete. Most of them have been suppressed. The teachings of the apostles were written as if they were from Christ, and also they have come down to us today through so many translations that 80 or 90 percent of them have been lost.

If the teachings had been written by Christ or somebody had taken notes of his teachings, they would have been pure Sant Mat. Those teachings would have been far different from what we have today. For example, you have just heard my discourse. It is only ten minutes since you heard it. If you go to a room to put on paper what you have heard, probably you may be able to reproduce with your best intelligence and efforts only 50 percent of what you have heard, and 50 percent will be your own wishful thinking, what you think had been said. Then if that discourse is to be translated into many languages, there will be left hardly 20 percent of it.

The problem with the Bible is that nobody took notes at that time. So many things were suppressed by the church and by interested peoples. Only that much is given to us which can keep us under their hold. As a result, there are so many missing links in the Bible. So in order to understand the Bible, we have to make a very thorough research to enable us to know the real teachings of Christ. Just by reading the Bible, you will not know his real teachings. But still, whatever is given to us today, if mystically we try to understand it, we definitely come to the conclusion that there is no difference between Sant Mat and the Bible.

359 Master, you just now spoke of the term 'light'. Can you tell us how it is to be understood? Can you just define it for us, what you mean by light?

With the help of the sound we have to find the direction of our house. With the help of the light we have to follow that path back to our house. For example, let's say from your house you go out for a long walk in the evening and it becomes pitch dark and you forget the direction of your own house. What do you do? You try to hear some sort of sound or voice coming from your house. Hearing that voice, you try to locate the direction of your house, and then when you try to go back towards your house there may be signposts: a fence, a barn, maybe another house and a yard. If you have a flashlight in your hand, with the help of that light you can see the way and go back to your own house. So, similarly, we have forgotten our real house, the house of our Father.

Father has kept a sound within every one of us. Father has kept a light within every one of us. When we come to this eye centre, we hear that sound. By hearing that sound we will know the direction of our house, and we will also see the light. By the help of that light we will follow that path. The soul has two aspects: the power to hear and the power to see. The power to hear is known in our Indian language as *surat*. The power to see is known as *nirat*. Surat hears the shabd, nirat sees the light. So we will hear the shabd and we'll also see the light.

You read in Saint John where he refers to that sound. He says, the word has created this whole universe.[72] And then he says, you do not know from where the wind bloweth, whether from the right or from the left.[78] I don't remember the exact words, but he very clearly talks about the sound, and he says you cannot know in the beginning from which direction it is coming. And then he talks about the light. He says, if your eye be single your whole body shall be full of light.[23] So we have to open that third eye, we have to withdraw back our consciousness to this eye centre. And when we open this eye, that single eye, that third eye, then we see the light within.

Every saint has talked about that light, that shabd or word. You go to a church: At the top of a church there is a bell. You always ring that bell before you start the service. And then you go into the church and what you see are candles – you will find the same thing in our temples. Every temple has a bell. You strike the bell and you go in, you will find candle lights inside, lamps being burned inside. You go to a mosque, and you will find the same thing there. You go to any Sikh temple, you will find the same thing there. The idea behind all this is that this body is a real temple, and we have to search for the sound and the light within this temple. Unless we make a search within this temple, we can never hear that sound, we can never see that light. Ultimately we have to go back to our Father with the help of that sound and light. And that light, that sound is within every one of us, irrespective of caste and creed.

Arresting the teachings

360 Master, two days ago when you were in satsang you were speaking about the golden frame or words like that. Could you tell us what you were talking about?

You see, there are two aspects of every religion: mode of living and spirituality. Spirituality is at the base of every religion. Then slowly and slowly, when it takes the shape of a religion, it also takes the shape of a mode of living. You can always distinguish a Muslim from a Hindu from a Sikh just by their mode of living. But the spirituality at the base of every religion is the same. I was trying to emphasize a point, that this mode of living has been made by us, and spirituality is imparted by the teaching. The teaching of every mystic is the same. But the mode of living differs with every religion, because we are the makers of that. And the mode of living is meaningful only when the spirituality is there. Without the spirituality in that religion, the mode of living becomes meaningless.

Say a painting or a picture is very beautiful – it's only then that the frame looks beautiful. Without the painting or a picture, a simple golden frame just looks ridiculous, it is nothing. It has no value. Its value is only along with the painting, along with the picture. Or you have beautiful jewellery; generally you keep it in beautiful cases. But without the jewellery, however beautiful those cases are, they are meaningless. So if the spirituality is lost in any religion and only the mode of living is left, it is meaningless. It's useless. It is only useful as long as the spirituality is there at the base of the religion. When the spirituality is lost, then simply following the mode of living leads you nowhere.

361 Master, what was the golden frame that you were talking about in satsang this morning?

Our organizations, our religions, our rituals, our traditions have meaning only along with spirituality. If the spirituality is lost, then they are just shells, just ceremonies. If the real teaching of Christ is lost, the whole religion becomes a shell. If Guru Nanak's teaching is lost, then that atmosphere which he tried to teach us, and that path which he wanted us to tread is forgotten and is not followed.

Then we are just following the rituals and ceremonies, trying to arrest his teachings into a religion. The ceremonies we perform by going to gurdwaras, temples and churches – they all become meaningless. They have their place along with spirituality if we follow the real teachings, if we live the real teachings. Otherwise all our religions become meaningless, and that spirituality is lost, that atmosphere is gone, and only rituals are left. Then I have to go to church once a week on Sunday, and for rest of the week we lock Christ and his teachings in the church while we come back home. The next Sunday we open it again and close ourselves in there for twenty minutes, and again we come back out and are lost in the world. That's all meaningless.

It is the same with every religion. I'm not referring just to Christianity. People think it is their duty to go every day to a gurdwara, to a temple and to read one book every day and then forget about it for the rest of the day. We don't know what the real teaching was at all. The ritual and our social traditions have become the reason for us to go to these places of worship. My father goes, my mother goes, so I have to go. And what the meaning is behind it, we don't understand.

The value in a mystic's teaching is to follow the teaching of the mystic. Its value doesn't increase by arresting his teachings into a religion. Their teaching is for everybody, for the whole creation. No mystic has said my teaching is just for Christians, just for Jews, just for Sikhs, just for Hindus, just for Muslims. They gave their teachings to everybody. We arrest their teachings into small organizations and then limit them in those rigid organizations, and in order to hold people we have them practice outer ceremonies. Do this, do this, do this, do this, hold to this dogma, hold to that dogma, just to keep them in the organization. The spirituality is lost.

We are cutting each other's throats, we are deceiving each other, betraying each other, hurting each other. Where is the teaching? Religions are fighting with each other. Where is Christ's teaching when we are cutting each other's throat? He said, if anybody slaps you on this cheek, turn the other cheek to him.[18] Where is that teaching? You know the history, what is happening in his name. There are so many schools of thought which are cutting each other's throat in the name of Christ. Has Christ taught us to quarrel or to fight or to kill each other? He never taught that. His teaching has become ritual, ceremony, tradition, organizations and dogmas. They have no meaning without spirituality. Whether the person who follows his teaching strictly is baptized or not is immaterial. Whether he goes to his church or not is immaterial. What matters is whether he is a real follower of Christ, of a mystic or a saint. But we are more interested in the conversion lists and which church we belong to. Nobody bothers with the teaching of the church, nobody tries to follow it.

So I was just harping on that point, you see. We should try to understand the mystics' teaching and try to follow it, try to live it. Don't arrest it into organizations, religions, communities or countries. Their teaching is for everybody. Nobody has a special right to claim that only he is in charge of a mystic's teaching. It belongs to everybody; it belongs to the whole creation. When we try to limit the teaching of the saints, we pull them down. We are not coming up to their level; we are pulling them to our level. Real followers try to go to their level.

362 Master, so many saints have come into the world, and when they've left the world, their followers have started a cult or an organized religion. Will this happen to Sant Mat one day?

Why not? If it's been happening to every mystic's teachings up to now, then why not to Sant Mat? It is already happening. Guru

Nanak came – he spread Sant Mat. Kabir came – he spread Sant Mat. Soami Ji came – he spread Sant Mat. Tukaram came – he spread Sant Mat. What is happening to their teachings now? Jesus taught Sant Mat – what happened to Christianity? So slowly and slowly, only the rituals will be left. The reality will be lost. Spirituality is not the heritage of one particular place or of a particular clan, or a particular line. It has to diminish at a certain point.

But is this through a breaking of the line of masters?

No, it's not a question of breaking. It finishes there and starts from somewhere else again. It's not a question of breaking that line. You see, a river may be flowing in a great spate – day and night the water is flowing. But if you cut its source, it will dry up eventually. As long as it is connected with the source, it's getting water, it will go on flowing. Once you cut it from the source, slowly and slowly the river will dry up. So the same thing happens with a spiritual line; when the source is cut, slowly and slowly it diminishes.

It's not essential that every master must leave a successor. If he doesn't, then people try to hold on to each other; they try to organize that group into some sort of a society and have their own laws and bylaws and rituals and ceremonies, just so that people can cling to that group. So they go on like that. The reality is lost. Only temples or books are left to worship.

It is not essential that once a line starts it will go on forever. It has its own limitations. It can happen to any line. It has been happening to every line practically. A seed is sown, and slowly and slowly a tree sprouts. It grows and grows and grows and grows. It becomes a huge tree. So many people sit under its shade, enjoy the shade of that tree, save themselves from the heat of the sun. But that tree has its own life span. Howsoever old it may be, it still has its own life span – five hundred years, one thousand years, two thousand years. It has to wither, and then the shade will go.

363 *Maharaj Ji, how does a line of masters come to an end and take up someplace else?*

Lord knows best. You see, waves always don't remain the same. The waves in the ocean, they're always shifting – sometimes here, sometimes there – they come and go in the sea. So sometimes mystics come someplace, then in another place, then in another place.

Is it true that as the organizations of the mystics' teachings begin to take root, dogma sets in and the mystics tend to go off to some other place?

To some extent that's right. Mostly the organization takes place after the mystics have died, because in their lifetime, they try to do their best to keep the teachings absolutely pure. But after their demise, definitely people try to arrest their teaching into organizations and dogmas and try to hold the masses to the teachings and yet forget the reality.

Could you make any comment about why India seems to be the birthplace of so much mysticism?

You see, mystics have been coming in every country. India has a background of spirituality, so they are known here. People write about their lives, about their teachings; they are read. And they're appreciated. In other countries, they may have gone unnoticed, unknown. Mystics have been coming everywhere.

364 *I have a question about worship and worshipping …*

What is the meaning of worship? What is your concept of worship? Worship means complete submission to another being, losing your own identity; to become another being is worshipping the other being. Or to develop that height of love which eliminates your ego and makes you one with the being – that is worship. So the worship of the guru means eliminating our ego, becoming one with the master. As Christ has said, I will come unto you and you will come unto me. We both become one. Then he says that we will become one with the Father, because I and the Father are one, so then you also become the Father.[129] That is worshipping the Father through him, the master. That is worship.

People's concept is that you go to a temple, you take some present or gift to the altar, and give that money and take some sweet things from there and put something on your forehead and come out of the temple, and you think you have worshipped the Father. That is people's concept of worship, and the same things are being done in synagogues and churches. That is not worship of the Father at all. To attend to that melody within, to merge your self into that divine light within – that is worship of the Father. No other worship pleases the Father. Because only that worship pleases the Father which eliminates the ego, your individuality, and makes you one with the Father. Ritualistic worship doesn't lead us anywhere. Guru Nanak says just what Christ has said – Christ said: Worship of the spirit is worship of the Father. No other worship pleases the Father.[84] It is the same as what Guru Nanak says: There's no worship of the Father without attending to your meditation, without attending to that divine melody within.*

365 In Sar Bachan *and* The Path of the Masters *one reads about the various deities that one must meet on the way up to Sat Purush. Are these deities also attempting to return to the source whence they have come?*

No. Certain deities have certain functions to stop you in the way. They are the agents of Kal, tricks of the mind. You have

* *Bin naavai hor pooj na hovee.* Guru Amardas, Adi Granth, M3, p.910.

read in the Bible that Christ also had the same experience inside when he said to Satan: Get thee hence, Satan.[6] Certain obstacles do come in our way – we have to cross them, and we need the help of a master to do that.

Are these deities souls which have originated from the same source?

Yes. Everything is soul, so to say. The whole creation is his creation. They are there for a certain object or purpose. He knows best.

They have no desire to return to him at all?

You think everybody has a desire to go back home in this life? You will find that in this world very few people really have a desire to go back to the Lord. Mostly we worship the Lord and we want to meet him not because we have love for him, but because we are unhappy without him. We want to escape from situations. We have become miserable in this world or we have certain longings and desires which we think only the Lord can fulfil for us. We worship him not for his sake, but for the sake of his gifts. Very few people have real love for him. We love people, we love objects of the world. We want the Lord to fulfil our desires, to give us those things. We think that if we do not worship him, perhaps we will lose in business, perhaps we will lose in our love affairs, perhaps we will not be honoured in our society, so we worship him. These are very strange motives for worshipping him. Actually, we should worship him because we want to go back and merge into him. The real longing, the real devotion, the real faith in him should be the basis for our worship.

Some people worship snakes, not because they love the snakes, but because they want to avoid their bite. They worship a snake out of fear of its poison. Similarly, many of us worship the Lord from that point of view, out of fear that if we do not worship him, perhaps we will lose a son or some near and dear one; or perhaps we will lose our health, fame, honour, business or wealth; or we have a desire to gain these things. God is not cruel. Even if you do not worship him, he will not make you lose anything. Perhaps he will give you much more. But we do want to worship him, to meet him, and to go back and merge into him. I often say, the basis of religion is love, not fear. You should never worship the Lord out of fear, but out of love.

366 My Christian background merged beautifully into Sant Mat, but there's one thing I do not understand. When Christ initiated his disciples, he connected them with nam, or the word or holy ghost. Why was it then necessary for him to send, after his death, the holy ghost on that special day when they had the tongues of fire above their heads and spoke in all the languages?

Actually, you see, this is something misunderstood and misinterpreted. What Christ means to say is that when I leave my body, I still will be there; my presence will be there in the form of the holy ghost.[121] And the holy ghost speaks the language of every individual; it is not the language of Christ that he speaks when he's in the body. The holy ghost speaks all languages of the world: It is the language of love between the shabd and the disciple.

But that is how they try to interpret it – that he spoke in so many languages. And everybody, all of his disciples, whatever language they may have spoken, they understood the holy ghost in that language. And that fire is nothing but the light which is in that holy ghost, which is in that spirit. That holy ghost, spirit or nam consists of that light and that sound.

So when he says that John the Baptist or he will baptize people with water and fire, this fire is nothing but light, and the water is nothing but the nectar, the living water – the same thing described in a different way, not that he spoke different languages. Everybody in his own language understood what the holy ghost had to say.

There's absolutely no difference in the teaching of Christ and the teachings of other mystics of the East or of the West. All mystics speak the same language; they harp on the same tune. They may come anywhere, in any country, at any time. They will show you the same path leading back to the Father. They will share with you the same spiritual truth, which enlightens you as to how to become one with the Father. It's very simple to understand. We all know the Father is one. Nobody says that Hindus have a different Lord, and Muslims, Sikhs and Christians have a different Lord. There is only one Lord. And everybody believes that he's within every one of us. And we all know that the path leading back to him is also within us. So how can we think that the Lord has kept a different path in Christians than in Muslims or Sikhs or Hindus? Those who try to search for him within contend that there is only one path – the path of light and sound.

Those who are trying to search for him outside in rituals and ceremonies, they're just lost in religions of their own. And that will lead them nowhere. The spiritual truth is the same. That is why Christ said: Right from the beginning till the end of creation, not a comma can be changed in the teaching, not a word can be eliminated, not a word can be added. It has remained the same; it will always remain the same.[13]

According to our background, according to the environment of the country or the people where the mystics preach, their approach may be different; but as for the path to which they are trying to point, there cannot be two. For intellectuals it will be one approach; for a simple person it will be a different approach. But the path will be the same. For example, if I talk to you from the Bible, you'll understand much better, but if I start talking to you from Buddhist or Muslim literature, you won't understand anything at all. It's not that they have different things to say. They may have the same message to give, but we can only understand it from our own background. Then, once we understand, we are above all these differences.

Christ talks about that sound, word, holy ghost. He says: The wind bloweth; we know not from where it cometh.[78] We hear it at the eye centre, but we don't know from where it is coming, we don't know its source. We don't know if it comes from the right or left. Then he says: If thine eye be single, thy whole body shall be full of light.[23] So we see that light at the eye centre. He talks about the sound and light. His parables are just to explain to us according to our background. And he says that you can find the Lord only within yourself, nowhere outside, and that you have to repent for your past deeds and seek forgiveness from the Lord;[3] you have to take a new birth.[77]

The mystic message, though very simple, is difficult to understand, because we are more concerned with the rituals and ceremonies. We don't try to find the real teaching of any mystic. These rituals and ceremonies are just like nursery school. When a child is sent to a school, for the first two or three years the teacher doesn't start teaching that child. Teachers just tell them how to pack their lunch, how to play, how to sit, how to clean their shoes, how to clean their knives and forks. The teachers want just to create interest in the child so that he will be happy to come to school. When they win his confidence, then they start teaching him the ABCs, and the child drops what he has been doing in nursery school.

So these rituals and ceremonies are nothing but nursery-school classes, elementary things to create the love of God in our heart so that we may get into the habit of worshipping the Lord, so that we may be filled with his love and devotion through these practices. Once you are filled with the real love and devotion, you don't stick to those things; you go way beyond that. The mystics' teaching is way beyond that, but we spend our whole life in the ritual and ceremony. We don't try to go beyond it.

367 *In the Ten Commandments, Moses commands us to remember the Sabbath day and keep it always.*[138] *In Sant Mat, isn't every day a Sabbath day?*

You see, these commandments were meant for those people in those times. He must have been explaining to them that at least one particular day you must keep for remembering the Lord and doing charity and other good works. But if you can make every day a Sabbath day, there's nothing like it. That doesn't mean that he preached meditation only on that particular day and no other day. We have Sunday, but we work every day, we rest every day. The Sabbath days may have had some significance in those days or in the traditional religion of the Jews. Saints try to preach their teachings to us in a way that allows us to remain in those traditions, and yet they inculcate the teachings of Sant Mat in us. They don't try to come in conflict with those traditions, but they put life in those traditions, spirituality in those traditions.

For example, there is a custom in India that on the first day of every month people go for holy baths to the rivers or holy tanks or the temples, and read and think that it is a very pious day, a good day. People were used to those traditions. So Guru Sahib wrote the *Barah Maha* in which he gave his teachings. That way, if you want to follow this tradition because you are used to following it, you can, but at least by following it you will also understand the teachings. What is *nam bhakti*? What is the purpose of our life? He gave the teachings in the context of those traditions. Generally saints don't boldly confront those traditions, unless they are absolutely meaningless or are taking us away from the path. They try to implant the teachings into those traditions.

368 *Your holiness, I have a question that is to me slightly embarrassing, but I am going to ask it anyway. Strictly speaking, I am not a satsangi, but I have heard that in India people make* arti *before a great one's picture. Am I permitted to?*

Brother, to some extent it is also embarrassing for me to answer your question, because we do not believe in any ritual and ceremony at all. Where originally did *arti* start? That ceremony which people do outside is just a reflection of what we see inside at the first stage. We see thousands of candles lit in the first stage and our soul dances when it sees that light. So, in order to exhibit what is inside, people started a ritual or ceremony. They light candles outside and just dance around the light, or take those lights around some picture or around some statue or around some of their idols. It is nothing at all but ritual and ceremony. If you want to really perform *arti,* if you are fond of it, you will have to go in and see all that and do all that – not outside.

369 *All the souls that go back to the Father – it's hard for me to grasp the fact that when we reach a certain place, that's it for eternity.*

There may have been many schools of thought, many other techniques and methods of withdrawing your consciousness to the eye centre, but from there onward it has got to be the same. It is the same for everybody in this creation, and it has always been the same. The essence of the mystics' teachings always has remained the same. That is the base of spirituality on which the teaching of the mystics stands and flourishes and blooms.

They come only to share with us their spiritual experiences, the path which we have to follow. They don't come to create any religions or divide us into small channels, into communities, or into religions or countries. That is why Christ said, I've come with a sword.[39] Their only purpose is to cut our attachments from this creation and take us back to the Father. Give it any name, call it any religion.

We generally don't understand the essence of their teachings and give ourselves to the rituals, ceremonies and dogmas, and try to arrest their teachings into small organizations, small institutions until slowly and slowly the teaching takes the shape of a religion. Any teaching of any mystic, when it comes to the hands of paid preachers, is bound to become a religion sooner or later because it becomes a question of bread and butter for them. That is why Christ warned his disciples: I've given you these teachings free, and you should give them to people free. Don't fill your pockets with gold and silver.[33] He didn't want any paid preachers at all.

370 *In this modern age, science and technology have made strides. And there are various religious groups and movements preaching the word of God, and their intention is to bring about peace in this world. But we do agree that we are far from peace. Despite the fact that all these teachings have been preached to our people, there is strife, discord, disharmony and a great deal of unpleasantness in the world. How do we reconcile this, in this modern age?*

You see, when any teaching is commercialized, discord is bound to come. In commerce, in commercialism, there is always jealousy, always discord. In love, there's no discord. I'm sorry to say that most of the cults and religions have become commercialized –

they are commercial shops, political shops. Their spirituality is lost. They're only holding on to the shells and the reality is lost. In order to hold the people, they invent all sorts of differences with others.

If there is one Father, as we all know, and he's within every one of us – nobody can deny that – then naturally the path leading back to the Father can only be one. It cannot be two. If we seek him within, then there is only one path for us. If you think you'll find him in a synagogue or a church, or in a temple or a mosque, then naturally we have our differences. But if we just sit at home and seek him within, then the question of any difference with anybody doesn't arise. Then we see him in his creation. And if we love him, we love his creation. If anybody hates anybody, he hates the Creator who's within every one of us. So if we are filled with love and devotion for the Father, the question of discord or hating anybody doesn't arise, because he's within everyone – whom is there to hate? Then we love the Father, not the people.

We love the Father who's within every one of us. Only if we see him within ourselves can we see him everywhere outside. But we don't search for him within; we try to search for him outside, and outside we do not find him. In order to have followers and to keep them, the priestly class always creates differences, pitting one sect against another, one religion against another, just to keep their list of conversions, nothing else. There's no spirituality left in those things. They're just empty shells. Religions have become social and political. So much blood has been shed in the name of God. Two nations fight – they pray to the same God, only to kill each other. This is not believing in him at all! We just deceive ourselves, and we are deceiving him, in whom we say we believe. They are just trying to justify their weaknesses by cutting each other's throats. If we really love him, the question of discord with anyone doesn't arise at all, because he shines within every one of us, and there is nothing in which he doesn't exist. So how can we hate anybody? How can we cut each other's throats? How can we malign anyone?

Christ says that if somebody slaps you on the right cheek, you should put your left cheek before him.[18] If our ideals are so high and we really believe in him, then why do we have these wars, nations fighting one against the other, cutting each other's throat? Why? We're just trying to either deceive him or deceive ourselves. We don't believe in God at all. We have made our own God, whom we try to worship.

371 *If the path to God is the same, then why do people fight?*

Inside of everyone there is love, because there is a soul. Whosoever has a soul – naturally everybody living has a soul in him – has that spark of love. Whether it ignites or not, that is a different question. A time comes when even the most hardened criminal also thinks about God, thinks about what he has done, about his own cruel actions. That is the spark of love which is within everyone. But our conscience has become so dead – we have become so blinded by these senses, by this ego – that we don't make use of it.

It's really very unfortunate. As long as we are in touch with that divine melody within, we are all influenced by the love of the Father. We see his reflection in everyone. We love all his creation, because we love the Creator. We don't want to hate anyone lest our Father be angry with us – we cannot afford his displeasure. So we love everybody. Actually, we love him in everybody. So the question of cutting anybody's throat doesn't arise. But when that spirituality is lost, that love for the Father is lost, and we give ourselves only to rituals, ceremonies and dogmas and try to arrest the teachings of the mystics, try to give them the name of an organization, a religion – then we become so rigid in those organizations, in those rituals and ceremonies – those so-called religions – that we become fanatics. We cannot tolerate anyone else at all. So we take pleasure in cutting each other's throat.

No mystic comes in this world to divide us or to create hatred, turning one against the other. When our mode of living becomes rigid, the reality is lost. We are all holding on only to the shells. And when we're just holding on to shells and we lose the reality, then we cut each other's throats. That is why there are so many killings in the name of religion. It's really a shame. In the name of the Lord, we kill each other. Actually, it is our ego. Nobody bothers about God at all – it is just our ego. God has been coming in a human form, and we have been killing him also – taking pleasure in killing him, because we are always dominated by ego. Otherwise, if anybody is really in love with the Lord, the question of killing anybody doesn't arise, the question of hating anybody doesn't arise.

372 Why is it that the hatred is there for all of the great saints? What was so offensive that made them be persecuted?

You see, their teaching touches the pocket of the organized priestly class. Why was Christ court-martialled by the Romans? Why were the Jews perturbed by him? When he went to their synagogue he turned out their tables. He said: You have made the house of God a place of merchandise.[76] You have commercialized this house of God. Naturally, it touches their pocket. So they won't tolerate that – nobody will tolerate it – it is their business. No organized religion tolerates the mystics. They're crucified on the charge of corrupting the public, corrupting the masses.

Yet they're so loving and so giving.

Yes. What was Christ's fault? He didn't want to rule the world. He didn't want to become a king. He didn't want any money. He didn't want any power. Why didn't they like him? What was his fault? In the same way, what was Sarmad's fault? In what way was he coming into conflict with the Muslim priests? People started following Sarmad, and the priests could not tolerate that people weren't coming to the mosque but were running after him. This is the fate of every mystic.

373 Why are saints persecuted?

You see, we always persecute the living and worship the dead – because it is so easy. And that is the history of all religions. While the mystics and saints were alive, nobody heard them. But when they leave this world, when they die, then we all worship them. Suddenly they become great for us. People were just like us when Christ was living, but how many heard him? There was no dearth of good people even then in the world, but how many heard him? That is the fate of all the mystics.

374 Master, in the United States I read an article about this group in California that is taking groups that are not Christian to the courts. They attacked Scientology; the next group was Eckankar; and now they're going after some scientists. They talk about God, the soul and the spirit, and accuse these groups of infiltrating the minds of children and taking them away from Christianity, away from Jesus. So I feel in the United States there is this large movement against anything Eastern now. When people come to my house and look at your picture, unless they know me, I don't really say what I'm doing because

I don't want them to think I am strange or weird. And I feel funny about that, because I don't want that kind of energy attached to me, people thinking that I'm weird.

You are frightened of persecution? Or of public opinion?

Not of public opinion. I feel that when I'm doing something I believe in …

Then believe it. Face the consequences.

And I am aware of all of the other things that are going on …

Voice: I think Christ said, if they persecuted me they will surely persecute you.

You see, if you read the Bible, Christ has made it very clear. He says, you will be brought to the officer, you will all be questioned about this, you will be persecuted, you will have to go through suffering for my sake. And then he said, don't prepare any defence. When you are there, automatically the defense will come to you.[35] So we have to face all sorts of things in life, and we should always be prepared for it. When Great Master started teaching here, Baba Ji's [Baba Jaimal Singh's] teaching was not very widely known in this area. He would go to a village and hold satsang in a house and there would be twenty, thirty people there. Hardly anybody would notice. But the Great Master started giving satsangs in all the big cities. He attracted a lot of devotees and at the same time a lot of enemies who belonged to organized religions – naturally they always get perturbed about the teaching of the mystics. So he faced all sorts of hardships, as you must have read in Dr Johnson's book. But he was never frightened. Even now, there is some inner conviction, inner experience in the mystics, and they don't bother about the consequences.

I guess I feel with you that if you were to say, "Okay, take my hand, now we're jumping in the ocean," I would take your hand and jump into the ocean. But it used to be that when people followed a master, they were killed.

It was the organized priests who opposed Christ and got him crucified – ultimately they put him on the cross. What was his fault? He didn't want power. He wasn't collecting any money. He wasn't collecting followers. He was just sharing his spiritual knowledge with the masses, putting them on the right path. But organized priests couldn't tolerate that. It probably cuts into their purse, which they were more concerned about. It affected their membership, so they got alarmed. Look at the history of any mystic; they have suffered a lot in the hands of the people, through no fault of theirs. History always tells us that we persecute the living and worship the dead. That is the history of all the saints and mystics. And that is why Christ prepared his disciples: For my sake, you will have to suffer a lot.[36] So much fear was there in his disciples that even Peter denied him. Read the Bible – even Peter, who was the most loving son of Christ, denied him.

ONE PATH, MANY RELIGIONS

375 Maharaj Ji, are you considered a Hindu?

I am just a human being, as far as I am concerned. We are all human beings. We are all sons of the same Father. We are a drop of the same ocean. We are concerned with the teachings of the saints, and we are to live in this world. You may consider me anything you feel like; or call me an Indian if I am to be confined to any particular country.

376 *Do you believe in all the religions of the world?*

I believe in the teachings of all the saints of the world. I don't know what you mean by religion. If by religion you mean the teachings of all the saints, then of course I believe in all the religions. If by religion you mean the exploitation of their teachings, then I don't believe in religions at all. You see, a religion can be different from the teachings of the saint on whom we are trying to base the religion.

Do you believe these religions are true?

If Christianity means the teachings of Christ and if Buddhism means the teachings of Buddha, then of course I believe in those religions. But if Buddhism and Christianity are something different from the teachings of Buddha and Christ, then I don't believe in them at all. If by Christianity we mean the real teachings of Christ, then certainly I believe in them, otherwise I wouldn't discuss the Bible.

377 *Someone wrote: "Let us not kid ourselves. I believe, and I think all satsangis believe too, that if the Radha Soami faith would advertise and let it be known that one does not have to quit his religion or his church to become a satsangi, then the membership in New York City would increase by leaps and bounds. But when a foreign religion is presented, people are timid and also are ashamed to become identified with an Oriental cult." Please express your opinion about these matters?*

Well, brother, you know that we are not interested in numbers. I am only interested in the seekers, in the real seekers, the true seekers, whether they are one or thousands. And our books are full of this assurance that in order to follow the path to

God-realization, in order to find the way within, in order to seek the Lord within, we have neither to change our religion, nor do we have to convert others to any other religion, nor do we have to leave our family or our duties. We have to live in the world and yet be not of the world. We are not to attach ourselves to all these things. Actually, I personally feel if we know the real teachings of the saints, the spirituality, the mysticism which they come to preach, and we follow that, we will become better Christians, we will become better Muslims, we will become better Hindus, and we will have deeper faith in our own religion, if we just learn or understand the real teachings taught by those saints.

Generally, we give importance to rituals and ceremonies and dogmas. Perhaps we think those things are the be-all and end-all of religion. The real essence of religion, the real teachings, the truth of such religion is lost. Saints always come to remind us of the truth and reality which is the basis of every religion. The question of changing from one religion to another religion does not arise. Every discourse, every book is full of the assurance that in order to meet or go back to the Lord, what is required is devotion, practice, spirituality, and the love of the Lord, not conversion from one religion to another religion. By converting ourselves, by leaving one religion or adopting another religion, we do not become entitled to meet him. It is the truth, the reality, the spirituality which will take us from here to the Lord. So saints always give importance to that truth, that reality, that spirituality. They never try to convert us.

And the question of advertising does not arise. We do not believe in advertising, as there is nothing commercial about these teachings. Sant Mat, or the path, or the Radha Soami faith – whatever name you may give it – is for the seekers, the real seekers who want to find him, who want to do spiritual practice in order to detach themselves from the world and attach themselves to the Lord. So I do not believe in such things nor do

I encourage any advertising. Those who really want spirituality always seek and always find it. And those who do not want it do not seek. Advertisements do not make any difference for them. I do not believe in advertising. Our books are very clear. They assure us that to follow this path, the question of changing one's religion does not arise.

378 It's been said that Sant Mat is not a new religion. I wasn't under the impression that it was a religion at all. Perhaps you can answer that one. Then, also, the books say that it is a philosophy which gives practical shape to the truth common to all contemporary religions.

You see, by religion we mean the organized religions such as Christianity, Buddhism, Islam or Sikhism. In that sense, Sant Mat is absolutely no religion at all. We have no rituals, no ceremony, no organization and nothing to bind us to any particular institution to claim that this is our religion. Sant Mat is no religion.

Sant Mat literally means the teachings of the masters, the teachings of the saints. And as I have explained many times, the teachings of all the saints in all the religions are the same. The rituals and ceremonies differ but the teachings of the masters – those who tell us their internal experiences, who tell us about the path leading back to the Father – that experience, that path, is exactly the same.

We people give shape to the teachings through organizations. Christ never created Christianity. After him, we formed a group and called ourselves Christians and gave this name to a religion. Buddha never created Buddhism. After he departed, his disciples collected together and brought his teachings into a narrow circle and called themselves Buddhists. The teachings and experience of all the saints – whatever country, creed and caste they may belong to – is exactly the same. It cannot be different. If the Lord is one, and he is within every one of us, and we have to search for the Lord within our own human body, how can you think that for Christians there is a different path inside to go back to the Father than for Muslims? Our structure is absolutely the same. If we find the Father within the body, then the path is the same. If we want to find him outside – in temples, synagogues or in the mosques – then we have different paths. But for the saints, the path is the same.

Every saint tries to tell us to search for the Lord within ourselves. For those who search for him within, the teachings are the same. They're not bound by any religion, they are not the slave of any religion, nor do they try to destroy any religion. Christ himself said in the Bible, I have not come to destroy the law.[12] No saint comes to destroy the teachings which already exist. They come only to refresh for us those teachings which we have forgotten.

The teachings of the masters have always been the same, but we forget these teachings. We give more importance to ritual and ceremony. They come again and try to take us out of the ritual and ceremony and point out the spirituality which is the base of every religion. They're only concerned with the spirituality which is within every human being. So there is no organized Sant Mat religion in that sense.

379 In speaking of the Christian religion that Christ founded, is Sant Mat in conflict with Christianity?

The teachings of Christ are not different from Sant Mat. At least in whatever little of the Bible I have read or have been able to understand, I find exactly the same teachings as the teachings I understand from other saints. He refers to the same light, he refers to the same sound, he refers to the same God, he refers to the same soul; he also refers to the body as the temple of the living God, to the many mansions which we have to cross before we can reach our home, to that single eye with which we have to see the light, to the door at which we have to knock and which has to be opened in order to get in. His teachings are exactly the same. If we do not understand his teachings or do not follow his teachings, it is we who are to be blamed, not him.

380 How does Buddha's state of nirvana, whose definition has been given as that which never appears and therefore never disappears, compare to the God-realization that you speak about?

Nirvana means release from birth and death, salvation. God-realization or salvation are different terms to explain the same thing.

But this is nirvana versus sansar. Isn't nirvana a state of being which does not even define such a thing as God or God-realization?

I think Buddha's teachings are not properly explained. Buddha is nowhere quoted as having said that there is no God. He only said, why worry about God? Look to your karma. But the entire teaching of Buddha is based on karma theory – a very rigid karma theory. What he said was, in effect, why worry about God? Look to your actions, what you are doing in this life.

He never mentioned God.

No, but he has not said anywhere that there is no God. Actually, I say we do not have the teachings of these masters as they really gave them. There is no book that Buddha wrote. There was no direct disciple of Buddha who put his teachings down in a book. The same is true of the Bible, which came to be written much later by the disciples of Christ.

But the Dhammapada is actually the book written during the time of Buddha?

It is very difficult to say. That is what we are given to understand, but history does not prove that. Actually, these saints were not at all recognized in their lifetime. Nobody bothered about them.

Buddha was, though?

Oh no. Very few recognized him. He had hardly ten or twelve disciples in such a huge world. What does it mean? The saints were hardly recognized by their neighbours.

Well, I was not there during those days, but I was under the impression that Buddha was very well recognized during his lifetime.

Of course, you were not there. It was Ashoka who, afterwards, gave his teachings to the world. Monks, about a hundred years after Buddha, thought of spreading his teachings. Not to say of Buddha, you take the case of Christ. How many disciples did he have?

Well, Christ had a poor following, I must admit.

With all his beautiful teachings, hardly twelve disciples. And some of the apostles did not have the privilege of being with him, though of course they were conversant with his philosophy. So what could they do? People do not recognize such great souls in their lifetime, and later on they try to determine what the teachings are, according to their own way of thinking. There is no history about these things.

I do not think there is any contradiction in Buddha's teachings.

There are different schools. I mean, the Buddhists have probably seventeen different schools.

Yes, I understand that part, but insofar as Buddha's teachings, or his system of relieving suffering, working out one's karma and entering nirvana, I wonder if it is understood?

By nirvana he means release of the soul from the mind. That is nirvana. But why get release of the soul from the mind? Just to merge back into the ocean. He does not mention the ocean, but when water, by evaporation, leaves the dirt, whether it is conscious of the cloud or not, it will go back and merge into the cloud. Now, if the water in the dirt is told, "Leave the dirt, for you are not dirt, you are something else," and it leaves the dirt, though it is not told at all about its origin – the cloud – even then it will go back and merge into the cloud. Similarly, perhaps the disciples were not plainly told about the Lord or about God. They were just told to look to their karmas and look to their nirvana, to get release of their soul from the mind. But where then will the soul go? Again, surely, to its origin.

381 *Maharaj Ji, recently here in Escondido we heard a high priest of the Parsees from Bombay talk. He was telling us about Ahura Mazda, and apparently that was basic to all religions, many, many years ago. I bought one of their books, and in it is stated that the last remnants of these ancient Persians went right down into the Punjab and into Bombay, there in India. And the rest of them, or the other religions, sort of took the main points and changed it around. Would Sant Mat possibly be one of these, through Guru Nanak? Would that be direct from the Ahura Mazda?*

No, sister. The saints never take the teachings from another saint and give another shape to it. I will tell you. Those people who travel on the path and reach their destination, all of them have the same story to tell. Whether the saint is born in the twentieth, or the eighteenth or nineteenth, or sixteenth or seventeenth century, in India or America, or any other country, he has the same story to tell. So regardless of who has written the story of that path leading to the ultimate destination, the teachings will always be the same. There may be a difference in explaining, keeping in view the background of that particular nation, or particular country, or particular people. But essentially the teachings will be the same; the kernel will be the same.

Supposing from America you went to India, and whatever countries came in your way, whatever obstacles you had in your way, whatever formalities you had to go through, whatever difficulties you experienced, and whatever enjoyments you had in the way, you write all that in a book. Another person goes and also writes what he sees and experiences in a book. A third person goes and does the same. Whosoever has taken that route to India, the experiences will be the same, but there will be a little variation in description here and there. Some will give a little more importance to Bangkok, some will give more importance to Burma, others will give a little more importance to Hong Kong; but actually, they have to explain the same things leading to the destination. There cannot be two different basic explanations from those who have gone there.

So it is not that the other writer takes from the teachings of the one saint and tries to make it his own religion. They have travelled the same path and they have told the same thing. After their departure, the people gave shape to those teachings in the form of religions, and they became the victims of organizations and such shells. If anyone with an unbiased mind will make a research, he will be told the same teachings. There cannot be two.

We have a lot of Parsees in our group from Bombay. In fact, in Beas we have a cosmopolitan colony. There is hardly any country or any religion which is not represented, because we do not believe in any creeds, dogmas, rituals or ceremonies. We believe only in the teachings of the saints and in putting them into practice.

Scriptures and holy books

382 *If all knowledge, all power and creativity – everything – comes from the perfect master, then the holy scriptures of all cultures are unnecessary. However, Master, these scriptures are your child too.*

You see, scriptures help us to accept the master. How do these scriptures come? The mystics write about their experiences, the obstacles in the way, for our guidance, for our enlightenment, for our encouragement – what to do, how to get rid of those obstacles and how to reach those destinations. These are just their experiences in the scriptures. But we can't make use of them just by reading them. It doesn't become my experience unless I also remove all those obstacles in my way. When I also reach the same point, the same destination, then it will also become my experience. So from scriptures I learn what I am supposed to do, what is the object of my life, what stands in my way and how I can remove it, what is the necessity of going to the master, what help I am going to get, and what my role is on the path. The scripture will strengthen our faith on the path.

383 *Can initiates of a perfect master learn anything from the Bible? Should we be reading it?*

I think there's more reason to read the Bible now, because now you can understand its real meaning. Initiation is a key, and through that key we can open the Bible, unlock its treasures, its mysteries, and find the real jewel there, the real mysticism.

384 *There is another thing in the teachings of Christ, that of a missionary angle. Some people take that as literal?*

That instruction he might have given to one whom he wanted to carry on his work.

But is it misinterpreted?

That is always the case with the instructions of every saint. It does not apply only to Christ. Saints are generally not recognized in their own time. It happens with every saint, and however little I have analyzed the Bible – and I am nobody to comment – I feel that in his lifetime his teachings were not noted or written at all. They were passed from mouth to ear. People just heard him. For example, you have just heard the discourse and you hardly remember 50 percent only fifteen minutes after you have heard what has been said. If you go to another room and try to write down what you have heard, how much would you have left? It would be perhaps 30 percent of what you have heard and 70 percent of what you think you have heard. And if you did not have the opportunity to hear it personally, but heard it later through someone else, and then you tried to explain to some other person what you heard and he begins to put it on paper, hardly anything will be left of the original. Then if that teaching, which the third person has written, is translated into different languages, how much will be left? Besides this, some people who have ulterior motives suppress certain things which interfere with their own way of thinking. How much of the original will be left ultimately?

That is the fate of the Bible, as far as I can understand. Nobody noted down Christ's teachings at the time he spoke.

They have just passed on what they understood, one to another, and then they wrote the book. Later it was translated into different languages. That is why it is not a continuous record of the whole of Sant Mat, nor Christ's whole teachings. Here and there in the Bible you do find his teachings, but you have to link them to understand his real teachings. Many mystic things are missing. There are many mysteries, illustrated in parables, and you need a teacher to understand the parables. Jesus himself said that he spoke in parables. His followers were hunted and persecuted, so he had to explain to them in mystical terms. Now we need some mystic to explain to us what he meant. If the people of his own time, who heard him personally, did not understand him – or else they would not have crucified him – how are we to understand him now, after so many centuries, particularly when his real teachings are also not being given to us in their purest or most complete form?

It is difficult to know the real teachings of Christ from the Bible; but still, here and there, we find that the mystical meanings are very clear. He explains to us that we have got to search for the Lord, and he emphasizes that the Lord is within us and that the search is to be made within the body. He tells us that our body is the temple of the living God[132] and that there are many mansions in the Father's house.[116] It is not only that you will find the Lord in the body, but you will have to pass through many stages and many mansions before you can reach him. Christ says that we will have to knock at a certain door before it opens, and when that door opens, we see light.[29] We have to hear the sound, the word, the holy ghost. We have to drink that living water, which will give us everlasting life.[96] These are all mystical terms which we must understand before we understand his real teachings. So we cannot just read the Bible from one end to the other and know his teachings. We have to fish here and there and go very deep into the Bible to understand the real teachings. One phrase is sufficient to set us thinking what he wants us to understand. It is not from just easy reading, like a novel, that we will know what he wants to tell us. That is why sometimes we are confused. Sometimes we do not understand what we are reading, but if we know the key, then whatever we read, the whole thing will be crystal clear to us.

And this is not the case only with the Bible. I know about the teachings of other saints who have written with their own hands. Not a word has been changed, yet their teachings are being misinterpreted – not rightly understood. Though the correct words are still there and in the original language, the basic concept has been changed by certain persons' own interpretations, for their selfish ends. Not to say of Christ, all saints have the same thing to tell us, but we want to lean back on the writings of past saints and want to corroborate. So they say: "All right, if you do not believe me, see your scriptures; see if that is there." The saints try to explain the teachings from every angle but we have to go very deep to understand the teachings.

In other words, we get off the track through our misinterpretation, so we always need a living master here to keep us on the track?

That is what I am trying to explain.

385 Would you say the Granth Sahib [Adi Granth] is one of the books closer to the Sant Mat teachings?

The fortunate thing about the Granth Sahib is that it was written by the gurus themselves, and it is being preserved to a word with the modern generation. Nothing has been changed. It cannot be said that this was not the teaching of the gurus, for they actually wrote that book. In their writings they have confirmed that this is their teaching. So that is something authentic, and the whole

Granth Sahib teaches us the philosophy of the saints – Sant Mat and nothing else. So the teachings in the Granth Sahib are not only close to Sant Mat, they are Sant Mat.

Is it being misconstrued like other books, or is it still coming out in true form? Or are the priests themselves misconstruing it?

That they do everywhere. You will find the same is true of the Bible and other scriptures. But actually, if with an unbiased mind you will make a research into the teachings of the Granth Sahib, you will come to the same point. What we are involved with is history, and that is never accurate, as nobody has made a research in it along that line. There is not a word in the Granth Sahib which cannot be explained and which is not true to the teachings of the saints. The Granth Sahib contains the writings of thirty-five contributors – six Sikh gurus and twenty-nine other saints and holy men. So it is a compilation of the sayings of all those saints.

How did it come into being? What is the history of the Granth Sahib? Guru Nanak gave his own teachings in poetry, and he used to recite them out of devotion and love. He never took up a pen and paper to write a book. Whenever he was in a mood of ecstasy and oneness with the Lord, his poetry just flowed out of him. And some saintly people noted down whatever he was saying. So his teachings eventually came into print. Similarly, the teachings of all these saints, till the fifth guru, came like this. But the written teachings of all the gurus were scattered. Guru Nanak's teachings – his poetry was taken away by his sons. His successor was not allowed to possess it. And the teachings and the poetry of the second guru were also taken away by his sons. The third guru was not allowed to see them, and he had no access to them, so none of the writings were available.

The fifth guru collected the teachings of all the gurus into one book. From the previous gurus' descendants, from their friends, wherever he could lay his hands on the teachings of his predecessors, he collected them and brought them into book form. Then he realized that if these teachings were given from his own masters, probably the world would think that these teachings were something new and different from the teachings of the previous masters of various castes and creeds, of previous times. So then he collected the teachings of all the saints that were available to him, in different languages. The writings of those saints who had lived even several hundred years before Guru Nanak were collected. All the teachings that he had collected, of various saints of various times and places, were the same as the teachings of Guru Nanak. He collected all of them and brought them into one book, called the Granth Sahib. So the Granth Sahib contains not only the teachings of the Sikh gurus, but also the writings of twenty-nine other saints and holy men.

The object of compiling the Granth Sahib was to tell the world that whatever his master had taught, the philosophy of God-realization was nothing new, and that there was proof of it in the writings of earlier saints. To prove that, he brought together their teachings into one book. Despite the fact that everything is there in black and white, people do not understand the teachings.

386 How can we know, before we ourselves can see the inner worlds, that Soami Ji's descriptions are correct? And can you speak about your own personal experiences verifying these descriptions?

Sister, that way we can challenge even the existence of God. How can we know that he exists? Physically there is no proof that God exists. But we take the corroboration from the mystics and saints when they speak the same language, describe the same experiences, give the same teaching, give us the same guidance and same signs and the same path. That shows what they tell us is right. That is why, when we discuss the teachings in our meetings, when we hold satsang, we quote so many quotations from different saints, to emphasize that point. Whatever one mystic tells us from a certain point of view, we try to give so many other quotations corroborated by other mystics, other saints, just to tell the truth. We try to show that whatever is being taught to us by one particular mystic, mystics have existed in different countries, they have taught in different languages, they have come in different times. They had no means to meet each other, and yet they speak the same language, share with us the same experiences, have the same truth to tell us. So naturally we trust them, trust what they say.

> *It seems to me that it would help, if one could hear from a living person that he also has seen these things. Can you, Master, tell us that you have seen?*

How would you trust him, if you don't trust the other saints and mystics? How would you trust him? Where is the surety of our trusting him? When we have no faith in the past masters, in their teaching, their philosophy, how then do we trust the living? We test the living by the teaching of the past masters; we cannot trust the past masters through a living master. It has to be the reverse. As we read in the Bible, how many people trusted Christ? Twelve? One betrayed, another deceived and everybody denied. How many people put faith in him? He told them the kingdom of God is within you.[3] How many people believed in him? He told them about the path of light and sound within. He told them, if thy eye be single, thy whole body shall be full of light.[23] Who believed him? Now we believe him. His contemporaries never believed him. He had to quote John the Baptist, he had to quote Moses to impress upon us the truths which he wanted to share with us because we had faith in Moses and John the Baptist, but not in him.

387 *In that vein, Master, has anybody done any study to determine whether or not Confucius was a master of any degree?*

It's very difficult to sit in judgment on anybody. We can only know and take advantage of their teachings. They talk about the path, they talk about the general aspects of Sant Mat, and that corroborates our belief, our faith, and strengthens our faith, and then we have to make use of all that by meditation. That is the only advantage of reading the books or works of other mystics and saints – just to corroborate our convictions. Otherwise, a few simple words of the mystic are enough to explain to us the whole teaching. But since we are intellectuals, we need so much corroboration from different mystics, different saints of different times, different countries, different religions, different nationalities – then the mind gets convinced. They're all harping on the same tune, singing the same song, so they must be right; I also should try to experiment with it. That is the only advantage of books, nothing else.

If a simple man can understand the straight teachings of a mystic, he doesn't need to refer to any book at all. He doesn't have to look to any other mystic at all. All books and literature are just to satisfy our intellect. All meetings are just to satisfy our intellect, convince us and then to create an atmosphere for meditation, that's all. Ultimately they will lead you to meditation. These are all the means, but if we don't attend to the end, the means are useless to us.

How the saints teach

388 We had a little German satsang today, which led to a few questions which have been translated. The first one is, I would like to know that if, as my fellow satsangis maintain, art and poetry are worthless, then why do the masters themselves – for example, Hafiz and others – give out their teachings in the form of poetry?

Mostly saints have given their teachings in poetry because they can reach us much better through poetry, through music. In many schools of thought, mystics sing their devotional songs because we are more receptive to that music. So through that music they reach our heart also, and we understand them better. And similarly, if anything is told to us in a poem, it reaches us quicker, easier, than if the same thing is told to us in prose. Mystics know our weaknesses, so they make use of those weaknesses to reach us. We are fond of poetry, we are fond of music, so they create those to reach us – anything which can reach our heart, which we can understand easily and which we are receptive to. Since everybody's fond of poetry and music, that is why they have given their teachings in poetry, and that is why they sing devotional songs, so that we can understand easier and better. There's no other reason.

Their main point, when they have talked about poetry, art and music, is that we should not become lost in these things. The real music is inside; that is that divine melody within, that silent music which is within every one of us. That is the real music. This music will be used as a means to that end. The whole problem is when people think that hearing or singing devotional music is an end in itself. That is wrong. And the same for poetry. Poetry is an expression of the poets' love and devotion. But it is just a means of expression – the real thing they are expressing is more essential. So we're not to get lost in the poetry – what has been said through the poetry is more important. Many mystics have even given their teachings just in straight prose, and it has the same effect, but we are less receptive to straight writing than to the poetry. But otherwise, the teachings are the same, whether they're given in poetry or prose.

389 Isn't the story of all the animals going into the ark possibly the Christian concept of the 8,400,000 species? This is the way I try to understand it for myself.

Stories are given to us to explain certain spiritual truths, but we give importance to the stories instead. When we were children, our mothers and grandmothers told us beautiful fairy tales at bedtime. We became so absorbed in those fairy tales, as if they were realities; now we have all forgotten those fairy tales, but the truths our mothers and grandmothers wanted to impress upon us, the lessons they wanted to give through these fairy tales – those last forever with us. That impression becomes part and parcel of our life. If we think of those fairy tales as reality, that was not their purpose. The purpose of those fairy tales was not to convey reality but to impress upon us certain spiritual truths, spiritual values. Now we are just giving importance to those fairy tales, not to the spiritual values or truths which they impart.

Similarly, the mystics and saints, also by using fairy tales, are trying to impress certain spiritual truths in our mind, trying to impress a certain spirituality in our hearts. For example, take the Bhagavad Gita. With a story, the author has tried to say so much about karma theory and so many other spiritual values. But nobody worries about the spiritual truth. People worry about Ram and Krishna and their personalities and they think they're real people and try to worship them, but nobody bothers about what spiritual truths their stories convey. So we are all giving importance to these fairy tales which we heard as children and have forgotten the spiritual truth which is behind them.

Similarly, read the Persian literature by Shams-i Tabriz or Maulana Rum – at every step they have a story to tell. They try to give us the spiritual truth through stories, because through stories we always remember the spiritual truth, and that was the approach the Great Master also took in satsang. To elaborate a certain spiritual truth, he would tell a beautiful tale, and we would remember, word by word, all those stories. And now, naturally we think about the spiritual truth which he wanted to impress upon us through a particular story.

Otherwise, if a mother starts telling a child a spiritual truth without a fairy story, he will not hear her at all. While hearing a fairy story, he's also slowly and slowly getting the truth which the mother or grandmother wants to impress upon the child. So similarly, mystics and saints have always been fond of stories and parables to explain certain spiritual truths. We remember those truths very easily with the help of those parables. Without parables, we would not be able to grasp as much. But as simple as we are, we give more importance to the stories and characters and have absolutely forgotten the teachings behind them.

Who knows now what spiritual truths the saints meant to explain to us by their stories. We are not worried now about what they wanted to tell us. We are only worried now about where the ark is and such things. It happens with every religion.

390 *Master, whenever we are attracted by a spiritual way of life, whether it be Catholicism or something else, there usually are some guidelines or religious concepts in each of these religions. Now the question is this: You have a concept such as the Ten Commandments, to give guidelines for a better way of life, and yet we don't have ten commandments, say, in Sant Mat, we have the concepts of lust, anger, greed, attachment, and ego, or vanity, and the vows. My question really is, if we were to be given the original concepts of those other spiritual guidelines, wouldn't they be about the same?*

People forget the teachings even forty, fifty years after a mystic gives them, and they twist them to suit themselves. And how can you expect the absolutely pure teachings of Christ to be conveyed to us today? I see right under my nose, in the Dera, in spite of my saying that everything is covered by meditation, that no ritual is required, that no place is to be worshipped, still people go to many houses here and prostrate here, prostrate there, drink water here, drink water there. They can't help it. They are twisting Sant Mat right under my nose, right under the mystic's nose. The teaching is being twisted here, and after two thousand years, what is going to become of it you can imagine yourself. Already houses are being turned into shrines; this is the human mind.

We don't like to know the real teaching of a mystic; we like to know what appeals to us, what we want him to tell us. We want to follow that teaching, not what he wants to tell us. Even if the real history, or the real teaching of Christ were to be revealed today from some old manuscripts, or even if scientists were able to catch the real words of Christ from the Sermon on the Mount, I think people would never follow it. They would never be able to leave what they are doing now. They would say, "No, you are not our Christ. This is what your teaching is." We want to twist the history in our own way. We want to accept what we like to accept. Our minds are not open at all. So God knows how much has been twisted in two thousand years, how many interested parties have given us his teachings, what shape it has taken today. And we think and accept every word in the New Testament as a word of law, and we interpret accordingly; it is wrong.

391 *Maharaj Ji, last night Professor Bhatnagar shared so much with us, and one thing that stuck in my mind was about the two brass kettles in the room, in terms of the relationship between two people and how they clang together. And about how hard it is, in relationships, since Adam and Eve. Last night was our wedding anniversary, and I was wondering if you could say something positive about marriage and the path.*

Well, sister, there was nothing wrong in whatever Professor has said about it. He doesn't believe in a sugar-coated pill. He thinks that unless the medicine is bitter perhaps it is not effective, and that is his individual approach. But all that he said was right. You can analyze this yourself. There is no special criticism of the ladies, you see, but it is each other's attachment, our individual attachment for each other, which pulls us back. Whether it is the husband or wife, it is immaterial. The soul, as you know, has no sex, and the soul should not be attached to anything in this creation. Unless the soul detaches itself from this creation it cannot go back to Father. That is why Christ said: I have come with a sword because I want to cut all your roots from this creation.[39] If you cut a tree from the roots it doesn't grow again.

Similarly, that is the purpose of the mystics in coming here. All the mystics and saints have the same message to give, the same spiritual truth to share with us, but everybody has a different approach, depending on the audience they want to reach. Some mystics have a very mild approach. Some mystics, unless they just shake you from the roots, you will not understand.

Kabir was one of those; Bulleh Shah was another example. People are so tied to their traditional beliefs, superstitions and traditional religions that unless they are shaken from the roots perhaps they won't understand at all. So some mystics have to just shake them before they can realize the importance of Sant Mat. And others may need just a hint to understand what the mystics or saints have to say. But all mystics have the same message; there's no difference in their spiritual experiences which they want to share with us or the spiritual path they want to show to us. They have to see the audience whom they want to reach.

Kabir, for example, had to preach in Benares, which was traditionally a priestly-class stronghold of exploitation, so unless he shook people from the roots, they wouldn't have understood him. Bulleh was born into a very aristocratic family and was very proud of his caste, of his tribal background. Unless he shook his own people from the roots, they wouldn't have understood him.

Other mystics have taken a very soft, very mild approach. Probably their audience was quite enlightened, so to say. Each mystic has his own individual approach, but each has the same spiritual truth to share with us. Yesterday I said that Kal is just – whatever you do, so shall you reap. Justice brings us back to this creation after every death. Justice means that whatever actions you have done, you have to come back to collect that harvest, which will keep you tied down to this creation. Another approach is: Kal is deceitful and always wants to keep us attached to this creation. It amounts to the same thing, there's no difference. Everybody has an individual approach.

392 *Master, we have heard you talk a lot about cutting off one's head. Professor Bhatnagar, a few nights ago, gave some examples. How do you make such a sacrifice? What does it mean to do this?*

Cutting off the head means eliminating your ego. You don't have to physically cut off your head. Don't be frightened about it. You see, generally when we're egoistic, we always raise our head, and when we are humble, we always bow. So cutting off your head means that you have to become humble. You have to eliminate your ego. And meditation is nothing but cutting off your head. That's the very strong phrase that's sometimes used. Every mystic has his own approach, but the teaching is the same. Mystics' approaches sometimes differ according to the people whom they're trying to teach. Kabir lived in Benares, which is the citadel of very orthodox traditional priests – the Brahmins. They make people do all sorts of rituals and ceremonies and austerities. Unless he shook people up, they would not leave all those traditional beliefs. Only after he shook them could they understand his teachings.

The deeper your roots, the more you have to water the field to loosen those roots before you can pull out the tree. Benares is still a citadel of the orthodox priests. People think that if you die there you will go to heaven, and if you don't die there, you will go to hell; and if you don't do this, you will go to hell, and if you do this you will go to heaven. People there have all sorts of beliefs. So Kabir had to shake them terribly. His language was very strong for those people – with milder language he could not teach them. The more asleep you are, the louder one has to shout to wake you up. If your sleep is not very deep, just a little knock will get you up. But if you're in a very sound sleep, very deep sleep, you have to be shaken before you can get up.

So that was Kabir's approach, because his audience was so deeply asleep. He had to use all sorts of language, very strong language, and sometimes he even frightened the people, so that they would leave all those rituals and ceremonies. There's no question of anyone cutting off his head; it just means eliminating your ego.

393 Don't different saints and mystics have different personalities?

Yes, mystics each have their own individual personality. But their basic teaching is the same, their basic approach to Sant Mat is the same. But it can differ with individuals, depending on whom they are talking to. Everybody who comes to them has a different background, so they have to deal with them according to their particular background, at the level of their background. Ultimately they have to put them on the path and help them on the path – that is their main object – but their approach can be different.

But the main object of every mystic is the same, there's no difference. Their teaching is the same, the path is the same, and their object of putting people on the path is the same. But sometimes people have to be shaken from their roots before they can understand Sant Mat.

5

Lost and Found

Lost in a maze

394 *Maharaj Ji, would you explain the story about a man who's walking around a room with ten doors and when he gets to the tenth door, he scratches his head and he misses it?*

The story is like this: Generally it is said that a blind, bald man enters an inn which has only one door. He's trying to find the door to come out of that inn, but since he's bald, when he gets to the door which can take him out, he starts scratching his head, so he again goes in the same circle. This story is told in reference to the human birth. We go through so many miseries in the lower species, and when this opportunity is given to us to get out of this prison of eighty-four, we just waste our time in sensual pleasures and worldly pursuits, and miss the opportunity again, and again move in the same prison.

395 *If one thinks of somebody like Einstein who discovered the theory of relativity, the theory was always there before he articulated it with his mind. In other words, it must have come from divine inspiration. And so in the same*

> *way perhaps there is something that is missing, a link – a missing link with the intellect that is still to come to one, spiritually.*

Well, brother, there is only one question in this life. Life itself is a question, and there is only one answer: how to get out of this circle of life forever. That is the only answer. This life itself is a question to us, and how to rise above this life and get that permanent life is the only answer. Neither is there any other question, neither is there any other answer. That is why Bulleh Shah says: These intellectuals have created this confusion. There is nothing in life to talk about, except God, but intellectuals have written so many books and created so much confusion for us. What is there to write about, what is there to talk about? There is only one God, and we have to go back to him.

396 I can't understand why we have to follow any one special path back to God.

We have to follow a special path because the Lord is within us, and so there must be a special path within us leading to him. God is everywhere, but we cannot see him outside unless we realize him within. He is living within us, and since we are all created alike, the path leading to him must be the same. Christ says that to worship the spirit is to worship the Father.[83] If you want to worship the Father, you must worship the spirit, you must withdraw your consciousness to the eye centre and be one with the spirit within. Then you will be able to go back to the Father. And that is the path. Unless we realize the Lord within ourselves, we will not be able to see him anywhere in the creation at all.

But once we realize him within, then we see him everywhere; the whole world is the temple of the living God. First your body has to become the temple of the living God; then you will see the Father everywhere, in everybody.

397 Master, when you say that some people are chosen, does that mean that there are some people who will not realize God?

Sister, if this creation is to continue, then everybody cannot go back to the Father. When he decides to put an end to this creation, then naturally they have no other place to go – they will all go back to him. But as long as he wants this creation to continue, how can everybody go back to him? In this room, every brick can't be at the ceiling. Some bricks are required in the foundation, and those bricks are holding up the bricks in the ceiling. So the imperfect souls in this creation are holding up the perfect souls in the creation. Because if the creation is to continue, everybody can't go back to the Father.

Guru Nanak gives a very beautiful example. He says: You have seen the puppet show and the person who demonstrates that show. He takes out everything from his bag and puts them on the table. And then to every puppet, there's a string attached from behind, and the puppeteer sits behind the screen. He's pulling from behind the screen, and all the puppets are dancing. Guru Nanak says there are two types of puppets – one is a gurmukh and one is a manmukh. One is God-minded; one is worldly minded. The puppet who is conscious that I am nobody to dance; there is somebody at my back who's pulling me and I am dancing to the tune of that person – those puppets belong to the Lord. And the puppets who think: Who can make me dance? I dance – they're full of ego. They're part of this creation. But both are dancing in this world.

When that puppeteer finishes the show, he collects all the puppets, puts them in the bag and goes away. The puppets have no other place to go. Their real place is in the bag, but as long as the show is there, the puppets have to dance. But when he puts an end to the show, the puppets have to come back to the bag. So as long as the creation is to continue, it has to be imperfect; it can't be perfect. The moment anybody becomes perfect, he merges into the perfect being.

Say there is a raindrop, and when it merges into the dirt it stagnates; it gives off a very foul smell, and it remains part and parcel of the dirt. The moment that with the heat it becomes pure, it leaves the dirt; it goes back to the clouds at once. So the soul is here only as long as it is imperfect. It is a drop of that divine ocean. The moment it becomes pure, it merges back into the Creator.

The soul is immortal. The soul doesn't die – but it can be caged, it can be imprisoned, it can be kept in captivity. But it doesn't die. You see, a diamond is precious, and it has so much lustre. But when you throw it into the mud, you neither know its price, nor can you see its lustre. Its lustre hasn't gone anywhere, nor has the dirt reduced its price. When you wash the diamond, its lustre will be the same; its price will be the same. It is the same with everybody's soul.

Every soul is potentially God. But having come to this creation, having taken the association of the mind, it has become absolutely dirty. It has forgotten the Creator. It thinks this creation is the be-all and end-all. The moment the soul gets a little light on its own origin and gets help to leave the dirt, it at once goes back to the Creator. That is why everybody tries to seek the Father – whether in the right way or the wrong way – because the inclination of the soul is always towards its origin. So the search is there with everyone. Whether we know the real path or we don't know the real path – that is a very different thing, but everyone is always seeking in some way because the inclination of the soul is always towards its origin.

You can never overcome your loneliness unless you allow the soul to go back towards its own source. You may have the whole world at your command, but you can't overcome the feeling of loneliness. There is a time when you feel that you're absolutely lonely in life. Nothing belongs to you. You try to deceive yourself by thinking that this belongs to me or that belongs to me, or I belong to him or he belongs to me. It's just a self-deception. Because the yearning of the soul is always there towards its own source, and this feeling of loneliness can never leave us unless we allow the soul to go back to its own source.

So that is why there is no perpetual happiness in this world. There can never be happiness in this world as long as we are part of the creation. We can only be happy when the soul goes back to its own Creator. Otherwise, these kings should have been happy, rich people should have been happy, healthy people should have been happy. Nobody is happy in this world. They all have transitory, temporary happiness for certain periods, but the reaction is so much that we become more unhappy. The real happiness can only be when we allow the soul to go back to its own source. That is why we search for the Father. That inclination is inherent in everybody.

398 *Master, when we are separated from the Creator and part of the creation, we seem to feel lonely, and then, to fill this loneliness, we create attachments. And the only way then to go back to the Creator seems to be to wait our turn until we know the futility of this mechanism. Is that our story, or would you like to tell us …?*

You see, it is a very simple thing: Once we are separated from the Father, we are part and parcel of this creation. Then we try to think this creation belongs to me, and we start putting in efforts to own our attachments or to be owned by them.

It's a natural instinct to feel lonely within yourself, because the inclination of the soul is always towards its own source, and this feeling of loneliness will never leave you unless the soul merges back into the Lord. So that feeling is in every one of us, irrespective of caste or creed or religion.

But in order to overcome that loneliness, sometimes we think: My wife belongs to me, my children belong to me, my friends belong to me, my country belongs to me. We just try to place our fingers on one another, and we try to think that they belong to me. Then we are attracted to other bodies, so we become attached to somebody else. We are always trying to put our fingers here and there and we deceive ourselves that probably I was wrong in that attachment, or wrong in that love, probably I'm right in this attachment, probably I'm right in this love. And though that never belonged to me in spite of my best effort, now this belongs to me. But all this is just a self-deception.

Actually, nothing belongs to us here in this world. Whatsoever you may have in this world, this feeling of loneliness will never leave you unless the soul merges back into the Lord. But for that feeling, but for that instinct of the soul towards its own source, nobody would find the Lord at all. If we don't miss him, if we don't feel the separation, if we don't feel lonely in this world, we will never think about the Lord at all. This is a natural instinct which the Creator has created in us. In his making us a part of this creation and remaining away from us, he has kept that link between him and us – the feeling which he has created in us to go back to him, the natural urge we have to go back to him. That urge forces us to find him, to seek him. But we try to satisfy that urge by putting our attention into the world, to worldly attachments, thinking that perhaps I will be able to fulfil the feeling of loneliness by belonging to these people, by owning those people. But we are disappointed and come back again, and again we try to go there, into worldly relationships. Then we start drinking, we start giving ourselves to sensual pleasures, just to overcome that feeling of loneliness. We go in a wrong direction.

But by his grace, the same feeling of loneliness – the urge to be one with him – may turn us towards the Father to overcome that loneliness. The feeling is the same. That urge is the same within every one of us. With his grace, this urge can be diverted towards him, and without his grace, this urge can lead you to the vices, to the sensual pleasures, and you may be lost in the creation again. But the Lord has kept that urge within every one of us.

It is a natural instinct of the soul towards its own source, which forces us to seek him or to find him; which tells us that whatever in the world may belong to you, you are not satisfied there, you're not contented there, you're not happy with them, you're not at peace with them. You have everything of the world, but still you want something more. In spite of everything that you need in this world, that feeling of loneliness does not leave, and will not leave us unless the soul merges back to its own source. That is a divine law, you see.

399 How should we best deal with loneliness?

Deal with it? We are all lonely in this world. It is a self-deception to think that somebody belongs to us, or we belong to somebody. It's just a self-deception. The time comes when we all realize the self-deception, when we wake up from our deep slumber. We are lonely because soul is the essence of that divine ocean, and this feeling of loneliness will never leave the soul unless it merges back into that ocean. This very feeling of loneliness is forcing us to follow the path which leads back to him. But for this nobody would bother about the Lord. This feeling of loneliness is forcing us on to the path and keeping us straight towards the Lord. So it is only a question of time until we realize that we are lonely. We think: I belong to mother, mother belongs to me. I have got sisters, brothers, so many friends, my wife, my children, my property, my wealth. I have so much. I belong to so much.

But in everyone's life an opportunity does come when one realizes that he is really lonely in life. Nothing belongs to him, and he also doesn't belong to anybody at all. I think that is a most fortunate moment when it comes in anybody's life. If at that time, by his grace, one goes to good company, you are on the path towards the Father. If you are dragged by bad company in order to overcome that loneliness, you will become a victim of the senses and you will fall down.

This loneliness can lead us towards the senses. This loneliness can lead us towards the Father. At that moment his grace is required. If his grace is there, then you will get an opportunity to be in such company or in such an atmosphere that you will be on the path to the Lord. Otherwise, in order to overcome that loneliness you will become a victim of the senses. Even then, you will never be able to overcome this loneliness. But you will, on the other hand, go on collecting more karmas and more sins.

The feeling of loneliness can be overcome only when we become one with the Father. Without that you cannot overcome this loneliness at all. This is a blessing in disguise, I would say. The sooner one can realize this fact – that one is lonely – the better it is for that person.

Then we will try to belong to the one who belongs to us, and to whom we can belong, and that is nobody but the Father, the Lord. He belongs to us, and we can own him. Besides him, nothing belongs to us, and we cannot own anything at all. That is just a self-deception. The sooner one can rise above it and realize it, the more fortunate one is, I would say.

400 *Master, I'm having a lot of difficulty celebrating life at the moment. I'm carrying a lot of pain. I feel the burden of living and want to go back to the Lord. How can I ease my pain?*

Sister, who doesn't want to go back to the Father? Who would like to stay in this world where we do not know when death may come, from whom death may come, and how death may come?

I hope it comes quickly.

Everybody is in separation from the Father – even if you stay in palaces and have all the luxuries of the world, you would still be miserable. As long as we are separated from him, nobody can become happy. Some are living comfortably in misery, others are living uncomfortably in misery. But everybody's living in misery as long as we are separate from the Father. If the beloved and the lover are separated, the lover cannot be happy no matter what you give him, no matter how comfortably he may be living. He may have all the gadgets of the world, but they don't please him at all. What pleases him the most is the beloved. As long as he is separated, there can be no peace for him. So as long as the soul is separated from the divine ocean, from the Lord, it can never find peace in this creation.

So I need to survive the way I am? Maybe change my attitude?

Well, we have to make best use of the opportunity which the Lord has given us. I often give an example of a child who goes to a fair while holding the finger of his father. Everything at the fair pleases the child. All the lights, the toys, the children playing, the sweet shops – everything pleases him. But if by mistake he drops his father's hand, then he starts crying in spite of everything which was pleasing him. Then he realizes he could derive all the pleasures from that fair only as long as he was holding the finger of his father. Without that support, without the hand of the father, all this is miserable for him.

So the whole creation is miserable for us if we are separated from the Lord. When we hold his hand, when our attention is towards him, we can go through this life without losing much of our balance. If we have absolutely forgotten him, then we live miserably in this creation. But if he's our focus, if he's our destination and we are trying to achieve that destination, then we can breathe in peace. Then we have consolation, contentment that we are going towards our home. So we go through this life. But if we have turned our back to our destination and are looking the other way, the more you look the other way, the more miserable you will be.

We try to find peace and happiness in worldly faces, worldly objects, and worldly pleasures. The more we try to seek there, the more miserable we become every day. We think we will be able to get happiness and peace from raising our standard of living in this world, from having all the sensual pleasures of the world; but the more we try to find, the more miserable we become every day. In spite of our civilization, with so much improvement and our higher standard of living, I think there are more deaths now, more suicides, more broken homes, more youths rebelling against their parents. There is no peace even in the home these days, no peace in the family, no peace in the country. Neighbouring countries are fighting, neighbouring communities are fighting, neighbours are fighting. It's because we have become self-centred. We think we don't need anybody, so we try to become self-centred, and we are becoming more miserable everyday.

Peace is only within us. The tendency of the soul is towards its own origin, and our soul is yearning to go back to the Father, but when there is so much weight over the soul it becomes helpless, becomes miserable. When you lift the weight from the soul, it will just go back like a needle attracted by a magnet. The needle is always attracted towards the magnet, but if there is a stone over it, what can the poor needle do? We are burdened with such a thick layer of karmas, layers of mind, that our soul is helpless in this creation.

The main purpose of meditation is to lift that weight from the soul, to make it light so that it automatically will go back to its source. The more weight that is being removed, the happier we are becoming. The more weight we feel on the soul, the more miserable we are becoming every day. And we are becoming burdened and burdened and burdened by these sensual pleasures and all these things – they are all burdens on the soul, so we are becoming more miserable. So we cannot seek happiness in this world; we can only seek happiness in his lap, by going back to the Father. The wife is always happy in the company of her husband. No matter what you give her – give her jewellery, give her all the respect, a beautiful house – all she needs is her husband. She can only enjoy these things if she is in the company of the husband. Otherwise, she cannot relish all that. Rather, they make her more miserable, and that is our position today in this life.

401 The Lord is an ocean of mercy. Our meditation moves him towards this mercy. Is that correct?

Well, brother, I'll give you a little example. A little child loses the hand of his father in a big bazaar, and he doesn't know his father's name or the address of his house. He knows nothing. He is weeping and crying and he can do nothing. Yet somebody will come and take that child. There are agencies that find lost children. Somehow they always can trace his parents. What led that child to his parents? His weeping and crying. He wept and cried without his father, whose address he doesn't know, whose name he doesn't know.

We also weep and cry without knowing our Father, without knowing his address, without knowing our home address or how to reach there. But this cry, the anguish within ourselves to go back to the Father, the longing within us to go back to the Father, the tears we shed in separation ultimately will lead us back to the Father. Somehow people will find out from the gesture of this child the parent's home, and the child will find his parents. So unless we cry within, unless we have that feeling of separation from the Father, unless we have that longing and love to go back to the Father, how can we go back to him? If we are sincere, if we are full of love and devotion, then we can throw all the burden on the Father to find out the ways and means to pull us to his level. What else can the child do who is lost in this creation, who has lost his Father, except cry? If he is playing with games, playing with other people, then nobody will even look at the child, nobody will bother about the child. Only his cry will attract people's attention. So if we are lost in this creation, nobody bothers about us. But if this creation doesn't entertain us and only the cries for the Father are heard, then he pulls us to his level.

402 Master, how can we help our fellow satsangis when they are having a hard time?

Everyone has a problem at every step in life, and there are a hundred and one types of problems. We are all full of problems. One has to struggle in life at every step and deal with these worldly problems. We should do our best, then leave the results to the Father. This world is full of problems – there's no dearth of human problems. Mostly they are our own creations – I don't say individually, but collectively. We have created these problems.

The Lord has given us enough earth to grow our food, enough material to live, enough places to live, but we do not know how to distribute these things, so we have created our own problems. We have exaggerated our needs in life so much that we cannot fulfil them, so we are always confronted with one problem or another. What do we need? How much can one eat? How many clothes do you need to cover yourself? How much shelter do you need? Calculate individually. Some have nothing, some have too much. So who has created these problems? Our demands, our desires in the world – there's no end to them, so there's always a problem at every step.

403 Life seems so painful. Why must we suffer so much?

You see, I don't know our concept of suffering. Suffering is a comparative word. If our suffering can pull us towards the Father, that's a blessing. If our suffering can keep the Lord in our heart day and night, and we have been able to tune ourselves to him, it's a blessing. It's not a suffering at all. It's just a comparative word.

Kings also think they suffer. They have a whole country to rule, but still they think they are suffering. The beggar, if he gets just his bowl of rice, a little thing to eat to fill his stomach, on that day, he doesn't think that he's suffering. But a king, with all his possessions around him, he thinks he's suffering, shivering in his shoes on his throne.

So it just depends on your point of view, it's just a comparative word. Otherwise, we're all suffering in this creation, suffering in separation from the Father. Separated from the Father, nobody can remain happy in this creation at all. Some are comfortably miserable; other people are just miserable. But we are all miserable in separation from him. We can never get peace within unless the soul goes towards the Father. Unless the soul becomes one with the Father, we can never be happy. No matter if the Lord gives us the whole creation at our feet, we can never be happy.

404 Can you give me an example of what is suffering in life?

Well, brother, look around. The whole world is suffering in one way or another. You go to a hospital and see individuals suffering. Just search within yourself and see how much we are suffering every day, how much we are in agony. If something is not achieved according to our heart's desire, we become frustrated and start suffering, start crying and weeping. All of that is suffering. And what more suffering can there be than when the soul is separated from its source?

But I accept that as suffering. Is it not enough for me to come to a higher plane?

There are two things: First, we want to escape from this world because we are suffering; second, we want to go back to the Father because we are in love with the Father. If we miss him and are so much in love and so full of devotion for the Father that we cannot live without him, that is one approach. Another is to escape from this world because we are suffering so much that we cannot stand this suffering, so we want to go back to the Father.

Whatever the approach is, it is good so long as we are trying to go back to the Father. But the basis of spirituality is love and not fear. We should not try to escape from this world because we are suffering. We should try to seek the Father because we cannot remain away from him out of pure love and devotion.

Love and devotion should pull us towards him. But if we do not have that love and devotion and that approach, the other approach is also not bad. There is so much suffering in this world that we must escape from it and go back to the Father. Whatever approach you may have, ultimately the result is the same.

405 To be without love in this world, would that be considered a type of hell?

What is the definition of worldly love? This love itself is a hell, because it ties us down to this creation – to hell – our so-called love. It's nothing but lust; a justification. We have very flowery words to explain our weaknesses – that's all. There's only one love, and that love is for the Father. There is no other love. That is everlasting love, eternal love. This other love is here today, and tomorrow you are standing in the courts, accusing each other. What is that love?

There is only one love. The soul can have no other love at all but for the Father. All other types of love are just self-deception. It's a question of realization, which everybody gets in life sooner or later – how much I have been deceiving myself, and how much I have been deceiving others. We neither belong to anybody, nor does anybody belong to us. We have come alone, we will go alone. And inside us we are always lonely, no matter what we have in this creation. When we cannot overcome this feeling of loneliness from within, then what is this love? Love should pull us out from this loneliness. Love should make us feel that somebody belongs to me and I belong to somebody. But where is that feeling? In spite of all we have around us, this feeling of loneliness doesn't leave us at all. It is the inclination of the soul towards the Father. Unless it is pulled to the level of the Father, you can never overcome this loneliness. That is real love. Otherwise, you can give it any name.

406 *You told my friend not to worry, that we were all alone in this world, and I wanted to know what exactly did you mean by that? I thought that you were always with us?*

That is what I'm trying to explain. We are born alone, we will go alone; and the one who belongs to us is the Father. Unless we go back to him, we will not be able to overcome this feeling of loneliness. That is why no matter how many friends we have, how many good relations we have, how much wealth of the world we have, when you sit alone, you will feel you're all alone in this world. Having everything, you are all alone. There's no contentment within you. Still you're yearning for something which you do not know, which you cannot account for. That is the natural inclination of the soul towards its own origin. Unless we let it go to its own source, we will not be able to overcome this feeling of loneliness.

407 *Is it true that the soul that truly yearns to go back to the Father will go back?*

That urge is always in every soul towards its own source. The inclination of the soul is always towards its own source. As to whether or not it's able to find the Lord, that is something different. That is why nobody has peace of mind in this world, and we all feel lonely. Whatever we may possess in this world, we are not able to overcome the feeling of loneliness. Sometimes, in order to overcome that feeling of loneliness, we give ourselves over to the senses. We think possibly that by running to the sensual pleasures we will be able to overcome the feeling of loneliness. Other people, realizing that they will not derive anything from the senses, turn to the Father, by his grace. But unless you miss something, you don't try to achieve it.

What is it that yearns? Is there something that does yearn to go back?

That is the soul. The soul is trying to become active; it can never be at peace unless it merges into its own source.

408 Maharaj Ji, the phrase "no pain, no gain"– what does that mean?

If you don't feel the pain of separation from the Father, you don't gain the Father. First, you have to feel the pain of separation from the Father. When you feel the separation from an object, you naturally try to find the object also. So then you gain the Father.

409 Is the fear of loneliness just a self-indulgence?

That is a God-given gift, I would say. That's his grace, if we are able to realize that fact and live with it and then try to overcome that loneliness by meditation. This feeling of loneliness may pull us to the senses or may pull us to the Father. To overcome this feeling of loneliness we become a victim of the senses or bad company. And to overcome this loneliness we become saints. This instinct has been kept by the Father within every one of us.

SUFFERING AND LONELINESS AS GRACE

410 How can we manage to have a calm or accepting attitude when suffering?

Take it as his grace and think more about the Father. When we are suffering, we think more about the Father than when we are in happy situations. So which is better from his point of view? Any moment when we remember him is to our credit. So only that is a moment of grace when we think about him, when we remember him. And when we forget him, that is not a moment of grace at all. So if worldly happiness makes us bow down before him and makes us remember him, that is grace. But if worldly happiness makes us forget about him, if he has given us so much that we are lost in the pleasures of the world and we forget the Lord even, that is not his grace. So grace may not be to our liking.

You see, when the child is sick, howsoever he may cry, the mother will never give him a chocolate or a toffee. She knows that it will aggravate his fever. The mother will put a bitter quinine in his mouth. Not that the mother doesn't love the child; the mother loves the child the most. But the child doesn't know what is best for him. He's unnecessarily crying for chocolate and doesn't want that bitter quinine because he doesn't know what is best for him.

The Lord knows what is best for us. So he will only give us that which pulls us to him. The master will not give us those things which make us forget the Lord and attach us to the creation. That is not his grace at all. Not that he wants us to suffer. He wants to save us from suffering. We don't even know what suffering is. We are only worried about these few moments of suffering here, but we've forgotten the suffering from birth to birth, from species to species – what we have gone through from age to age. The Lord wants just to save us from all that, and we are only concerned with these few moments of pleasure, and we think the Lord is unhappy with us, that he doesn't want us to enjoy this life.

411 *Well, is it correct to assume then that once you are initiated everything that happens to you is for your own spiritual good? That everything that happens is helping you to go back to the Father?*

At least we should take it in that light. It may be a bitter pill to swallow sometimes. Because, you see, it's good from the Father's point of view, not from the worldly point of view. Our concept of his grace is something very different. We think that if he gives us a very good partner and a good house and a lot of money and a good reputation in this world, if we are worshipped by people, then the Father's grace is very much on us. But his grace may come in a different way. He may take your wife from you or your child or your friend. And you may become frustrated by this world and turn back to the Father. That may be his grace, to pull you out of all the attachments of the world and make you realize the reality, which you never would have thought about otherwise. You were so much engrossed in your own love, your achievements and your own wealth that you have practically forgotten him. That is not his grace. His grace is what pulls you back to him, and that may be a very bitter pill. Our concept of his grace is something very different – it is always from the worldly point of view.

412 *Master, if you ask the master before you meditate if he can do what he can, if it's his will, is that wrong?*

That is right. Of course we are all beggars. What is grace? Grace is that which detaches us from the world and takes us back to the Lord, our true self; that is grace. Grace doesn't mean asking the Lord to fulfil worldly desires or worldly ambitions. That is not grace. If he gives us worldly things, worldly wealth, or we get attached to those worldly things and those attachments keep us back from the Father, that is not grace.

It's very difficult actually to accept the grace of the Father. His grace is that which detaches you from one another, detaches you from worldly objects, worldly faces, and attaches you to him. But our concept of grace is if he gives us wealth, a good wife, good houses, a good job, and a good atmosphere to live in. We think that is his grace, but those things may make you forget him. That may not be his grace at all.

His grace is that which takes you back to him, which keeps him always in your mind, which creates his love and devotion in your heart – that is his grace, what we call a blessing in disguise. For example, we may be attached to someone, and we suddenly know the reality and we try to detach ourselves from that person. That may be his grace. From the worldly point of view, we feel the separation, we cry about the separation, we don't accept it as grace. But actually that's his grace, because we are remembering the Lord now and we have realized the reality of the world, and now we are detaching ourselves from the people and objects of the world and are now trying to find him, to lean on him, rather than on the world. That is his grace.

But our concept of grace is always what looks pleasant in the world. And it's no doubt good to think positively, but that may not be his grace at all. Anything which takes our mind away from the world and creates his love and devotion and yearning in our heart to go back to him, that is his grace. But they may not be pleasant incidents, pleasant events.

413 Master, has this loneliness anything to do with the marking of the Lord?

You see, when he has marked you, he creates that loneliness – the intensity of that loneliness in you, the intensity of that urge in you – and gives you a better company, better society, better atmosphere, better environment, which turns your direction towards him. The feeling is already there. It was dormant, but when he marks you, when he allots you to come back to him, then that urge becomes more and more intense and you get a certain environment, certain facility, certain opportunity. And in that atmosphere, you turn towards the Father. This is how he moulds you, moulds our direction towards him.

414 *If this life is a dream, then why is the pain we feel so very real?*

Well, sister, in dreams also you feel pain. You cry. You weep. You also feel happiness. You feel so many things in dreams. You may have nightmares as well as pleasant dreams. So this is why we feel miserable here. Dreams are not always pleasant.

415 *Well, if life is a dream, why is it so necessary to make a great effort?*

You want to be one with the reality. We are miserable here, being separated from the Father, so we want to escape. If we were happy here, we wouldn't think about the Father at all.

They are the fortunate ones who, having come to the creation, are missing the Creator; they're missing the Beloved. They're the fortunate ones, the blessed ones. So the teachings are always for the blessed ones, for the fortunate ones. Those who are happy in this dream, they will remain part and parcel of this dream, and those who are the blessed ones, who realize the transitory nature of the world and want to go to their everlasting home, their permanent abode, they will feel his separation. They will miss him. They will try to get to him.

HAPPINESS

416 *Master, I had an uncle who was a millionaire, and there were very few millionaires, and he had everything anyone could want in a material way, but he drank himself to death.*

Yes, materialism doesn't give any happiness to anybody. If it did, the kings would have been happy, the people at the top would have been happy. They are even more miserable than us. We get normal sleep, they have to sleep by pills and injections. Happiness is something different; that we get from within, that we don't get in outside things at all. We try to search in the outside things. The more we search for it outside, the more miserable we are becoming today. If we search for it within, then naturally we are liable to get it.

The West has started thinking that with all this to their credit, they have not become a happy nation. So they are now looking towards religion. And when they look to religion, they want to see reasoning, and probably the orthodox religions cannot satisfy their intellect and reasoning. There are only dogmas which they have to accept. It doesn't appeal to the reasoning of the mind. They are so logical and so intellectual that they want reasons; they want to be intellectually satisfied. They don't want to be carried away by traditions. So naturally they look to the East to find that. But there's exploitation also by the East. But still, happiness you can't get from anywhere outside.

417 *Master, quite a few people seem to think that there's some kind of spiritual awakening or a new desire for spiritual knowledge in the West. Is this really so? Are we in an Aquarian Age?*

I don't know, brother, what astrologers say, but when you are at the bottom of a hill, you are very anxious to reach to the top – you're excited to find something at the top. When you reach the top, you have no option but to look down. You are feeling frustrated that you have come all this way and not found what you were looking for. In the West, people have achieved everything material. They have even gone to the moon. But in spite of all the big achievements to their credit, they have found that they have not become a better or a healthier or a happier nation. They are lacking something, they are missing something. There are more mental cases, more broken homes, more agony and unhappiness in their society.

If all this materialism has not given them that mental peace, they think perhaps their pursuit of peace is in the wrong direction. Now they are turning inward – to religion, to spirituality, and that is a big thing. They have realized that if by going to the moon and having all these material achievements to their credit, they have not been able to find happiness, then their pursuit of happiness is in the wrong direction. They are living in agony, but comfortably. They're comfortably unhappy, but they have realized that they're unhappy. So they are coming towards religion and spirituality. So there is some sort of awakening, I must say.

But in the East, it is now becoming just the reverse. They think perhaps by reaching to the top, they'll become happy. So they are running more towards materialism to find peace and happiness, and the West, generally speaking, is leaving materialism, so to say. They try to find peace now in religion or through spirituality. And when they go to the religions, orthodox, traditional religion doesn't satisfy them, because they have become too intellectual, and they can't accept things just on faith. Reasoning is there; the scientific mind is there. They aren't satisfied by the dogmas, by the traditional approach of a particular religion. So they run here and there; they try to go deeper, and when they try to go deep, then they come to these spiritual movements here and there and try to know everything. There is definitely a type of awakening taking place.

Is this why there are so many young people coming to Sant Mat?

It is actually a revolt against the age, against the hypocrisy of the elders, I must say. Young people have become very intellectual, very scientific-minded. They must satisfy their reason, and probably traditional religions and their elders' way of life does not satisfy their reason at all. They think there is more hypocrisy in their way of living. So they are a little more truthful and honest, I must say. But they do not know where to go. Sometimes they are also misled or exploited: They might do drugs; they might live a free way of life. But definitely there is a revolt. They want something. Sometimes they don't know what they are wanting, but they're not satisfied with their old way of living. So they may find their way to the right path someday, but there's definitely an awakening in the youth.

418 Master, is it the attachments to the material world in the West that's resulted in there being more satsangis in India than there are in the Western world?

Well, brother, I can tell you there's absolutely no difference between East and West. We are all in the same world. I don't think that the West is more attached to material things than Eastern people. I sometimes feel that probably they have reached to the top and they have started looking down now; they have achieved every possible human comfort and even reached to the moon, and they're disillusioned with all that. Now what? Even after reaching the moon, you've not become happy or a better people or a better nation. There is something missing in our approach, so they have started looking towards spirituality. But the East, due to its hunger and poverty, probably think that they will get something by reaching to the top. So they're running after those things which the West is discarding now.

So there's no difference between East and West. Seekers are seekers and the Lord's grace can be anywhere – it is not bound by the East or West. I don't think that Western satsangis are more attached to material things than Eastern people. Eastern people may be hankering more for them than Western people, I would say. It depends upon the individuals.

419 *Maharaj Ji, the mind keeps asking questions, but perhaps you would explain to us briefly why, in the past, it has been so difficult for even masters to find the path, it would seem. Whereas recently it almost seems like Sant Mat has been thrust upon us, as the whole programme seems to be so rapidly accelerated in the last fifty or a hundred years, perhaps?*

The person who is miserable, he would like to find peace and happiness and try to get out of that misery. If somebody is drowning, naturally he will put out his hands and feet to get out of that water. So perhaps we have become more miserable with this modern civilization, by becoming self-centred or by being possessed by all these modern gadgets. So naturally we want to get out of our misery, and so are we are searching, seeking. Moreover, we have realized that we are unhappy in spite of all the modern comforts – having even reached the moon – so that is to our credit. We have not been able to find peace anywhere in the comforts of the world, so we have started searching within now.

Perhaps, having pursued peace in the wrong direction, we are turning back and trying to search for that peace within ourselves. So that is why more people are turning towards spirituality now. A man thinks that if I have a beautiful house or a good wife and something good to eat and a big bank balance, perhaps then I'll be happy. But after achieving all those things, if he still remains miserable, then naturally he feels frustrated. What have I gotten all these things for if I am still miserable like this?

So then he realizes that his search for peace has been in the wrong direction, and I think that stage has come with us. When we are at the bottom of a hill we think perhaps we are going to get something at the top of a hill. And after tiring ourselves and toiling so hard, when we reach to the top of a hill we feel frustrated if there's nothing there. Then we look down again. So I think now we are looking down. We have achieved all the comforts in modern civilization. We have practically everything now that we can think of. When we find that still we are not happy, naturally we realize that perhaps our pursuit has been in the wrong direction. So we have started searching now within, in religion, in other things. So now everybody is searching here and there.

420 A man named Walter Russell once said that God said to him: All men will come to me in due time, but theirs is the agony of waiting. Is this a correct statement?

Do you not think there is agony in waiting? We are all going through that agony of waiting. Every soul is the essence of the Lord. Unless we go back and merge into him, we cannot escape this agony. Just analyze the people here in the States. You have all the material objects to your credit – what have you not got for your comfort! But still you have not been able to say no to agony or unhappiness. I think you have perhaps added to it.

421 Maharaj Ji, do you sometimes have feelings of nostalgia for the past or the old days which are so different from the way it is now – nostalgic feelings for simpler times?

Well, we always want change. I have seen people living in very big cities. They run to the villages for weekends, and people living in the villages, they run to the big cities for the weekend. People in the villages think probably: God knows what we are missing by not staying in the big cities. But people in the big cities are so tired of the pollution and noise that they run to the small villages just to have a quiet weekend. We always want change. We are never satisfied with what we have. That is human nature. We used to have candles in our houses. Now we have electricity and beautiful chandeliers, so we get tired of the chandeliers and electricity and go to restaurants where they have candlelight. Why? With great difficulty we have come to use electric lights, so why go to candles now? We are never satisfied with what we have, whatever we may have. We always want change.

422 *Nobody in this world is really happy. But you can see that a person can find happiness simply by doing their duty, or staying at home or at work, particularly if the work is something which helps other people, such as being a nurse or a doctor. I've met dedicated people who seem to derive a lot of satisfaction from the type of work that they do.*

Well, brother, no doubt mystics try to depict the darkness of this creation. But for that, we wouldn't want to escape from it, we wouldn't want to go back to the Father. But as I said a few days ago, why curse the darkness? Light the candle, and then there will be no darkness. No doubt the world is unhappy. We see misery all around us, but we can build our own happiness within ourselves, and then wherever you go you radiate happiness. Happiness is within. It is not in sensual pleasures or anywhere outside. You will never be able to achieve happiness outside at all. No matter how much job satisfaction you may get, how much social work you may do, whatever professional work you may do, you will never get happiness in these things because the soul has a yearning for its own source. Unless you let the soul go to its own source, it will never be happy.

No matter what we have in this creation, how comfortably we may have been placed in this creation, how devoted a wife you may have, what beautiful, smart, loving and obedient children you may have – you may have all the wealth of the world – but you will never get happiness from these things. Still you will find something missing, and you will always feel: What am I missing? I have everything in this creation. Still you will find that feeling of loneliness within you. You are not happy within yourself, in spite of all that you have. This is the inclination of the soul to its own source. Unless you let it go to its own source, you will never be happy.

So happiness lies in worship of the spirit within and nowhere else. Happiness doesn't lie outside at all. It is a self-deception to think that I can be happy here, I can be happy there. If I have this, I'll be happy. If I have that, I'll be happy. It is a self-deception. And the moment comes in everyone's life when we do realize that nothing belongs to us, and we don't belong to anybody at all. So unless we belong to the One to whom we really belong and who belongs to us, we can never be happy. And that One is the Father, the Lord.

The mind tries to seek happiness in the senses, in worldly achievements, worldly fame, worldly authority, worldly wealth. The more you try to seek happiness there, the more frustrated you become every day because your pursuit is absolutely in the wrong direction. You are running away from your goal. In order to achieve the goal, you are actually going away from the goal, so you become more miserable. If you run towards your real goal, only then can you be happy. So the more we try to seek this outside happiness below the eye centre, the more we are running away from our goal. When you try to seek it above the eye centre, you are running towards your goal, and you are becoming happy. Unless we try to achieve the goal, we can never be happy. And seeking happiness outside is running away from your goal. So how can we be happy?

423 I don't understand when the verse says we are never happy here. It seems that we are definitely happy sometimes.

He challenges us by saying that in this creation, whatever our pleasures are in this creation, there's always a fear at the bottom of that pleasure. When you get married, you're always worried: What if my wife leaves me, becomes unfaithful, deserts me, or I annoy her? You see, there's always a fear, and wherever there is a fear at the base of a pleasure, it can never be a pleasure. It's only a question of time before it is converted to misery. You have a child, you're so happy, but you're always concerned he may become sick, he may die, he may become a drug addict, he may get into bad company, he may not attend to his education. You're always worried. You carry out a coup, and you become the dictator of a country. Then you're always concerned about your life, that there may be a coup at night and you may be put before a firing squad someday. So where is that happiness? When we get wealth, we worry about taxes, about thieves, about cheats. Our friends betray us, so where is that happiness? There is a fear at the base of every happiness. Unless that fear is removed, there can be no permanent happiness.

That is why mystics say that no matter what you do in this creation, you can never be happy. No matter what you get, you'll be miserable. If you want happiness, that is within you, that is in love and devotion for the Father. In our love there is a jealousy, but in love and devotion for the Father, there is no jealousy at all. We rather become happy if we meet any lover of the Lord, we become very happy that I have met some good lovers of the Lord, but if you meet other lovers of your love object, you become jealous. That love is something very different from this worldly love.

So we can only get happiness when we are filled with love and devotion for the Father, not otherwise. If you are happy within, then you will radiate happiness. If you are miserable within, you will radiate misery everywhere you go. You always share what you have; you can't share what you don't have. You go to a miserable person, he will make you miserable in two minutes. You go to a happy person, howsoever miserable you may be, and you will just come away smiling because he shares his happiness with you. A miserable person will share misery with you. So we have to obtain that happiness within ourselves and then we will radiate happiness in this creation.

424 Can you talk about happiness in the life of the disciple?

What is happiness? It's when you have no worry, when you're relaxed. When are you happy? When you are in the lap of the Beloved. The real happiness can only come when the soul shines and becomes one with the Father. Before that there's no happiness at all. Every happiness has misery underneath it in the worldly sense. There is no constant or permanent happiness in this world at all. A child is born, and then we are frightened that he may die any day. He may become ill, he may become sick, or he may become crippled. There's always fear in that happiness. When we earn wealth, there is always fear that we may lose it. Banks may fail. There may be income tax cases or so many other raids on our money. So that happiness is no happiness. There can be happiness only where there is no misery under it. And that happiness can exist only when the soul shines and becomes one with the Father. Before that there's no happiness at all in this world. It's self-delusion, self-deception. We try to think we are happy.

But then when we try to analyze it, we realize we are very miserable. We are all living comfortably in misery in this world. Nothing else. Some people are living uncomfortably in misery, others are living comfortably in misery. But there's no happiness at all in this world. When you don't know where you may die, when you may die, how you may die, then how can you be happy? When there is so much uncertainty at every step, how can one ever be happy?

So real happiness comes from within, when the soul is yearning towards its own source. The more it is nearer to the Father, the more happy it will be. The more it is away from the Father, the more miserable it will be. So those who are going nearer to the Father, they are happy within, and they radiate happiness in the world. Those who are away from the Father, they're miserable and they radiate misery in the world. So the real happiness is only in the love and devotion of the Father and nowhere else. You can't find that happiness at all anywhere.

So meditation gives you that bliss, that peace, that happiness, that contentment within you. We are trying to seek happiness outside, in worldly objects, worldly possessions, worldly people. And the more we look there, the more miserable we become every day because our pursuit is absolutely in the wrong direction. Only if we try to find happiness within can we succeed in becoming happy. Nobody can find happiness in the sensual pleasures – there's frustration after that. The real happiness is only in meditation, nowhere else. The seat of the soul and mind is at the eye centre. As long as mind is pulled down toward the senses, we are unhappy. When the mind is pulled out of the senses to the eye centre and its tendency is upward, we start becoming happy. So happiness starts from here upward. And misery starts from here downward. Real happiness is only in meditation, nowhere else.

425 Can we experience joy in this life?

You see the wars, people cutting each others' throats. Read the newspaper. Listen to the radio. What is happening? Is it joy? All the bombs, tanks and bullets are being made day and night – is it for joy? We are deceiving ourselves that we are enjoying ourselves. Constant fear of death is there. It can come from anyone at any time, at any place. Then where is that joy? It is a self-deception. Are we at peace with ourselves? Close your eyes and find out – are we happy? Where is joy without happiness? We are always at war with our own self. Conflicts are always there. A wife cannot see eye to eye with her husband; a husband cannot pull on with his wife. There are differences between children, father, parents, mother, friends, country, races. Where is the joy? Where is that peace which you are trying to find in this creation? There is no peace.

But still we try to escape from the worries of the world, problems of the world, misery of the world. The attempt to meditate is trying to escape the misery of the world. The more you open your eyes and try to find joy outside, the more miserable you become, the more unhappy you become. We are becoming more frustrated every day. Aren't there more mental cases now than before? Aren't there more cancer cases than before? Isn't there more hunger in some countries than before? Where is the joy? More divorces, more broken homes. Where is that peace which we are searching for outside? We just live in illusion and self-deception. The more we try to find peace outside, the more miserable we are becoming every day. If there is any joy, it is within us. It cannot be outside at all.

426 You have spoken of happiness – becoming one with God. But what about accomplishments in this world? There are a number of people who have done great things, but who have ended up being very unhappy. How do you feel about that?

You mean people who have achieved great things and yet are unhappy?

Yes, well, take someone like Voltaire, who undoubtedly was miserable all his life, yet he made a great contribution.

Well, brother, you are proving my point that whatever we may do in this world, we can never be happy. We will get the desserts of the good deeds that we do, but we will have to come back to reap the fruits of those good deeds. At the most you can go to heaven. You may get a much richer birth, a better birth, but true happiness you will claim or can get only when you go back to the Father. Worldly achievements can never give you permanent happiness. You may be a king, you may be a ruler, you may do good in the world, but your good deeds alone will never take you back to the Lord. However, you will definitely get their fruit or reward. From a C-class prisoner you will become an A-class prisoner. Instead of iron chains you will be bound with golden chains. From small huts you will be taken to palaces. That is all, nothing else. All the same, you will remain a prisoner.

Yesterday I gave an example that all philanthropists do good to the prisoners by improving their lot, but in spite of everything, the prisoners remain prisoners. Another man comes with the key of that prison house, he opens the gate and sets all the prisoners free. Saints just come for that purpose, to set us free from the world. They do not come to solve our problems. They come to help us to rise above these problems. You can never clear the thorns of the world, but you can definitely put strong shoes on your feet and the thorns will not affect you. Saints give us the faith to live in this world and yet not to be affected by this world. There are great philanthropists in this world, great people who have come and gone. Spirituality is something completely different.

427 *After one has reached a civilized human level, is it possible for the consciousness to lose all of this and to be born again as a monkey, or something of lesser consciousness?*

I do not think this modern civilization has made us better humans. Certainly I do not agree with you. Compare ancient history with modern civilization and you cannot say that we do not fight now, or that there are no bad habits in us, or that we do not slander anybody, we do not murder anybody. First people used to fight with swords, with their hands; now with one bomb you kill thousands. I do not consider that modern civilization has made us better humans at all. We do not have better human qualities because of this civilization. The object of civilization and of a better standard of living is to make us happy. That should be the main criterion of civilization – health and happiness. You cannot say that we are happier and healthier than our forefathers were. They were living just under the shade of a tree, but perhaps were much healthier and happier than with all this steel and concrete, where we are prisoners now.

428 *Would you say, Maharaj Ji, that we are moving from one type of civilization to another type of civilization, that we are now farther away from oneness?*

Yes. People are more miserable now than our elders used to be. We have more anger in us than they had. Their problems were confined within thirty, forty miles of this universe. Our problems are spread throughout this whole world.

Hasn't communication brought us closer to one another?

Closer together for what? For hating each other, for jealousies, for becoming miserable? We have not become happier by becoming closer to each other. In earlier times, people's problems were few because they were only concerned with thirty, forty miles around where they lived. Our problems are worldwide now. You get up in the morning and you read a newspaper: There is a war on the other side of the world in which so many people have died. There is an earthquake somewhere in which so many people have died. A river has washed away so many villages. There is an air crash, there is a train crash. Right when you start the day, you have all this news before you and you are bothered by the problems of the whole world. But in that civilization where there were no newspapers at all, hardly any news reached from one person to another, and they were only concerned with what was happening within an area of thirty or forty miles.

We are more aware of the world situation, but that doesn't mean that we have become happier. We are more aware of each other's problems, but that has not made us happier. The question is whether we are happier than our elders, healthier than our elders.

429 *I would like to understand your logic, sir, but I am overwhelmed by the number of humans, with intellect equal to my own, who prefer the modern progress to the old-fashioned peace and happiness.*

That is what I say; but it is for us to think whether we are improving or are going down. I do not say that they do not prefer it. Everybody likes to be a better human, but whether we are or have become better humans or not, that is what we have to find out. I think the day will come when we will realize that we have to say good-bye to this modern civilization and we will have to go back to the natural way of life to get more peace and better health. I think that consciousness is coming within every one of us that we have reached the top, and now we feel disillusioned with this civilization. With all this material achievement to our credit, are we happier than before, healthier than before? Rather, we are so frustrated that it is agony for anyone to analyze oneself.

430 But I also think that more people are now aware of mysticism or spirituality than in olden times?

That is right. You can give credit to the modern civilization for this because this modern civilization has made us more frustrated and unhappy. So we try to seek peace and lean more towards mysticism, more towards spirituality. In this way you can give modern civilization credit, as it is the cause of our seeking real happiness now.

Improving the world

431 Man has to redeem man, so what part does man play in this evolutionary process?

Brother, man is only to help himself. We can help others only when we have helped ourselves. If we are not in a position to help ourselves, we cannot help others at all. If we have nothing, how can we give anything? Sometimes we try to help others, but instead of helping others, we are making ourselves miserable. We mix with them so much that we share their misery instead of sharing our love with them. We do not have anything within us, so we cannot give what we do not have. By trying to be helpful before we are able to help, we find that we have made ourselves miserable with their plight. We must help ourselves before we can help anybody else. We must have something within us to give and to share with others. If we are empty, how can we give? In order to help humanity, in order to help anybody else, we must rise to that stage where we can help and shower our grace right and left. Then only can we help them, otherwise it is self-deception, and we will only share their agony and misery without being of any help to them at all.

432 *If we attain that highest bliss, how can we humans be happy if we know that our dear ones, or even humanity as a whole, are still suffering? When we still remember such horrible things, how can we be happy?*

Well, sister, are we happy without achieving that highest bliss? Now we see the suffering of humanity right and left; everywhere we see people suffering terribly; they are miserable. Are we happy? No. When we go back to the highest bliss we will be happy. At least then we will have something to share with others, and we can help them to get rid of their suffering. So when we are happy, we also make them happy. But when we do not have anything within us, we cannot share anything with them. And if we do try to help them before we are able to rise above these things, then instead of helping them we only succeed in sharing their miseries and worries, which helps neither them nor us. We only make ourselves miserable and torture ourselves, but if we make spiritual progress and rise above all that and have the real devotion and bliss of the Lord, we are in a position to help them and we are also happy. In other words, we merge into the Lord and become the Lord.

Now you may say, how can the Lord be happy when the whole world is suffering? This world has to go on like that. When it becomes perfect, it will cease to exist. We may think that people are suffering unjustly, but they are all reaping the fruits of their own karmas. How can we be happy when so many of our fellow brothers are in prison houses? We do not feel concerned about them at all because we think they have done something for which they must pay. But we would like to improve them so that they may not do these things again and may not have to go to the prison house again. So we help them from a practical point of view. Similarly, when we get the bliss of the Lord, at least we will be happy and then we can also share our happiness with others and make them happy. We can lead them to the path of bliss, of wisdom, and they also can become happy.

433 Master, how can we share our teachings with leaders of the United Nations?

Sister, we should worry only about ourselves, not about others. We must help ourselves. You cannot solve the problems of the world. You cannot clear all the thorns of the world but you can put shoes on your own feet, so the thorns of the world won't bother you. As Christ has told us, we can rise above these problems.[25] We cannot explain anything to these politicians or to the world or to the public, but we can explain to ourselves. We cannot make other people pure, but we can make ourselves pure. We must make ourselves pure first. We must be a burning and a shining light instead of worrying about other people. Why should you worry about others?

Because they are my brothers and sisters.

You will be able to help them when you become an example for others. Then they will automatically be influenced by you. You can help them only when you are in a position to help yourself.

For example, there are five or six students in a medical college. One student always studies and reads and confines himself to his room. The other students continually play on the grounds and complain that he is selfish when he won't play with them. They taunt him. But that student is working hard. Then that student becomes a doctor. He has helped himself. Now he is in a position to help them also. If he had simply thought: If I study, they will call me selfish; I must be one of them – he would not have helped himself and he would not have been in a position to help them. However, he never worried about the criticism of his friends. He helped himself. He became a doctor. He became qualified. And once he had helped himself, he was then in a position to help them also.

So we must help ourselves. As Christ said, be a living example. When the candle is on a rock, it gives light to everybody. When it is under a bushel, under a basket, it doesn't give light to anyone.[11] If you become a light, automatically other people will benefit from you. You cannot improve the world, but you can improve yourself.

The relationship of the soul with the Father is individual. It is not a collective relationship. Everybody has an individual relationship, a direct relationship with the Father. Just try to develop that relationship within yourself. Improve yourself. Why worry about others? So many civilizations have come and gone, and we are still a part and parcel of this creation. We should think about ourselves.

But we are always watching everything that happens. Can't we help in some way to give the truth, since people are so anxious for it?

Experience the real truth first and then share that truth with them. You can't share the truth without first experiencing it.

434 *Maharaj Ji, this question is about world affairs. I would like to point out that man has accomplished quite a lot in limiting poverty.*

Well, brother, eliminating poverty is different from making people happy. Does social welfare make people happier than before?

There is an expression: Man does not live by bread alone. But bread comes first, Maharaj Ji.

Yes, bread comes first, but you can't live by it alone. You also need something else. If only bread is given to you and nothing else, then you are living comfortably in misery. If only bread could give us peace and happiness, then it would have been very easy to achieve it. Then I think all Americans would have got it. Our problem is that we are trying to find that peace outside. We think that by having all these worldly comforts perhaps we can be happier. The more we try to find peace in those things, the more miserable we are becoming today. You may have more mental cases in your country, more suicides, more hospitals and patients than perhaps we have in India, though we have very poor people. I don't say that we shouldn't try to give bread to the poor – we should. We should try to solve the problem of poverty, but that won't make people happy.

My 21-year-old daughter said to me – when I pointed that out to her – that that is a negative, selfish philosophy based on pleasure, and I had quite a job to explain to her that it wasn't really.

We don't say that we shouldn't be helpful to others, charitable to others. We have a free langar, a free hospital, free facilities here at the Dera. Nobody's lacking for want of money here at all. But this is not the be-all and end-all of why we are here.

435 Our world is always at war. Do you agree?

Yes, brother, unfortunately the world is at war because we are at war with ourselves. If we are able to obtain peace within ourselves, wherever we go we'll radiate peace. When we are at war with ourselves, wherever we go we spread war, ego, possessiveness, selfishness. So we are not happy with ourselves. We are miserable due to these weaknesses, and we make other people miserable by declaring wars and battles and all that, being victim of these weaknesses.

So we cannot pick up the thorns of the world, but we can definitely wear strong shoes so as not to be affected by them. No matter what you do, people will always be at war. History doesn't encourage us. We read the history of five, six, seven thousand years ago – before that we don't know anything. We see that tribes have always been fighting with each other, countries have always been fighting with each other, people have always been fighting with each other, families have always been having family feuds. This has always been going on, and this will continue.

You cannot reform the world. But you can reform yourself so that you are not affected by peoples' fights, their quarrels, because everybody is being dominated by the mind. As long as the mind is ruling us, there will always be war. This is ego which puts us against one another. And due to that ego, we are part of this creation. So how can we avoid this? This will continue. We have to rise above all that so that we are not affected by these things. We should try to obtain peace within ourselves. If we are able to get peace within ourselves, we will radiate peace wherever we go.

You go to a miserable man and in two minutes he will make you miserable. You go to a happy person and in two minutes he will make you forget all your worries and problems and make you happy. Because you always radiate what you have.

Because people have nothing but conflict within them, they are always at war. Everybody prays to the same Lord. Both sides are fighting, and they are praying to the same Father to help them kill each other. What more mockery can there be? We are praying to the same Almighty to kill each other.

So we can't improve the lot of the world. That is why Christ said that I have not come to create peace, I have come with a sword.[39] Don't think that by my coming, this world will become a place of paradise. This world will remain as it is. I want to cut all your roots which pull you back to this creation so that you may never come back to this wretched creation. Christ says, that is my purpose in coming to this world.

So mystics don't come as social reformers, economic reformers, political reformers, or to improve the lot of the people. They come to take us away from this creation. That is their main mission.

436 *In the past it seems like political powers have been threatened by saints and their followers. Do you think there's any danger of that in the foreseeable future?*

Saints don't interfere in politics. They're not interested in any authority; they're not interested in the politics of any country. Saints belong to the whole universe, to everybody. They're interested only in the marked souls, regardless of their country, nationality or creed. They only collect them. They're not interested in anybody else.

437 *Some people seem to think that they can say and do just as they like and justify it by saying it's my karma …*

Every nation justifies war. Every nation justifies killing, knowing very well that they are deceiving themselves. They talk about peace; they are preparing for wars. So far no nation has admitted it started a war. Read the history. Every nation justifies declaring war, fighting, bombing, killing. This is human nature, sister. We all justify our actions. Otherwise, we can't live with ourselves. We become miserable within ourselves. We get a little consolation by justifying our weaknesses, our follies, but that doesn't mean that we get rid of them. We are just fooling ourselves.

438 *Now, I want to come back to the topic of the Ten Commandments. The Israelites were wandering aimlessly, and were the Ten Commandments not meant to put the people in check?*

Then why are we fighting in this world? What have the Ten Commandments done for us today? Have we improved? Have the Ten Commandments been obeyed? Without a living master it is impossible to obey the first two commandments, for he alone can give us the key and teach us how to love God and worship him, and how to love our neighbour as ourselves.

It brought us a little way, I mean we went one little step?

I ask: Have we improved?

Not a notch?

Brother, I'll tell you. I have already told you that so many saints have come into this world. Not only Moses, but so many other saints have come. Have we improved as human beings? I do not find it so. We boast about killing hundreds of thousands with one bomb. Our ancestors only used to stab each other. Probably they could kill one or two in a lifetime. We have killed hundreds and thousands every day. Our ancestors used to kill one bird for their food. Our machines kill millions every day. We boast.

You say we have improved. We have improved because we are living in palaces instead of under trees.

439 Master, it seems like there's more temptation and immorality in the world lately ...

The mind is a very faithful servant of its master, and the mind is always running to the senses, and the mind doesn't want any soul to escape from this world and go back to the Father. So the morality of the world has practically always been the same. Sometimes history reveals it; sometimes we know, sometimes we don't know. Sometimes it's a little higher, a little lower, but if we had been moral and spiritual we would not be here today. We are here as part of the creation because we have not been sufficiently spiritual in the past.

Peace

440 As Jesus said: By their fruit ye shall know them. Does that mean how we act regardless of our intellectual ability, or that, whatever man is, we should love one another?

Brother, when do we love each other? When we have a pure heart, when we have devotion in our heart, then only we will love each other. The nearer we are to the Lord, the nearer we are to each other. The more that devotion and love of the Lord is within us, the more we find we are closer and nearer to each other. The more we are away from him, the more we drift away from each other. When Christ said, love one another,[115] we forget the real essence behind that. We can love one another only when we see the Lord in one another. When we have love of the

Lord within us, we will love one another. Then we do not love persons, but love the Lord within each one of us. We are not lost in individualities and personalities then. We are lost in our love for the Lord. When we are in tune with him, we find him within everyone. When we find him within everyone, the question of superiority and inferiority does not arise; the question of ego does not arise; the question of hatred does not arise. So in order to love one another we must have that love, his love, within us. Then we will find we are also close to each other.

I mentioned somewhere, perhaps in Chicago, that everybody tries to find peace in this world. At least according to what I read in the newspapers, every nation, every country is anxious to create peace in the world. The approach, however, is either political, economic or social, and we can never achieve peace in the world as long as we are trying on those levels. We can never convert all countries and nations to one ideology along those lines. If, on the other hand, our approach becomes spiritual, we can come much closer to each other. But the difficulty is that we do not try to approach each other from the spiritual angle. If everyone realizes that he is to love the same Lord, and we know the same Lord is within everyone of us, and if everybody would make an effort to seek him within, then as we are nearer to the Lord, we will be nearer to each other, and nations and countries will automatically come closer to each other. If our object is one, if our love is one, then we will love one another. If we forget him, ignore him, do not try to know who he is, and yet we want to create peace in the world, we can never succeed on that basis, no matter how hard we may try. History at least does not encourage us from this standpoint.

In order to have this outside peace we must have peace within ourselves. And we can have peace within ourselves only when we are in tune with the Lord, when we are nearer to our destination, when we are nearer to him. Then there will be no ego or hatred or malice against each other. Rather, we will find love in every one of us and we will be much closer to each other, as we will be on the same spiritual platform.

Now we want to create peace with the help of arms, with the help of superiority, with the help of social reform, by changing the political structure of the world, converting people to the political ideology of our own way of thinking. We can never achieve it that way. Politicians may try their way during their whole life, but they will never achieve it. To even think so is just a self-deception. We are talking of peace and preparing for war. We are not living at peace in the world nor with ourselves.

If we want real peace we must search for it within ourselves. The nearer we are to our destination and home, the more we will find that peace within our own selves, the more we will find peace in the whole world, and the more we will be closer and nearer to each other. Generally, when you meet satsangis, those who are travelling on the same path, you do not need an introduction; you feel so close to each other. You just meet and you feel that you have known each other for ages. Why? The objective is the same. Love is the same. The destination is the same. You are all nearer to the Lord, so you are all nearer to each other.

In order to find peace we must look for it in the right direction. Unless we merge in that light, unless we become a part of that light about which Christ said, if thine eye be single, thy whole body shall be full of light[23] – unless we see that light within us, unless we merge into that light, we can never get peace. But nobody tries to open that eye, nobody tries to see that light. We are ignoring – rather, we ridicule and mock anybody who talks about that light, or about that single eye or third eye. So how can we get peace in this world?

441 Do those who hanker after happiness and peace require a guru equally, the same as in mystical work?

As I said in one of my lectures here, everybody wants happiness. There is hardly anybody who does not want peace. But the question is whether the place where we are trying to search for peace is the place where peace can be found. If we want peace politically, economically, socially, we will never achieve it. History does not encourage us. We will always be at war with each other. So many social reformers have come into this world, so many statesmen and world politicians have been here, but we are not better humans, nor are we enjoying more peace. We are always fighting against each other. I think our approach is wrong.

If we try to find peace spiritually, on the spiritual platform, we will get peace within ourselves and we will radiate peace everywhere we go. If we are to find peace, we have to seek peace within our body. Unless you seek peace within yourself, you will never find peace outside. The nearer we humans are towards the Lord, the closer we all will be to each other. The more we forget him, the more we are deviating from each other, the more we are hating each other. So, if we really want peace, let us go back to the same goal, the same source or origin, the same destination. The closer we come to him, the closer we come to each other. That is why Christ said, love one another.[115] And we can only love one another when we love the Lord, when we love our own destination, when we stand on the spiritual platform. But in our search for peace we are ignoring the spiritual platform.

Even our politicians want to use the spiritual platform, not from a spiritual point of view but from a political point of view. They are interested only in power and votes, and not in you and me. They do not mind killing thousands and hundreds of thousands in order to gain power. Not that they are spiritual, but that they want to use the name of religion for their own selfish ends and means. But who listens to you and me?

We can find peace only within ourselves. Unless we seek that peace within ourselves, we can never be happy even in this world. Sometimes you are in agony, you are at war with yourself, you are unhappy, even if you live in a palace. You may have a thousand dishes before you, you may have many happy people around you, but you are not happy – nothing appeals to you. But when you are happy within yourself, then you find love and joy even from anything you pick up; every step you take, you just dance with happiness.

I often give an example: A child goes to the World's Fair, holding on to his father's hand. Everything in the fair appeals to the child. Somewhere children are playing, somewhere there are trained porpoises and whales performing, music, electric lights and so many other things to enjoy that the child probably thinks that he is getting happiness out of all that he sees and hears in the fair. But the moment he loses hold of his father's hand and is lost in separation from the father, then he begins to weep. The same things are still going on in the fair, but nothing appeals to him. Then he realizes that he could get peace and joy from this fair only as long as he was holding the hand of his father. Similarly, we have only one Father, as is mentioned in the Bible. As long as we remain in his will, we are holding his hand, we love him, we are devoted to him, we are in communion with him, or we are trying to seek him or are on our way to him, we will be happy and we will also find peace while in this world. The moment we forget him, or lose hold of his hand, this whole world will be nothing but an agony.

Any number of politicians or social reformers may come into this world, but they will never be able to create peace in this world at all, merely on political and social levels. But if peace is attained on a spiritual level, then everything else is included, and that peace alone is permanent.

442 *I wondered how mind can kill the ego in me and still continue the contribution to making the world a better place to live in.*

You see, if you are able to obtain peace within yourself, you will be able to radiate peace wherever you go. If you are miserable within yourself, you will do nothing but spread misery anywhere you go. And we can only obtain peace within ourselves when we are able to eliminate ego. As long as we are in the realm of ego, we are all miserable. Whether we are living uncomfortably in misery or comfortably in misery, we are all in misery. We can never get peace. No matter what you have in this world, what you possess in this world, you can never be happy. You can have the whole world at your command, but you can never be happy in this world. Otherwise, these kings would have been happy, these maharajas would have been happy, these rulers and dictators would have been happy.

We sleep six, seven hours at night, but they have to depend upon these injections and tablets to sleep. We have to worry just about our family, our wife and children, but they have to worry about a whole nation, a whole country. So we can never obtain peace outside at all. We can only obtain peace within ourselves – not by possessing things but by detaching ourselves from those things. If we want more and more, more and more, we can never be happy. If we are leaving those things and are taking our mind out of all that, we can become happy. Ego means more possession, more possession, more possession.

Guru Nanak says: One who doesn't need anything in this creation, he is the king of the kings. And Christ also has said the same thing, that it is more difficult for a rich man to go to heaven than for a camel to pass through the eye of a needle.[61] In other words, it is impossible for one who is attached to the riches of the world to go back to the Father.

Ego doesn't give us happiness. Only when we eliminate ego will we be able to obtain happiness within ourselves. And once you are happy, wherever you will go you will make people happy. You go to a humorous person, a happy person – he will make you happy in two minutes. You go to a miserable person, in two minutes he will make you miserable.

So you can improve nations, you can improve the environment, you can improve everybody around you by improving your own self. This world can be a better place to live in if we are able to obtain that peace within ourselves. We can never come together on an economic platform, a political platform, or a social platform. But we can always come together on a spiritual platform. The Father is one; our soul is the essence of the same Father; we are travelling on the same path; our destination is the same; so we are the same and we can all become one on that level. At no other level can we become one. That is why there is so much conflict between nations, between countries, between tribes.

That is why Christ said that I have not come to create peace, but have come with a sword.[39] I want to detach you from this creation; I don't want to improve your standard of living in this world. That is not the purpose of the mystics. They come to detach us from this creation. And we can only get detached from this creation when we are able to eliminate the ego. Christ says: If you build your treasure in heaven, you will go to heaven. If you build your treasure in the world, you come back to the world.[22] Building your treasure means if you are attached to this creation you always remain part of this creation. If you are lucky enough to attach yourself to the Creator, you will go back to the Creator.

So unless we are able to eliminate our ego, how can we go back to the Creator? How can we improve the lot of this world? We will never be able to obtain that peace and happiness in this creation, no matter what we have, what we achieve.

443 *There is so much vivisection done in Western science. In experiments, animals are cut up while still alive and feeling. How can it ever be for the sake of human beings to torment other beings?*

It is this world. For everybody, there's a struggle for existence. We are all cutting each other's throats. The bigger insects eat the smaller insects. Fish eat all the insects in the water. The big fish eat all the small fish, and so on. On land, lions eat what they like and man kills the lions. We are all bloodthirsty. Humans are bloodthirsty for each other, cutting each other's throats. It's a struggle for existence. But God has created this creation that way. There never has been peace in this world. People have always been fighting with each other. Thus far nobody has been able to know what for.

The ego says, "This is mine, this is mine, this is mine." And yet these things never belonged to anyone. They never went with anyone at death – they are still here. The same land which Alexander wanted to make his still exists, but Alexander doesn't exist. Hitler wanted to conquer the whole of Europe. He's not here; Europe is still here. It is possessions, ego, attachment, which make us kill each other – the struggle for existence, for possessions. If we realize that everything belongs to him and nothing belongs to us, we would never even hurt anybody. Then we would see that the Lord is in every one of us. As Christ said: Love thy neighbour.[67] The whole creation becomes our neighbour. We see him everywhere in this creation. Guru Nanak says that if the love and devotion for the Father comes in you, then the whole creation becomes your family. Then you will have the same love for the whole creation as you have for your own limited family, and you will see that Lord in everyone. But as long as ego is there, attachment is there, we can't cease cutting each other's throats.

A hundred United Nations may come and go, but they cannot eliminate ego from a man. There can be no peace in this creation at all, no matter what they do. First people used to fight with their hands, then with sticks, then with spears, then with swords, then with guns, then with tanks and now with bombs. Still they are fighting. What for? Nobody has been able to know what for. What do they gain after that? Nobody knows. It is ego. That same ego makes us kill animals for our food. And that same ego makes us kill each other. We just want excuses to kill each other. This belongs to the Muslim. This belongs to the Hindu. This belongs to the Sikh. This belongs to the Christian. Each thinks the other has no right to exist. We have become bloodthirsty. Yet nobody gains anything in this creation. People come and go, but the creation still exists. There's no answer to "Why?" It's only ego. So unless we eliminate ego from within ourselves there can be no peace in this world. We can have peace within ourselves but we cannot create peace in the world. We cannot pick up the thorns of the world, but we can definitely wear shoes and not be affected by them. We can rise above these things, but we cannot stop people from killing each other.

I said that even humans are cutting each other's throats, what to say of animals. Whom will you stop? Everybody is killing each other. This whole creation is such. That is why saints say that this world is not worth living in for you; this place has not much worth for you at all. Leave this creation. We should go back to the Father. We will not find peace in this creation at all. Nobody knows who kills whom, when, where, how. Nobody knows.

444 *Master, I have a question. It's not mine, somebody told me to ask you. There is a lot of talk of nuclear war now, that the end of the world will come soon. Can you comment on that?*

Well, if the Lord wants it, who can stop it? You see, there has never been peace in this creation. We read history and see that countries and people have always been fighting. Our method of wars or battles has become different but otherwise we have always been fighting. This is human nature. We have always been fighting. If we are not fighting with anybody else, then we are fighting with our own selves. We are not at peace with ourselves. We are always at war with our own selves.

There can never be peace in this world, no matter how much the United Nations or any other organization may endeavour to create it. There can never be peace in this world because people don't have peace within themselves. Unless we are able to develop that peace within ourselves, there can never be peace in this creation at all. At least history does not encourage us. Human conflicts are always there. There is no peace in our family life, no peace with our children, no peace with our neighbours. That is the human mind. That's why Christ said, blessed are the peacemakers.[10] Those who have been able to obtain peace within themselves will radiate peace. Go to a miserable person and he will make you miserable in two minutes; you go to a happy person and he will make you happy in two minutes. So unless we develop that peace within ourselves, how can we radiate peace? We are full of war within ourselves, and we are talking about creating peace in this world? It's impossible – just a self-deception.

445 *Is there any purpose to life on this planet earth, other than just to get out of it to find happiness? I mean, is the whole history …*

All other things are secondary to this happiness. If you are unhappy, you may have a whole kingdom at your disposal, but it's no use to you. Ask a sick person – if you give him a lot of wealth, if he lives in luxury, what use is that wealth to him if he is crying day and night because of his physical pain? What use can he make of it? If somebody has no digestion at all, and you tell him that you have brought him so much delicious food – eat as much as you can – what use is that food to him if he can't feel hunger and has no digestion?

The main purpose of this life is to obtain that peace and happiness within ourselves. That is the purpose of every religion. That is the purpose of every society. That is the purpose of every home. The husband wants to make his wife happy, the wife wants to make her husband happy, the mother wants to keep her children happy, children want to give peace to their parents. The foundation of nations and societies and religions is based on that, to find peace, to live in peace and happiness.

Well, then, why are we going to the moon? Isn't there an objective? Are we not reaching for something more abstract as a society? Aren't we going to reach the stars, physically?

Because we are not searching for peace in the right direction. We are searching for peace in the opposite direction. So we are becoming more miserable.

You mean we won't discover a better world one day?

The one who can give us peace – the Lord – we ignore him. We have turned our back to him. That which makes us miserable – this creation, the love of this creation – for that we are hankering day and night. So how can we obtain peace? Everything is subordinate to peace. No matter what you have in this creation, if you are miserable, it is no use to you at all.

I am miserable because I don't know the truth; not because I'm poor or anything, but because I don't know the truth. I don't know the truth about life.

That's what I say, we are miserable because we don't know the truth. And truth is only one. All other things are perishable. There's only one truth – the Lord. Everything else is just an illusion, just perishable. We are living in illusion, hankering for this illusion, and not trying to find that truth. Saints give an example drawn from traditional Indian family life: If a wife is separated from her husband, no matter how much wealth you give her, how many ornaments you give her or what a beautiful home you give her, no matter how much you respect or humour her, she can never be at peace. All she needs is her husband and his love. Other things are meaningless without her husband and his love. She can enjoy all these things only as long as she has her husband's love and his company. Without that, these things make her miserable. The soul is the wife and the Father is the husband. Only the love of the Father can give us peace and happiness, nothing else.

446 Maharaj Ji, when we come on the path, is this supposed to bring us peace and harmony within ourselves?

Well, sister, peace and harmony come from within. It does not come from anywhere outside at all. You have to find that peace within yourself. Peace will come only from within yourself, when you are living with yourself, when you are happy and contented within yourself. Then naturally you will be at peace. If you still have doubts and are unresolved about the teachings, naturally you can't be at peace. When you know this path is meant for you, you are going to practice it, you are going to achieve it, then you will build that peace within yourself. Peace has to come from within you, nowhere else.

What is peace? When we have no desires. When we have no anxiety. As long as your mind is creating desires and you are trying to satisfy those desires and you are not able to satisfy those desires, you can never be at peace. Only when you become desireless can you be at peace. And you can become desireless only if you get something better than the sensual pleasures, because the mind is always wanting something. When we get diamonds we won't worry about silver or anything else. When we get something within much better than the sensual or worldly pleasures, then automatically your mind leaves the sensual pleasures. Then you are at peace. As long as the tendency of the mind is downward from here toward the senses, howsoever much we may indulge in those senses, we will never be at peace. But when we are able to withdraw ourselves from the senses to the eye centre and become one with that audible life stream or that shabd, with that divine light within, then automatically your mind will be at peace.

The more you are going towards your home, the more you are on the path to your destination, the more you will be at peace. The more you are driven away from your destination, the more you are going astray from your destination, the more you will be at war with yourself. You will be unhappy and miserable.

Our destination is from the eye centre upwards, not downwards. So when the tendency of the mind is downwards, we can never be at peace, even if we have all the riches of the world. The whole world may be at your command, but you can never be at peace. When you are able to withdraw from all these senses and come to the eye centre and you are on the path leading towards your home, to your destination, then you will get relief, then you will be at peace. One can never be at peace in a foreign land. One can only be at peace in one's own home country. Our real home is where the Father lives. As long as we are separated from him we can never be at peace. The whole world may be at our command, but we will never be satisfied, we will never be happy. We will always crave something, we will always feel frustrated. That is why Christ has said: Come to me and I'll give you rest.[45] A man who's always moving, always walking, he can never be at peace. Only a man who can rest can be at peace. When we are always shifting from one flesh to another flesh, from one birth to another birth, from one species to another species, when we are always moving, always a slave of one body or another, then how can we be at peace? We can only be at peace when we escape from this moving, or transmigration of the soul, and are able to go back to our own source. Only then we can be at peace, not before.

447 *The Bible says: A merry heart is a good medicine, but a broken spirit dries up the bones.*[2]

Sister, the Bible is full of mysticism, full of spirituality, but nobody tries to make a research about it. Christ very beautifully said that your prayer will never be accepted by the Lord if you do not first forgive everybody.[16] As long as you have malice in your heart, or hatred against anybody, or ill-feelings, your prayer will never be accepted by the Lord. If you want to pray to the Lord, first go and ask for forgiveness from the one you have injured. When he forgives you, then your prayer will be heard by the Lord. Only the pure-hearted can reach him. And only a pure heart can be a merry heart, can be genuinely happy. When we are always thinking of cutting each other's throats, nation against nation, religion against religion, country against country, tribe against tribe, how can we have peace and be really happy or merry? We should not have hatred or malice towards each other. There should be no thought of revenge, even if we feel that we have been injured. Did not Jesus say that if someone smites you on one cheek you should turn the other? We have to develop that love and devotion for the Lord within ourselves. Then we will follow these teachings automatically, which will give us peace within ourselves. And when we find peace within ourselves, we will have it all around us.

If such is everyone's approach, we can all, on a spiritual platform, become one; we are all one. But if you think you will be able to convert another nation to another ideology of living, you can never do it. If you think you can convert the whole world, you can never do it politically. There has never been one ideology in this world, politically. Read the history of the world. So our endeavour is to try along the spiritual line. First we have to reform ourselves. If you try to pick up the thorns of the world, you can never succeed, but if you put strong shoes on your feet, no thorns will bother you. Similarly, we can never solve the problems of this world, but we can always rise above them. The saints just give us the strong shoes – they give us the essence of spirituality to help us find peace within ourselves and radiate peace wherever we go. When we have joy within ourselves, we find joy and beauty all around us; and if we do not have joy or peace or happiness within ourselves, even the most beautiful thing does not appeal to us. So we have to reform ourselves rather than reform the world.

448 Maharaj Ji, do you foresee that there will be a time in the world when there'll be so much love, there will be so much of Sant Mat, that there will be no more wars?

Sister, if this creation is to continue, we cannot get rid of these wars, because if creation has to continue, it has to be imperfect. The moment anybody becomes perfect, he goes back to the perfect one. That soul doesn't stay in the imperfect world at all. We are only here because we are imperfect. If he doesn't want this creation to continue, then of course, we all become perfect and go to the perfect one. But if this creation is to continue, then you can't help it, mind has to be here. It has to be imperfect. As long as we're imperfect, there'll always be feuds and wars. You can't help them. At least history doesn't encourage us. Whatever history we have been able to trace or know, it has always revealed one against the other, in one form or another.

Because that is the mind – the mind has always been at war. Nations to a great extent can come nearer to each other on the platform of spirituality, never on the platform of social reforms, economic reforms, or political reforms. We can never have the same way of thinking economically, politically or socially. We can never all think alike. But on the spiritual platform we are one and we can become one; we can come nearer to each other because our pivot is one God, and everyone looks to him. On the platform of spirituality, we are one. Then we don't appear as belonging to certain races, countries, social orders, economic orders, or political orders. We just appear as all lovers of one Beloved, and then we are all nearer to each other.

So if we really want peace in this world, we have to come together on the platform of spirituality. No matter how politically developed a nation may become, no matter how much it may raise its standard of living – that doesn't mean that those nations with a very high standard of living don't create war. Rather, they are responsible for creating more wars because they want to keep their own standard of living high. And how can they keep it unless people fight? So their standard of living is high at the cost of other people's loss. They always want to sell their goods so that their standard of living remains high; so they always like other nations to fight. Actually, nobody is sincere about creating peace in this world.

If we are filled with love and devotion for the Father, all qualities of compassion, of being kind and good to each other, loving to each other, automatically come in us. One who is filled with his love, he will never hate anybody, because he will see the Lord in everybody. He will never notice that someone is a Russian, an American, a South African, an Indian. He sees only the Lord in everybody. We are ignoring this spiritual side today, and trying to build peace on political platforms, on social and economic platforms, and they have no base. It's like building on sand. Otherwise, rich nations would have been able to obtain peace, but they have not. Probably there's more crime in them than in poor countries. There may be more mental asylums, a higher suicide rate in those countries than in the poor countries. They have compromised with certain spiritual truths in order to raise their standard of living. If we build a spiritual platform – but it is impossible for the whole world to build one spiritual platform – only then can we come nearer to each other.

Marked souls

449 *How do we know if we are making the proper search for God?*

It is the accumulated effect of our karma. In whatever way we search for the Father, if we are honest and sincere, we invoke the grace of the Father to mark us, to put us on the right path. Then we are marked by the Father – we are drawn towards a mystic or a saint and automatically we follow the path. The marking is not done as a result of one or two lives, but because of many lives. It is always by the grace of the Father that we come in contact with any saint or mystic.

450 *Could you say something about how the master recognizes his own sheep?*

Because the marking is done by the Father, and he knows the marking is done by the Father. Only those sheep will come to him who have been marked for him. No other sheep will come to him at all. Someone may be living right under the master's nose, but he does not have any faith in him, so he will never come to him. He will never take him as the master. Only the marked one will come – though he may be living thousands of miles away from him. So the master does recognize his own sheep. Christ said: I speak in parables because everybody is not meant to understand them. Only those who are meant to understand them, only they will understand.[49] The teachings are not for everybody. The teachings are meant only for those who are marked to understand, who are allotted by the Father to understand. Others will not even understand the teachings.

451 *Can we visibly ascertain whether we're ready or not for initiation? Some of us seem to be in such terrible disrepair when we come to the master.*

Nobody is initiated unless he has to be initiated. Neither the disciple has any choice, nor the master has any choice. All souls belong to the Father, and the master is engaged only to collect those souls, to bring them back to the Father. They don't belong to the master. They belong to him who has marked them for a particular shepherd. So when the shepherd whistles, all who are marked for him automatically flock around him. He has no right to refuse any and they have no option but to go to him.

Even though after initiation it seems that there are many satsangis who deny the path and just want to …

Whatever you may say, I have frankly told you the facts. Nobody has any choice. Read the Bible very thoroughly and you will know it. Christ says: I don't do anything of my own. I do what my Father wants me to do. I've no will of my own at all. And I've no right to refuse anybody.[120] And when I whistle my sheep recognize my whistle. They run to me.[104] They also have no option. You see, in a hundred people you know the voice of your husband. If you call for him, even out of the hundred, at once he will recognize your voice and you will recognize his voice. His voice differs from everybody else's. You will at once recognize without seeing him that your husband is speaking there. Because you are linked with him, you know his voice.

That is why Christ says that my sheep know my whistle, they know my voice; they know me. The Lord is giving them the understanding to know me, and they will automatically come to me. And if they come to me I have no right to refuse them, because I don't do anything on my own at all. I do what he wants me to do. Sometimes sheep do come to the shepherd but they run away, they go astray. He again picks them up and again brings them back to the fold. And that is why Christ gave the example: If there are a hundred sheep and one goes astray, the shepherd runs after even the one sheep. He's not content to have ninety-nine.[57] Why should he bother about that one black sheep who is always running out of the fold? The master runs after even that one sheep and physically lifts that sheep and brings it back to the fold again because he loves all of them. And he's responsible for them all. Christ has not given us these parables just to amuse us. They have very deep spiritual meaning behind them. Ultimately no sheep is allowed to go astray. It has to come to the fold.

452 Is it coincidence when we meet a master?

There's no coincidence in Sant Mat. Everything happens according to a divine plan. You don't meet a master as a coincidence;

you don't come to the path as a coincidence. You don't select your parents just by coincidence; you don't select your brother and sister just by coincidence. There is some karmic relationship which brings you to that. There is some string at the back which is being pulled – why you are being asked to play that part on this stage. There is no coincidence here. Whatever has to happen has already happened. We are just spectators of our destiny. Those who have to come to the path will come automatically. Those who are not meant to come to the path, you may break their heads with all your knowledge explaining it to them, but they will never come to the path. As Christ said, my sheep know me and I know my sheep. When I whistle, they all flock to me because they know me.[104] So when the mystics come, all allotted souls automatically flock around them. They know their master and he knows them. They don't gather by coincidence. Christ said, I pray for them, not for the world,[128] because he's responsible only for those allotted sheep who have been entrusted to his care by the Father.

It's a very beautiful example Christ gave, you see. The sheep always belong to the landlord, who engages a shepherd to look after the sheep. The shepherd is responsible to the landlord for all his sheep, to look after those sheep. So similarly, souls belong to the Father, and mystics or saints are his shepherds. They are sent to look after those allotted sheep who belong to the Father. So the master is responsible only for those allotted to his care, not for everybody.

When Christ knew that he was going to leave his disciples physically, that he would be no more with them to guide them in this world, he prays to the Father: According to your instructions, I have put them on the path. I have looked after them. Now, since you are calling me back, I pray to you to look after them.[129] He is responsible only for those allotted sheep. And those allotted sheep won't come to him just by coincidence. The marking is done somewhere else; we only listen to his whistle and flock around him.

If you have a little experience of seeing shepherds grazing their goats or sheep, you will see that there are two or three flocks and two or three shepherds. When a shepherd whistles, only his particular sheep will go to him – they will not go to another shepherd. There are maybe five thousand sheep brought together and they may belong to three different folds and three different shepherds. When one shepherd whistles, only those sheep which belong to him will come to him – the other sheep won't even listen to his whistle. That is why Christ says that my sheep know me and I know them, so when I whistle they all flock around.[104] There's no coincidence on the path at all.

453 *If a soul is initiated in this life, the soul is with the master. But if the soul has to come back a second time, then from birth, even before initiation, the guru will be with the soul?*

The guru will always be guiding that soul and ultimately will bring that soul to the path. The guru will not leave that soul; the guru will be with that soul right from birth. Some of you may have experienced that even before we heard about the path, when we knew nothing about the master or the path or anything, we always felt some guiding hand with us, always – which was something of a mystery to us. And then suddenly we find we have come on the path without searching, without any intellectual research, without reading, without ever having felt the necessity for a master or a desire to go back to the Father. Suddenly, in a few days circumstances develop, and we find that we are on the path. For us it is sudden, but for the master it is not sudden. We are not allowed to go so astray that we will not come back to the path. So master has to take care of that soul right from the beginning. Actually, right from the initiation, master never leaves that soul so that it may not go astray at all. He's always there in one form or another.

As you have often seen, a boy flying a kite lets out the string as much as he can, but he always keeps hold of the string. When he finds the kite is flying out of control, he just pulls it back. When he starts seeing that the kite is probably coming down too fast, he starts pulling it tight and again it goes up. So similarly, master always holds the string in his hand, and will never allow us to go so astray that we may not be able to come back to the path again. Even if we go astray, there's always a limit. We are brought back. The guiding hand is always there, right from birth.

454 Is it always a disadvantage, spiritually, to be born in the West, far away from the physical master?

There's no disadvantage at all. You see, we are all the same. The human mind is the same, whether it is in the East or in the West. You will find many noninitiates near the Dera. They are born in India – and not only in India – but living right in the neighbourhood. They may even be attending satsang. They have never thought about initiation. So for the Lord, there's no West and East. Maybe for you and me there is West and East, but not for the Lord. Christ said that my sheep hear my whistle, my sheep recognize my whistle and they all flock around me.[104] So when he calls, all the allotted and marked souls flock around the master. There's no question of East and West.

455 I don't quite understand. It is said that a soul, before it gets initiated, is marked. A person to be initiated is marked. Why is it necessary to really understand everything intellectually, if we feel the pull enough to ask for initiation? If a person is marked, it shouldn't make any difference if he is intellectually …

No, you see, when the marking is there from the Lord's side, then all things start moving in that direction, and then you realize suddenly that you know everything. There is nothing new on the path. All your questions get dissolved or satisfied, and you are prepared to sacrifice everything for that path when you are marked. Otherwise it won't appeal to you. Christ said: I speak in parables. Somebody asked him: Why do you speak in parables? Why can't you be straight? He says: Those who are meant to follow me, only they will understand my parables. Others won't understand them.[49] Those who are marked will understand. Others won't understand him at all.

456 *You read in the books and so on about how you have to have some merit, that the soul has performed so many good works or has suffered so much. But so many people in the world are suffering, and many people are much better than some satsangis, so how does master choose whom he initiates?*

It's not essential that only good people become satsangis. Who goes to the doctor? A healthy person or a sick person? You read in the Bible what Christ said: Only the thirsty will go to the well.[96] One who thinks he is good, he will never try to find a master at all. One who feels he's bad and wants to improve will search for him. Now whether what we call 'good' is really good or not is a very moot point – it's difficult to say.

You see, we are on the path due to our past karmas, his grace, his marking, and he knows best whom to mark. People who look too good to us, we don't know what they have been doing in the past to deserve all that, that they have become good in our eyes. And people who are so-called bad, we don't know what good they have done in the past. And yet, unfortunately, they look bad in our eyes. So everybody has individual karmas, and the marking is done by the Father.

You can't put any limitation on the Father – whom to mark and whom not to mark. He knows best whom to mark. If we can find out his criterion for marking, then we are limiting his power. But he is limitless. Only the marked one will come. The allotted soul will come, not otherwise. And the soul comes to become whole, to become good in the eyes of the Father, not in the eyes of the world – because those souls don't want any appreciation from the world. Worldly appreciation will pull them back into the creation. Fatherly appreciation will pull them to the level of the Father.

So it's very difficult to say who's good and who's bad. Everybody, according to their own karmas, has a certain allotted part to play on this stage. One who realizes that he's playing a part is good. One who doesn't realize that he is playing a part – he thinks he's doing it: "Who can make me play? I do everything" – he's bad, howsoever good he may look to us, to the eyes of the world. One who has been able to eliminate the ego and realize that there's somebody else at the back pulling us and we're dancing to his tune, he's good. One who thinks: "I am dancing; who can make me dance?" – he's bad, bad in the sense that he will come back to this creation. And the other person is good in the sense that he will go back to the Creator. He has eliminated his ego and realized his self.

So you see, we all come to the path to become good, to become whole. That is why Christ said: You have become whole – go and sin no more, lest a worse thing fall upon you.[85] You have become whole since you have been put on the path. You're now in the process of becoming whole, provided you don't sin anymore, don't add more to your karmas – lest a worse thing happens to you. What kind of worse thing can happen to a soul? Taking another birth, coming back to some other body, that is the worst which can happen to a soul – remaining separated, condemned to be separate from the Father. That can only happen if we don't become whole and go on adding to our sins, adding to our karmas.

So when he puts us on the path, he puts us on the path to becoming whole, to becoming good in his eyes. Whether the world crucifies you or condemns you or shoots you, it's immaterial. They can't crucify your soul. They can't shoot your soul. They can't put your soul behind bars. They can destroy the body, that's all. But 'good' we have to see from the soul's point of view.

457 Master, when I look at the people who are living in my neighbourhood, I can see many good people, people who do their duty smilingly, who are full of love and devotion and so on. And then when I look at myself I see so many weaknesses, and yet the Lord has chosen me to let me go home. This is totally incomprehensible to me.

He knows best whom he has to mark. He doesn't have to mark the best. He can mark the worst also. He knows best. Everyone is better than us. Nobody is worse than us, when we look within our own self, because we know where we stand. We don't know about anybody else. Everybody's good. It depends upon from which angle you see him. Nobody's bad. If you rub someone on the wrong side, naturally he will react. Everybody's good, nobody's bad.

I feel sort of helpless because I think I got something for nothing.

Sister, only a patient goes to a doctor. A healthy person doesn't go to a doctor. Only a thirsty person will find a well. If he doesn't need to drink the water, he won't touch such a well. He knows best whom to mark. Who are we to judge? It is not one life that can tell us whether we are worth being marked or not. God knows since when we have taken birth, and since then we have been moving about here in one form or another. So it is grace that he has put that seed of love and devotional pull within every one of us. Let us respond to it, let's make use of it. What do we know about other people? We know nothing about anybody. We need to be concerned only with ourselves.

458 *When you met your master, did you know right away, when you saw him, that he was your master without a doubt?*

I was born in the family. I didn't have to select him, to choose him. I knew him right from my birth.

And you just accepted that?

More than that. You see, to us, Sant Mat has come through the master. To you, the master has come through Sant Mat. It makes a difference, a lot of difference. You are convinced by the teachings and then you look to the preceptor who gives you that teaching. But we look to the preceptor, and whatever he gives is the teaching for us.

459 *Master, are all souls destined to go back to the Father? And, if not, where do they go?*

Sister, if all souls were destined to go back to the Father, then the question of marking wouldn't arise. When the Father says only those will go back who are marked by him, then automatically they will go back. If the creation is to continue, then all souls can't go back. If this creation is not to continue, then there is no other place to go but back to the Father. But as long as this creation is to continue, some souls have to stay; there is no other alternative. If this building is to be built, some bricks have got to be used in the foundation. They must be in the foundation to hold the bricks on the ceiling, on the roof. Every brick can't be on the ceiling. Some bricks must be there in the foundation.

So every soul can't go back to the Father. Only those who are marked by him will ultimately go back to the Father, because if he wants this creation to continue, it has to be imperfect. The moment anybody becomes perfect in this creation, he merges back into the perfect being. He becomes one with the perfect being. We can only remain in this creation as long as we are imperfect. So that is why what we call evil exists, because this world has to be imperfect. It's a combination of the good and bad.

460 *Those people who wish to be drawn, meet a master and receive initiation – why should the Lord want some to be drawn more than others?*

I think we should give some sort of discretion to the Lord. We can't bind him to any conditions. If he's free, then we can't restrict his choices or discretion. He's free. He knows best whom he's to mark and when to mark and how to mark.

But those who are marked will eventually get pulled to a saint?

Whosoever is marked, automatically will be pulled sooner or later. We think that we have found the path, but the one who's bringing us to the path is behind us, and we suddenly find that we are on the path. What have we done to find it? If you analyze yourself, you realize: What have I done to search for the path?

Suddenly you find you're on the path. The one who is guiding you is behind you, and you don't know when he's guiding you to that and how he's guiding you to that. Actually, from a higher point of view, we're all puppets. You can't blame anybody – we're all puppets. There's absolutely no free will, absolutely none.

Christ has gone so far as to say that even the hairs on your body are numbered.[38] And hair is an insignificant thing. Whether you have ten less or ten more, it hardly makes any difference to you. But it means that you have not even the slightest amount of free will.

And Guru Nanak says: Without his order, even a leaf doesn't move. When the wind blows, so many leaves are moving. Whether they move or not, what difference does it make to anybody? But he says even this leaf can't move without his order. So what free will is left?

Guru Nanak gives a very beautiful example. One who shows you a puppet show has one big bag and all the puppets are in the bag. He just pulls them out and puts them on the stage. At the back of every puppet is a string, and the puppet master behind the screen is pulling each one from behind the screen. All the puppets are dancing. The puppets think that they are dancing. Who can make them dance? They do not realize the strings behind them and the person who's pulling at the back of the screen.

So he says: The realized soul knows that there's a string behind me and somebody is pulling the string and I am dancing to the tune of that person. The unrealized soul thinks, "Who can make me dance? I dance." He is dancing with his ego. To the person who's seeing the show, there's no difference, since they're all dancing. But there's a difference in their dancing. One has realized that there's somebody at the back who's pulling the strings. The other hasn't realized that there's a person who's at the back. That's the only difference between a gurmukh and a manmukh. They both live in this world and pass through all sorts of activities in life. But one has realized that he's absolutely a puppet, that somebody is behind him making him dance, and he has submitted himself to him – he is dancing according to his tune. The other is just a slave of his ego and thinks, "I am dancing." Both are dancing in this world.

461 *I've heard you say Sant Mat can't be taught but has to be caught.*

If you say you are able to catch Sant Mat by intellect, you are wrong. There is some other power within you who forces you and puts you on the path. Then you are helpless but to follow the path. The pull is from within. The pull is not anywhere from outside. It is not by your own intellect or by your own desire to go back to the Father that you are able to meet a master or find the path. That hidden power is always working from behind, and you get such circumstances that you find that you know the path, and everything becomes so clear to you that you want to follow it.

Then what you are saying is that Sant Mat catches you.

Sant Mat catches you. You don't catch Sant Mat at all. We don't worship the Lord; the Lord creates that feeling, that desire within us to worship him. That is why every day we discuss that marking is first done by the Father, and that marking creates that desire to follow the path, to go to the mystics, to live in their teachings and to change our way of life. That marking is responsible for all this, and that marking is not in our hand. That is in the Father's hand.

Well, then all the willpower and the desire to meditate and to read the books, even to see the master, is all put in there by the Lord?

Yes. I've given the example sometimes that if you are hungry and there is no food on the plate, what will you eat? And if there is delicious food on the plate and you have no hunger, even then you won't eat. If you have hunger and there also is food on the plate, only then will you eat. It is not in your hands to create that hunger and to put that food on your plate. It is in the Lord's hands to give you that hunger and to put the food on the plate. You can take credit only for the fact that you are eating.

Master, sometimes it feels that the Lord gives us the hunger, and the food is on the plate, but then the plate is kind of separate from us …

Yes, he does that to generate more hunger in you so that you may relish the food. Otherwise you won't relish it. If a man is not hungry and you bring delicious food before him, he will find a hundred faults with the food. But if the real hunger is there, he will never find fault with the food. He eats in gratitude. So these are the ways of the Lord, how to generate more hunger in us.

462 *What about those people living in various parts of the world who have never had the opportunity to meet or make the acquaintance of a living master? What chance have they got?*

It is for the Lord to mark people, to put them on the path. It is not in anybody's hands. That is why Christ says that only those who are meant to understand my teachings will understand my parables. My teaching is not for everybody.[49] Only those whom my Father wants will be pulled by me. They will automatically be drawn by me. I don't go to collect them. They will be pushed by the Father to me. And I am nobody to refuse them. So the marking is to be done by the Father, and he will collect only the marked ones. When Christ prays to the Father, after finishing his work, he says I pray for them, I do not pray for the world. He says, I am not concerned for the whole creation – that is your job. I pray for those whom you have allotted to my care, whom you have marked for me.[128] I pray only for them, because I am concerned only with them, not for everybody. Mystics don't come for everybody. That is between them and the Lord. Mystics come for that particular group of people whom the Father wants to be collected.

And if this creation is to continue, then souls must stay here. Everybody can't rush back to the Father. If this creation is to continue, it has to remain imperfect. That is why, in spite of the best social, economic, and political reformers, the world has not become perfect in any way. The moment anybody becomes perfect in this imperfect world, he goes back into the perfect one. He merges back into the perfect one. So we are here because we are imperfect. So if he, the Lord, wants this creation to continue, then souls have to stay here. Everybody can't seek him or go back to him. They will never even think about him. It is entirely in his hands.

I give this example: If the Lord doesn't give you hunger, you don't feel like eating. And if he gives you hunger but there's nothing on your plate, what will you eat? Now it is in his hand to give you the food on the plate and also to give you the hunger. Then you think you are eating. You can take credit for the fact that you are eating, but actually hunger is making you eat, and that food is so delicious that you can't help eating it, because the hunger is there.

Our hunger is given by the Father, and the food on our plate is given by the Father. So we think we are worshipping him. Actually, he's making us worship him. Because if he doesn't give us hunger, how can we eat? How can we worship him? So whom he wants to worship him, he will give them the hunger. That is why Christ said, if you are thirsty, come to me.[96] The Lord will give you the thirst, and then automatically you will search for the well. If you are not thirsty, you are not concerned with the well. It is in his hands to make you thirsty or hungry; it's not in your hands. So everybody can't worship him. Even if you have hunger, if there is nothing to eat, what will you eat? So it's entirely in his hands. If he wants this creation to continue, then there is no option – the souls must stay here. Everybody can't go back to him; everybody can't worship him in the right spirit.

But eventually everyone worships him?

I can't say everybody will worship him, but eventually everybody may go back to him when he dissolves the whole creation. When he finishes the whole play then the souls will have no other place to go. As Guru Nanak gives in an example of dissolution: A person comes to put on a puppet show; he takes all the puppets from his bag; he puts them on the table. And then he pulls all their strings and they are all dancing, and people are amused. But when he finishes the show, he puts all of the puppets back into the bag and walks away. So we are all puppets and we are dancing. But when the show finishes, the puppet has no other place to go but back into the bag. In dissolution we have no other place to go but back to the Father, whether we worship him or not.

463 *Maharaj Ji, if the master knows our karmas and our destiny, and yet we're initiated – if he knows that we're weak, but he gives us the teachings anyway – do we have any means of making an effort to follow the teachings? Is that when he helps us, if we make an effort?*

Master only initiates those who are marked. He is not concerned at all with how many karmas we have, how loaded we are under the weight of karma. He initiates only those who are marked by the Father for him, not anybody else. There may be many souls more pure than the satsangis, but they may not be initiated at all. The Father knows best whom to mark. Christ makes it very clear in the Bible. He says: I don't do my own will at all, because I have no will of my own. I live in the will of my Father.[88] I do only what he wants me to do. I do not do what he doesn't want me to do. He's not concerned that he should select only the pure ones and reject the sinners. When a washerman washes clothes, he doesn't refuse the dirty clothes. He has to wash all the clothes given to him for washing. Some clothes may need more attention than others, but he has to wash them all. So the master has to collect all the marked ones allotted to his care, whether they are good or bad. He has to look after the marked ones, and it is for the Father to see whether to mark them or not.

464 *If we are marked souls and this marking is due to our past good karma, do we have any reason to be proud of our past good karma? Why are we the marked souls?*

The marking is done by the Lord, and he knows best whom to mark and when to mark. Rather than feel proud, we should be humble and grateful for having been marked. If the Lord's grace is there, we should be more humble and grateful. As to why he marks certain souls, he knows best. We can't limit his power, we can't limit his discrimination. He can mark anybody he likes. We should only accept and do our bit, our duty.

There must be quite a difference in karma between being marked and not being marked.

Naturally there's a lot of difference. Once one is marked, naturally one becomes entitled to go back to the Father sooner or later. Others have to remain part of the creation until they are marked. So that is absolutely in the Lord's hands. If we can determine the conditions under which the marking is done, then we're limiting the power of the Father. But we can't limit his power at all. He's all-powerful. He knows best whom to mark and what pleases him. He knows best.

465 *The decision that makes us decide to accept the teachings – where does that come from? From the soul?*

No, that comes from our karma, the fruits of our association and sincerity in the past birth, to meet the Lord. It is due to our real and sincere longing to meet him. Then it is for him to put us on the path. What we have to do is to have a real longing to meet him. Whether we are following the right or the wrong path, if our longing is sincere, then the onus is not on us but on him to put us on the right path. So all these things taken together shape our destiny on the path. That is what we call the grace of the Lord. It is through his grace that we get the opportunity to come on the path. Actually, we have worked our way and thus invoked his grace to come on the path in our previous birth, and that is how we find ourselves on the path in this life.

466 *Master, is it fair to say to a wife who is not a satsangi that she is a marked soul?*

Well, brother, the Lord knows whom he has marked, but we shouldn't push our way of thinking on anyone if one is not interested. We become very enthusiastic and start pushing too much, so much that people react and run away from us. It has to come from within for everybody. You can give them the means to understand the teachings, if they're interested. You can give them books to read. You can answer all their questions. You can help them understand, but don't push too much. Our problem generally is that we start pushing too much. We become so happy that we want everybody to be like us, which is very wrong. We were also like them first. We can just give them the opportunities and facilities to understand and not unnecessarily feel too worried or excited about it or push too much. But if a seeker is genuine, we must try to give him all sorts of help. Then we should not hesitate, we shouldn't withhold anything.

467 *If we know somebody who is good, should we try to guide him to the path, or should we just let him go naturally?*

If you love somebody, you can lovingly guide that person. If you think he's interested, definitely you can lovingly guide him, but don't try to force Sant Mat on him; don't try to convert him. It must come from within him. But you can definitely give assistance, give help and offer facilities to him to know.

468 *Maharaj Ji, some initiates seem to think we are supposed to be perfect in this group, so they just get the wrong impression. I consider, in Sant Mat, the practice for spiritual development a personal responsibility. I am only responsible to myself. Is that correct? And it is up to me to realize that spiritual development – I have to see the best way that I can and act in the best manner that I can. I cannot tell anyone else whether they are on the right track or not. Is that correct?*

Brother, there are two things. With some people, we are so much attached, we are so much in love, as we call it, so much interested in them that we cannot bear to have them go in a different direction, so we try to persuade them affectionately. The idea behind the affection and love for them is not to show off that they are wrong and I am right, or why do you not do as I am doing – that idea should not be there. We should be so interested in them that we can take the liberty to tell them that perhaps they are wrong and that it would be more beneficial and helpful to them if they come to this side. But we should never force anybody, and we should try not to hurt anybody. If they want to go to any side, let them go anywhere.

The conviction, the love, must come from within themselves, for only then will it be solid like a rock; otherwise, it is merely built on sand. In the latter case, the decision would be due to your emotional influence, your atmosphere, and when your influence is not there, they would again go astray. That is of no use. We simply should tell them the advantages of being on the path ourselves, and that it is up to them to make up their own mind about what is best for them. We are mainly concerned with ourselves, but we have certain responsibilities in this world towards our friends and relations and others, so we try to guide them; but if they do not feel like being guided, we should not feel perturbed about it.

469 I am asking this question for a brother who lives in West Africa. His family is rather like families in India, I think. He's got not only the father and the mother and the children but also uncles, nieces, brothers and sisters, and he feels it's quite a burden to be the chief of such a family. So his question is this: In what way does the master's grace help the family members of a satsangi? This disciple knows of course that, as the master says, it is the strength of his own attachment to the master which could influence his family members. But as he feels that his own attachment is not strong or deep enough, this is the reason why his question is about master's grace.

Well, brother, our relationship with the Father is an individual relationship. It is not a family relationship with the Father. It is the individual soul's relationship with the Father. So any soul can be marked, right in a big family whose members do not even care to know about the Father, and yet that soul can rise to the level of the Father. The relationship of the soul is with the Father. It is not a family relationship at all.

As for helping the family members, actually it is our attachments to family members that bother us because we are so attached to them. We want them to take advantage of the teachings. If we are attached to the shabd and nam within, and they are attached to us, then they will indirectly get an advantage because we go where our attachments are. We will find our way to our master because we are attached to the shabd and nam within. Our family members are attached to us, so their attachment will lead them to us sooner or later, wherever we may be. But if on the other hand we are attached to them, and we are not attached to the sound and light within, their attachment will pull us down to their level. So in order to help our own relations, our kith and kin and our beloveds, we must attach ourselves to the sound and light within and detach ourselves from them. Only in that way can we help them.

470 We have been told that when a satsangi passes away, his soul is met by the master. We have loved ones who, to the best of their ability, have been devoted to the Lord and have lived within his will to the best of their knowledge; but unfortunately, they were not initiated in Sant Mat. My question is: When they pass away, who meets their soul?

If one is sincere and honestly devotes time to and has love and affection for the Father, he will definitely get the advantage of that sincerity. Whether he's doing wrong or right is immaterial; honesty of the mind is there. His heart is honest. He wants to go back to the Father, and he does whatever he can to please the Father. Now it is on the Father to mark him and put him on the path.

471 *Maharaj Ji, if all of us are marked by the Lord to come to the feet of the master in our life, how is it that some come late and some come early?*

Everybody has a time to come to the path. There are so many karmas that stand between us and the path which we have to follow. Unless those karmas are cleared, we can never come on the path. We can never feel the necessity for the path or the master or even the Lord. When that time comes, automatically everything will be adjusted and shaped accordingly so that we suddenly find that we are on the path.

472 *Why do some satsangis in this life have to go through three or four various religions and different paths before they come to the Radha Soami path, whereas others come directly to the Radha Soami path from their first religion, which they were born into?*

It is very simple. Each seeker is being driven to the path according to his own karma. For some it is the first time on the path. For some it is the second time. With some it is the third time, while with others it is the fourth time. So everybody does not start right from point A. Some have already started – they just pick up the thread and get going. Naturally everybody has to take a start from where he left off. You may have read in the Bible about the sower and the seed. Some seeds just fall on the ground, which is not ploughed and which is not worth yielding any fruit at all. So the seed lies there, and when the rain falls, it comes out a little and withers again. Some seeds fall on the rocky land, but also wither after coming up. And some seeds fall on absolutely fertile land which is properly cultivated. They alone yield fruit.[48] But the seed is sown everywhere, and sooner or later the seed definitely yields fruit. Every seed takes its own time to give fruit. So we cannot say that all of us start from the same step. Some are on the first step, some have already travelled a few steps, some are just about near the top and need only a little push to go ahead. So everybody has his own way of starting.

473 *Those of us who encounter seekers and lend them some Sant Mat literature, and they have experiences with saints but do not become initiated outwardly – what happens to them?*

This is all due to sanskaras, which means the fruit of actions in their past life. They have worked their way on the path and ultimately they will be led to the path again. Even though some satsangis – seekers, that is, the initiates or those who are to come to the path – begin to have experiences much earlier, they do not realize what it is. They cannot understand. Sometimes they think that something is wrong with them. Actually, one who is to come to the path is being guided right from the beginning. There are always visions here and there, to keep them straight. Many people have visions or certain inner experiences, even if they do not understand all that. The Lord has his own way of bringing people to the path.

474 *Are we protected by the Lord only after initiation? Suppose we are still seekers?*

The protection of the Lord is everywhere. When we sincerely want to follow the path, when we sincerely want to go back to the Father, his protective hand is always on us. We should not worry about not being protected before initiation. Those souls who are marked to be initiated, who are allotted to a mystic, are protected right from birth in one way or another. Protection starts right from birth. They are not allowed to go so far astray that they cannot come back to the Father. When you fly a kite, you always have its string in your hand. The kite is flying in the sky. But whenever the person holding the string pulls that string back, the kite is pulled back. Similarly, every allotted soul that has been given over to the care of the master is always protected by him right from birth, even if that soul is not yet initiated.

475 *Sometimes in the Radha Soami literature, or it may be in some of the discussions, we have been referred to as being prodigal sons, which indicates that we came down here by our own choice, rather than being sent down by the supreme Lord. Will you comment on that?*

How could we have a choice, when we were with the Lord? Choice comes through the mind, and there is no mind there. We have been sent. We have been given a mind, to be pulled to and function in this world. But we had no mind there. The question of our choice did not arise there. If the universe had to be created, some souls had to be sent, whether they liked it or not. It is not advisable to discuss these things. For example, you may have heard or you may have read – but I do not want to give much importance to it – that some souls were quite willing to come, and others were quite reluctant to come. Generally, it is said that saints come for those souls who were reluctant to come into this world, and that is considered to be one-tenth of the number of souls sent here. So only one-tenth will make their way back to the Lord and nine-tenths will stay back here to carry on the universe. That is why everybody will not be attracted towards the Lord. Some souls are required for the universe to go on, unless the Lord wants to finish this whole play. Otherwise, if all the souls were to go back to him, there would be an end to this universe. So the saints come for those marked souls. The one-tenth are the marked souls for which the masters come, to take them back to the Lord. They are known as the marked souls. I did not want to discuss this question.

476 To what extent does a living master involve himself in the lives of nonsatsangis, in the world of nonsatsangis?

I do not follow your point. Why should they interfere in the works of nonsatsangis? Do you mean how much interest do they have in nonsatsangis? You see, actually they only have an interest in the initiates, in the disciples whom they put on the path. They're responsible for them not only here, but also in the hereafter, as you read in the Bible. But nonsatsangis who are attached to satsangis are also helped in many ways. Because a satsangi is attached to that spirit within, and with the help of the spirit he will be able to make himself whole, or make himself clean and bright. If an initiate is attached to a bulldozer and a nonsatsangi is attached to him, through that disciple this person will also find, someday, his way to the bulldozer.

If we want to help the nonsatsangi we must first help ourselves. We should not be attached to them; we should be attached to that voice of God within. When we are attached to that voice of God, if these people are attached to us, then, through us, they will find their way to the voice of God. But if, on the other hand, we are not attached to the voice of God, if we are attached to them, their attachment can pull us to their level. Otherwise, our attachment to the Father and their attachment to us can pull them to our level. In that way they are helped.

Christ made it very clear in Saint John. He says: I do not pray for the world. I pray only for them whom you have allotted to me.[128] He says: The world is not my concern at all. The world is your creation. You look after it as you think best. I'm concerned only with those whom you have allotted to me. So mystics or saints are concerned only with their own disciples, with their own initiates, not with anybody else. But others are helped through the initiates in this way.

477 Is there a link in between the initiate and the master?

Yes. As you have read in the Bible, Christ has referred to it somewhere by saying that I have been sent by the Father and I have been sent only to collect those whom he has marked.[128] I have just come to collect my sheep and take them back to the Father. Every saint is sent into this world for particular souls – allotted souls – and those souls alone will come to him. They alone will have faith in him. They alone will be receptive to his teachings. They alone will practice meditation and go back to the Father. So it is always with the grace of the Father that a disciple is drawn to the master, and the master initiates him and he works his way back to the Lord.

GRACE TO BE PULLED

478 It seems as if the master loves us more than the Lord does, because, in a way, the Lord rejected us by separating us from him and throwing us down into the well of this creation. But then, the master finds us and leads us back home.

I can tell you that without the Lord's love, we can never get out of the well. We think we worship him, we think we love him, but actually he is the one who is pulling us from within. He is the one who's giving us all this atmosphere and these arrangements so that we can think about him. He's the one who puts us on the path, and he is the one who is leading us, and he is the one who is forcing us to meditate and to burn the rubbish that we have collected during this span of life or in previous lives. He is doing everything. So we can't say that he has no love. But for love, he wouldn't do all these things. We only think we are without his love when we find ourselves miserable in this creation and separated from him.

That is why Christ says: I have come to save you, not to condemn you, because you are already condemned.[80] We are condemned, no doubt. What more condemnation can there be than that we are separated from him and we are part of the creation and not part of the Creator? That is the condemnation that all of us are facing. So he says, I have come to save you, and the one who has come to save us from this condemnation has been sent by him. So even if the master loves us, he doesn't love by his own will. The Father wants the master to love us, the Father wants the master to fill us with love and devotion for the Lord. But for the Father, we wouldn't find the love of the master – we wouldn't even find the master. So you can't say that master is more loving than the Father, because master would not be there but for the Father.

In Saint John, Christ makes it very clear. He says there was a man who was with God whose name was John.[73] So when the Lord wants us to eliminate this veil of darkness from within and see him, then he sends somebody from his own level to our level. Only when he sends somebody to our level – one who has the privilege of being at our level and also at the level of the Father – only with his help can we eliminate that veil of darkness and become one with that light which he has kept in every one of us. Unless he sends someone to our level, and he gives the privilege to that person of being at our level and also at the level of the Father, how can we eliminate this veil of darkness and how can we see the light? The Lord is the doer of everything.

So you can't say that master is loving and the Lord is not loving, because master would not be there but for the Lord. And all the love that we find in the master – it is by the grace of the Lord that we find that love in the master. Not everybody finds that love in the master. People crucified Christ. People beheaded the saints. They put them into prison. They tortured them. They didn't find any love in those masters. If we find that love in the master, it is all his grace. He has made us receptive so that we can feel that love from the master. But for the Lord's grace, we would not feel that love even in the master. It is all the Lord's doing.

479 Does everyone get the same amount of grace, each disciple?

Do you mean, does everyone have the same type of karmas, is everybody attending to meditation in the same way? Is everyone living the same way of life? It has to differ. It depends upon us. His grace that has put us on the path is there and he's going to lead us back to the Father. Some people are able to just crawl, some people are able to just move, some people are able to walk, and some people are able to run, but everybody ultimately reaches the destination. As Christ said: Many are called, few are chosen.[65] That doesn't mean that whoever has been called will go back to the Father at the same time. Whoever is initiated is called. But few are chosen to go back to the Father in this very lifetime. Others will come back again, they'll be called again, and then they may be lucky to be chosen.

It depends upon people's individual karmas. Everybody doesn't have the same-size load. Everybody has a different-size load. Some people have a lot of dirt in the house, other people keep their house absolutely clean. You see, all wood catches fire. But some wood is so moist that it takes a very long time to dry before it can catch fire. Other wood is so dry that you hardly need to touch a match to it and it just catches fire. All wood is the same. All wood will catch fire, but some pieces take more time. So, many are called, but everybody doesn't have the same amount of karmas, the same-size load of karmas, and then how do we know whether it is our first birth on the path, the second time on the path, or the third time on the path? So it differs, depending on the individual. We can't put any seniority on it. The first may be the last, and the last may be the first – that is what Christ said.[62]

For example, some saints ultimately become masters. They came to the path at the age of seventy. Other people may have come at the age of just twenty, but the person who came at the age of seventy, he's the one who became the master. Sometimes the candle is absolutely ready; you just need a matchstick to light it. For others, you have to collect the wax and mould it to make a candle before you can light it. So it depends upon the individuals.

480 Master, why did we have to come to this earth? Couldn't we have stayed with our Lord in heaven?

Sister, I don't think we had any desire to come to this world or that we were ever consulted when we were made part and parcel of this creation. The Lord has projected himself in this creation, and he's everywhere. So it is his *leela*, his play, that we are part and parcel of the creation. We were never consulted about whether we would like to come here or not. He has sent us, but now since we are away from him, and we are living in separation, we are miserable. We are trying to go back to him and become one with him again. It is not in our hands at all.

Becoming one with him is in *his* hands. Nobody can worship him unless he pulls us from within. When he wants us to come to his level, only then will we worship him. In other words, he worships himself through us.

Whenever he wants us to come to his level, he will create that desire in us, that longing in us, that pull in us to become one with him. And then we will become mad in our search for him; we will become restless to become one with him. Without his grace, nobody can worship him. I often give an example: If we are not hungry, no matter however delicious the food on your plate may be, your hands won't move at all. If, on the other hand, you are very hungry, but there's nothing on your plate to eat, again your hands naturally won't move. But if you are hungry and food is on the plate, then your hands automatically will move. It is not in our hands to have that hunger; it is not in our hands to have delicious food on the plate – that is in the hands of the Father. He gives the hunger; he gives that thirst; and he gives the means to quench that thirst, to satisfy that hunger. Everything is in his hands. Without his grace nobody can worship him.

481 *Maharaj Ji, what brings us to the path except the grace of the Lord, in the sense that nice people doing good for others keep coming back into this world and continue to do good for others, even though they may do it in a pleasant life? But some of us find this desire for the Lord and this yearning. What have we done to deserve it? Is it something we have done that the Lord gives us this grace, or are we just lucky?*

No, no. We have earned it. We have earned it in the sense that we have been very honest in our efforts to meet the Lord, whether we have been trying in a wrong way or in a right way;

the longing, the real yearning to meet him was within us. In whatever way we worship the Lord, that helps us in getting his grace, and he will put us on the path.

482 *But can you obtain that grace through longing alone – just by craving and longing to know the truth?*

That's right. And that craving and longing also is from the Lord. He's pulling us from within, and when he creates that longing and pull within, he will also give us the facilities, environments and opportunities to put us on the path, to satisfy that longing. He creates the longing and he is the one who will satisfy that longing, too.

483 *Master, in your analogy you compared the intellectual to a simple-minded person. Would you say the same thing if you were comparing an intellectual to a lover?*

Lover?

Lover of the Lord, compared to an intellectual.

You see, an intellectual person can also be a lover of the Lord; a simple person can also be a lover of the Lord. Everybody can be a lover of the Lord. The soul yearns for its own source, so everybody can be a lover. Unless you're a lover of the Lord, you won't try to search for him. An intellectual person will search for the Father when he feels the pull within, when he feels the longing within. A simple person will also search for the Father when he feels that pull and longing within. Unless the love is there, nobody will search for the Father at all. It's not a question of simple-minded people or intellectual people. Love can be with anyone.

484 When a marked soul is born, who administers his karma until he is initiated? Is the answer the same if he was initiated in a former birth?

A combination of many good karmas entitles us to be marked by the Father. When we are sincere about going back to the Father, we are doing our best – whether we are doing wrong or whether we are doing right – then the only thing left is for the Father to put us on the right path. When we are sincere and honest in our search, then the Father marks us. Marking by the Father means he gives us the opportunities, facilities and environment to be in the company of holy people – to be in the company of a mystic. And through them we learn the path and we try to follow that path. So marking naturally is done by the Father. Saints only come to collect the marked sheep, the allotted task given to them by the Father. Marking is done by the Father.

Actually, without his grace, without the Lord's grace, we would never think about him at all. We think sometimes that we are searching for the Lord, we are trying to worship the Lord, but actually he's within us, every one of us. He's pulling us towards himself. He's creating that love in us, that urge to go back to him. Without his grace we would never even think about him. We would never have the opportunities, the facilities, the environment even to talk about him. He puts us on the path, and he brings us in the company of mystics or saints.

485 By grace, do you mean the will of the Lord?

Brother, give it any name. Call it his will, call it his love, call it his grace, call it by any name. Mere words do not count. His grace is his grace. It is his mercy, his grace, his blessings that put us on the path, and we refer to all this as his grace. The name makes no difference.

486 What can we do to have faith that we are on the right path?

Sister, we have discussed this question many times in our meetings. Actually, a disciple can never pretend faith. It is for him to put us on the right path, to bring us face to face with him. When we are sincere, when we want a master, we will automatically follow the right path. He will create such circumstances that we will find that we are on the path. If we are following the wrong master, we will eventually slip out of that and find ourselves in the lap of the right master. Automatically, the Lord will put us right. All we need is sincerity and honest longing to meet him, to follow him; then it is for him to put us on the right path. There are outward signs too, but still the intellect can be deceived. Even though the books are full of all these hints, still the intellect may be deceived. So for guidance, we can depend only on him, nothing else.

Association with a master

487 Do most American satsangis have past human lives in India?

It is difficult to say about Americans, or Indians, from the East or West, but those in foreign countries usually have had some sort of association with some saint in a previous life that leads them to the path in this life. Whether we are born in America, or in India or anywhere else, it is certainly the accumulation of certain good karmas which really makes us deserving and marks us for the path. It is not just by coincidence that we come to the path or to a master. We are led in that direction. Though we may think it is coincidence, it is as the effect of those karmas that we are automatically led to the path. Wherever we may be born, ultimately our karma will bring us to the path when that time comes.

488 Who takes care of us before we are initiated?

The Lord, the master, say anything, but it is that power, the shabd. When we come to the path in this life, it may not be for the first time. We may have some sort of association or we may have devoted a lot of time to the Lord in our previous birth. We may be deserving it, or in a previous life we may have met a master and did not have faith or did not practice, and we had to come again for that purpose. Or we may have covered a certain distance and have to start from there. It is difficult to analyze, but generally we have had past association with saints – we have met them; we created links with them and are drawn towards them.

489 If we have a maximum of four lifetimes in order to get to Sach Khand, and if we don't make it this time around or the next time around, and you are not around to reinitiate us, how does the soul get back or get hooked up with the sound current again? Do we have another master, or do we just realize it?

How has the soul come now to the feet of the master? Is it by your own efforts or by some other means? Did you start searching for the master right from your birth? Circumstances led you in such a way that you were drawn toward him. If the seed has been once sown, it is the master who finds the disciple. The disciple can never find the master. The master will automatically find his disciple, wherever he may take birth.

Is it possible then that you could be picking some of us up another time around?

All masters are the same. All waves of the ocean are the same. The body is not the master; shabd is the master. The master will project from the shabd in the physical form somewhere, and his allotted souls automatically will be drawn to him. Even in this life, there may be many souls who may be here for the second time or third time. They don't recollect anything about their past. They know nothing about any association with any mystic. The body of the mystic cannot be the same. Because the shabd is the master, the shabd automatically will pull the marked ones again.

490 *Master, if a disciple after initiation – let's say it's his first life – dies and then comes back and has to live another life on the earth plane, how does that disciple come on to the path? Is that disciple initiated again? What happens when at that point they return?*

It is not in the hands of the disciple to come on the path. Automatically he'll find himself on the path. He doesn't need to do anything at all.

Will that disciple learn meditation from a new master in that second or third birth?

He must come back to come in contact with some master. Once he takes birth he must come in contact with some other master and he must follow the path. But he doesn't have to do anything. He doesn't know even about his past. He will automatically find himself coming on the path.

But one disciple could presumably have two or three masters in a series of lifetimes?

I'm not talking about the same lifetime, I'm talking about the next birth.

Yes, later on.

All masters are the same. There's no question of two or three masters. They're all waves of the same ocean. You can't differentiate one wave from another wave at all; they all have their roots in the sea. They're just part of the sea – there's no difference between the waves and the sea. The masters are all waves of the same ocean, because the body is not the master; that creative power is the master, the creative word is the master.

491 *Once a person has come in contact with a spiritual master, in his physical form, will he come in contact with the master in every reincarnation?*

Once he is in touch with that spirit within, that spirit is the master, and the spirit will never leave the soul until that spirit takes the soul back to its own destination. All masters are the same. Every wave rises from the ocean and settles down into the ocean. All masters are the same. If the soul is initiated, put on the path, and is not able to make progress back to the Father in this life, it may have to come back to this worldly environment. But it will automatically meet a contemporary master. And the same soul will be initiated again, and be led back to the Father. The soul does not have to find the master again. The soul will automatically be drawn by the new master.

492 *When you're born again, do you have to find a new master each time?*

Well, sister, all masters are the same. The master will find you automatically. You don't have to find any new master. The new master will find you. All masters are waves of the same ocean. The shabd and nam is our real master. When that shabd and nam takes its abode in any flesh, he becomes our living master. And he also leaves that body, just as we leave. But through our bodies, when the soul creates that contact with the shabd and nam within, that shabd and nam will pull the soul back to its own source. So the real master is not the flesh, it is the word which is our real master – that holy ghost or shabd and nam. That is our real master.

Guru Nanak says: Shabd is your real master, and your soul is the real disciple.* This body is not the real disciple and the master's body is not the real master. The word or shabd or nam which has taken abode in the master is the real master, because that shabd or nam pulls our soul back to its own source. This flesh we leave here, and the master's flesh will stay here, too. The real master is that shabd and nam.

493 Master, it says in one of the books that if a person comes in contact with a master before initiation for the purpose of initiation, that master is responsible for the soul if he happens to pass away before he was initiated. Can you explain this to me?

If you are attached to the master, you want to be initiated by the master, you have to go where the master goes. You go where your desire is, where your attachment is. So you ultimately will find your way towards the path in the next birth. You will build some good sanskaras which will help you to get initiated in the next birth. But the master is only responsible for those whom he initiates. As I discussed from the Bible: Who can look to the master for help? Whom will the master prepare for the last day and meet at the time of death at the last day? Those who have been initiated by him during his lifetime, and who live his

* *Sabad guroo surat dhun chelaa.* Guru Nanak, Adi Granth, M1, p.943.

teachings, who follow the teachings. They will be looked after, here and hereafter.[92]

494 *Master, we have read that in order to be initiated in this life, a satsangi must have had the good fortune to have been in the company of a mystic or a master in a previous life?*

This may be one of the reasons for getting a human birth, but there may be other factors also.

It is not necessary to have been in the company of mystics?

No. We may have earned a lot of merits by doing a lot of good karmas, by our sincerity of devotion. We may have been lost in rituals and ceremony, but we were very sincere, so then we may have earned coming on the path. This may be the first time we have come to a mystic, and with others it may be the second time. They may have had association with a mystic in the past, and that is why they got a second birth and got initiated. Others may never have seen or known about the mystics at all in their previous births. So many factors are responsible which bring us to the path.

495 *Maharaj Ji, I think it was Kabir who said: If one comes into the presence of a perfect master, innumerable karmas are wiped away.*

There are so many karmas which are keeping us in this world. Many karmas are cleared in the company of a mystic because we are influenced by the aura or by the company of that saint. That company, the association with that saint creates such a deep impression on our heart and mind that ultimately we come back to that saint. So naturally all karmas are washed when, with the help of a saint, we start following the path. When we come on the path, we are at once detached from the world. Now it's only a question of karmic adjustment. But our permanent relation with the world ceases to exist when we come to the path. So in that sense, all those karmas are washed.

As Christ said, that seed may fall on barren ground, but the seed has to sprout. Whether it sprouts for a short time or for a longer time or gives any fruit, a seed is a seed.[48] Similarly, the association of a mystic definitely helps us, in this life or in the next life. But that association, the karmic relationship which we create with a master, the deep impression we carry on our mind due to the company of a mystic, definitely leads us to the path, ultimately.

496 *If it is decided at the time of death that we should take another birth, how do we find another master?*

You don't have to find any master at all. The master will find you himself. We never find any master; we are just pulled to a master.

497 *How can we know for sure, when we first come to the path, that we will reach our destination?*

When you catch the first end of the road, you become pretty sure that you will reach the other end of the road, that your destination will be achieved. You'll be able to travel on the road and find your destination. You may not have reached it yet, but your hopes are always there, and you are happy that you have found the road, at least, which leads to the destination. So coming to the master, seeing the master, meeting the master, is actually catching the road leading to the destination.

6

Role of the Master

What is a master?

498 *For the benefit of those seekers that may hear this tape and for the benefit of us who find it hard to put into words the phenomenon of seeing the master, would you be so kind as to give a small gist on who we have come to see, on who the master really is?*

Our real master is shabd, that holy ghost, that spirit, that logos or word which is within every one of us. That is our real master, that creative power which has created the creation. But unless we find someone in whom the word has taken its abode and he connects our soul with that word, we cannot be brought in touch with that word within.

Our main object is to go back and merge into the Father. The relationship of the soul with the Father is that of love and devotion. This relationship is not based on any religion or any colour or creed or any caste. It's based on pure love. Soul is a drop of that ocean. Only on the strength of our love and devotion can we go back to the Father; but we can only love whom we have seen, whom we have met, with whom we have mixed. How can we love the Father, whom we have never seen, about whom we have only heard? We love our children – we have given birth to them. We love our parents – they have brought us into this creation. We love our brothers and sisters – we have common blood running in our veins. We love our wife, our friends – we have had a mental association, an emotional association with them for so many years. We love our country, we love our religion – our mind has been conditioned right from birth about these things.

But these loves are all perishable. They cannot last long. Even our body leaves us – it lasts only for a short period. Only our love for the Father can remain, but we cannot love him because we have not seen him. So we try to seek the company of mystics or saints, who fill us with love and devotion for the Father, who lead us back to the Father, who give us strength and support and drag us towards the Father. So we love him. Ultimately, the master and we become one with the Father. That is why we seek the company of those mystics, because we have seen them, we know them, and their love is transformed into the love of the Father.

That is why Christ said: If you love your father and mother more than me, then you're not worthy of me. Unless you become worthy of me you cannot become worthy of the Father.[42] Unless you become me you cannot become the Father. So we have to become worthy of the master and then we become worthy of the Father. It is a strong channel between us and the Father, a strong means which pulls us back to the level of the Father.

We wouldn't need a master at all if we could worship the Lord directly. But if we have not seen him, then we cannot worship the Father directly. So we need a mystic or a saint who is at our level, like us, who can influence us with his love and his devotion, who can lead us on the path which leads back to the Father. We need living mystics, living saints, because old mystics, old saints, have already become one with the Father. So for us they have become as unapproachable as the Lord himself.

They're at the same level as the Lord. So why not worship the Lord directly, instead of worshipping him through those who are as far away as the Father himself? If we need a master, we need him at our level.

We need the company of the mystics so that we can be filled with love and devotion for the Father, mystics who can lead us back to the level of the Father. They come from the Father. Being here, they're one with the Father and they take us back to the Father. All sheep belong to the Father. The mystics just come as shepherds. Souls are marked by the Father. The saints come and whistle, and all their allotted souls automatically collect around them with one excuse or another. They don't have to go searching for them. The marking is done at a different level. The shepherd recognizes his own sheep.

499 *Sages and saints have come in many lands and throughout the ages. Did they come of their own will or were they sent by God?*

You read in the Bible, in Saint John, that there was a man who had come from God, who was sent by God and whose name was John.[73] In many places Christ also speaks of the Father which hath sent me.[88] So it means that whenever the Lord wishes, he himself sends the saints to collect his marked souls, the souls which he has allotted to them. Saints do not come into this world of their own will. They are always appointed and sent by the Father. By themselves, neither do they preach nor do they want to initiate anybody. They are always deputized by the Father.

500 *It is said that the master doesn't function below the eye centre at all, the way we function through the senses.*

Our real master is shabd. And shabd is always here at the eye centre. So master functions here, because shabd is here. Everybody's master is sitting inside, and everybody's master is functioning in their body. Naturally shabd is here at the eye centre, so it functions here and upward.

In the disciple?

In the disciple.

What about the master himself at the physical level?

Of course he has to come to the physical level also.

Below the eye level?

Yes. Otherwise he cannot work at all. As Christ said: I can take this body when I want to, I can leave this body when I want to.[108] It's not physical death at all. It means I can withdraw my consciousness to the eye centre when I want to; I can come into the body when I want. He says, my Father has given me this privilege, that I can function in the body and I can function with him.[91] Then he says, through that spirit or voice of God I can descend into the body and ascend back to the Father.[108] Like on a ladder you can come down to the ground level or ascend to the roof top. So a saint says, "I can descend back to the body when I want to, and I can ascend back to the Father when I want to. I have access there and I have access in the body too."

But the master can be in the body and out of the body at the same time?

Not only master, every one of us is in the body and out of the body. We're hardly in the body, we're mostly out of the body. We're either thinking about sitting here or about England, about America – your body doesn't leave here; you're always out of your body even when you're here.

501 *Maharaj Ji, certainly perfect masters or great masters are above emotions; why do they show emotions, such as happiness, and smile and laugh, that type of thing?*

Because they are in the body and they have to work with the mind, and these are all instincts of the mind.

You see, they have a loving nature, a kind nature. A loving person will always have emotions, a kind person will always like to be helpful, and anybody's misery will affect his heart. He's so kind and loving that he cannot bear to see the suffering of other people. That is not a drawback – it's a quality. They have no suffering of their own – their suffering is that of their people. Mystics are good, kind-hearted and loving and want to be helpful to others, so naturally the suffering of others is close to their heart. They're not affected by it – they're not attached to them when they go – but they are helpful and loving.

I remained for a pretty long time with the Great Master because as a child I was brought here to the Dera. And there were so many tragedies in the family. My brother-in-law died, my grandmother died, and so many other people. I never saw a tear in the Great Master's eyes. He was always smiling, always laughing. But in his last days, after the partition, a lot of refugees were coming from Pakistan – mostly satsangis – who had very woeful tales to tell. And the Muslims on this side of the border were also leaving their kith and kin – leaving India – and had very woeful tales to tell.

The first time I saw a tear in Maharaj Ji's eyes, he was standing on the roof of the satsanghar in Amritsar, and a lot of refugees were flocking there, with their small bundles – some with camels, some with a donkey, some with a bullock, whatever the poor people could get. The whole place was crowded with their small bags and bundles. Maharaj Ji was giving darshan from the rooftop, looking at these people, and I saw moisture in his eyes. In my whole life, I had never seen any tear in his eyes, not even a drop. So when he came back down he sat on the bed, and Mr Shadi, who was his attendant, sat beside him and said, "Maharaj Ji, you seem to be upset." Maharaj Ji said, "I just can't face the misery of these people. They're so good and loving, but look what they have to suffer." And then he closed his eyes and we were asked to leave the room.

Besides that, I don't recollect ever seeing a tear in his eyes.

502 Is there any difference between the spirit and the master?

When that spirit is in the flesh, it is our living master. That spirit, that word, which is in the flesh, that is our master, not the body. Both the disciple and the master will leave the body. But neither the master nor the disciple ever dies. The real master is the spirit, the word, and the real disciple is the soul. But unless the soul is in the flesh and unless that spirit or word is in the flesh, the soul cannot be brought in contact with the spirit. Only through initiation by a living master can the spirit within pull the soul of the disciple back to the Father.

503 I have been taught that there is no difference between the satguru and the Lord. Now, if this is true, why do people not believe in them?

People do not believe even in the Lord, so there is no question of their believing in his sons. It does not mean that if a thing is true it has to be accepted by everybody. Truth is rarely accepted.

504 Maharaj Ji, do the saints have a short cut inside?

They have a short cut in the sense that they have immediate access to the Father. After having reached sainthood, they do not have to pass through all those stages on their way to the Father. Christ also indicated that he could leave the body when he wanted to and he could take it up again when he wanted to, as he was always with the Father[108] and he and the Father were one.[111]

505 *When Christ said that he sees the Father both day and night, does he mean that he sees him through the physical eyes or does he mean that he sees him at the eye centre?*

This is spiritual seeing. He is one with the Father. He is at his level. When he sees him within, he sees him everywhere in every part of the creation. The Father is not a man. He is a power, a state of consciousness. So Christ says he is always at that level, at that state of consciousness where the Father is.[111] Therefore he sees him everywhere and in every part of the creation, within himself and outside of himself. Not with his physical eyes. That is a different eye. This involves a different understanding of the whole situation.

506 *When you refer to saints now in your answers, are you referring to gurus? There are other saints, are there not?*

There are many saints. A saint is a saint, wherever he may be. *Guru* is a Sanskrit word, and it means teacher or master. *Guru* also means one who brings light into darkness. That is the literal meaning of guru, teacher or master, because he gives us knowledge, wisdom. After all, these are just words. All real spiritual gurus are saints, but all saints may not be gurus or masters.

There is a technical difference between a saint and a guru. A saint is one who has reached a certain spiritual stage and has become one with the Lord. He may not be authorized to initiate people upon the path. But a guru, having the same spiritual status, is authorized by the Lord to teach, to initiate and take the souls back to God. Jesus says in the Bible that the Father hath given authority to the son to execute judgment[87] and to give unto you that meat which endureth unto everlasting life, "for him hath God the Father sealed."[90]

For example, an advocate and a judge both have the same legal qualifications, but whereas the judge is authorized to pass judgment, the advocate with the same qualifications has no such authority. But the words saint and guru in everyday language carry the same meaning.

507 Do the five names represent several different gods?

No, they are not gods. You can call them certain powers inside. As regards Moses, he makes it very clear that you should not worship anybody but the one Lord. Everyone's ultimate destination is that one God. All teachings are always given keeping in view the times and the people to whom these are given. In the time of Moses people were worshipping many idols and images. Therefore Moses said that there is one God and only he is to be worshipped.[138] He did not want to eliminate the masters. Masters do not show their identity to be different from that of the Lord at all. They say, I and the Father are one. The Father is in me and I am in the Father.[113] So the Lord himself establishes the contact between the soul and himself through the masters.

But this image of yours? I mean no disrespect to you. I love you very much.

I will tell you now what is the image of the Lord. It is not the body. Our real master is the word, logos, shabd, nam, the audible life stream or whatever name you give it. The body we need in order to explain certain things, and after the saints leave the body it does not mean that they do not remain our masters. Still they are masters. If the body were the master, then how could he remain our master after he has left the body? The body is not the master. The master is that power, that shabd manifested in human form; but the form itself is not that power or shabd, which is the real master. Through the body we are in touch with the shabd. Masters are nothing but the waves of the ocean of the Lord. The relationship of the master and the Lord is the relationship of the wave with the ocean. Waves come from the ocean and merge back into the ocean. The wave and ocean are one. Christ says, I and the Father are one.[111] He does not say that his image is different from the Father. He tries to explain that saints are the waves of the same ocean; the saints and the Lord are one.

We are all little awakened waves?

Yes, that is right.

ALL MASTERS ARE ONE

508 *Master, I've heard that the discourse this morning was exceptionally beautiful. I wonder if you could tell us something about it?*

Sister, I was harping on the same tune. I have the same subject matter to discuss every day practically, in one form or another. You see, I often say that all mystics have the same spiritual truth to share with us. Their approach may be different, according to the background of the people, to the listeners whom they are trying to reach, trying to approach. But they have the same spiritual truth to impart to us. No mystic comes with any short cut or with any new method.

Everybody tells us the same thing – the Lord is within every one of us, we have to search for him within ourselves, and the path leading back to the Father is also within us. That path you will only find when you come back to the eye centre. This is the door of our real house and you have to open this door and then you have to follow that light. You have to know the direction of your house with the help of that sound, and you have to follow the path with the help of that light, and stage by stage you come back to your destination.

You read the works of any mystic. You read the Bible, you read any Persian mystic, Arabic mystic, Eastern mystic. They have the same spiritual truth to share with us. Nobody has ever said there are two Gods. Nobody has ever said that you find him outside the body. If he's one and he's within every one of us and we have to find him within, then naturally the path leading back to him can be only one. It cannot be different with different nations, different countries, different peoples. It has got to be the same. So every mystic is harping on the same tune. No matter what instruments they play on, the same music will come out.

509 I have heard it said in the books, and it is stated repeatedly that all masters are one. Would you comment on that? Also, could you give us a guide perhaps as to what we can do to improve our ability to receive your darshan?

I'll attend to your first question. You have seen the waves in the ocean. They all arise from the ocean. They merge back into the ocean. Every wave is different from one another, and yet they have roots in the same ocean, they are part of the same ocean, so they are all one. Anything you throw into any wave, the wave will take it to the bottom of the sea. The sea is the same; no matter which wave carries that article, it will carry it to the bottom of the sea. So all masters are just waves of that ocean. We submit ourselves to the masters, and they carry us to that ocean. They are all the same. And yet they are different from each other. They have their roots in the same ocean, and they become one with the ocean. Our real master is shabd; it's not the body.

That is why Christ referred to the word made flesh.[74] We search for that flesh where the word has taken its abode. Because ultimately the word will pull the soul back to the level of the Father. It is not the body of the master which pulls us, pulls the body of the disciple back to the Father. The master's body will stay here; the disciple's body will stay here. They will never go back to the Father. The soul is the real disciple; the shabd is the real master, whether it comes in one body or another body or a third body. It is immaterial because the bodies will all stay back. But that shabd, that creative power, is one and the same. So all masters are the same. That is why Christ said: Ultimately, there will be one shepherd and one fold.[107]

510 *This is what confuses me: If the master is the word and the word keeps coming – still, there's reference in the literature to masters having some identity other than being purely infinite being. In other words, there's reference in some of the Radha Soami books to the fact that Great Master would be back in two or three hundred years and that he was going to be bringing certain souls with him.*

It would be very difficult for people to understand at this stage. Masters are waves of the same ocean. They are just like a wave which rises from the ocean and merges back into that ocean. There is no difference between the waves and the ocean, so those particular souls may come back again and yet they are one with the Father within. They are sparks of the same fire. For example, you have so many sticks. Light the sticks and bring their ends together and the flame is one. Can you differentiate that this fire belongs to this stick and that to another? You can't. The fire is one, though it has come from different sticks. So the masters are all one with the Father, and the real master is the word. The Great Master coming again does not mean he will come in the same surroundings and in the same body.

511 *Maharaj Ji, in* With the Three Masters, Volume One, *the Great Master is quoted as saying that the satguru, after initiating an individual, hands him over to his own guru. He himself does not take the responsibility. Because the guru cannot help the individual, the guru's guru or even the guru of his guru's guru helps him. They are very jealous about the reputation of their ministry. Would you care to elaborate on that?*

The idea is that the whole line of masters is one. Master merges himself into his own master, who merges himself into his own master. They're all waves of the same ocean. So any wave can take anything to the bottom of the sea. There's no difference at all. The master who initiates, he always hands over all his disciples to his own master because he is only doing work at the command of his master – not by himself. He takes the responsibility on himself if he has himself initiated anybody. If he is initiating on the command of his master, then he just hands over everything to his own master. And they're all taken care of. Christ has said: Not only must I look after my own disciples, I must also look after the disciples of my predecessors.[107] Ultimately, he says, there will be one fold and one shepherd. Whether you come from the right or left, it doesn't make any difference. But as far as the disciple is concerned, he's only concerned with his own master. His own master will do everything for the disciple. What happens internally is not the concern of the disciple at all.

512 *Have any of the saints, although in this line on the way back to God, the sound current path – have any of them*

reincarnated? Have they reincarnated and been other saints at another time?

You mean to say when once a saint, he comes back again as a saint? Sister, all saints are one. They are related to God as a son to a father. Christ said, I and the Father are one. He that hath seen me hath seen the Father.[111] The relationship of a saint with the Lord is that of a wave to an ocean. Saints are all one. They are waves of the same ocean. There is no question of that particular personality coming again. That power comes. It may come in anyone. That power is the same; it is not the body. They come to preach the same philosophy, the same spirituality, and merge back into the same ocean again.

513 *Maharaj Ji, the master himself is a timeless thing, or entity. Time has no bounds on him. He must, I presume, watch the soul that he's going to initiate go through this beginning of creation to whenever they must leave this creation permanently. Where is the necessity for those souls to go through such an immense length of time, which we're not even aware of, except in only a sort of fragmented state? Why so long? And is this his work?*

For the Lord, there is no time. As you just said, there's no time limit. For you and me there's a time limit. But not for him. He has been assigned to collect a certain number of souls. So he has to collect them. As I said, all masters are the same. That doesn't mean the same entity will come every time to collect the leftovers.

514 *Your Holiness did speak of different kinds of master and saints, and that some had a degree of karma, and perhaps would be in a different category?*

I was trying to explain how many categories of saints there are. How one attains to that state, I will explain. Either he is directly sent by the Lord; by the grace of a saint he has come to that height, as by gift or inheritance; or he has worked hard, just as some people work very hard to become rich. I was trying to explain the different categories, how they come – whether they are sent directly by him, or by the grace of the saints they have become saints, or by their efforts they have reached that state. But when they reach that state, their way of thinking will be the same and their teachings will be the same. There can be no difference in their teachings. Whether they are born in the East or in the West, they have the same thing to teach us. It is really very easy to understand.

The Lord is one. Nobody denies this fact. Nobody dares to say something different than this. And we have to seek him within. Everybody has to search for the Lord within himself. How can we logically think that for one part of the world there is one way of finding him within themselves, and for another part of the world there is another way of finding him within themselves? If he is one, he is in every one of us and the way leading to him is just one. It cannot be two. There is a difference in our interpretation, there is a difference in our understanding, there is a difference in our rituals and ceremonies, a difference in our dogmas. As to how much the priestly class can sway us, hold us – that may be a different thing. But, the path leading to the source, our own original home, which is gained by devotion to the Lord within everyone of us, is absolutely the same. There cannot be two. If with an unbiased mind we start making a research into the teachings of any saint, born anywhere in the world, we shall find his pure and simple teachings of spirituality to be the same as those of other saints.

We are racially prejudiced against each other. We always think this master is higher than that master, and nobody tries to understand the real teachings of a master. If we understand the teachings we will find that all masters are the same; there is no difference in them. But we always like to feel superior in one way or another. And when these masters come, they want to teach, but people take pleasure in crucifying them, beheading them, slaying them, flaying them alive, putting them on red-hot plates, and so forth. When they go, the people weep, cry, build big monuments and big churches. This is what history tells us.

Because we do not give any importance to their teachings, we generally are worried about their history, where they were born, how they were born, who their parents were, who their children were, what miracles they performed. We are just lost in these organizations and these stories. Nobody tries to tell us their purest spiritual teachings. Have we been able to digest those teachings within ourselves or not? If not, what is the drawback? Why can we not digest those teachings? Why cannot those teachings become a part of our life? Nobody cares to find answers to these questions. If we make those teachings a part of our life, we will rise above all these prejudices and everybody will look the same to us then. We will never look at each other as an American, an African, an Indian, a Christian, a Hindu, or a Sikh; we will all look to each other as humans, sons of the same Father, struggling to go back to the same original home. We come much closer to each other. But nobody tries to look from that angle at all.

We have our own goggles, our own coloured glasses through which we want to look. We do not try to remove them, we do not try to throw them away, we do not try to look at things with the naked eye. We are so much under the influence of these political priests, or of these dogmas or rituals, organizations, that even if we feel it, we do not raise our voice. We know what has been done to those who have raised their voices. But what is given to us today in the shape of religion is not the real spiritual teachings of the saints. Their teachings are much deeper, much simpler. The teachings for realizing the Lord are so simple, so very simple that we do not understand them. It is the habit of the human mind to create problems and then try to solve them, and take pleasure in solving them. We cannot accept simple thinking in a simple way. The truths are so simple that we cannot accept them. If anybody takes three hours to explain the same simple thing, you say you have understood it. If he tells you in two words, you do not understand at all what he has told you. We have complicated ourselves so much with the intellect that we cannot accept simple truths.

515 *Is there any case of a master being called to a country by an initiate who was deep enough in his sincerity to call the master on his own?*

I do not exactly follow your question.

In America, there might be people, a very select few, with an intense desire for the master, who could establish a relationship between themselves and the master in India. The master would be inclined to visit them rather than their going to India?

I follow your question now. A master can be anywhere, in any country. India is not the only heritage for masters. When we are really sincere within ourselves – we want to follow the path but are worshipping the Lord by a wrong method, not the right sort of meditation – it is for the Lord to put us on the right path. What we need is a real yearning and devotion for him. Then it is his responsibility to work out how to put us on the path. He has his own ways and means of bringing people to the path, whatever country they belong to, or in whatever country they take their birth. He knows how to draw those souls. He knows how to collect those sheep. For him it does not make any difference whether it is America, India or other countries. He just picks up from where he is to pick up. A master can be born here, a master can be born in any country. They are not known in the West because the West has never bothered about them; it's not that they have never been in the West. It has no tendency to know them or study them or do research into their lives. In India, which is a little spiritually minded, the masters have become known through their devotees or writers. Any country may have masters, must be having masters. But people have never bothered about them. It's not that they never had them; they have just forgotten or never recorded those chapters in their history.

516 Is there only one spiritual teacher for all?

There may be many. Spiritual teachers are not confined to any particular caste or religion or to any particular country or state. They can be anywhere and there can be any number.

> *You say there are many teachers; there may be many teachers, but then how can an individual know when he has the right teacher?*

It is extremely difficult, to tell you frankly; because we try to judge them on an intellectual level and depend on that to guide us rightly. But still there are certain ways. We have got to see them in order to satisfy our intellect as to whether one is a right teacher or a wrong teacher, according to our limited intellect. There are signs for that. But even with all that we can be misled. Even with all our intellectual findings, we can be misled and follow the wrong teacher also. It is the grace of the Lord that puts us in touch with the right teacher. Actually, without the grace of the Lord, we can never meet the right teacher. There are signs which we have to see; but they are seen only with our intellect, so to say, and our intellect can deceive us.

Do these signs differ and vary with each individual?

Not much. I do not think you have read our books, for certain things are described in them. But that is also written with intellect, to satisfy the intellect, and intellect can deceive us even there. In fact, we can depend only upon the grace of the Lord.

517 Will there be a living master in the United States some day?

The Lord knows best. Masters are not confined to any caste or creed, or any country or nation. The Lord can send them anywhere, any time. That is entirely up to him. When he finds the need for doing so or he finds the ground prepared, he may send a master.

518 Why are not any masters in the Western world? I mean why are not any masters born in the Western world, like there are in India?

Are you sure they are not born in the Western world?

Well, I mean, we do not know about them.

That is what I say. Your people are not interested to know if they are in your own sphere. Because the West has always tried to investigate the history, the material achievements, the scientific achievements, your trend has always been to this side, giving great importance to those people who have invented those things. You have just ignored your own mystics. You have never bothered to know about their history or their teachings. On the other hand, the background of the East has always been spiritual. They have ignored the scientific outlook, the historical outlook on life, or the economic or social part of life. They have always been devoted to mysticism. So their main research, main history, is directed towards spirituality, towards mystics. They know about their mystics; they have been able to explain the teachings of their mystics; they have been able to advertise their mystics, so to say. Your people have been able to advertise your scientists, your historians, your other people. Mystics have not been confined to any particular country, or any particular nation. There are many mystics, even in this country here [U.S.A.], but they have been ignored. Nobody has heard of them, nobody bothered about them, nobody tried to know their history, nobody tried to do any research in this line. When the spiritual consciousness will awaken in this country, they too will find, naturally, their own mystics on this side. There is no reason why they should not be here.

519 Has there ever been a woman guru?

In the Indian history of the mystics there have been many women saints. We have many famous, great women saints. Definitely. The soul has no sex at all. The body has sex. As I told you, the word is the master, not the body. And the word can be in anyone. It makes no difference whether it is in a woman or whether it is in a man.

520 Master, I'm wondering, actually worried about whether the line of masters will end in my lifetime.

You see, water – if it stays too much at one place – it stagnates. If it's always moving water, it's always pure. So you can't bind down spirituality to any particular place, particular country, particular sect, particular community. It shifts and goes from place to place. But there are always masters in this world, here and there.

521 Are masters aware of each other?

To some extent they are.

Are they aware of new masters?

You mean when they reach that stage, do they know each other? Yes, they do. They are just waves of the same ocean, of that power. The body is not the master. We need a body to explain to a body. The master needs a body. The disciple needs a body.

522 Who, in your opinion, was the first master? And who was his master?

You mean by first master, the first since the creation of the earth? The Lord himself!

A physical man, a physical man?

Many masters have come to this world, many masters will still come into this world. If we try to make a story-telling search perhaps it would lead us nowhere. We are always concerned with our own master. He is the Lord to us. He is God to us. We have to look just to our own master and nobody else. We are not concerned how many masters have been in this world before, or how many masters are present, or how many masters will come after us. We are only concerned with our master, and he is everything to us.

I agree with you there but you did not answer my question.

But I do not understand your question. You are interested in the history of how the mastership began?

No, I meant this: If it takes a living master to bring you back to God, then how did the first master make it, if he did not have a master?

The Lord was his master. He sent him.

NEED FOR A LIVING MASTER

523 *Maharaj Ji, I understand that only love and devotion lead us back to the Father, to our eternal home, but we are told that we should love only the Creator and not the creation. And I don't understand; I also love my family and my children. Is it only an attachment, a karmic attachment?*

Well, brother, the relationship of the soul to the Father is that of love. What is love? To merge into another being, to lose your own identity and to become another being: that is love. Ultimately the soul has to merge back into the Father, has to become the Father and to lose its own identity. So that is why Christ said, God is love.[136] It has the characteristic of a love, where you do not exist anymore, only the Lord exists. That is love. When we are attached to worldly faces, worldly objects, then where is that love for the Father? Mind is the same. It cannot remain attached to so many people. Christ said in the Bible: If you are attached to your father and mother more than me, you are not worthy of me.[42] Worthy of me means worthy to become me. Unless you become me, you cannot become God. We cannot love God because we have not seen him. How can we love him whom we have never seen, when we don't know what he looks like, when we don't know where he lives, what type of face he has, or if he has any face at all?

We love worldly faces, worldly objects. We have common blood with our brothers, with our mothers, with our sisters. We have companionship with our wife, with our friends. We love our property that we have bought with our hard-earned money. We love our religions, because we are born in those traditions. But how can we love the Father, whom we have never seen, whom we have never known, when we don't know what he looks like?

Worldly love will pull us back to its own level. Only the love of the Father can take us back to the level of the Father. So saints say that when the Father wants to pull us from this creation to his own level, he sends his sons to our level, and he marks us or allots us to that mystic, to one of his sons. So when we are drawn to the company of a mystic or a saint, whom we know, whom we see, in whom we develop faith, from whom we ultimately learn love and devotion because he talks about the Father, then our soul's natural instinct is to go back to the Father. Christ said: I and my Father are one.[111] Why does he say that? If you love me, you will love the Father; if you love the wave, you love the ocean. Because the wave cannot be separated from that ocean. The wave you can see; the ocean you cannot see. So he says: If you love me, if you have seen me, you have seen the Father. If you come unto me and I come unto you, ultimately you will come unto the Father, because I and the Father are one; there is no difference between us.[120]

So the Father creates his own love in us through his sons, through his mystics. And the mystics attach us to the shabd and nam within, by which they detach us from this whole creation and attach us to the Father. They don't need our love at all. They only build that much faith and love in us so that we may get attached to the shabd and nam within. We follow their advice, we follow their footsteps, their teachings so that we may withdraw ourselves from the senses and attach ourselves to the divine melody or shabd and nam within.

And that love of shabd and nam within is so much higher and purer that we automatically forget worldly love, worldly faces, worldly objects. That is the nature of the mind. If you find something much more beautiful, you automatically run away from the other things to which you are attached. That better attachment automatically detaches us from worldly faces and worldly objects. So mystics, with the help of shabd and nam, detach us from the whole creation and permanently attach us to the shabd, to the divine Father within. This is his divine law, cosmic law, by which he pulls us to his own level from this creation, which he has created, which he has designed. Only he can pull us back to his own level.

I often say that if you have no hunger, no matter how delicious the food may be before you, you will never eat. And if we are hungry and there is no food on the plate, we have nothing to eat. But if there is food on the plate and we also have hunger, our hands automatically move to our mouth, we start eating. It is not in our hands to have that food on the plate and to have that hunger and thirst. He gives us that food, he gives us that hunger and thirst, and we are eating and drinking by his grace, to satisfy our hunger and thirst for the Father. Everything is in his hands. He worships himself through us and pulls us to his own level. That is what Jesus has said, and that is what the Indian mystics are trying to teach us.

524 Master, is it possible to love another human being at this point?

Sister, we can only love what we can see, what we can touch, what we know, what we can possess to some extent. We can only love what we think can belong to us or to whom we can belong. We have only a concept of the Lord. We neither know what he looks like nor do we know anything about him, so how can we love him? Actually, we love our own concept. So we don't really love the Father at all. That is why Christ said: Unless you love me more than your parents or your relations, you are not worthy of me, because by loving me, you become worthy of me and by becoming worthy of me, you become worthy of the Father.[42] He says: I have seen my Father, you have seen me, so through me, you have seen the Father.[119]

That is why we require this medium of the living master. Because we can love them, we can know them, we can see them. The masters who left us long ago, no doubt they were great masters, great mystics, and they were one with the Father. But for us they are as far away as the Father himself. We know nothing about the Father, nor do we know anything about past mystics. How can we love them when we don't even know what they looked like?

We have pictures of those people. Take the picture of Christ. I have had the opportunity to go to so many countries. Every country has a different picture of Christ, a different concept of Christ. African countries, Spanish countries, English countries, and German countries – they all have different concepts of Christ. They have made his features according to their own features, as if he was born there, amongst them. It's impossible to know anybody, to love anybody who never existed during our lifetime, who existed two thousand years ago.

Christ said: You love the flesh, because that word has taken abode in that flesh.[74] Our love can then be transferred to the love of the Father. By loving that flesh you actually love that word which is in that flesh. Ultimately, our guru is that word which is in that flesh. The soul is the disciple, and the word is the master. The body is not the disciple, the body is not the master, because the body will stay here. These five elements we have taken from here, we will leave them here. They will not go with us anywhere.

The soul is the disciple, the soul has to go back to the Father, and the soul has to be in love with that divine melody within. So through the flesh, we bring the soul in contact with the word within. And that is why we need a living master. Either we don't need any master at all, or, if a master is required, it must be a living master. There is no alternative.

525 *Maharaj Ji, I was wondering if you could explain something to me from last night's reading. When you were reading from Saint John, explaining the conditions when the master would raise the disciples up on the last day, you said that they would have had to receive initiation, that – according to all of the teachings of the masters – they would have had to have seen him.*

You can't receive initiation without seeing. Seeing means when he's in the flesh and you are in the flesh and you are initiated by that master. Then you have seen him. And then you have to follow the teaching, live the teaching. Christ said: Then I will raise them on the last day.[92] So after initiation, even after the master leaves the body, your relationship is permanent. You have created that contact forever with the master. The contact never breaks. He's living for you forever. Now Christ is not in the flesh, so we cannot make use of him. If we leave this body and the master is living, even then we can't make use of the master. So he needs to be living in the body and we need to be living in the body.

And then he puts us on the path. That is the first condition. Second, he said: You live in my teaching, you follow my teaching. He explains that attaching yourself to the shabd and nam within is living in the teaching. He said: Those I will raise on the last day, and they are my disciples indeed; they are my real disciples. In the end he prays only for them. He makes it clear to the Father that by them he means those whom I have put on the path, those who have been entrusted to me by you, who have been put in my care by the Lord. Christ says: I pray only for those who are allotted to me, who are stamped for me.

I am responsible only for them, not for others at all.[106] He makes it very clear in the end, in his prayer to the Father.

526 *Will you please explain the difference between a living master and a dead master? Because once you're a master, whether you are alive or dead, so to speak, you have ended your karma. Is it still very significant for you to care about or believe in your dead master?*

Well, brother, I follow your question. Once you have accepted a master and he puts you on the path, that master never dies for you at all. Your master is always living for you, provided you have 'seen' him, that is, provided you are initiated by that master, put on the path by him. Then even if he leaves the physical body, he never dies for you.

At the time of initiation, he sits within you. He becomes part and parcel of you, and he always guides you back to the Father. But those past masters whom we have never seen in the body at any time cannot be our masters. If you read the Bible thoroughly, especially Saint John, Christ very clearly shows the necessity of a living master. He says: As long as I am in the world, I am the light of the world. Night comes when nobody can work. I must finish my work while it is day.[102] While a saint is in the flesh, he can initiate us and put us on the path. He can guide us. But once the day ends, once he leaves the body, he can no longer help us.

A master actually means a living master. Why is there a necessity of a master? Because we cannot be at the level of the Lord. Only somebody at our level can give us the way to go back to the Father, can fill us with this love and devotion, can put us on the path, can guide us back to the Father. It is necessary to go to a master because we cannot be at the level of the Father, and the Father in his real form, whatever it is, cannot come to our level. So that is why we need a medium, a master.

Now, if our master has gone permanently to the level of the Father [before we become his disciples], how can he guide us? Where then is the necessity of the master in the first place? Why not look to the Father directly for guidance? We cannot get the help of the Father, because the Father is away from us. He is not at our level. That is why we want somebody who has come from the Father to our level, and who is also at the level of the Father. Only he can lead us back to the Father. That is the necessity of the master. If we could reach the Father directly we would have no need of a master, but we cannot. So if the person whom we claim to be our master is beyond our level, then how can he guide us? How can he take us back to the Father?

Every mystic tries to impress upon us the necessity of the living master. But often, after the death of a certain mystic, we just put our faith in that mystic who left the world long ago. That is why Christ is trying to impress upon us in Saint John: You all look to Moses, you all look to John the Baptist to come and help you and guide you.[54]

He says to the seekers, and not to those who were initiates of John the Baptist: He was a burning and a shining light. But he was privileged only for a season to guide you.[89] Now if you want to go back to the Father, you have to follow me. You have to take a new birth through me. If John the Baptist or Moses could help them, where was the necessity of Christ? John the Baptist was there before him; Moses was there before him. There was a need for Christ because John the Baptist or Moses was no longer with the seekers. That was why he gave them that sermon. The same holds true today in regard to Christ, because he is also not at our level. So if we want to go back to the Father we must seek someone who is in the body now and also has access to the Father. Only he can help us to eliminate the veil of darkness and lead us back to the Father.

527 *Master, speaking about going back, is it absolutely necessary to go back with the master? Can one reach up to the various planes by his own efforts?*

We always need a teacher. We are so much under the sway of the mind, of the senses, that unless there is somebody to shake us from the roots, to take us back to him, we can never reach him. We are in a deep, deep sleep. We are all dead. We need somebody to put life in us. We need somebody to give us that eye with which we can see inside; we need somebody to give us that ear through which we have to hear, somebody to give us that living water by which we have to come back to life again, from death. Christ also referred to that living water, to the single or inner eye, to the inner ear, when he said, ye have ears to hear but ye hear not,[69] for it is the inner ear with which we hear inside. He also raised the dead to life, which means that he awakened the spiritually dead, while in the human body. He was the spiritual teacher of his time. Call him anything, but we definitely need a teacher to know that science of spirituality. And inside it is impossible to travel at all on the right path without a teacher.

Why do you say it is impossible?

Because there are so many more and greater temptations and obstacles in our way inside. Even in this world we always lean on somebody to help us, to give us advice when we get confused, lost, frustrated and when we weep. And inside it is much more difficult. It is impossible to go without somebody to guide us, somebody to lead us back to our home. If from the States you want to go to India, you do not, just by your own intelligence, reach India. You see a travel agent. You collect all sorts of information. You read books on the subject. You go to somebody who has been to India to get all the information you can and all the help you can before you start on your journey. Then you have to purchase your tickets and have to rely on a conveyance to get there. Just by your own efforts you will never get there. How many helping hands you get on the way to reach that place! So, when we want to return to our home, how much more help we need to go back to him.

Well, if there is help here, is there not help there also? Would there not be help at each plane? We find people here in the world willing to help.

If there is help here, there will always be help there, provided we have definite help here.

If a yogi, by his own efforts, were to reach the first plane, would he not find adequate help there to reach the next plane?

No, the yogi must have been taught by somebody how to reach the first plane. He is not a born yogi.

Well, the world is full of teachers. They say in India there are thousands of teachers who are teaching some …

Get hold of anyone you feel like, but in any way, you need a teacher. I am not telling you which teacher you should choose, but my answer is that you need a teacher.

In other words one should adopt one teacher and hold to that teacher until he reaches some realization?

Well, we have to make a search for a teacher, and when we get hold of a teacher, then we have to hold on to him. Then we should not leave him.

528 *Is there any way for a person who is not yet initiated to try to train the mind to focus before they can meditate? Would it be a detriment for him to do so?*

No, there is nothing detrimental about it. Everybody should try to control the mind, whether he is an initiate or not. But the question is the method – how to control the mind? Some people read books and think that they can control the mind with hatha yoga or by doing some physical, mental or breathing exercises. But if you do not have a proper teacher to teach you these exercises, you may get into difficulties. You can even damage your mind. You may lose your mental balance, because you do not know how to do them properly.

You see, we start by reading the books. We try to do it. But there's nobody to guide us when some complication arises and the book doesn't say anything about that. That is why it is always good to have a teacher. But that does not mean that without a teacher one cannot attempt to control the mind. When one attempts to do so, then naturally one will run to a teacher also.

529 Is there no other way to God-realization except with the help of a master?

Brother, for whatever we learn in this world we always need some teacher, someone who has the knowledge of that subject. You have met so many doctors, so many advocates, engineers, and none of them have become doctors, lawyers or engineers simply by going to the laboratory or by reading books. Even after spending many years in schools and colleges, they have to go for practical training before they can make any headway in that line. For this worldly knowledge, worldly gain, we have to go to teachers, to learn from them. And spirituality is the most difficult subject. For this we need a master, a teacher in spirituality. He tells us why we have to meet the Lord and where the Lord is; how to find the Lord; what is between us and the Lord that keeps us away from him; and how to remove these coverings, these barriers between us and the Lord. You may call him master, teacher, elder brother, friend. These are just names given to recognize somebody in this world.

The word 'master' should not confuse us at all. We may call him a teacher or by any name, but we must have somebody to put us on the path, to tell us about the path. There are so many obstacles in the way. There are so many temptations to lead us astray. Unless there is somebody to guide us and keep us straight on that path, we can never travel on it. This is what we know outside. Internally, it is even more difficult to travel without a right guide, without a proper teacher. There are so many temptations inside. We find so many stumbling blocks when we concentrate and come here, at the eye centre, to follow our spiritual journey inside. Without a guide we will be lost. When we need a teacher in this world to learn so many things, why should we not need a teacher to go in and follow the real path to our home? If there had been no need of having a master, then there should have been no need of any saint to come to this world.

You know how we are influenced by the company we keep. If we keep the company of good people, they influence us, as we also like to be like them. If we keep the company of bad people, we are influenced by their bad thoughts, and we go astray along with them. So we need a master to build that atmosphere of devotion around us in order to follow that path and to go within. We do not achieve anything in this world without a teacher or a guide, so how can we achieve God-realization without an inner teacher or guide?

530 *Master, I know that Professor L. R. Puri has written extensively comparing Sant Mat teachings to other religions and occult sciences and other forms of mysticism. A lot of us have read in Theosophical writings that there is a world brotherhood called the White Brotherhood and*

a hierarchy of adepts, or masters, that are responsible for the evolution of the earth and the earth change. Could you say something about that? Is that true?

I don't believe in masters who are hidden somewhere in the Himalayas or in those who are trying to control our destiny or trying to help us from there. A master who wants to help us must be at our level, in the flesh. Those masters who have become one with the Father have become the Father. They are as far away from us as the Father himself. Since the Father cannot be at our level we must have a master who is at our level. That is why we need a living master, because a living master is at our level; but at the same time, he is at the level of the Father. After his death, the master becomes one with the Father and is as far from us as is the Father himself. If we can worship the Father directly, then where is the need for the master? The master must be living so that he can help us, guide us, and lead us back to the Father.

So I don't believe in masters who are hiding somewhere in the Himalayas, trying to control our destiny from there. In the Bible and in the writings of other great mystics, they are always impressing upon us the necessity of a living master who is at our level. Unless the master is at our level, he's of no use to us, even if he's hiding in the Himalayas.

Can more than one person be their successor?

There can be. That depends upon the master. If he wants to have more than one successor, he can appoint more than one. There can be more than one master at one time.

531 *You say we must have a living master. For some people Jesus or the Buddha may be very much alive to them. Do these people have to eventually find a master in the flesh before they can return to the Father?*

Well, brother, before I answer that question, we must understand the necessity of the master. Why should we have a master? Why not worship the Father directly? We cannot worship the Father because we do not know him, we have not seen him, and he's not at our level. We do not know what he looks like. So we cannot love him, we cannot worship him. We love only those people whom we see, whom we hear, whom we feel, whom we know. So since we do not know the Lord, we do not know how to worship him or even how to love him. We love the mystics, our saints, because we think they have come from God to our level. We think that our love for them will be converted into love for the Father. We merge into them. And since they're already merged into the Father, through them we also will merge into the Father.

As Christ said, if you love your father and mother more than me, you're not worthy of me, worthy to become me.[42] Unless you become me, you cannot become the Father. So only through me can you become the Father because I am at your level. If our saints or mystics are not at our level, they have already gone to the level of the Father. So why not then worship the Father directly? Where is the necessity of the master? Those saints are as unapproachable to us as the Father himself. When they are at the level of the Father, they have become the Father. So where is the necessity to bring any medium between us? Why not worship the Father directly? If those mystics are not with us, then how can we make use of them?

So if we don't believe in the living master, we don't believe in the necessity of any master at all. That is my belief. Past masters have become as unapproachable to us as God himself. We do not know what they look like. We do not know them, we have never seen them. So the same problem is there. Where then is the necessity of the master? Why not worship the Father directly? That is why we feel the necessity for some living guidance.

532 *Maharaj Ji, would you comment on another quote of Christ's where he says abide in me and I in you, and then he says that unless the branch is connected to the vine it cannot bear fruit.*

What he means to say is that you merge into me and I merge into you. Unless you merge into me you will never be able to merge into the Father at all. He says, if a branch is cut from the trunk of a tree it can never yield fruit.[123] The trunk, main trunk, is the mystic, the master. The branches are the disciples. They can only bear fruit as long as they are attached to the trunk. Once you cut any branch from the trunk it will not yield fruit at all. So he says if you are separated from me, if you are cut away from me, if you go away from me, you will not be able to bear any fruit at all. As long as you remain my branch, as long as you are attached to me, to the main trunk, you will bear fruit. That's very simple.

533 *When one has professed to be a Christian and has no cause to doubt, the question arises that if one has got to be a satsangi, which master would be correct, and how could one serve both?*

But are you sure Christ is your master just by your becoming a Christian? That is the main thing. If Christ is your master, or when you become a Christian he becomes your master, then you do not need a master. If it is just a deception in your mind that he is your master, and actually he is not, then you need one.

Sister, the real teaching of Christ is something quite different from just embracing Christianity. According to the teachings of Christ, we have to find a living master; the only way in which we can really follow his teachings is to be in the fold of a living master. Christ initiated certain people and took them to his abode. He indicated that as long as I am in the world, I am the light of the world.[102] He said very beautifully: Now I am with you, but after a little while I shall leave you and then again I shall be with you. Now you have so many doubts, but when I shall be with you after a little while, you shall have no doubts.[127] These are all mystic things. When Christ said that he was going to leave them, he meant only as far as the physical form was concerned. And that was said to certain disciples of his, not to you and me today. When he said to his disciples – those whom he had initiated in his lifetime – a little while and ye shall see me, he meant that he had not only initiated them in the physical form, but that after he had left the physical form he would be with them in his radiant form inside, permanently. Now you see me in the flesh and you have doubts, he said, but when you will see my radiance inside, after a little while, then you will have no questions. He explained all this beautifully to his personal disciples, pertaining to himself as their living master. You and I cannot make use of that personality now. If we are really followers of Christ's teachings, we have got to find a living master. We have got to know the teachings of Christ from him, and to follow those teachings, and then we can be led to Christ too, if we are interested to meet him.

Somehow we are just involved in personalities and do not give any attention to, nor do we try to understand the real teachings of the personalities. If we understand the real teachings of Christ, the personality, we will know what he wants us to follow. He did his work and he left certain teachings for us to follow, but we are not paying any attention to his teachings. We are still trying to think about him, his personality. His disciples living in his time could benefit by his physical presence; but you and I cannot make use of his physical presence. We can only make use of his teachings, and in order to follow his teachings, we must have a living master. Then only can we be true Christians and then only are we following his teachings. From what little I have read in the Bible, this is very clear.

Christ also said that we have got to merge back into the Lord: I and the Father are one, I am in the Father and the Father is in me.[113] He indicated that our soul is the essence of the Lord. Unless our soul merges back into the Lord, it will not get release from birth and death. He also explained that the Lord is not anywhere outside, but that he is within the human body: Know ye not that ye are the temple of God, and that the spirit of God dwelleth in you?[132] Also, ye are the temple of the living God. The living God is within you, so you have to seek the Lord within your body. You have to make a search in this manner, not outside. Then he told us, in my Father's house are many mansions.[116] We have to pass through many stages before we can reach our destination. Then he hinted that we have to knock at the door of our house: Knock and it shall be opened unto you; seek and ye shall find.[29] You always knock at a door from outside, and the door is opened from inside. We are outside, the door is inside, here at the eye centre. We have to withdraw the consciousness up to this door of our house and knock here. The method of knocking is to concentrate here, hold our attention here, and the door will be opened from inside. There we seek, and we shall find the path leading to our destination. Being on that path, we will find the Lord, whom we are seeking in the body. These are all mystical terms which we have to understand.

We also find in the Bible that Christ said: If thine eye be single, thy whole body shall be full of light.[23] When we knock at that door, the single or third eye, that eye is opened and we see that light. Until we merge into that light, we cannot travel on this path. Until then we are full of darkness and we cannot know or see our destination. Christ also talked about the word or logos when he said: The wind bloweth where it listeth, and thou hearest the sound thereof, but canst not tell whence it cometh, and whither it goeth; so is everyone that is born of the spirit.[78] By this he is referring to the holy ghost, that audible life stream, the holy spirit, the sound current that is within every one of us, and we can be in touch with that only after we knock and open this door, the single eye or third eye.

Then Christ indicates that the dead will rise, the deaf will hear, the blind will see and the lame will walk when they see that light, when they hear that wind or sound within.[130] We are all blind and deaf as well as spiritually dead and lame, but when that inner eye is open, we shall really see, hear and be alive and walk straight on the path leading back to the Lord. The dead shall hear the voice of the Son of God; and they that hear shall live.[86] Before we come to that realization, we have eyes and see not and we have ears and hear not. We do not see the Lord. What is the definition of a blind man? One who cannot see something that is in his presence. We all know that the Lord is within every one of us. He is within every sphere, but we do not see him – neither inside nor outside. So, we are blind people. When that inner eye is open and that inner ear is open, we see that light and we hear the sound, that silent music. He says, and the dead will rise. We are all dead. As far as the world is concerned we are living, but as far as the Lord is concerned, we are dead, we have forgotten him. We have given ourselves wholly to this world, so we are dead as far as he is concerned. But with that living water which he gives us inside, we become alive again, are raised from the dead. Then we are dead as far as the world is concerned and we are living as far as the Lord is concerned.

These are all mystic terms in the Bible which we have to understand. Just by becoming Christians, you do not become Christ's disciples. You need somebody to explain all these mystic terms. The Bible is not just straight reading like a novel. In order to know the teachings, you have to dig deep, here and there. So many things have been suppressed, so many things have been misinterpreted, so many things have been forgotten and lost. We have to link, take out parts from here and there and knit the parts into a whole garment; then we can know the real teachings. You do not become his followers merely by rituals and dogmas, running to the churches and being baptized. You have to do much more to become his real followers, to become real Christians. Everybody has to become a real Christian before he can go back to him. Everybody is stranded here. We are all trying to be real Christians. You call his teachings Christianity, and others will call his teachings Sant Mat, or the science of the soul; but a true Christian is a traveller on the same path. They are all his teachings.

True saints do not suggest differing ways of meditation. There is only one way of meditation. The Lord is one, he is within every one of us, and we have to seek him within. The path leading to him cannot be different for you, different for me or different for another person. The path must be the same. Those who follow the path are the real Christians, whether they are Hindus or Sikhs or Christians or Americans or Indians. Whoever follows the path is the real disciple of Christ, the real disciple of Nanak, the real disciple of the Great Master, the real disciple of Kabir and all true saints. These are only different names. Every saint comes and teaches us the same principle, gives us the same teachings of spirituality. No saint brings his own teachings to us. As Christ said, the Father in me doeth all things.[120] They just come to fish out the marked souls, to collect the sheep assigned to them by the Lord and take them back to the Lord, to do their allotted task. Their mission in life is to put these souls on the path, and those who come on the path become their real followers.

It is just for our mental satisfaction that we say I have become a Christian or I have become a Sikh. These are just political religions, just ways of living in the world. You are what you are, and it hardly makes any difference what dress you wear, what clothes you wear, whether you dress Indian style,

American style or African style; your body is the same. You cannot change; these are just coverings, which you call Christianity or this faith or that. As long as you are doing the real practice of meditation, searching within, these coverings make absolutely no difference. In these days we are just lost in these rituals and ceremonies, forgetting the real teachings of the saints, fighting each other – Christianity against Hinduism, Hinduism against Sikhism and vice versa – and taking pleasure in fighting. We think that by doing so we are followers of the saints, but we do not question whether they own us or not. At that stage we are just slaves of the mind and senses, nothing else, and are only deceiving ourselves in thinking otherwise.

534 *Then what about the first of the Ten Commandments, Sir: Thou shalt have no gods before me.*[138]

Yes, there is only one God. We believe in that God and we worship that God.

But you seem to imply that one must have a master.

Yes, one must have a master. Masters are sent by the same one God. The only difference is that in the past people followed the instructions of the living master of their time, and we are under the guidance of a master of our own time. Perhaps you are a little confused: "Can there be any master besides Christ?" is perhaps what you mean by your question – am I right?

Well, yes. I sort of believe in one God …

We all believe in one God.

Then we should not even worship Christ?

We all believe in one God. The master believes in that same God. We only need help, a living guide, a teacher, a master, give it any name, just to return to the one God. Otherwise there is no sense in going to a master, if we are not being led back to the Lord.

It is just a quick way to make contact?

There is no question of a quick way. That seems to be the only way. If we believe that Christ was or is the only master, we must also have some consideration for the people who came before Christ. Who was their master? How could they go back to the Lord? The Lord could not be partial to those who lived during the life of Christ and not show anybody else the way to come back to him.

I was not implying that. I think all the teachers had a place and had something to do.

Yes, the teachings of all the saints are the same. There cannot be two different teachings. The Lord is one and he is within every one of us. We are all seeking him within our own body. When our human structure is the same how can there be a different path for a Christian, for a Muslim or a Hindu in this same body? The path leading to the Lord is the same in every human being. Our interpretation may be wrong; our understanding may be wrong, but there cannot be two paths for those who seek him within. For those who search for him outside, there may be hundreds and thousands of paths. So there is absolutely no difference between the teachings of Christ and other saints. What do you mean by Christianity? Perhaps the actual teachings of Christ may be a little different from the modern conception of Christianity.

535 Is the teacher within?

The teacher is always within, but unless you meet him outside you can never find him within. To find that teacher who is within you, you also need a teacher. But the real teacher, of course, is within. Our real master is within. He is always there to guide us. But to reach that teacher within, we need a teacher outside.

Why?

Just to reach that teacher who is within us.

Is it possible without a teacher on the outside?

No, it is neither practical nor possible.

Is it possible to be unaware of that? That there may be a guide, a teacher on the outside, but I am unaware of it?

We have to search for the teacher.

But if I realize the teacher within?

There is nothing like it, if one can; but it may be self-deception.

How will one know that it is a self-deception?

For that also you need a teacher to tell you.

I need a teacher to tell me that that is self-deception?

That is right. Otherwise you can be misled. You can be deceived. Your mind may be playing tricks with you.

But the mind may not have anything to do with it?

It may not, but also it may have. In order to differentiate whether the mind has anything to do with it or not, we need a guide.

How does one differentiate?

That is why I say we need a guide, to know that.

Well, in our lives there are many teachers, you know, as we see them grow great and noble?

That is right. That is right in every sphere of life.

And they are our gurus as we go along, so they are adequate in their way?

That is right. In their own line.

To have one who is alive is better, of course?

For our spiritual development, we have to find a living spiritual teacher. In order to become a doctor, we need a teacher who is a doctor. In order to get some other knowledge, you need a teacher in that line. In order to gain spiritual development within ourselves, we need a living spiritual teacher.

536 Can a chela, a disciple, reach Sahansdal Kamal without initiation?

Yes. I do not say up to Sahansdal Kamal, but with our efforts, our personal efforts without a guide, we can reach up to a certain stage, but then there is a block. We cannot go ahead. We can see a light, we can hear the sound to a degree, but by our own efforts or by just following the instructions given in books, we will be stuck there and unable to go ahead.

How far can one go without initiation?

That again depends upon the karmas of the individual. Whatever little progress we do make without a master is due to many factors of our past births. This is very difficult to describe. We do make some, but very limited progress.

Then we do not need the sound current to reach Sahansdal Kamal, because you said yesterday that one could reach Sahansdal Kamal ...?

No, I said that you could make progress to some extent by your own efforts; but you do not make much progress inside by your own efforts. You need a master. The master is nothing but the sound, and sound is nothing but the master. Our real master is sound, the word, the bani, the shabd, the nam – give it any name. The master just takes the form from that sound, and merges back into the sound.

Now you say we cannot reach Sahansdal Kamal without initiation?

Sahansdal Kamal is not as small as this universe. It is a big region. You may reach the rim of the lower portion with your own efforts, yet you may not reach Sahansdal Kamal itself. Sometimes you may see a reflection of what is there and you think that you have seen the whole thing. Actually, it is just a reflection, as you see that of the sun in the water. Definitely, by your own efforts, you can make some progress up to a certain extent; but that, too, only with exceedingly great effort. Beyond that, you can make no further spiritual progress by yourself. And then, by your own efforts, you have no way of knowing whether you are going in the right direction or in the wrong direction. You have got to have somebody to guide you.

PURPOSE OF THE MASTER

537 *Do you know your disciples personally or impersonally? For example, when you see me, do you know everything about me – my troubles, my doubts, my past, my future? I am asking this because I doubt, I don't know how to discriminate when people say master knows everything. Could you please explain?*

You see, master is a medium between the soul and the Lord, and he is concerned with the soul – to help it to develop, to reach to the level of the Father. The soul, being in the body, and being a slave of the mind, is ensnared in karmas. So it has to go through certain types of karmas – otherwise nobody stays in the body. That is known as destiny.

Whether master knows, whether master doesn't know, it makes absolutely no difference. Master definitely helps the soul to develop spiritually, not from the material point of view. Our concept of grace and help is all material – worldly ambitions, worldly achievements, worldly fulfilments – but that is not the purpose of the master. That is already destined – we have to go through our destiny.

Master is concerned with what way the soul spiritually develops. He gives the source of strength to the soul to spiritually develop within so that it is transported to the level of the Father and gets released from the mind and thus from birth and death. That is his duty. Our real master is shabd, which is within every one of us, and there is nothing which is hidden from the shabd. If he is the Creator, he is also all-pervading and all-knowing.

That word which has created the whole creation is our own master and that is within every one of us. So he is the Creator; he is all-knowing, all-pervading; nothing is hidden from him. In the flesh, master has realized that word within, and we are connected through him to that word.

538 Why do saints and mystics always seem to emphasize the darkness and ugliness of the world, rather than the beauty?

What is the one thing which belongs to you? The Father. Why don't you try to make him your own? When you get peace within, you'll get peace outside. That is their approach. They know the reality. It's not that they don't see beauty in this world or that they only try to explain the back side of the picture. But they also have to show us the back side of the picture: These faces are so beautiful, but from the back, those pictures are nails and cardboard. The saints know both sides of the world. They know that peace within, and they know that misery within. They know the reality.

Why do their teachings appeal to us? Because we need corroboration from them; they don't tell us anything new. We are miserable. The moment they describe the misery of the world, we always see it at once – this saint is right, we are miserable; I have just been deceiving myself, fooling myself into thinking that somebody belongs to me. They are right – there is something within us which tells us that what they say is right. And when anybody corroborates our feelings we become happy at once, and we believe in him and then we try to overcome that loneliness. So that explains their approach. It's not that saints see only the dark side of the world; they also know the beautiful side of the world.

That is why Christ said, love thy neighbour.[67] He never said hate thy neighbours because they are miserable. Love thy neighbour – love the Creator who is in everybody in this creation. He said that there are only two commandments. The whole teaching comes down to those two commandments. The saints' approach is different, but they're guiding us to the same goal – the worship of the Father, that only he belongs to you. Nothing else belongs to you in this world, so don't deceive yourself. It's just a question of time before we realize what belongs to us. They try to help us to rise above our self-deception. That is why they sometimes go a little far in condemning the misery of the world.

If a tree has many deep roots in the ground, and you want to uproot that tree, you need a very strong wind. You also need to moisten the roots to loosen them so that a strong wind can easily do its work. We have so many roots in this creation, with all our past karmas. We are so engrossed in the pleasures of this world that unless the saints shake us from the roots, we'll never be able to uproot ourselves from this creation. So they sometimes use very drastic steps; their approach is very, very strict I would say, because they want to uproot us from this creation and take us back to the Father. A small tree which hardly has any roots can be blown down by even a little wind. But those trees that have very strong, long roots going deep into the ground need a very special wind, and they need a lot of watering and moistening before they can be uprooted.

So the saints' teachings are for everybody – for those people who have small, shallow roots and for those people with very deep roots. They can't divide their teaching and say this teaching is for these people and that teaching is for those people. So they have to describe things in a general way. That is why sometimes they go to the extreme when describing the misery of the world. And they're not wrong about that; they're right.

539 Why is it so difficult to take our attention off the objects of the world and devote it to the master?

Why is it difficult? Because we are so attached to this creation. We are so attached to the sensual pleasures and to this creation that it becomes difficult for us to have that love and longing for the Father. The shabd detaches us from the creation, pulls us from the world, and attaches us to the Creator. That is why Christ said, I have come to make them blind, those who see, and I have come to give them eyes, those who are blind.[103] It seems contradictory, but it is not. Those who only see the world and do not see the Father, I've come to make them blind to the world. They are so attached to this creation that they do not look to the

Father at all. My purpose for coming to their level is so that they may look within, so that they may become blind to this creation and see the Father. And I have come to those who are blind to give them eyes. Those who are blind to the Father, who do not see the Father, neither within or outside, I have come to give them eyesight. So the purpose of the mystic is to detach us from the creation and attach us to the Creator, and only shabd can do that. When we attach ourselves to the shabd, it pulls us by the roots, pulls us from the creation and attaches us to the Creator.

540 Why is a master more than a priest or a preacher? Why is he more valuable to one seeking spiritual salvation?

In the beginning we should just take him as a preacher or a teacher or a guide. And when we go in, we will realize what he does for us. We automatically see what he is. In the beginning we are just to take him as a guide, as a friend, as a leader, somebody to put us on the path. Then we ourselves will realize more and more why we need him.

You see, everywhere, in every line, we need a teacher. You want to do law, you want to do engineering, we have so many teachers to put us on the path. And we always give them due respect and are grateful to them for being so helpful to us. All that we are as an advocate or as a lawyer, it's all due to our teachers. In the same way, we need a master, we need a guide, to put us on this spiritual path, to lead and guide us on that path. And when we realize what that path is, what the beauty of that realization is, we automatically know what we have to be, how we have to be with him. There is nothing that we have to force ourselves to admit to, nor do we have to take a certain thing. All this comes from within, and whenever it comes, it comes from within. The realization is within.

The way I have interpreted that question of this gentleman here is, the master is the thing itself, the light itself; and the preacher is the one that talks about the light, only talks about it or tries to describe it?

The master does not only describe it to us, he actually leads us inside, and ultimately we merge back into him and he merges back into the Lord. We all become one. Everybody is a wave of that ocean. A wave comes from the ocean and merges back into the ocean along with whatever has been consigned to it.

541 *In this country – I do not know if it is the same in India – some people say that they have initiation inside and do not need any outer master. What can you say to them?*

Sister, you have seen India, you have seen America. You can compare it better now that you have seen both. I have seen only one, and I am trying to see the other now. We definitely need initiation by a master to put us on the path. Initiation is not a ritual; it is a guiding factor in our life. The master is always there. He does not just forget about us after initiation. He is always there to guide us and lead us. So, whether we need him or not, he is always there to lead us and help us. Ultimately the initiation and the master and the audible life stream and devotion and the Lord and the soul become one. These are just means to go back and merge into him.

542 *Master, you said that once the chela has attuned himself to the sound current, the sound current will draw him up to the source from which he has come. Well, if the sound current will draw him up to the source, what is the purpose of the master?*

The purpose of the master is to connect him to the sound current and to be with him all through, so that he may not fall into the temptations, he may not be driven away from the real path. There is no difference between the master and the sound current inside. The sound current is your master. Every human being needs a master who is in the human form, to connect him with the sound current inside. We need someone in the human form who has made that contact and is himself merged in the sound current, and that someone is the living master.

543 *The books say that the master connects us with the sound current. That is not quite clear to me. It seems to me that if we were disconnected from this force we would not be alive, if you see what I mean. Is not the sound current the very life within us?*

The sound current is the very life within us. It comes here with our mind, and the mind is scattered in the whole world, through the nine apertures of our body. We have to retrace it back up to this point, between the eyes, and be in touch with the sound. The master will put you on that path and will bring you in contact with that sound. The sound is always there. That sound current is always in the body, because that is the soul itself. Ultimately, the sound, the soul and the Lord are all one. But the master will put our mind in touch with that sound, with that vibrating sound, here at the eye centre. He will put us on that path, and we will practice and make the effort with his help and guidance.

544 *With all the trouble in the world, some people think it's selfish to seek the Father.*

Even if you don't search for the Father, there will still be trouble in the world. Even if you all try to do your best, I don't think you'll be able to improve the lot of the world. Many social reformers, many mystics and saints, many kind-hearted, noble and good rulers have come to this world; but I don't think they have been able to change the fate of the world. It's becoming worse every day. The purpose of the saints is not to reform the world. It is to take us back to the Father. They impress upon us the fact that this world is miserable, and not a place for us to remain in. Whatever you may get in this world, you can never be happy. The inclination of the soul will always be towards its own source, and unless the soul merges into that source it can never be happy in this world.

Those people who, from a material point of view, are fortunate enough to have everything at their command, are not denied anything by the world, who have wealth, health, honour and fame, are still missing something. They have everything at their command, but no peace of mind within. They still feel lonely. This loneliness is the inclination of the soul toward its own source. Unless you let your soul go back to its own source, you will never be able to get peace of mind, nor will you ever overcome the feeling of loneliness. So if you go on trying to improve the lot of the world, you cannot be happy at all. You can only be happy when you're able to go back and merge into the Father.

In Saint Matthew, Christ said, I have not come to create peace.[39] Don't think that by following my teaching you will find this place a paradise for you to live in. This place will remain as wretched and miserable as it is. My purpose is to detach you from this world and take you back to the Father. You're attached to this world, you have built your treasure in this world, and you have to come to this world because your heart is in this treasure which you have built here.[22] You are attached to everybody in the world, and these attachments are pulling you back to their own level. So unless I cut these attachments by use of the word or the holy ghost, you will not be able to go back to the Father at all. So that is why mystics come to this world. Social reformers have their own duty to perform. They're most welcome to do it. Everybody has been allotted some work by the Father. Let the social reformers do their best to reform the world. But the purpose of the mystic is to take us away from the world.

The Great Master used to give us this beautiful story. He said: There were many prisoners in a prison. It was summer, and very hot. The prisoners had no cold water to drink. So a philanthropist spent money to give them sweet, cold drinks. Another philanthropist thought that they were not getting enough good food. So he spent still more money and tried to give them delicacies and sweet dishes. He was also doing his best to improve the lot of the prisoners. And the third philanthropist had even more money. Winter was approaching and it was very, very cold. He gave the prisoners woolen clothes. So each philanthropist tried to do his best to improve the prisoners' lot. But with all their philanthropy, with all their help and social reforms, the prisoners were still imprisoned in their cells. They couldn't get out. They were still miserable; only their standard of living had risen. From class C they had become class A prisoners. But all the same, they were still prisoners. Finally a fourth person came who had the key to the prison. He opened the door and set them free. That is the purpose of the mystic. He comes with the key to this prison and his key is that spirit, that word, which God has kept within everyone of us.

Mystics attach us to that spirit or holy ghost and free us from the cage of this body, the prison of this world. Other duties are being performed by social reformers. I have nothing against them. The world has always been miserable. At one time, we lived under trees, in caves. Now we are comfortably miserable. But all the same, we are miserable. With all the social reforms, with a high standard of living – I don't think any other country can boast of a better or higher standard of living than America – you know your lot. We are comfortably miserable in our palaces of concrete. So the purpose of the mystics is to take us out of this prison and back to the Father. That is their mission.

545 *Do you think that the time will come when the people will know how to control the elements? Now what is your feeling about that? Do you think that we have someone like that coming?*

Perhaps, I do not know. But saints never come to make this world a paradise. That is not their mission at all. They come to take the marked souls back to their home.

Saints never come to make this place a paradise. Had this been their mission, world conditions would have been improved as so many saints have come. Christ was here and so many great saints were here. Still, I do not think we have improved in any way. We may boast that within this modern civilization we are far better than our ancestors, but if we think dispassionately, we cannot but conclude that we are not superior human beings or better than our ancestors. We have the same crime, we have the same wars – even on a bigger scale – the same jealousies, the same throat-cutting of each other, all silly evil things we are doing. I do not think we have improved in any way. Those people, perhaps, had more human values than we have now. So, if with all the coming of the saints we have not improved, then where is the guarantee that if more saints come, our lot would improve? As long as the human mind is there, conditions will remain the same.

Mind always puts conflict upon conflict – race against race, country against country, man against man. That is the nature and tendency of the mind. So we cannot ever think of making this world a paradise. We can think and know that we can rise above the problems of the world, so that these problems of the world never bother us at all. And that is exactly the mission or the purpose of the saints. They just come to pick up their sheep from here and there, merge them into the shabd and thus merge them back into the Lord. That is their only object of coming into this world. They are unconcerned with the world. They are unconcerned with this modern civilization. They have to live like other people, but they are not at all affected by these things which are going on around us, because it is not in the least their business to interfere in all this. They are not the social reformers. They just come to create devotion, faith and love within us for the Lord and to take us back to the Lord. That, entirely, is their mission.

546 Maharaj Ji, yet Christ said in the Sermon on the Mount: Blessed are the peacemakers. Could you comment on what that means?

You see, actually he's praising the lovers of the Father, those who are able to obtain peace within themselves. He says they are the blessed ones because only they can radiate peace. If we have misery within ourselves we will radiate misery. You go to a miserable person, he will make you miserable; you go to a happy person, he will make you happy. Because we give what we have within. So he says, blessed are the peacemakers[10] – those who are able to obtain peace within themselves. They're one with the Father and they're contented, they're happy, they're at peace and they're in a position to create peace in the world – that is, give peace to other people, to other disciples. So they are the blessed people, the fortunate people.

He's not referring to any politician or anybody, he's only referring to the devotees of the Lord. They are the real peacemakers because only through them are we able to obtain peace within ourselves. In this world there can never be peace. At least history doesn't encourage us at all. There never has been peace, there can never be peace; as long as the mind is there, conflicts will be there.

So, as I often say, we can't collect the thorns of the world but we can definitely wear shoes so that the thorns won't bother us. We have to obtain peace within ourselves; we can't create peace in this creation at all. But we can live in this creation in a peaceful way, because we can obtain peace within ourselves. And that peace we can only obtain when we are filled with love and devotion for the Father. So Christ says, they are the blessed ones who fill us with love and devotion for the Father.[134] They are the peacemakers: They live with peace and they create peace, they radiate peace.

547 *I read in some of the Sant Mat books that Shams-i Tabriz was flayed alive and Jesus was crucified. I was just wondering why masters of that spiritual stature have been subjected to that kind of physical violence?*

It is really very unfortunate that all these saints had to go through all these tortures. It is simply because the worldly people never like them, and their teachings are a little bold. Saints do not come to create any religions – they do not come to conform to all the rituals and ceremonies which we are used to, because that is a profession for the priests. And when they preach the real teachings of saints, naturally, those professionals do not like it. As a result the saints generally have to face all sorts of troubles and tortures. Otherwise, they never do anything which we cannot understand. They are never harmful to society. If you read the history of their lives, you will find that their only "fault" is that they want to save us from the cycle of birth and death, they want us to detach ourselves from the worldly possessions and the worldly loves, and they want to attach us to the Lord. They do not accept money. They do not interfere in any religion. They do not recruit people to fight one nation against another.

Saints only awaken the love of the Lord within us, but people are so much tied to each other, so much tied to their creeds and are such slaves of old rituals that they feel that probably the saints are heathens. "What are they going to do with us?" they ask. So they crucify them, kill them, flay them alive, try to torture them in so many ways. And when those saints leave, then the very same people weep for them, worship them; but while they were living nobody recognized them – nobody gave them their due. After the saints go back, then again the people come under the sway of the priests, the professionals, I would call them. Those professionals, in the name of those very saints, again want to keep the people under their sway. Again the people, of course, in the manner prescribed by the priests, worship them and love them. In this way these professionals will not let the people understand the real teachings of those saints, which would enable them to worship and love God within themselves, as designated by him, through his saints.

548 Would you say that the death of Socrates was another example?

Yes. If you start analyzing and quoting, you will find almost every saint had to go through the same fate. It is only because people do not understand them and do not like them and so become prejudiced; otherwise they can find no fault. Saints have never committed any crime against society. They are the best citizens, to whatever country they may belong and whatever society they may be born into. But they are a little bold, in order to shake people from their roots, to which they are so badly tied. Actually, these people think they are the devotees of the Lord, but they are not. They are devotees of the organizations. They are devotees of the professionals. They are devotees of the old rituals and ceremonies. The real philosophy, real spirituality, which is the base of every religion, they absolutely forget. The saints again come to remind them of the purpose of that particular religion, the purpose of spirituality. The professionals or priestly class never liked it, so the saints had to face all these tortures at their hands.

549 Do you think that Jesus being crucified – assuming that he was – had any significance? Other saints have died naturally, I assume, but he was martyred?

No, sister. I do not agree with you. The fate of all the saints has been the same. You know only of Christ. I have read the lives of so many saints who had to meet the same fate. The world does not tolerate them. People are so much in fear, so much attached to each other, so much enslaved by dogmas, rituals and religions that they cannot bear them. Saints do not appeal to them, so they want to do away with them. At least three or four gurus were crucified the same way, and some Muslim mystics were burnt alive. Some saints were flayed alive; others were made to sit on red-hot iron plates; still others were put alive in boiling water. If you read the history of the saints, you will find that it is really terrible what they had to face. Now people worship them. Still, I think they are not worshipping them in the true sense; for the condition, the lot of the saints, is still the same. If Jesus were to come among us today, perhaps he would meet the same fate.

My question was that in his death, did he do something for us? As remission for sins?

Perhaps he was setting an example that, having everything with him, he did not want to use his power. That may have been the lesson that he wanted to give us – the lesson to resign ourselves to the will of the Lord – thy will be done.[21] He knows best.

550 Can a real true saint promote his longevity?

They do not like to. They are always in tune with the Lord. They do what he wants them to do. They can, if they want to, but they do not like to, so they never do it. They have their allotted task to perform and when that is finished they are eager to go back.

551 I do not think you have the Christian point of view. They are sleeping in the grave until Resurrection Day!

Well, let them. It will be quite a mess when all of them get up. [Laughter] I think that is a wrong interpretation. What we mean by sleeping is that we are asleep as far as the Lord is concerned, because we have forgotten the Lord. We are sleeping under the spell of this maya or illusion, these attachments. We have forgotten our real home, the Lord, our destination. And when we come to the master, we sleep as far as the world is concerned and awake as far as the Lord is concerned. When Christ said that the dead will rise,[114] he meant that we are all dead as far as the Lord is concerned. We have forgotten him. We have forgotten our real home, and we will be resurrected from the dead, get that everlasting life, when we get in touch with him. Then we will be dead as far as the world is concerned. Now we are dead as far as the Lord is concerned. Saints come to put life into the dead. That does not mean decaying dead bodies, but the living dead. We, who have forgotten him, are all dead though living in this world. When we are in touch with the shabd, we attain eternal life. So the question of these dead bodies in the graves rising again does not arise at all. Those bodies have decomposed, they are finished. To think that they will come back to life again is just a self-deception, I would say.

552 *Maharaj Ji, my father, I'd like to know the meaning of when we are told that Christ died for our sins, and what is meant by the word 'resurrection'.*

Well, sister, when the Bible says that Christ died for us, it means that every master has to share the karmas of his disciples. Unless the master helps his disciples and shares their karmas, no disciple can go back to the level of the Father. So they help them to account for their karmas, and they even share their karmas. As Christ said: I stand as a ransom for my disciples to the negative power.[64] So every master dies for the sins of his disciples; this means that he helps them to clear their karmas, to clear their sins. That is his mission in life.

And Christ gives a very beautiful example. If there are a hundred sheep in a flock and one sheep goes astray from the herd, the shepherd, leaving ninety-nine, runs after that one sheep and even physically takes that sheep on his shoulder and brings it back to the fold. The sheep is unable to walk and is astray from the fold. But it is the duty of the shepherd to look after all hundred of the sheep. He is responsible to the landlord for all hundred of the sheep, not just ninety-nine sheep. So if any sheep goes astray, for any reason, the shepherd goes after that one sheep and physically brings it back to the fold. That is what the master's duty is. They share our karmas, if we are incapable of clearing them. So naturally they die for our sins.

And as far as resurrection is concerned, our account is taken care of at the time of death. There's no particular time of resurrection. Everybody has his own resurrection. His account is computerized at the time of his death – where he is to be born, where he is to go according to his karmas. He finds his own place inside, in those mansions, or he may find his place back in this creation. But his karma is accounted for immediately at the time of his death.

553 *You actually have more protection after you have been initiated than before, because you have the master in the radiant form with you at all times?*

You see, every disciple has to go through his destiny. If you think that you will escape from your destiny and that the master will protect you by removing you from your destiny – that is wrong. You have to meet your destiny. The protection is spiritual. The soul is not allowed to go astray from the path. It is protected in the sense that ultimately it will go back to the Father and become one with the Father. That is the real protection master gives to the soul within. This is not physical protection. It doesn't mean that if we become initiated, we are not going to meet with an accident or we are not going to become ill or that tragedy will not happen in our family. That is a wrong concept of protection. Everybody is born with a certain destiny, and we have to go through it. But we get so much strength within ourselves to go through that destiny smilingly, without losing our balance. That help is there, but it doesn't mean that we escape from our destiny. We have to account for what is due to Caesar.[66] We have to account for all our actions, all our karmas. Unless we account for all our karmas, the soul cannot escape from the realm of Kal. So protection is of a very different kind. It's a spiritual protection; real protection of the soul. People always try to interpret it in a physical way.

554 *Master, we have heard that the master protects us, that he is our protector, and I was wondering what our attitude should be? I know that we shouldn't think that we can do dangerous things and that the master will make it okay. But should we have the attitude that the master is our protector?*

Master protects you from going astray from the path, from going to hell – from coming back to this creation again. That is his protection. It doesn't mean that if you have to meet a car accident that you will not meet a car accident. This protection doesn't mean that if you have to bear losses in a business, you will not bear losses in a business. That is no protection at all. He gives protection to the soul. Master takes care of that soul so that it may not be condemned again to this creation. He has his own ways and means of protecting it. We have a wrong concept of protection. We think that if we don't meet with an accident we are protected, if we don't fall ill we are protected, if we don't lose in business we are protected. Even from these things you may be protected, according to your karmas, according to your destiny. Even if you don't worship the Father, you will get whatever is in store for you. The real protection is of the soul, that it may not be condemned again to this creation. For that, master stands as a ransom to Kal. He takes charge of the soul and sees that all karmas of the soul are cleared, so that it can shine and go back to the Father. It is the soul that gets protection, or guidance, whatever you may call it.

555 *Last night I think I heard Professor Bhatnagar read that when a disciple suffers, the master suffers more than the disciple. Does that mean that when we are suffering physically and mentally, the master is also suffering?*

Don't worry about the suffering of the master. Let him play his own role. We have to play our own role. When a tree doesn't yield any fruit, is the gardener happy? Doesn't he suffer so that the tree can yield fruit? He feeds it all sorts of nutrients, he waters it and does all sorts of things with that tree. He wants that tree to yield fruit because he has planted it. He has aligned himself with the tree.

THE MASTERS' MIRACLES

556 Does God at any time send miraculous cures, or miraculous healing? As Jesus is said to have raised Lazarus from the dead?

Well, brother, I have told you that saints can do whatever they like. There is absolutely no restriction on them, but they generally do not like to break the laws of nature. All these miracles that we credit to the saints, generally, hardly 5 percent of them have been performed by the saints as miracles. They may seem like miracles to us, but they are not. We make up stories to exaggerate them. From what I have read in the Bible, I do not think Christ performed as many physical miracles as people think he did. He gave eyes to the blind; ears to the deaf; power of speech to the dumb; but that does not pertain to physical miracles. We are blind. In spite of having eyes, we do not see the Lord. He gave people inner eyes to see the Lord; inner ears to hear his music, the word of God, the shabd or audible life stream. These are not physical miracles at all; they are spiritual miracles.

Saints are not jugglers who come to make miracles in this world. They do not try to perform miracles, but miracles do happen in their lives. I do not deny that. They are capable of performing all these miracles because they are so tender-hearted and so much in love with humanity and with the Lord that they sometimes do interfere with our karmas. Then they take the burden on themselves, and we call these things miracles.

But that is not their purpose of coming into this world. We always give more importance to the miracles they perform and none at all to their teachings. Their main purpose of coming into this world is to teach spirituality and how to live a life of love and devotion. They want to give all of us that inner sight; they want to give us the power to hear within; and they offer us that living water, the nectar within, which can give us life forever. They want to take us back to the Lord. That is their main miracle, which we confuse with these outside physical miracles, which is not their purpose at all.

As I said, miracles do happen in their lives. They can and do perform them. I am not discussing Christ in particular, because it is true of all the saints. Christ may have performed all those miracles. I do not deny that. But that was not his main purpose of coming into this world. And, in spite of Christ's performing all these miracles, do we not see the blind in this world now? Are there no diseased now, no lepers, no dumb or lame people now? Are not our hospitals filled with sick people? Saints do not come to cure our physical ailments, as that is not their mission in life.

I often give the example of a jail. where there are many prisoners. One philanthropist comes and finds that these prisoners do not get good fresh water to drink, so he buys some good cold drinks for them. He is doing good for the prisoners. Another philanthropist comes, who perhaps has a little more money. He gives them good food. He is also doing good for them and trying to raise their standard of living. He is doing good according to his limited capacity. A third philanthropist comes and finds that winter is fast approaching and the prisoners do not have good clothing. He spends a little more money in trying to help them still more by giving them beautiful warm clothes, to save them from the coming severe winter. He also is doing good. Each philanthropist is doing his best, while the standard of living of every prisoner is just becoming higher and higher. But, all the same, they are still in the prison. A fourth philanthropist comes who has the key of that jail and the power and authority to use it. He opens the gate and sets all those prisoners free. He is the best philanthropist.

In the same way, saints come into this world with the key, this world being a big jail that we are all in, each person serving his own sentence according to his karma, fate or destiny, whatever you want to call it. So saints just open the gate for us and set us free to go back to the Lord. Nothing can compare with their mercy and grace.

Saints do not come merely to improve the life of the prisoners. They do not come to raise our standard of living in this world. They come to set us free from this world and take us back to the Lord. That is their mission in this life; that is their purpose in this world. So we should always try to know the teachings of the saints, the real mystics – the mystic way that the Lord wants us to follow: how to get out of this prison, how to get out of this world, how to go back to him. We should try to seek their teachings in their books and not give so much importance to where they were born, what their miracles were, what they did, who their parents were, whether they had a teacher or not. We should not get ourselves confused in the history of these matters; that is not the purpose of our lives.

We should always keep in view their real teaching, which is their purpose in coming into this world. They have to have a mother and a father; they have to be born in some country or another; they have to be governed by one ruler or another; so we should not worry about these things at all. We should try to make a research of their real teachings, the purpose of their coming; for then we can make the best use of their coming. Otherwise, we fail to do so.

557 *Master, when we feel that master has performed some small little miracle on our behalf, which might be explained as coincidence but we know that this was not a coincidence, is it all right to share it with other satsangis, or is it not to be discussed?*

Well, sister, as far as the principles of Sant Mat are concerned, masters don't come to perform any miracles at all. But miracles sometimes do happen in their lifetime. They're so tender-hearted, kind-hearted, that sometimes they help us go through certain situations, and you can call them miracles. But actually that is not their mission in life, to perform miracles. They perform spiritual miracles, so to say. We who are slaves of the senses, slaves of karma, slaves of this world, who are bound to this world – they detach us from here and take us back to the Lord. That is the greatest miracle they can perform, and that is their main mission in this life.

But miracles do happen in the lives of saints, sometimes, rarely, here and there. Mostly we exaggerate stories after they leave this world because we want to give them importance and we want to discuss their greatness. Human nature is like that. We exaggerate things a little or we think they were miracles. For us they become miracles, but for the saints such occurrences are only guidance to keep us straight on the path so that we may not go too much astray. Sometimes the sheep in a flock go a little astray, and the shepherd whistles to get them back into the fold. That is his duty; it is not a miracle that he has got the sheep back into the fold. Master also guides us and keeps us straight. To us that looks like miracles sometimes.

558 *So, the doing of miracles, all of this has nothing to do with the kingdom of God?*

No. Miracles do happen. Saints are generally very kind-hearted, but performing miracles is not their mission in life. Sometimes miracles do happen in the lifetime of saints, but they do not intentionally want to do it. They do not want to deviate from the laws of nature. If Christ had done all those miracles intentionally, he would not have said: Thy will be done.[21] He would not have said that we have to submit to the will of the Lord. It means that we should face our fate karmas with his grace, boldly and gladly. Whatever is in our lot, we have to face that. Saints do not like to interfere with that, but miracles do happen. I do not say that they do not perform them. They do happen, but they do not give any importance to these things. The supernatural powers do come within us when we meditate, but saints do not want us to use those supernatural powers, because one always does so at one's own cost. If we begin to use them, we will lose all that we have. So Christ also told Satan: Begone![53] He did not want to be tempted by all those supernatural powers.

559 *Master, what is your theory regarding healing of the sick?*

If you are a doctor, do it. Help people.

I mean, according to the Scriptures, Jesus has so frequently healed the sick with the crack of the whip.

Brother, he has healed the sick souls. He did not make a practice of healing the physically diseased people. These are wrong interpretations. He has given eyes to the blind.[103] That refers to the spiritual, inner sight, for we are all blind as long as we do not see the Lord, as you have just heard in the discourse.

560 *Master, about Christ: We know that perfect saints, perfect masters, do not, generally, perform outward miracles. What would be the explanation for the many miracles which Christ performed, or reputedly performed?*

Well, brother, miracles do happen in the lifetime of mystics. But it is not their main purpose to come to this world to perform miracles. As far as Christ is concerned, he did perform certain miracles – saints are so kind-hearted and compassionate – but mostly what look like miracles aren't miracles at all.

If you read Saint Matthew very thoroughly, it is clear that Christ performed spiritual miracles; he gave them spiritually, not physically. He says, the dead are raised.[130] That doesn't mean that he raised the dead from the grave. It means that as long as our attention is below the eye centre, we are dead, just living in a grave. The whole body he calls a grave. Those whose consciousness is below the eye centre, who have absolutely forgotten the Father and have become slaves of the senses, they are dead. They are being raised in that they are being made conscious of the Father, they are being filled with love and devotion for the Father. Christ says, the lame can walk now.[43] We are so crooked, we do not even know how to walk straight in the world. We are always trying to cheat each other, deceive each other. Our actions are crooked. So, he says, those people have become absolutely straight; they have become honest, truthful, loving. They have learned how to walk straight in this life. So these are not physical miracles that Christ performed. I don't deny that he performed miracles in his lifetime, but not as many as are attributed to him today.

And then, he may have used that means to attract crowds, in order to give them the teachings. He may have realized that he could not reach people with his teachings unless he was able to collect them together and win their confidence. In Saint Matthew it says that his reputation spread all over, in Jordan and Israel and so many other places. People came to him. Their purpose in coming to him was only a physical healing. The Bible says that seeing the multitude, he went to the mountain and thus he spoke.[7] His purpose was not to heal those whom he collected, but to give them the teachings. Although he may have collected them with this excuse, his purpose was not to physically heal them. He gave them the sermon, the teachings. And when you read the Sermon on the Mount, you see there is nothing, nothing in it about miracles.

So miracles may have happened in his lifetime. I don't deny that. But people just remember the miracles and forget the teaching. And then, what is a miracle to you may be just a coincidence to another person. And for a third person, it may be just an ordinary thing. So-called miracles are only comparative.

MASTERS ARE ABOVE KARMA

561 Do masters have karma?

You see, whoever comes into this world will have to have karmas to live here. Without karma nobody can exist in this world. Even a saint needs a mother. A saint needs a father. He will have brothers, sisters, and many people to come across. Without karmas, he would meet no one. We can't take a step without karma in this world. But saints are not a slave of these karmas; karmas are not their masters. They have to take on karmas in order to come to our level in this world, but they are not slaves of karma. They can leave this body whenever they want to. They can avoid any karma they want to. They can take on anybody's karma to help, to share that person's karma. But we, who are slaves of our karmas, can't do that. And we can't get rid of our own karmas if we don't want to face any particular karma. But masters are above karma. So whoever exists in the body, whoever comes into the flesh, has no option but to take on karma, because without karma nobody can exist in this world.

562 Is the suffering that a master goes through purely physical, and does it not affect him in any other way?

No, he shares people's suffering, whether it's physical or mental. However happy you may be, if someone comes to you and starts telling his woeful story, won't you feel for him? Just in the ordinary human way? We may have no suffering of our own, but we are so moved by the suffering of another person that we mentally start suffering along with him after hearing his woeful story. So whether we help him or not, we definitely share his misery and his mental suffering. Though that suffering is not ours at all, out of sympathy, out of compassion and regard for another person you suffer along with him.

So masters come on a mission of mercy. They have no load of their own, but they're so kind-hearted and merciful that they also suffer along with their disciples because they want to help them. They have to hear everybody's woeful tale, everybody's miserable story, everybody's problem. Nobody will come and share his joy with him. Everybody has to share his tears with him. So naturally one is also affected to that extent.

563 Are the great masters who are supposed to be perfect and are karmaless, but who are sacrificed and condemned – they are crucified in one way or another – does that not mean that they have karma? Otherwise they could not be crucified.

There are many reasons for it. Sometimes they have to set an example to the world. Sometimes they take the karmas of the disciples on themselves, and make their own body endure them. And yet if they want to escape it, they can escape from that situation.

In what way do they escape it? What do you mean, with crucifixion for instance?

They can escape it if they want to. They are all-powerful from that point of view. But, do they actually want to be crucified? Who wants to be crucified? Not even a master. They just do not bother. It does not hurt them at all. You see, the physical body is not the master. They leave the body. When they leave the body every day, at will, it makes no difference what you do with their body. Crucifixion takes place only as far as the world is concerned, as far as our physical eyes are concerned. A saint actually cannot be crucified.

564 Do saints not have to come back?

They are sent back. There is no question of their having to come back. They are sent for a particular purpose, not because they come by karmas or they are being pulled down or they want to come back to this world. They are sent by the Lord to bring certain souls back to him.

565 But does even a perfect master need a living master? Or is it merely a formality?

How has he become a perfect master? From imperfect you become perfect. When you are born, you are imperfect. When you go to the master, you become perfect. So you need a master to become perfect. If you weren't imperfect, you wouldn't be born. Imperfect means we must bring some karmas in order to take birth.

For a perfect master too?

He will become perfect when he is brought in touch with the word made flesh. Until then, he is not perfect. When he is brought in touch with the word made flesh, he becomes perfect. The necessity is there for one who brings him in touch with the word made flesh.

For example, there are many types of rich persons. Some people were labourers on the roads and they became multimillionaires. Other people were lucky to be born with a silver spoon in their mouths and they became multimillionaires. Whoever has the wealth is a multimillionaire irrespective of how he got it, whether by birth, whether by inheritance, whether by work. Some people are lucky to get the grace of their master, and they become a master themselves, whether they have worked for it or not. Some people inherit that wealth from their master – that is for him to decide how he makes them. But when one is born, he can't be perfect. He can never be part of the creation if he is perfect. He has to become imperfect to some extent, in order to take birth.

And from where comes the karma of a perfect master? If he is perfect, he has no karma.

A saint is not bound by karmas, but he has to come with some karmas, otherwise how will he get a father or a mother or a sister or a brother? It is not a question of just his own individual karma; it also concerns the karma of so many others with whom he is going to associate.

He is master of his karma. Christ said: I can take the body when I want to, I can leave the body when I want to.[108] That means, I am not in the body due to the force of my karmas; I am not a slave of the karmas. I am master of the body. But when I am in the body, I have to go through the karmas. He has a mother, he has a father, he has a brother, he has associates. Karmas are there, but he is not a slave to them.

566 *When we read history, we find saints often have to suffer in this world. Was it due to their own karma, or did they have to suffer for the sake of others?*

The Lord has his own ways and means to make the saints known in the world, to give us his teachings. There is always a divine law behind this. Saints have no karma of their own. Christ indicated that he could leave his body when he wanted to and he could take it up again when he wanted to,[108] meaning that he was immune from karma. It is not the karma, but the will of the Lord that binds the saints to the flesh.

Christ also said that he stood as a ransom for the allotted souls.[110] By 'ransom' he means whatever the souls owe to the prince of this world, Kal, the negative power. The saints hold themselves responsible for that debt. They may take it on their own body, or they may make the disciple pay for it, because all karmas of the disciples must be cleared before they can go back to the Father.

Saints have no karmas of their own. They take the karmas of their disciples, and it may be a divine law to make the saints known to the world. If Christ had not been crucified, I don't think his teachings would have spread so much in this world today. He is known today because he was crucified. But actually, saints have no karmas of their own.

567 *Maharaj Ji, yesterday a person asked me if a guru can sometimes give away part of his grace to anybody else, and would he be any poorer for it in his spiritual life? And I said, "No, he has such an abundant reservoir that he would not, by giving away a portion of it." This person then asked me, "Then, why should a master suffer from any disease, or be unwell, physically, at the time of his death?"*

Saints sometimes do take the karmas of their disciples, and being in the domain of Kal, they themselves have to account for those karmas on their bodies. That is why we feel that they are suffering physically, from a health point of view. Actually, they are above the cycle of karmas and can clear any karma. They do not like to break the law of nature, being in the domain of Kal. So we may think they are suffering. Really, the soul is not at all bothered with what the body is going through.

There is never a deficiency of what they give. The more they give, the more it grows. It is just like love. The more we are helpful to others, the more we feel like helping others, and the more it grows every day. The question of deficiency does not arise. Being in this world, they do not like to break God's law. So sometimes they help their disciples by taking their karmas on their own bodies. The soul does not suffer at all.

568 Why do sant satgurus like Kabir, Mansur, Gobind Singh and others suffer violent deaths? Or suffer lingering diseases like Sawan Singh and Jagat Singh? Are they still in possession of some karmas of their own that have to be paid, or do they pay some of the karmas taken off their disciples to promote their spiritual progress?

Both are right. As I explained yesterday, there are three types of saints. Some come from the supreme Father just for this purpose. They are ready. They need only the light of a match to light that candle. Everything is there: The oil is there, the wick is there, everything is ready. They need only a spark to become a lighted candle. And for others, everything has to be collected: A wick is to be collected and wax is to be collected and it has to be moulded, made into a candle, and then lit. It also becomes the same type of candle when lit. In the first category are those who come direct from the Father and in the second class are those who work their way up and those who become masters by special endowment, as by gift or inheritance from the Lord. Saints come for the purpose of enlightening us and merging us back into him. Then those saints also make other disciples and bring them up to the same level. They make them saints to carry on their work.

All saints have some karma to go through in this world, for without karma there can be no physical body; but mostly it is the portions of the karmas of their disciples that they take on themselves. They help their disciples in many ways; physical ways, mental ways, spiritual ways. Sometimes we think they are suffering. They are not suffering. They are helping us; they are sharing. Some of their karmas may be their own also, but they are not affected by those karmas. They can pay them in a second. Karmas do not pull them. They have to have karma in order to live in this world, just as everybody has to have some karma to live in this world. Because karmas are under them, they control karma; they are not victims of the karma.

When a saint comes into this world, he must have a mother and a father. He has to live, he has to work. Nothing can be done without karma. But he is not a slave of the karmas. He can refuse to take on or he may share the karmas of his disciples or others because saints are very soft-hearted, kind-hearted and always like to help. They even help people at the expense of their own bodies. So both things are right.

One flame lighting another

569 *Is it necessary for a line of gurus destined to be perfect saints to leave a written word, a will, before they pass on, to let the disciples know?*

It is not essential that every master must have a line. Some masters have no line at all and some masters are destined to have some line. It entirely depends upon the will of the Lord. You can't fix the rule, that every master must have a long line. They may or may not have, and they know best how to appoint somebody.

570 Are there other living masters besides you?

Well, brother, I do not consider myself a master. I am here by the order of my predecessor. My only qualification is that I have been entrusted with a duty to perform by my master, and I am trying to do my duty to the best of my ability. There may be many masters in the world.

571 Do you personally have a living guru?

No. My master has departed, but I was initiated by him during his lifetime.

572 Master, in the introduction to the English version of Sar Bachan *it is mentioned that Soami Ji meditated for seventeen years in a dark back room before he brought out the teachings of Radha Soami, which implied that he had no early teacher in that life. I was eager to know if this indicates that he was one of those masters you spoke of, in a class of those who came directly from God?*

Sister, generally the disciples of every saint refuse to believe that their own master ever had a master. This is out of respect for their own master. They think that their own master was so great that he never needed a teacher. Actually, Soami Ji had a teacher. I do not want to enter into controversy about history or other points, but Soami Ji definitely had a teacher who put him on the path, who gave him all that he wanted to give him, internally and externally, and Soami Ji continued the practice before he taught, before he put people on the path. Similarly, Guru Nanak had a teacher, Kabir had a teacher, but no disciples of any master will believe that their master needed a teacher. In our fondness, we think that probably our master will not be considered great if we admit that he had a teacher. That is exactly cutting at the root of the very teachings of those masters, to say that they never had a master. Every teacher needs a master. Before he becomes a teacher he is a disciple. If the disciple then comes to that stage, he also can become a master. I do not agree that Soami Ji never had a teacher. Soami Ji had a teacher, whether they admit it or not. But I do not wish to enter into controversy with anybody.

573 Did Jesus have a master?

I am not a student of history. Historians probably have to prove who the master of Jesus was. Perhaps John the Baptist has said that he baptized Jesus. I do not know who the teacher or master of Christ was, but he must have had a teacher. We do not degrade a master to whom we give sole respect by accepting the fact that he had a teacher. We rather praise such masters by doing so, because they prove the knowledge, the wisdom, the path, that everybody needs a teacher, and they are the first to give an example to the public that we need a teacher. It is for the historians to say who was Christ's teacher; but definitely he did not get all the beautiful teachings that he tried to give us without a teacher. Saints may have a formal teacher, just to prove to us that a teacher is necessary, but every master has had a teacher. As I explained yesterday, if the candle is ready, it needs only a match to light it. For the other, we have to bring the wick and the wax, and mould it, make a candle, and then light it. So all those guides of souls, who come into this world to teach us, they are all ready. They just need a lighting from another candle, another master, to become a full master. But all the same, they need a teacher, and they have a teacher. This is the law of the Lord.

574 What did the Great Master mean when he said that the man who comes after me will have powers tenfold?

John the Baptist said the same thing in the Bible: The one who's coming after me is greater than me.[75] Since no disciple can be greater than a master, mystics always prepare a way for their successors.

Unless a master talks highly of his successor, the successor can never be successful at all. Because the master's disciples will not care about the master's successor. To them, the successor is just another disciple. So every master always highly praises his successor.

575 Does even the first in a line of mystics need a master?

Of course, every mystic has a master. Sometimes history reveals their names, sometimes history is silent, doesn't know about it. But every mystic has a master to begin with. It has been discussed so many times. Some souls just come ready, they only need a spark to be lit, and then they are ready to give light to others. Some have to come to that level of consciousness to experience that light and then become mystics. Some have to work hard to come to that level; some just come in this world, but even they need a little spark.

If the oil is there, the wick is there, then all that is needed is a little match. But if first you have to make a container, then you have to bring oil, then you have to make a wick, then you have to put them together, and then you light it, that candle also will give you the same light, even though it has taken time to become that candle. Guru Nanak says: One candle has given light to another candle.* The candle was already there, but another candle is required to give it light before that candle can be used to also give light.

It's not essential that every mystic must tell us who his master is. They're not concerned or bothered about the history of their life, how they got their spiritual progress or light within, who put them on the path. They're only concerned with giving us the teachings. That doesn't mean that they had no master.

Followers of Guru Nanak say Guru Nanak had no master; followers of Soami Ji Maharaj say he had no master; followers of Kabir say that he had no master; followers of Christ say he had no master. It's a wrong concept. People probably think that if they accept that their master also needed a master, then their master perhaps is not very great, which is a wrong concept. There lies the greatness of the master. Christ makes it very clear that unless you are born again – brought into contact with shabd – you cannot go back to the Father.[77] If we need a new birth – initiation – then he also needed a new birth.

Every mystic definitely has been associated with some mystic to get that light, to experience that light. But we think that if we accept that our master also needed a master, perhaps he is not very great. That is absolutely wrong.

Can there be more mystics in the world?

Yes, there may be many mystics in the world. There is no dearth, but very few will be teachers, very few may be stamped or given the authority to teach. No mystic will teach anyone unless he gets the authority from the Father to do it. As Christ has made clear in the Bible: I don't do anything for my own glory, I have

---

* *Deepak te deepak pargaasia tribhavan jot dikhaaee.* Guru Nanak, Adi Granth, M1, p.943.

no will of my own; I do what my Father wants me to do.[100] I have been stamped by the Father.

As you know, in those days, and even now, the president has to stamp or sign a contract when you're employed to do any job, which gives you the authority to do that job. A judge and an advocate, a lawyer, have the same qualifications. But if a lawyer writes a judgment, it will not be accepted. He can't acquit anybody, he can't imprison anybody. But the judge has been appointed by the president. His judgment is accepted; he has the authority to acquit someone or to put anybody in prison. Their qualifications are the same, but the judge has the authority, not the lawyer.

Similarly, a professor and another person may have the same academic qualifications, but one has been appointed by the university to teach students. So only he will teach; the other person won't teach. It's not that he's not as intelligent as the professor. We are only concerned with the professor, who has been given the authority to teach us. We can make use only of the professor's knowledge, not anybody else's.

So there may be many mystics in the world, but only those who are appointed by the Father, stamped by the Father, given authority by the Father, can put people on the path.

Index to Bible Quotes

According to the King James Version of the Bible

1 **Psalms 37:11** But the meek shall inherit the earth; and shall delight themselves in the abundance of peace. [*i*.266]

2 **Proverbs 17:22** A merry heart doeth good like a medicine: but a broken spirit drieth the bones. [*i*.399]

3 **Matthew 3:2** And saying, Repent ye: for the kingdom of heaven is at hand. [*i*.70, *i*.87, *i*.97, *i*.128, *i*.239, *i*.309, *i*.333, *iii*.259]

4 **Matthew 3:10** And now also the axe is laid unto the root of the trees: therefore every tree which bringeth not forth good fruit is hewn down, and cast into the fire. [*i*.125]

5 **Matthew 3:16** And Jesus, when he was baptized, went up straightway out of the water: and, lo, the heavens were opened unto him, and he saw the Spirit of God descending like a dove, and lighting upon him: … [*i*.84]

6 **Matthew 4:10** Then saith Jesus unto him, Get thee hence, Satan: for it is written, Thou shalt worship the Lord thy God, and him only shalt thou serve. [*i*.306, *ii*.215]

7 **Matthew 5:1** And seeing the multitudes, he went up into a mountain: and when he was set, his disciples came unto him: … [*i*.507, *iii*.403]

8 **Matthew 5:4** Blessed are they that mourn: for they shall be comforted. [*i*.25, *i*.290, *ii*.102, *ii*.366, *iii*.63, *iii*.65, *iii*.70, *iii*.77]

9 **Matthew 5:5** Blessed are the meek: for they shall inherit the earth. [*iii*.231]

10 **Matthew 5:9** Blessed are the peacemakers: for they shall be called the children of God. [*i*.395, *i*.493, *iii*.417]

11 **Matthew 5:14** Ye are the light of the world. A city that is set on an hill cannot be hid. **15** Neither do men light a candle, and put it under a bushel, but on a candlestick; and it giveth light unto all that are in the house. **16** Let your light so shine before men, that they may see your good works, and glorify your Father which is in heaven. [*i*.381]

12 **Matthew 5:17** Think not that I am come to destroy the law, or the prophets: I am not come to destroy, but to fulfil. [*i*.322]

13 **Matthew 5:18** For verily I say unto you, Till heaven and earth pass, one jot or one tittle shall in no wise pass from the law, till all be fulfilled. [*i*.308]

14 **Matthew 5:21** Ye have heard that it was said by them of old time, Thou shalt not kill; and whosoever shall kill shall be in danger of the judgment: … [*ii*.59]

15 **Matthew 5:23** Therefore if thou bring thy gift to the altar, and there rememberest that thy brother hath ought against thee; **24** Leave there thy gift before the altar, and go thy way; first be reconciled to thy brother, and then come and offer thy gift. [*iii*.134, *iii*.261]

16 **Matthew 5:25** Agree with thine adversary quickly, whiles thou art in the way with him; lest at any time the adversary deliver thee to the judge, and the judge deliver thee to the officer, and thou be cast into prison. [*i*.124, *i*.399, *iii*.257]

17 **Matthew 5:28** But I say unto you, That whosoever looketh on a woman to lust after her hath committed adultery with her already in his heart. [*i*.113]

18 **Matthew 5:39** But I say unto you, That ye resist not evil: but whosoever shall smite thee on thy right cheek, turn to him the other also. [*i*.302, *i*.314, *iii*.363]

19 **Matthew 6:1** Take heed that ye do not your alms before men, to be seen of them: otherwise ye have no reward of your Father which is in heaven. **2** Therefore when thou doest thine alms, do not sound

a trumpet before thee, as the hypocrites do in the synagogues and in the streets, that they may have glory of men. Verily I say unto you, They have their reward. [*iii*.156, *iii*.403]

20 **Matthew 6:6** But thou, when thou prayest, enter into thy closet, and when thou hast shut thy door, pray to thy Father which is in secret; and thy Father which seeth in secret shall reward thee openly. **7** But when ye pray, use not vain repetitions, as the heathen do: for they think that they shall be heard for their much speaking. **8** Be not ye therefore like unto them: for your Father knoweth what things ye have need of, before ye ask him. [*ii*.134]

21 **Matthew 6:10** Thy kingdom come. Thy will be done in earth, as it is in heaven. **11** Give us this day our daily bread. **12** And forgive us our debts, As we forgive our debtors. [*i*.497, *i*.505, *ii*.437]

22 **Matthew 6:21** For where your treasure is, there will your heart be also. [*i*.275, *i*.392, *i*.490, *iii*.297, *iii*.299, *iii*.331]

23 **Matthew 6:22** The light of the body is the eye: if therefore thine eye be single, thy whole body shall be full of light. [*i*.209, *i*.239, *i*.299, *i*.309, *i*.333, *i*.388, *i*.476, *ii*.15]

24 **Matthew 6:24** No man can serve two masters: for either he will hate the one, and love the other; or else he will hold to the one, and despise the other. Ye cannot serve God and mammon. [*ii*.105, *ii*.111, *ii*.302, *iii*.10, *iii*.161, *iii*.299]

25 **Matthew 6:25** Therefore I say unto you, Take no thought for your life, what ye shall eat, or what ye shall drink; nor yet for your body, what ye shall put on. Is not the life more than meat, and the body than raiment? **26** Behold the fowls of the air: for they sow not, neither do they reap, nor gather into barns; yet your heavenly Father feedeth them. Are ye not much better than they? **27** Which of you by taking thought can add one cubit unto his stature? **28** And why take ye thought for raiment? Consider the lilies of the field, how they grow; they toil not, neither do they spin: **29** And yet I say unto you, That even Solomon in all his glory was not arrayed like one of these. **30** Wherefore, if God so clothe the grass of the field, which to day is, and to morrow is cast into the oven, shall he not much more clothe you, O ye of little faith? **31** Therefore take no thought,

saying, What shall we eat? or, What shall we drink? or, Wherewithal shall we be clothed? **32** (For after all these things do the Gentiles seek:) for your heavenly Father knoweth that ye have need of all these things. [*i*.263, *i*.380, *ii*.131, *ii*.133, *ii*.144, *ii*.451, *iii*.201]

26 **Matthew 7:1** Judge not, that ye be not judged. [*iii*.250]

27 **Matthew 7:3** And why beholdest thou the mote that is in thy brother's eye, but considerest not the beam that is in thine own eye? [*iii*.244]

28 **Matthew 7:6** Give not that which is holy unto the dogs, neither cast ye your pearls before swine, lest they trample them under their feet, and turn again and rend you. [*ii*.254]

29 **Matthew 7:7** Ask, and it shall be given you; seek, and ye shall find; knock, and it shall be opened unto you: … [*i*.288, *i*.329, *i*.476, *ii*.159]

30 **Matthew 7:11** If ye then, being evil, know how to give good gifts unto your children, how much more shall your Father which is in heaven give good things to them that ask him? [*iii*.202]

31 **Matthew 7:17** Even so every good tree bringeth forth good fruit; but a corrupt tree bringeth forth evil fruit. **18** A good tree cannot bring forth evil fruit, neither can a corrupt tree bring forth good fruit. [*i*.121]

32 **Matthew 7:21** Not every one that saith unto me, Lord, Lord, shall enter into the kingdom of heaven; but he that doeth the will of my Father which is in heaven. [*iii*.80]

33 **Matthew 10:8** Heal the sick, cleanse the lepers, raise the dead, cast out devils: freely ye have received, freely give. **9** Provide neither gold, nor silver, nor brass in your purses,… [*i*.312]

34 **Matthew 10:16** Behold, I send you forth as sheep in the midst of wolves: be ye therefore wise as serpents, and harmless as doves. [*iii*.178]

35 **Matthew 10:19** But when they deliver you up, take no thought how or what ye shall speak: for it shall be given you in that same hour what ye shall speak. **20** For it is not ye that speak, but the Spirit of your Father which speaketh in you. [*i*.317]

36 **Matthew 10:22** And ye shall be hated of all men for my name's sake: but he that endureth to the end shall be saved. [*i*.318]

37 **Matthew 10:28** And fear not them which kill the body, but are not able to kill the soul: but rather fear him which is able to destroy both soul and body in hell. [*iii*.41]

38 **Matthew 10:30** But the very hairs of your head are all numbered. [*i*.130, *i*.131, *i*.413]

39 **Matthew 10:34** Think not that I am come to send peace on earth: I came not to send peace, but a sword. [*i*.51, *i*.58, *i*.312, *i*.339, *i*.384, *i*.392, *i*.490, *ii*.405, *iii*.5, *iii*.203, *iii*.279]

40 **Matthew 10:35** For I am come to set a man at variance against his father, and the daughter against her mother, and the daughter in law against her mother in law. [*iii*.279]

41 **Matthew 10:36** And a man's foes shall be they of his own household. [*iii*.280]

42 **Matthew 10:37** He that loveth father or mother more than me is not worthy of me: and he that loveth son or daughter more than me is not worthy of me. [*i*.201, *i*.222, *i*.442, *i*.461, *i*.464, *i*.473, *iii*.22, *iii*.279]

43 **Matthew 11:5** The blind receive their sight, and the lame walk, the lepers are cleansed, and the deaf hear, the dead are raised up, and the poor have the gospel preached to them. [*i*.192, *i*.506]

44 **Matthew 11:25** At that time Jesus answered and said, I thank thee, O Father, Lord of heaven and earth, because thou hast hid these things from the wise and prudent, and hast revealed them unto babes. [*i*.265]

45 **Matthew 11:28** Come unto me, all ye that labour and are heavy laden, and I will give you rest. [*i*.399]

46 **Matthew 12:31** Wherefore I say unto you, All manner of sin and blasphemy shall be forgiven unto men: but the blasphemy against the Holy Ghost shall not be forgiven unto men. [*ii*.103, *ii*.336, *ii*.368, *iii*.30]

47 **Matthew 12:47** Then one said unto him, Behold, thy mother and thy brethren stand without, desiring to speak with thee. **48** But he

answered and said unto him that told him, Who is my mother? and who are my brethren? **49** And he stretched forth his hand toward his disciples, and said, Behold my mother and my brethren! **50** For whosoever shall do the will of my Father which is in heaven, the same is my brother, and sister, and mother. [*iii*.221, *iii*.280, *iii*.292, *iii*.294, *iii*.303, *iii*.306]

48 **Matthew 13:3** And he spake many things unto them in parables, saying, Behold, a sower went forth to sow. 4 And when he sowed, some seeds fell by the way side, and the fowls came and devoured them up. 5 Some fell upon stony places, where they had not much earth: and forthwith they sprung up, because they had no deepness of earth. **6** And when the sun was up, they were scorched; and because they had no root, they withered away. 7 And some fell among thorns; and the thorns sprung up, and choked them. 8 But other fell into good ground, and brought forth fruit, some an hundredfold, some sixtyfold, some thirtyfold. [*i*.424, *i*.440, *ii*.420, *ii*.421]

49 **Matthew 13:13** Therefore speak I to them in parables: because they seeing see not; and hearing they hear not, neither do they understand. [*i*.403, *i*.408, *i*.415, *ii*.370]

50 **Matthew 13:24** Another parable put he forth unto them, saying, The kingdom of heaven is likened unto a man which sowed good seed in his field. **25** But while men slept, his enemy came and sowed tares among the wheat, and went his way. **26** But when the blade was sprung up, and brought forth fruit, then appeared the tares also. 27 So the servants of the householder came and said unto him, Sir, didst not thou sow good seed in thy field? from whence then hath it tares? **28** He said unto them, An enemy hath done this. The servants said unto him, Wilt thou then that we go and gather them up? **29** But he said, Nay; lest while ye gather up the tares, ye root up also the wheat with them. **30** Let both grow together until the harvest: and in the time of harvest I will say to the reapers, Gather ye together first the tares, and bind them in bundles to burn them: but gather the wheat into my barn. [*ii*.438, *iii*.6, *iii*.121, *iii*.372]

51 **Matthew 15:4** For God commanded, saying, Honour thy father and mother: and, He that curseth father or mother, let him die the death. [*iii*.307]

52 **Matthew 15:24** But he answered and said, I am not sent but unto the lost sheep of the house of Israel. [*ii*.7]

53 **Matthew 16:23** But he turned, and said unto Peter, Get thee behind me, Satan: thou art an offence unto me: for thou savourest not the things that be of God, but those that be of men. [*i*.505]

54 **Matthew 17:12** But I say unto you, That Elias is come already, and they knew him not, but have done unto him whatsoever they listed. Likewise shall also the Son of man suffer of them. **13** Then the disciples understood that he spake unto them of John the Baptist. [*i*.467]

55 **Matthew 17:20** And Jesus said unto them, Because of your unbelief: for verily I say unto you, If ye have faith as a grain of mustard seed, ye shall say unto this mountain, Remove hence to yonder place; and it shall remove; and nothing shall be impossible unto you. [*ii*.124]

56 **Matthew 18:3** And said, Verily I say unto you, Except ye be converted, and become as little children, ye shall not enter into the kingdom of heaven. [*iii*.205]

57 **Matthew 18:12** How think ye? If a man have an hundred sheep, and one of them be gone astray, doth he not leave the ninety and nine, and goeth into the mountains, and seeketh that which is gone astray? [*i*.404, *ii*.428, *iii*.4, *iii*.6, *iii*.18, *iii*.132]

58 **Matthew 18:13** And if so be that he find it, verily I say unto you, he rejoiceth more of that sheep, than of the ninety and nine which went not astray. **14** Even so it is not the will of your Father which is in heaven, that one of these little ones should perish. [*iii*.4]

59 **Matthew 18:20** For where two or three are gathered together in my name, there am I in the midst of them. [*iii*.106, *iii*.115, *iii*.126]

60 **Matthew 18:26** The servant therefore fell down, and worshipped him, saying, Lord, have patience with me, and I will pay thee all. [*iii*.258]

61 **Matthew 19:24** And again I say unto you, It is easier for a camel to go through the eye of a needle, than for a rich man to enter into the kingdom of God. [*i*.267, *i*.392, *iii*.143, *iii*.146]

62 **Matthew 19:30** But many that are first shall be last; and the last shall be first. [*i*.97, *i*.430, *ii*.274, *ii*.350]

63 **Matthew 20:16** So the last shall be first, and the first last: for many be called, but few chosen. [*ii*.275, *ii*.421, *ii*.423]

64 **Matthew 20:28** Even as the Son of man came not to be ministered unto, but to minister, and to give his life a ransom for many. [*i*.498]

65 **Matthew 22:14** For many are called, but few are chosen. [*i*.429]

66 **Matthew 22:21** They say unto him, Caesar's. Then saith he unto them, Render therefore unto Caesar the things which are Caesar's; and unto God the things that are God's. [*i*.47, *i*.83, *i*.89, *i*.103, *i*.109, *i*.499, *iii*.225, *iii*.354]

67 **Matthew 22:36** Master, which is the great commandment in the law? **37** Jesus said unto him, Thou shalt love the Lord thy God with all thy heart, and with all thy soul, and with all thy mind. **38** This is the first and great commandment. **39** And the second is like unto it, Thou shalt love thy neighbour as thyself. **40** On these two commandments hang all the law and the prophets. [*i*.174, *i*.393, *i*.485, *ii*.58, *ii*.102, *ii*.450, *iii*.130, *iii*.261, *iii*.389]

68 **Matthew 26:42** He went away again the second time, and prayed, saying, O my Father, if this cup may not pass away from me, except I drink it, thy will be done. [*iii*.73]

69 **Mark 8:18** Having eyes, see ye not? and having ears, hear ye not? and do ye not remember? [*i*.284, *i*.289, *i*.468, *ii*.30, *ii*.206]

70 **Luke 6:48** He is like a man which built an house, and digged deep, and laid the foundation on a rock: and when the flood arose, the stream beat vehemently upon that house, and could not shake it: for it was founded upon a rock. [*ii*.397]

71 **Luke 11:21** When a strong man armed keepeth his palace, his goods are in peace: ... [*ii*.298]

72 **John 1:1** In the beginning was the Word, and the Word was with God, and the Word was God. **2** The same was in the beginning with God. **3** All things were made by him; and without him was not any thing made that was made. **4** In him was life; and the life

was the light of men. **5** And the light shineth in darkness; and the darkness comprehended it not. [*i*.27, *i*.29, *i*.116, *i*.175, *i*.178, *i*.284, *i*.298, *ii*.14, *ii*.230]

73 **John 1:6** There was a man sent from God, whose name was John. [*i*.428, *i*.443, *ii*.14]

74 **John 1:14** And the Word was made flesh, and dwelt among us, (and we beheld his glory, the glory as of the only begotten of the Father) full of grace and truth. [*i*.451, *i*.464]

75 **John 1:27** He it is, who coming after me is preferred before me, whose shoe's latchet I am not worthy to unloose. [*i*.516]

76 **John 2:16** And said unto them that sold doves, Take these things hence; make not my Father's house a house of merchandise. [*i*.315]

77 **John 3:3** Jesus answered and said unto him, Verily, verily, I say unto thee, Except a man be born again, he cannot see the kingdom of God. [*i*.309, *i*.517, *ii*.16, *ii*.23, *ii*.24, *iii*.352, *iii*.377]

78 **John 3:8** The wind bloweth where it listeth, and thou hearest the sound thereof, but canst not tell whence it cometh, and whither it goeth: so is every one that is born of the Spirit. [*i*.298, *i*.309, *i*.476]

79 **John 3:14** And as Moses lifted up the serpent in the wilderness, even so must the Son of man be lifted up: **15** That whosoever believeth in him should not perish, but have eternal life. [*ii*.234]

80 **John 3:17** For God sent not his Son into the world to condemn the world; but that the world through him might be saved. **18** He that believeth on him is not condemned: but he that believeth not is condemned already, because he hath not believed in the name of the only begotten Son of God. [*i*.428, *iii*.11, *iii*.16, *iii*.26]

81 **John 3:29** He that hath the bride is the bridegroom: but the friend of the bridegroom, which standeth and heareth him, rejoiceth greatly because of the bridegroom's voice: this my joy therefore is fulfilled. [*iii*.418]

82 **John 4:14** But whosoever drinketh of the water that I shall give him shall never thirst; but the water that I shall give him shall be in him a well of water springing up into everlasting life. [*i*.200, *iii*.151]

83 **John 4:23** But the hour cometh, and now is, when the true worshippers shall worship the Father in spirit and in truth: for the Father seeketh such to worship him. [*i*.344, *ii*.24]

84 **John 4:24** God is a Spirit: and they that worship him must worship him in spirit and in truth. [*i*.305]

85 **John 5:14** Afterward Jesus findeth him in the temple, and said unto him, Behold, thou art made whole: sin no more, lest a worse thing come unto thee. [*i*.201, *i*.409, *ii*.22, *ii*.155]

86 **John 5:25** Verily, verily, I say unto you, The hour is coming, and now is, when the dead shall hear the voice of the Son of God: and they that hear shall live. [*i*.477]

87 **John 5:27** And hath given him authority to execute judgment also, because he is the Son of man. [*i*.448]

88 **John 5:30** I can of mine own self do nothing: as I hear, I judge: and my judgment is just; because I seek not mine own will, but the will of the Father which hath sent me. [*i*.418, *i*.443, *ii*.348]

89 **John 5:35** He was a burning and a shining light: and ye were willing for a season to rejoice in his light. [*i*.467]

90 **John 6:27** Labour not for the meat which perisheth, but for that meat which endureth unto everlasting life, which the Son of man shall give unto you: for him hath God the Father sealed. [*i*.448]

91 **John 6:38** For I came down from heaven, not to do mine own will, but the will of him that sent me. **39** And this is the Father's will which hath sent me, that of all which he hath given me I should lose nothing, but should raise it up again at the last day. [*i*.444]

92 **John 6:40** And this is the will of him that sent me, that every one which seeth the Son, and believeth on him, may have everlasting life: and I will raise him up at the last day. [*i*.439, *i*.465, *ii*.29, *ii*.396, *iii*.34, *iii*.352]

93 **John 6:44** No man can come to me, except the Father which hath sent me draw him: and I will raise him up at the last day. [*ii*.6, *ii*.10]

94 **John 6:53** Then Jesus said unto them, Verily, verily, I say unto you, Except ye eat the flesh of the Son of man, and drink his blood, ye have

no life in you. **54** Whoso eateth my flesh, and drinketh my blood, hath eternal life; and I will raise him up at the last day. [*iii*.43]

95 **John 6:63** It is the spirit that quickeneth; the flesh profiteth nothing: the words that I speak unto you, they are spirit, and they are life. [*iii*.46]

96 **John 7:37** In the last day, that great day of the feast, Jesus stood and cried, saying, If any man thirst, let him come unto me, and drink. **38** He that believeth on me, as the scripture hath said, out of his belly shall flow rivers of living water. [*i*.329, *i*.408, *i*.416]

97 **John 8:28** Then said Jesus unto them, When ye have lifted up the Son of man, then shall ye know that I am he, and that I do nothing of myself; but as my Father hath taught me, I speak these things. [*iii*.38, *iii*.40]

98 **John 8:32** And ye shall know the truth, and the truth shall make you free. [*iii*.260]

99 **John 8:34** Jesus answered them, Verily, verily, I say unto you, Whosoever committeth sin is the servant of sin. **35** And the servant abideth not in the house for ever: but the Son abideth ever. [*i*.151]

100 **John 8:50** And I seek not mine own glory: there is one that seeketh and judgeth. [*i*.518]

101 **John 9:1** And as Jesus passed by, he saw a man which was blind from his birth. **2** And his disciples asked him, saying, Master, who did sin, this man, or his parents, that he was born blind? **3** Jesus answered, Neither hath this man sinned, nor his parents: but that the works of God should be made manifest in him. [*i*.98]

102 **John 9:4** I must work the works of him that sent me, while it is day: the night cometh, when no man can work. **5** As long as I am in the world, I am the light of the world. [*i*.191, *i*.466, *i*.475]

103 **John 9:39** And Jesus said, For judgment I am come into this world, that they which see not might see; and that they which see might be made blind. [*i*.486, *i*.505, *iii*.403]

104 **John 10:4** And when he putteth forth his own sheep, he goeth before them, and the sheep follow him: for they know his voice. [*i*.404, *i*.405, *i*.406, *i*.407, *ii*.322, *iii*.43]

105 **John 10:8** All that ever came before me are thieves and robbers: but the sheep did not hear them. [*ii*.236]

106 **John 10:14** I am the good shepherd, and know my sheep, and am known of mine. [*i*.466]

107 **John 10:16** And other sheep I have, which are not of this fold: them also I must bring, and they shall hear my voice; and there shall be one fold, and one shepherd. [*i*.451, *i*.452, *ii*.237, *ii*.428, *ii*.451, *iii*.10, *iii*.98, *iii*.101, *iii*.292, *iii*.306]

108 **John 10:17** Therefore doth my Father love me, because I lay down my life, that I might take it again. **18** No man taketh it from me, but I lay it down of myself. I have power to lay it down, and I have power to take it again. This commandment have I received of my Father. [*i*.107, *i*.444, *i*.447, *i*.510, *i*.511, *ii*.215, *ii*.229]

109 **John 10:27** My sheep hear my voice, and I know them, and they follow me: … [*ii*.6]

110 **John 10:28** And I give unto them eternal life; and they shall never perish, neither shall any man pluck them out of my hand. **29** My Father, which gave them me, is greater than all; and no man is able to pluck them out of my Father's hand. [*i*.511]

111 **John 10:30** I and my Father are one. [*i*.169, *i*.195, *i*.207, *i*.447, *i*.449, *i*.453, *i*.462]

112 **John 10:34** Jesus answered them, Is it not written in your law, I said, Ye are gods? [*i*.171]

113 **John 10:38** But if I do, though ye believe not me, believe the works: that ye may know, and believe, that the Father is in me, and I in him. [*i*.448, *i*.476]

114 **John 11:25** Jesus said unto her, I am the resurrection, and the life: he that believeth in me, though he were dead, yet shall he live: … [*i*.497]

115 **John 13:34** A new commandment I give unto you, That ye love one another; as I have loved you, that ye also love one another. [*i*.386, *i*.389, *iii*.134, *iii*.145, *iii*.363]

116 **John 14:2** In my Father's house are many mansions: if it were not so, I would have told you. I go to prepare a place for you. [*i*.276, *i*.329, *i*.476]

117 **John 14:3** And if I go and prepare a place for you, I will come again, and receive you unto myself; that where I am, there ye may be also. [*ii*.216, *iii*.35]

118 **John 14:4** And whither I go ye know, and the way ye know. [*iii*.31, *iii*.67, *iii*.69, *iii*.72]

119 **John 14:9** Jesus saith unto him, Have I been so long time with you, and yet hast thou not known me, Philip? he that hath seen me hath seen the Father; and how sayest thou then, Shew us the Father? [*i*.464, *ii*.55]

120 **John 14:10** Believest thou not that I am in the Father, and the Father in me? The words that I speak unto you I speak not of myself: but the Father that dwelleth in me, he doeth the works. **11** Believe me that I am in the Father, and the Father in me: or else believe me for the very works' sake. [*i*.81, *i*.404, *i*.462, *i*.478, *ii*.55]

121 **John 14:16** And I will pray the Father, and he shall give you another Comforter, that he may abide with you for ever; **17** Even the Spirit of truth; whom the world cannot receive, because it seeth him not, neither knoweth him: but ye know him; for he dwelleth with you, and shall be in you. **18** I will not leave you comfortless: I will come to you. **19** Yet a little while, and the world seeth me no more; but ye see me: because I live, ye shall live also. **20** At that day ye shall know that I am in my Father, and ye in me, and I in you. **26** But the Comforter, which is the Holy Ghost, whom the Father will send in my name, he shall teach you all things, and bring all things to your remembrance, whatsoever I have said unto you. [*i*.307, *iii*.33, *iii*.69]

122 **John 14:20** At that day ye shall know that I am in my Father, and ye in me, and I in you. **21** He that hath my commandments, and keepeth them, he it is that loveth me: and he that loveth me shall be loved of my Father, and I will love him, and will manifest myself to him. **23** Jesus answered and said unto him, If a man love me, he will keep my words: and my Father will love him, and we will come unto him, and make our abode with him. [*ii*.194, *ii*.225, *ii*.231, *iii*.29, *iii*.37, *iii*.42, *iii*.44, *iii*.46, *iii*.95, *iii*.294]

123 **John 15:4** Abide in me, and I in you. As the branch cannot bear fruit of itself, except it abide in the vine; no more can ye, except ye abide in me. [*i*.474]

124 **John 15:20** Remember the word that I said unto you, The servant is not greater than his lord. If they have persecuted me, they will also persecute you; if they have kept my saying, they will keep yours also. [*iii*.248]

125 **John 15:22** If I had not come and spoken unto them, they had not had sin: but now they have no cloke for their sin. [*i*.93]

126 **John 16:7** Nevertheless I tell you the truth; It is expedient for you that I go away: for if I go not away, the Comforter will not come unto you; but if I depart, I will send him unto you. [*iii*.66, *iii*.67, *iii*.72]

127 **John 16:16** A little while, and ye shall not see me: and again, a little while, and ye shall see me, because I go to the Father. **17** Then said some of his disciples among themselves, What is this that he saith unto us, A little while, and ye shall not see me: and again, a little while, and ye shall see me: and, Because I go to the Father? **18** They said therefore, What is this that he saith, A little while? we cannot tell what he saith. **19** Now Jesus knew that they were desirous to ask him, and said unto them, Do ye enquire among yourselves of that I said, A little while, and ye shall not see me: and again, a little while, and ye shall see me? **20** Verily, verily, I say unto you, That ye shall weep and lament, but the world shall rejoice: and ye shall be sorrowful, but your sorrow shall be turned into joy. **21** A woman when she is in travail hath sorrow, because her hour is come: but as soon as she is delivered of the child, she remembereth no more the anguish, for joy that a man is born into the world. **22** And ye now therefore have sorrow: but I will see you again, and your heart shall rejoice, and your joy no man taketh from you. **23** And in that day ye shall ask me nothing. Verily, verily, I say unto you, Whatsoever ye shall ask the Father in my name, he will give it you. **24** Hitherto have ye asked nothing in my name: ask, and ye shall receive, that your joy may be full. **25** These things have I spoken unto you in proverbs: but the time cometh, when I shall no more speak unto you in proverbs, but I shall shew you plainly of the Father. [*i*.47, *i*.475, *ii*.127, *ii*.235, *iii*.59, *iii*.62, *iii*.99, *iii*.190]

128 **John 17:9** I pray for them: I pray not for the world, but for them which thou hast given me; for they are thine. [*i*.405, *i*.416, *i*.426, *i*.427, *ii*.355, *ii*.369, *ii*.371]

129 **John 17:11** And now I am no more in the world, but these are in the world, and I come to thee. Holy Father, keep through thine own name those whom thou hast given me, that they may be one, as we are. **22** And the glory which thou gavest me I have given them; that they may be one, even as we are one: **23** I in them, and thou in me, that they may be made perfect in one; and that the world may know that thou hast sent me, and hast loved them, as thou hast loved me. [*i*.110, *i*.305, *i*.405]

130 **John 20:9** For as yet they knew not the scripture, that he must rise again from the dead. [*i*.477, *i*.506]

131 **1 Corinthians 15:31** I protest by your rejoicing which I have in Christ Jesus our Lord, I die daily. [*ii*.226, *ii*.244, *ii*.245, *ii*.246, *ii*.247]

132 **2 Corinthians 6:16** And what agreement hath the temple of God with idols? for ye are the temple of the living God; as God hath said, I will dwell in them, and walk in them; and I will be their God, and they shall be my people. [*i*.174, *i*.239, *i*.329, *i*.476, *iii*.170]

133 **Galatians 6:7** Be not deceived; God is not mocked: for whatsoever a man soweth, that shall he also reap. [*i*.50, *i*.54, *i*.56, *i*.75, *i*.115, *i*.125, *i*.132, *i*.138, *i*.151, *ii*.59, *iii*.224, *iii*.260]

134 **Ephesians 1:3** Blessed be the God and Father of our Lord Jesus Christ, who hath blessed us with all spiritual blessings in heavenly places in Christ: ... [*i*.494]

135 **Ephesians 2:18** For through him we both have access by one Spirit unto the Father. [*i*.29]

136 **1 John 4:8** He that loveth not knoweth not God; for God is love. [*i*.284, *i*.461, *ii*.97]

137 **1 John 4:16** And we have known and believed the love that God hath to us. God is love; and he that dwelleth in love dwelleth in God, and God in him. [*i*.289, *ii*.102]

138 **Exodus 20 (The Ten Commandments)** **1** And God spake all these words, saying, **2** I am the LORD thy God, which have brought thee out of the land of Egypt, out of the house of bondage. **3** Thou shalt have no other gods before me. **4** Thou shalt not make unto thee any graven image, or any likeness of any thing that is in heaven above, or that is in the earth beneath, or that is in the water under the earth. **5** Thou shalt not bow down thyself to them, nor serve them: for I the LORD thy God am a jealous God, visiting the iniquity of the fathers upon the children unto the third and fourth generation of them that hate me; **6** And shewing mercy unto thousands of them that love me, and keep my commandments. **7** Thou shalt not take the name of the LORD thy God in vain; for the LORD will not hold him guiltless that taketh his name in vain. **8** Remember the sabbath day, to keep it holy. **9** Six days shalt thou labour, and do all thy work: **10** But the seventh day is the sabbath of the LORD thy God: in it thou shalt not do any work, thou, nor thy son, nor thy daughter, thy manservant, nor thy maidservant, nor thy cattle, nor thy stranger that is within thy gates: **11** For in six days the LORD made heaven and earth, the sea, and all that in them is, and rested the seventh day: wherefore the LORD blessed the sabbath day, and hallowed it. **12** Honour thy father and thy mother: that thy days may be long upon the land which the LORD thy God giveth thee. **13** Thou shalt not kill. **14** Thou shalt not commit adultery. **15** Thou shalt not steal. **16** Thou shalt not bear false witness against thy neighbour. **17** Thou shalt not covet thy neighbour's house, thou shalt not covet thy neighbour's wife, nor his manservant, nor his maidservant, nor his ox, nor his ass, nor any thing that is thy neighbour's. [*i*.448, *i*.479, *ii*.54, *ii*.58]

Subject Index

Addresses for Information and Books

INDIAN SUB-CONTINENT

INDIA
The Secretary
Radha Soami Satsang Beas
Dera Baba Jaimal Singh
District Amritsar, Punjab 143204

NEPAL
Capt. S.B.B. Chhetri (Retd.)
Radha Soami Satsang Beas Nepal
Gongabu 7, P. O. Box 1646
Kathmandu
☎ +977-1-435-7765

PAKISTAN
Mr. Sadrang Seetal Das
Lahori Mohala, Larkana, Sindh

SRI LANKA
Mr. Chandroo Mirpuri
Radha Soami Satsang Beas
No. 45 Silva Lane
Rajagiriya, Colombo
☎ +94-11-286-1491

SOUTHEAST ASIA

FOR FAR EAST
Mrs. Cami Moss
RSSB-HK
T.S.T., P.O. Box 90745
Kowloon, Hong Kong
☎ +852-2369-0625

MALAYSIA
Mr. Bhupinder Singh
Radha Soami Satsang Beas
29 Jalan Cerapu Satu, Off Batu 3 ¼
Jalan Cheras, Kuala Lumpur 56100
☎ +603-9200-3073

THAILAND
Mr. Harmahinder Singh Sethi
Radha Soami Satsang Beas
58/32 Ratchadaphisek Road, Soi 16
Thapra, Bangkok Yai, Bangkok 10600
☎ +66-2-868-2186 / 2187

INDONESIA
Mr. Ramesh Sadarangani
Jalan Pasir Putih IV/16, Block E 4
Ancol Timur, Jakarta
DKI Jakarta 14430

Yayasan Radha Soami Satsang
Jalan Transyogi KM. 5, Jatikarya
Pondok Gede, DKI Jakarta 17435
☎ +62-21-845-1612

Yayasan Radha Soami Satsang
Jalan Bung Tomo
Desa Pemecutan Raya
Denpasar, Barat 80116
☎ +62-361-438-522

PHILIPPINES
Mr. Kay Sham
Science of the Soul Study Center
9001 Don Jesus Boulevard
Alabang Hills, Cupang
Muntinlupa City, 1771
☎ +63-2-772-0111 / 0555

SINGAPORE
Mrs. Asha Melwani
Radha Soami Satsang Beas
19 Amber Road, Singapore 439868
☎ +65-6447-4956

ASIA PACIFIC

AUSTRALIA
Mr. Pradeep Raniga
Science of the Soul Study Centre
1530 Elizabeth Drive
Cecil Park, New South Wales 2178

NEW ZEALAND
Mr. Tony Waddicor
P. O. Box 5331, Auckland

Science of the Soul Study Centre
80 Olsen Avenue, Auckland
☎ +64-9-624-2202

GUAM
Mrs. Hoori M. Sadhwani
115 Alupang Cove
241 Condo Lane, Tamuning 96911

HONG KONG
Mr. Manoj Sabnani
Radha Soami Satsang Beas
3rd Floor, Maxwell Centre
39-41 Hankow Road
Tsim Sha Tsui, Kowloon
☎ +852-2369-0625

JAPAN
Mr. Jani G. Mohinani
Radha Soami Satsang Beas
1-2-18 Nakajima-Dori
Aotani, Chuo-Ku, Kobe 651-0052
☎ +81-78-222-5353

KOREA
Mr. Haresh Buxani
Science of the Soul Study Group
613, Hopyeong-Dong
R603-18604 Sungbo Building
Nam Yangju, Gyeong Gi-Do
Nam Yangju Kyung-gi
☎+822-315-117-008

TAIWAN, R.O.C.
Mr. Haresh Buxani
Science of the Soul Study Group
Aetna Tower Office, 15F., No. 27-9
Sec.2, Jhongjheng E.Rd.
Danshuei Township, Taipei 25170
☎+886-2-8809-5223

NORTH AMERICA

CANADA
Mr. John Pope
5285 Coombe Lane
Belcarra, British Columbia V3H 4N6

Mrs. Meena Khanna
149 Elton Park Road
Oakville, Ontario L6J 4C2

Science of the Soul Study Centre
2932 -176th Street
Surrey, B.C. V3S 9V4
☎ +1-604-541-4792

Science of the Soul Study Centre
6566 Sixth Line, RR 1 Hornby
Ontario L0P 1E0
☎ +1-905-875-4579

MEXICO
Radha Soami Satsang Beas
Efrain Gonzalez Luna
2051 Col. Americana
Guadalajara, Jalisco 44090
☎ +52-333-615-4942

Radha Soami Satsang Beas
Circuito Universidad S/N
Lomas Del ProgresoEL Pitillal CP 48290
☎ +52-322-299-1954

UNITED STATES
Mr. Hank Muller
P.O. Box 1847, Tomball, TX 77377

Dr. Vincent P. Savarese
2550 Pequeno Circle
Palm Springs, CA 92264-9522

Dr. Frank E. Vogel
275 Cutts Road
Newport, NH 03773

Dr. Douglas Torr
P.O. Box 2360
Southern Pines, NC 28388-2360

Science of the Soul Study Center
4115 Gillespie Street
Fayetteville, NC 28306-9053
☎ +1-910-426-5306

Science of the Soul Study Center
2415 Washington Street
Petaluma, CA 94954-9274
☎ +1-707-762-5082

CARIBBEAN

FOR CARIBBEAN
Mr. Sean Finnigan
R.S.S.B. Foundation
P. O. Box 978
Phillipsburg, St. Maarten, N. A.

Mrs. Jaya Sabnani
1 Sunset Drive South
Fort George Heights
St. Michael BB111 02, Barbados

BARBADOS, W.I.
Mrs. Mukta Nebhani
Science of the Soul Study Center
No. 10, 5th Avenue
Belleville BB11114
☎ +1-246-427-4761

CURACAO, N.A.
Mrs. Hema Chandiramani
Science of the Soul Study Centre
Kaya Seru di Milon 6-9
Santa Catharina
☎ +599-9-747-0226

ST. MAARTEN, N.A.
Mr. Prakash Daryanani
R.S.S.B. Foundation
P. O. Box 978, Phillipsburg
☎ +599-547-0066

GRENADA, W.I.
Mr. Ajay Mahbubani
P.O. Box 820, St. Georges

GUYANA
Mrs. Indu Lalwani
155, Garnette Street
Newtown Kitty, Georgetown

HAITI, W.I.
Ms. Mousson Finnigan Pierre
P.O. Box 2314, Port-au-Prince

JAMAICA, W.I.
Mrs. Reshma Daswani
17 Colombus Height
First Phase, Ocho Rios

ST. THOMAS
Mrs. Hema Melwani
P.O. Box 600145
USVI-VI00801-6145

SURINAME
Mr. Ettire Stanley Rensch
Surinamestraat 36, Paramaribo

TRINIDAD, W.I.
Mr. Chandru Chatlani
20 Admiral Court
Westmoorings-by-Sea, Westmoorings

FOR CENTRAL & SOUTH AMERICA

Mr. Hiro W. Balani
Paseo De Farola, 3, Piso 6
Edificio Marina
Malaga, Spain 29016

CENTRAL AMERICA

BELIZE
Mrs. Milan Hotchandani
4633 Seashore Drive
P.O. Box 830, Belize City

PANAMA
Mr. Ashok Tikamdas Dinani
P.O. Box 0301
03524 Colon

SOUTH AMERICA

ARGENTINA
Ms. Fabiana Shilton
Leiva 4363 Capital Federal
C.P. 1427 Buenos Aires

BRAZIL
Mr. Guillerme Almeida
RUA Jesuino Arrvda 574/51
Sao Paulo 04532-081

CHILE
Mr. Vijay Harjani
Pasaje Cuatro No. 3438
Sector Chipana, Iquique

Fundacion Radha Soami Satsang Beas
Av. Apoquindo 4770, Oficina 1504
Las Condes, Santiago

COLOMBIA
Mrs. Emma Orozco
Asociacion Cultural
Radha Soami Satsang Beas
Calle 48 No. 78A-30, Medellin 49744
☏ +574-234-5130

ECUADOR
Dr. Fernando Flores Villalva
Radha Soami Satsang Beas
Calle Marquez de Varela
OE 3-68y Avda. America
P.O. Box 17-21-115, Quito
☏ +5932-2-555-988

PERU
Mr. Carlos Fitts
P.O. Box 18-0658, Lima 18

Asociacion Cultural
Radha Soami Satsang Beas
Av. Pardo #231
12th Floor, Miraflores, Lima 18

VENEZUELA
Mrs. Helen Paquin
Radha Soami Satsang Beas
Av. Los Samanes con
Av. Los Naranjos Conj, Res. Florida 335
La Florida, Caracas 1012

EUROPE

AUSTRIA
Mr. Hansjorg Hammerer
Sezenweingasse 10, A-5020 Salzburg

BELGIUM
Mr. Piet J. E. Vosters
Driezenstraat 26, Turnhout 2300

BULGARIA
Mr. Deyan Stoyanov
Radha Soami Satsang Beas
P. O. Box 39, 8000 Bourgas

CYPRUS
Mr. Heraclis Achilleos
P. O. Box 29077, 1035 Nicosia

CZECH REPUBLIC
Mr. Vladimir Skalsky
Maratkova 916, 142 00 Praha 411

DENMARK
Mr. Tony Sharma
Sven Dalsgaardsvej 33, DK-7430 Ikast

FINLAND
Ms. Anneli Wingfield
P. O. Box 1422, 00101 Helsinki

FRANCE
Mr. Pierre de Proyart
7 Quai Voltaire, Paris 75007

GERMANY
Mr. Rudolf Walberg
P. O. Box 1544, D-65800 Bad Soden

GIBRALTAR
Mr. Sunder Mahtani
RSSB Charitable Trust, 15 Rosia Road
☏ +350-200-412-67

GREECE
Mr. Themistoclis Gianopoulos
6 Platonos Str., 17672 Kallithea, Attiki

ITALY
Mrs. Wilma Salvatori Torri
Via Bacchiglione 3, 00199 Rome

THE NETHERLANDS (HOLLAND)
Mr. Henk Keuning
Kleizuwe2, Vreeland 3633AE

Radha Soami Satsang Beas
Middenweg 145 E
1394 AH Nederhorst den Berg
☎ +31-294-255-255

NORWAY
Mr. Manoj Kaushal
Langretta 8, N - 1279 Oslo

POLAND
Mr. Vinod Sharma
UL. Szyprow 2M12, 02-654 Warsaw

PORTUGAL
Mrs. Sharda Lodhia
CRCA Portugal
Av. Coronel Eduardo Galhardo
No.18 A-B
Lisbon 1170-105

ROMANIA
Mrs. Carmen Cismas
C.P. 6-12, 810600 Braila

SLOVENIA
Mr. Marko Bedina
Brezje pri Trzicu 68, 4290 Trzic

SPAIN
Mr. J. W. Balani
Fundacion Cultural RSSB
Fca Loma del Valle S/N
Cruce de Penon de Zapata
Alhaurin De la Torre, Malaga 29130
☎ +34-952-414-679

SWEDEN
Mr. Lennart Zachen
Norra Sonnarpsvägen 29
SE-286 72 Asljunga

SWITZERLAND
Mr. Sebastian Züst
Weissenrainstrasse 48
CH 8707 Uetikon am See

UNITED KINGDOM
Mr. Narinder Singh Johal
Radha Soami Satsang Beas
Haynes Park
Haynes, MK45 3BL Bedford
☎ +44-1234-381-234

AFRICA

BENIN
Mr. Jaikumar T. Vaswani
01 Boite Postale 951,
Recette Principale Cotonou 01

BOTSWANA
Dr. Krishan Lal Bhateja
P. O. Box 402539, Gaborone

CONGO
Mr. Prahlad Parbhu
143 Kasai Ave., Lubumbashi

GHANA
Mr. Murli Chatani
Radha Soami Satsang Beas
P. O. Box 3976, Accra
☎ +233-242-057-309

IVORY COAST
Mr. Veerender Kumar Sapra
Avenue 7, Rue 19, Lot 196
Trechville, Abidjan 05

KENYA
Mr. Surinder Singh Ghir
Radha Soami Satsang Beas
P.O. Box 15134
Langata 00509, Nairobi
☎ +254-20-890-329

LESOTHO
Mr. Sello Wilson Moseme
P. O. Box 750, Leribe 300

LIBYA (G.S.P.L.A.J.)
Mr. Abhimanyu Sahani
P.O. Box 38930, Bani Walid

MADAGASCAR
Mr. Francis Murat
Lote 126B
Amnohiminono, Antanetibe
Antananarivo 101

MAURITIUS
Dr. I. Fagoonee
Radha Soami Satsang Beas Trust
69 CNR Antelme /Stanley Avenues
Quatre Bornes
☎ +230-454-3300

NAMIBIA
Mrs. Jennifer Carvill
P. O. Box 449, Swakopmund 9000

NIGERIA
Mr. Nanik N. Balani
G.P.O. Box 5054, Marina, Lagos

RÉUNION
Ms. Marie-Lynn Marcel
5 Chemin 'Gonneau, Bernica
St Gillesles Hauts 97435

SIERRA LEONE
Mr. Kishore S. Mahboobani
82/88 Kissy Dock Yard
P.O. Box 369, Freetown

SOUTH AFRICA
Mr. Gordon Clive Wilson
P.O. Box 1959
Randpark Ridge, Gauteng 2156

Radha Soami Satsang Beas
P.O. Box 5270, Cresta 2118
☎ +27-11-792-7644

SWAZILAND
Mr. Mike Cox
Green Valley Farm, Malkerns

TANZANIA
Mr. Manmohan Singh
99 Lugalo Street
Dar-Es-Salaam 65065

UGANDA
Mr. Sylvester Kakooza
Radha Soami Satsang Beas
P. O. Box 31381, Kampala

ZAMBIA
Mr. Surinder Kumar Sachar
6 Mutondo Crescent
Riverside, Copper belt, Kitwe

ZIMBABWE
Mr. Gordon Clive Wilson
P.O. Box 1959
Randpark Ridge
Gauteng 2156, South Africa

MIDDLE EAST

BAHRAIN
Mr. Iqbal Kundal
P.O. Box 76091 - Juffair

ISRAEL
Mr. Michael Yaniv
Moshav Sde Nitzan 59
D.N. Hanegev 85470

KUWAIT
Mr. Vijay Kumar
Yousef AL Badar Street
Bldg 28, Block 10, Flat #8, Salmiya

U.A.E.
Mr. Daleep Jatwani
P.O. Box 37816, Dubai
☎ +971-4-339-4773

Books on This Science

SOAMI JI MAHARAJ
Sar Bachan Prose
Sar Bachan Poetry

BABA JAIMAL SINGH
Spiritual Letters

MAHARAJ SAWAN SINGH
The Dawn of Light
Discourses on Sant Mat, Volume I
My Submission
Philosophy of the Masters (5 volumes)
Spiritual Gems
Tales of the Mystic East

MAHARAJ JAGAT SINGH
Discourses on Sant Mat, Volume II
The Science of the Soul

MAHARAJ CHARAN SINGH
Die to Live
Divine Light
Light on Saint John
Light on Saint Matthew
Light on Sant Mat
Quest for Light
The Path
Spiritual Discourses (2 volumes)
Spiritual Heritage
Spiritual Perspectives (3 volumes)

BOOKS ABOUT THE MASTERS
Call of the Great Master – Daryai Lal Kapur
Heaven on Earth – Daryai Lal Kapur
Treasure beyond Measure – Shanti Sethi
With a Great Master in India – Julian P. Johnson
With the Three Masters (3 volumes) – Rai Sahib Munshi Ram

MYSTICS OF THE EAST SERIES
Bulleh Shah – J. R. Puri and T. R. Shangari
Dadu: The Compassionate Mystic – K. N. Upadhyaya
Dariya Sahib: Saint of Bihar – K. N. Upadhyaya
Guru Nanak: His Mystic Teachings – J. R. Puri
Guru Ravidas: The Philosopher's Stone – K. N. Upadhyaya
Kabir: The Great Mystic – Isaac A. Ezekiel
Kabir: The Weaver of God's Name – V. K. Sethi
Mira: The Divine Lover – V. K. Sethi
Saint Namdev – J. R. Puri and V. K. Sethi
Sant Paltu: His Life and Teachings – Isaac A. Ezekiel
Sarmad: Martyr to Love Divine – Isaac A. Ezekiel

Sultan Bahu – J. R. Puri and K. S. Khak
The Teachings of Goswami Tulsidas – K. N. Upadhyaya
Tukaram: The Ceaseless Song of Devotion – C. Rajwade
Tulsi Sahib: Saint of Hathras – J. R. Puri and V. K. Sethi

SPIRITUALITY AND SANT MAT

Honest Living – M. F. Singh
In Search of the Way – Flora E. Wood
The Inner Voice – C. W. Sanders
Liberation of the Soul – J. Stanley White
Living Meditation: A Journey beyond Body and Mind – Hector Esponda Dubin
Message Divine – Shanti Sethi
The Mystic Philosophy of Sant Mat – Peter Fripp
Mysticism: The Spiritual Path – Lekh Raj Puri
The Path of the Masters – Julian P. Johnson
Radha Soami Teachings – Lekh Raj Puri
A Spiritual Primer – Hector Esponda Dubin

THE MYSTIC WAY AND WORLD RELIGIONS

Adventure of Faith – Shraddha Lietz
Buddhism: Path to Nirvana – K. N. Upadhyaya
The Divine Romance – John Davidson
The Gospel of Jesus – John Davidson
The Holy Name: Mysticism in Judaism – Miriam Caravella
Jap Ji – T. R. Shangari
The Odes of Solomon – John Davidson
The Prodigal Soul – John Davidson
The Song of Songs – John Davidson
A Treasury of Mystic Terms, Part I: The Principles of Mysticism (6 volumes) – John Davidson, ed.
Yoga and the Bible – Joseph Leeming

BOOKS ON MISCELLANEOUS THEMES

Empower Women: An Awakening – Leena Chawla
Life Is Fair: The Law of Cause and Effect – Brian Hines
One Being One – John Davidson
A Soul's Safari – Netta Pfeifer

VEGETARIAN COOKBOOKS

Baking Without Eggs
Creative Vegetarian Cooking
The Green Way to Healthy Living
Meals with Vegetables

BOOKS FOR CHILDREN

The Journey of the Soul – Victoria Jones
One Light Many Lamps – Victoria Jones

For Internet orders, please visit: www.rssb.org

For book orders within India, please write to:

Radha Soami Satsang Beas
BAV Distribution Centre, 5 Guru Ravi Dass Marg
Pusa Road, New Delhi 110 005